MW01113595

Hong Kong Studies Reader Series

Series Editors
Brian C. H. Fong
Academy of Hong Kong Studies
The Education University of Hong Kong
Tai Po, Hong Kong

Tai-Lok Lui
Academy of Hong Kong Studies
The Education University of Hong Kong
Tai Po, Hong Kong

Stephen Chiu
Academy of Hong Kong Studies
The Education University of Hong Kong
Tai Po, Hong Kong

In recent years, Hong Kong society has undergone significant political, economic and social changes. Hong Kong Studies, as an interdisciplinary field of area studies that takes "Hong Kong" as a central subject of analysis, has become the focus of attention for both locals and non-locals from different backgrounds. There is a growing demand from local and non-local students, school teachers, scholars, policy researchers, journalists, politicians and businessmen to understand the development of Hong Kong in a more systematic way. The *Hong Kong Studies Reader Series* is designed to address this pressing need by publishing clear, concise and accessible readers to key areas of Hong Kong Studies including politics, history, culture, media, etc. The series aims to offer English-Chinese-Japanese trilingual guides to anyone who is interested in understanding and researching Hong Kong.

More information about this series at
http://www.palgrave.com/gp/series/15923

Stephen WK Chiu • Kaxton YK Siu

Hong Kong Society

High-Definition Stories beyond the Spectacle of East-Meets-West

Stephen WK Chiu
Department of Social Sciences
The Education University of
Hong Kong
New Territories, Hong Kong

Kaxton YK Siu
Department of Sociology
Hong Kong Baptist University
Kowloon, Hong Kong

ISSN 2523-7764   ISSN 2523-7772   (electronic)
Hong Kong Studies Reader Series
ISBN 978-981-16-5706-1   ISBN 978-981-16-5707-8   (eBook)
https://doi.org/10.1007/978-981-16-5707-8

This Palgrave Macmillan imprint is published by the registered company Springer Nature Singapore Pte Ltd.
The registered company address is: 152 Beach Road, #21-01/04 Gateway East, Singapore 189721, Singapore

For the Hong Kong and Hongkongers We love

PREFACE

"Why bother to write another book on Hong Kong society?" A colleague asked when she heard of our plan. "It will go out of date the moment it hits the shelf of bookstores" is her reason.

By the end of 2019 when we were completing this book, indeed it looked like her words rang ominously true. As a result of the government's attempt to reform a bill extraditing criminals to the Mainland, Hong Kong had since the summer been caught in the furnace of protests where tens of thousands of people (or up to two million at one point according to the organizers) marched on streets in such numbers and frequency unheard of in its history. Thousands of masked protesters wearing black, most of them young, stood off with police on the streets in the nights, burned roadblocks, paralyzed the subway system, vandalized shops perceived to be pro-establishment (including the Starbucks franchise), and threw Molotov cocktails at the police officers.

The common feeling on both sides of the protest is that Hong Kong has turned upside down and never be the same again. "There is no turning back" is the prevalent sentiment. Politicians, observers, and academics alike are scrambling to catch up with the bewildering array of events breaking out almost every week, among others, "singing with you" (和你唱) protest in shopping malls, formation of human chains across the city, and the violent "black bloc tactics" by protestors.[1] On the other side, police use of force also escalated; thousands of canisters of tear gas and plastic bullets were rained down on protesters, water cannons were deployed,

[1] https://time.com/5672018/glory-to-hong-kong-protests-national-anthem/

occupied universities were besieged, and even live rounds were shot, just to name a few. Even foreign governments were involved. In November 2019, the American Congress passed the Hong Kong Human Rights and Democracy Act, which was sternly opposed by the Central Government of the People's Republic of China (PRC), who stood firmly behind the SAR Government.

So why bother to write this book? The events in 2019 and what followed were far too close for the real history to be written. Sociologically, what were the causes that mobilized people to the street? What was the impact of the July 21 indiscriminate attack on protesters and commuters by a "white-clad" mob in Yuen Long? What happened before HKUST student Chow Tsz-lok fell to his death from a carpark on November 3? What were the "deep-rooted" causes, socially or politically or economically speaking or all, that led to the outbreak of the events? The public called for a Commission of Inquiry with statutory investigation power to find out the truth of these and many other issues surrounding the movement, like the one published after the Kowloon Disturbances in 1966, but the government had steadfastly rejected the suggestion. It may take years before the truth on many of such questions could be found.

This book is not about the protest movements in 2019 and its aftermath. But this does not mean that we do not need a book like this one. Whenever we are teaching courses on Hong Kong society, students' lack of background knowledge on Hong Kong is startling. Not only many of them do not have any sense of history of the city, but their understanding of what contemporary events leading to the current scenario is also very limited. They appeared to be concerned only with the here and now, and that worries us. Although we have misgivings about the current official discourses on the "deep-rooted contradictions", we do think that it is important to talk about the socioeconomic contradictions that serve as the backdrop to the current malaise in Hong Kong, as well as the political contradictions directly responsible for the mobilization we had seen. One point we agree on is that to understand the present-day Hong Kong, deeply engulfed in social and political crises, we need to acquire knowledge of the city past and present.

To do this, we need a framework that is much broader in scope. Hong Kong was haunted by not just one spectre, but two since the early settlement years after the Unequal Treaties, as - it had stood at the fringe of two empires, the British and the Chinese. Ever since then, the story of Hong Kong has often been told as a spectacle, a wonderful story of

East-meets-West. At the confluence of the empires, Hong Kong has been construed as a product either as the spread of Western civilization to the East, or the legacies of the Chinese culture under Western rule, or as some kind of crosscurrents of the two.

Drawing from Latin *spectaculum* "a show", and *spectare* "to view, watch", the etymology of spectacle is derived from Middle English from about 1340 as "specially prepared or arranged display". It is considered here therefore that the Hong Kong story has often been told as a "display" of the ideological forces that sought to construct what is special, "spectacular" or at least note-worthy about Hong Kong. As such, all these "stories" are not necessarily incorrect but incomplete, that "display", with various accentuations, certain facets of the experiences of the settlement (we use settlement rather than city because it was certainly not a city two hundred years ago) over the past few hundred years and especially the last one hundred something years.

We are not fighting an ideological battle to replace one story with another (hence this is not an exercise of "exorcism"), but rather would like to dig deeper into the experiences of the people who had and have lived here and see where gaps and misses are, and whether we could present stories of people and their lives in this settlement in a more "complete" representation. Certainly these are also "our" stories, as the authors are both born and raised in Hong Kong. That is also why "we" also want to tell our stories, not just from our own vintage point, but from the experiences of all those we grow up together with, the booms and busts, the joys and sorrows, and the hopes and despairs.

This book borrows the concept of "high-definition" from digital broadcasting technology to highlight our unique approach to Hong Kong society. The dictionary meaning of high definition is "a high degree of detail in an image or screen". In present-day usage, the term is usually associated with latest digital television system—high-definition television (HDTV)—using higher resolution to give a sharper image than conventional lower resolution "standard-definition television" (SDTV) system. To us, the idea of "high-definition" (i.e., high degree of detail) and its contrast with "standard definition" capture the gist of our approach and provide a sharp and innovative way to craft our Hong Kong stories. Now of course the standard in television technology is already ultra-high-definition (UHD) with 4K resolution of about 4,000 pixels, but we have decided to keep the more commonly used imageries.

This book intends to highlight the contrasts with many common and taken-for-granted stories, myths and representations of Hong Kong—to which we consider only "standard-definition" with lower degree of detail. Many of these standard-definition Hong Kong stories lack proper connections with the grounded personal experiences and macro social contexts. Consequently, not only do these stories preclude us from having high enough "resolution" to watch multiple layers of experiences from walks of life of Hong Kong people, but they also prevent us from understanding how global transformation impacts on local people's experiences, as well as understanding Hong Kong's significance in the global system.

Each core chapter of this book examines a popular visual imagery of Hong Kong, highlights the processes of and interactions among global transformation, social history and personal experiences, and opens up discussion about the accuracy and validity of the imagery. The main goals of the book will be to: (a) present fine-grained Hong Kong stories in high definition through analysing "state-market-civil society" dynamics from three levels of analysis: global, regional, and local; (b) critically evaluate the different popular imageries, conceptualizations, and discourses held by the public and in the extant literature about Hong Kong society; and (c) update the literature and new development on Hong Kong politics and society, and portend the future of Hong Kong society.

With these in mind, we have penned ten chapters. We have tried to make the individual chapters stand on its own and could be read separately, but certainly cross references have to be made from time to time.

With the aftershocks of the 2019 events still reverberate and appear to be changing Hong Kong completely at this moment, we are indeed standing at the crossroads of the history in which a hugely unpredictable future unravelling in front of us.

Tai Po, Hong Kong   Stephen Chiu

ACKNOWLEDGMENTS

This book was written with sweat and tear—for six years of writing, the authors sweated their hands days and nights to finish this long overdue project; for so many midnights, the authors burst their tears in front of televisions, witnessing the Hong Kong story they were crafting changed beyond recognition. Occupation on streets, violence in university campuses, tear gas over the sky, dramatic melody heard inside shopping arcades—hundreds or thousands of television imageries touched their central nerves, overwhelmed their hearts and minds. The initial motive for writing this book was nothing sentimental. But as locally-born and raised academics, after the past six turbulent years of Hong Kong society, we could not help but have the final product of this project tinged with our personal sentiments.

Somehow, these sentiments drove us to finish this difficult project, and accomplished something more than we set out at the beginning. Back in April 2015, when teaching just ended, together with Kent Lee, the three of us were working then at the Chinese University of Hong Kong, were reviewing our semester. As always, one of us moaned about the difficulty of finding suitable readings to go with our lectures for the courses on Hong Kong society. The last broadly used textbook was written in the 1980s, and the most recent compilation of essays was from the 1990s and 2000s (another one did appear in 2018). Journal articles and book chapters on Hong Kong society usually focus on giving an overview of a particular topic. So the idea of why not writing a textbook of our own got thrown out. After six long and turbulent (for Hong Kong) years and countless delays, we managed to deliver the manuscript in May 2021.

Unfortunately, at the end Kent had to drop out because of other personal commitments, but his role in this project is fondly remembered.

For a project of this nature, the list of acknowledgements is always extensive. Together we would like to recognize our debts to generations of scholars working on Hong Kong studies. Without their original work, a book of this nature would never have been possible, and we all know that in many cases researching on Hong Kong is more a labour of love than a wise career move. Throughout the long period of labour before the delivery of the manuscript, the editorial team from Palgrave was always besides us offering their unwavering support even in times of our procrastination and delays. Gratitude should also be registered to Brian Fong, who organized this important book series for Hong Kong studies. Special thanks should be extended to Lai Tsz Chung, who provided crucial and excellent research, writing and editorial assistance at our final stage of producing this manuscript, especially his collaboration with us in writing the social movement chapter. Without his assistance and contribution, this book should not be able to be delivered to the press on time. We would also thank Stefan Hung, Agnes Ku, and the Hong Kong Public Records Office for their generous permission to use their photos in this book.

Stephen Chiu: The first one I need to thank is David Levin, my teacher and mentor, who introduced me to the sociological world of industrial societies, social class and industrial relations. Special gratitude should go to Tai-Lok, lifetime friend, collaborator and colleague, and because together we have travelled much of our academic journey towards better understanding of the Hong Kong society. Our "happy hour" (with Hong Kong-style tea and coffee) has always been a source of inspiration. I would also like to thank cohorts of students who care to talk to me and push me to think about why young people are looking at Hong Kong so differently from some quarters of the mainstream. In particular, Joycie, Hang, Trevor, CD, Michael, Nan, and Natalie have been at the heart of much of my work in the past decade, reminding me of the joys and excitement of "doing" sociology. Another note of thanks goes to Victor, who knows more about Hong Kong films than I do and kindly agreed to include a co-authored chapter here.

Kaxton Siu[1]: Special thanks goes to Stephen, who not only has invited me to join this important book project, but also taught me how to be a Hong Kong studies scholar. Indeed, without the two years working with

---

[1] The corresponding author of this book.

him at the Chinese University of Hong Kong, my academic journey would have been much more difficult. I would also like to thank my MPhil thesis supervisor, Alvin So, who patiently mentored me to finish my first Hong Kong studies research. Gratitude should also be extended to my Hong Kong studies research collaborators—Julian Groves and Ho Wai Yip, who accompanied me to have ethnographic adventures in Hong Kong public housing estates to study marginal youth with outreaching social workers. I also owe a debt to Agnes Ku and Ma Ngok, who respectively taught me Hong Kong culture and Hong Kong politics during my undergraduate years. A note of thanks also goes to Tony Wong Hon Tung and Samuel Li Shing Hong for their excellent research supports.

We would also like to thank the Research Grants Council of Hong Kong (PolyU 256141/16H, and PolyU 156068/18H) and the Education University of Hong Kong Start-up Research Grant (RG42/17-18R) for supporting this book project. Last but not least, this book is dedicated to generations of Hong Kong people who have devoted themselves to this previously-dubbed "borrowed place, borrowed time" city. We also want to thank all the younger generations who are seeking to dream and build a better Hong Kong. This project would not have been undertaken if not for these diligent predecessors and visionary youngsters.

Although we have tried our best to catch up with the explosive growth of social scientific literature on Hong Kong in the last few years, it is almost certain that we must have missed a lot of pixels in painting our big picture. Added to this is the dramatic unfolding of events in Hong Kong every day in front of us, making it hopeless to capture adequately for a work of this nature. Still, we humbly hope that this book will serve as a steppingstone for future scholars and students into the field of Hong Kong studies, helping them to embark on their journey into the quest for deeper understanding of the city. The responsibilities for any omissions and errors are, of course, entirely ours.

May 2021   Stephen Chiu and Kaxton Siu

Meeti...j at Tai Po Market between Sir Henry Blake and the gentry and elders of the New Territories communities at which the Governor explained the principles upon which the le.... territories would be governed. Gentry and elders assembled to greet the governor and his party, 2 August, 1899.

Plate 1.1 Meeting at Tai Po Market between Sir Henry Blake and the gentry and elders of the New Territories communities at which the Governor explained the principles upon which the leased territories would be governed. Gentry and elders assembled to greet the governor and his party, 2 August, 1899. By HKSAR Government Record Service, 04-03-057a. Source: Colonial Office Photographic collection, National Archives. Part of CO 1069/446, p.45 (Crown Copyright expired; Originally black and white.)

Plate 1.2 Foreign domestic helpers in their Sunday gatherings in Central. (Credit: Agnes S. M. Ku)

Plate 1.3   Old tenement buildings (*tong laus*) and residential skyscrapers in To Kwa Wan. (Credit: Agnes S. M. Ku)

Plate 1.4   One of the many rallies during the Anti-Extradition Bill movement in 2019. (Credit: Agnes S. M. Ku)

Plate 1.5   Child standing in front of a Lennon Wall of protest propaganda during the Anti-Extradition Bill Movement in Tai Po. (Credit: Stefan CF Hung)

CONTENTS

LIST OF FIGURES

LIST OF TABLES

CHAPTER 1

Hong Kong as a Crown Jewel of the British Empire: Colonial History and Legacy

When the British Empire finally sank beneath the waves of history, it would leave behind it only two monuments: one was the game of Association Football, the other was the expression of 'Fuck off'.
—Richard Turnbull, *the penultimate Governor of Aden, quoted in Ferguson (2004)*

1 INTRODUCTION

Sir Turnbull's observation about football as a legacy of British imperialism is correct in the case of the former 'colony'[1] of Hong Kong since it is still the most popular sport, of both the participant and spectator varieties. His other point regarding the use of language does not apply. While English is the most commonly used second language for many Hong Kong people, the f-word is certainly not as widely used as the more powerful and colourful Cantonese vulgar language. What then, did the British Empire really leave Hong Kong people and society?

The British did not come to Hong Kong in pursuit of a noble cause. But when they left, they took pride in their contribution to modernizing Hong Kong and making it a world-famous success story. This chapter

---

[1] It should be noted that in 1971, the United Nations General Assembly adopted Resolution 2908 by a 99:5 vote to remove Hong Kong and Macau from the U.N. list of Non-Self-Governing Territories. The word colony is used interchangeably with 'colony' and readers are reminded of such interpretation.

© The Author(s), under exclusive license to Springer Nature Singapore Pte Ltd. 2022
S. W. K. Chiu, K. Y. K. Siu, *Hong Kong Society*, Hong Kong Studies Reader Series, https://doi.org/10.1007/978-981-16-5707-8_1

traces Hong Kong's pathway to modernity. It examines narratives of the origin of modern Hong Kong, focusing on the oft-mentioned positive aspects of "the British colonial legacy". This chapter provides an overview of Hong Kong's social and political history, and brings in some untold stories giving us a fuller picture of the colonial social structure and state-society relations from the global, regional and local perspectives.[2] While recognizing British colonizers' contributions to Hong Kong's success, we highlight the darker sides of colonial rule. This chapter ends by revisiting the debate of "colonial modernization" to capture the two faces of British colonial impact.

The dominant standard-definition image about Hong Kong's modernization is—the making of modern Hong Kong owed much to the helping hands of the British. In this view, British governance did turn colonial Hong Kong into a peaceful society without much conflict.[3] Ironically, nostalgic references to colonial times have been seen in recent street protests, including the "dragon and lion" flag borrowed from the colonial Hong Kong banner. Simultaneously, some have argued colonial legacies such as rule of law and freedom of speech have been subjected to challenges in recent years. It is high time we review the imprint of British colonial rule on Hong Kong.

We do not dispute the generalization that British colonialism contributed to the development of Hong Kong. Nonetheless, this standard-definition image of Hong Kong precludes us from discerning many dark sides of British rule. It conceals the conflicts and contradictions in the society (Lui & Chiu, 1999) such as sub-standard living conditions, its sweatshop label due to poor labour regulations, a lower-than-average investment in tertiary education compared to other OECD countries, slow progress of democratization (Pepper, 2008)—not to mention the gross disparities in income and wealth distribution.

This chapter closely examines several standard-definition images in modernization narratives presented from the perspective of the colonial endgame. While British colonialism is inseparable from many of the economic and political "achievements" (especially the former) of contemporary Hong Kong, its legacies are real rather than imaginary. We would like

---

[2] As some of the major post-World War II political and social events will be covered in the forthcoming chapters, this part places more emphasis on the pre- World War II history.

[3] A similar positive standard-definition image of colonial legacies has been recycled in the post-colonial era, nourishing radical localism in Hong Kong's civil society (see Chap. 5).

to remind readers, however, there is many more to the Hong Kong story than the standard colonial narrative.

1.1   Assessing Colonial Legacies and Postcolonial Development

Hong Kong's significance as a former British colony[4] and its standard colonial modernization narrative lies in the increasing interest among historians and social scientists in assessing the legacy of European colonialism in general and the British Empire in particular. As Nunn (2009, p. 66) observes, "an exciting new literature has emerged empirically examining whether historic events are important determinants of economic development today". Seminal works of this literature converge on particularly fateful events in most Third World countries' history, namely, European colonialism and the impact of colonial rule on domestic institutions persisted after independence. All these works basically share as their theoretical starting point the new institutional economics espoused by North and Thomas (1973) and North (1981, 1990). Where they diverge is the aspects of colonial rule they consider critical in shaping institutional legacies bestowed on the colonized and how such legacies shape postcolonial development. Four major themes stand out in the debate: development of the legal system, development of growth-promoting institutions, impact of colonial institutions on postcolonial development, and adoption of economic models in the colonies.

Development of the legal system: La Porta et al. (1997, 1998) highlight the differences between the British common law system and Roman civil law. The British common law-based system, in their view, once transplanted to the colonies, offered a higher level of protection to investors and economic activities than Roman civil law did. A contrast is drawn in this connection to the British Empire versus the continental European ones (Spain, France, and Portugal). They argue since the legal origin of colonies is largely exogenous to country characteristics, it is a potential instrument to estimate how investor rights are protected on financial development. Accordingly, countries with a common law origin offered

---

[4]It should be noted that in 1971, the United Nations General Assembly adopted Resolution 2908 by a 99:5 vote to remove Hong Kong and Macau from the U.N. list of Non-Self-Governing Territories, hence cleared the sovereignty dispute by 'officially' announced that Hong Kong was not a colony but an entity under colonial rule. Readers should interpret the word 'colony' throughout this book with reference to the above terms and timelines.

better protection to investors, leading to larger debt and equity markets and hence more robust long-term economic development.

Development of growth-promoting institutions: Acemoglu et al. (2001) also focus on the impact of institutional legacies of colonial rule on long-term growth but they discount the effect of the identity of the colonial rulers. They look instead at how early situations significantly affected the kind of institutions evolved across former colonies. They argue that colonies with a more habitable and less deadly disease environment had greater European settlement; hence colonial rulers would develop more growth-promoting institutions to protect property rights under colonial rule, largely for their fellow colonial compatriots' benefits. Early European mortality rates are used as a proxy for institutions; a strong negative relationship is found between initial settler mortality and current institutional quality. Second-stage analyses then confirm the positive effect of domestic institutions on per capita income. Engerman and Sokoloff (1997, 2002) approach the issue qualitatively and arrive at a similar conclusion about how initial resource endowments and the suitability for large scale cash crop plantations contribute to the adoption of slavery and hence different development paths among the colonies of the Americas.

Impact of colonial institutions on postcolonial development: Mahoney's and Lange's works leverage from a more sociopolitical perspective by comparing the British and Spanish empires and examine the differential effects of domestic institutions in the colonies (Lange, 2004, 2009; Lange et al., 2006; Mahoney, 2010). They focus on the so-called "great reversals" in the long-term development of the colonies long espoused by dependency theorists. Those most economically-advanced territories before colonialism often became the least economically-developed after colonialism and vice versa (Lange et al., 2006, p. 1413). They contend that much of the economic history literature, most influential being Acemoglu et al. (2001), emphasizes the conditions within the colonized areas and their factor endowments (broadly conceived) as the determinants of colonial institutions and that in turn determined postcolonial developments.

Adoption of economic models in the colonies: Lange et al. (2006) contend that colonizers' identity and the economic models they bring to the colonies have shaped the developmental legacies they left behind. Through a sociological analysis of 39 former British colonies and 18 former Spanish colonies, they distinguish two ideal-typical economic models adopted by colonizers: the mercantilist and the liberal. The British adopted a liberal model; the Spanish the mercantilist. For the Spanish colonies, the more highly-developed the mercantilist institutions with predatory states and dysfunctional markets are, the less potential there will be for postcolonial development. A developed form of British colonialism, by contrast, introduced inclusive institutions (e.g. the rule of law and freedom of speech, effective administration, and competitive markets) that would promote development in the postcolonial period. Thus, for both colonial models, the effects of the more extensive form of colonialism were exactly the opposite. The more developed colonial institutions were in the case of the Spanish colonies, the more postcolonial development was hindered, while the reverse is true for British colonies.[5]

Hong Kong and other former British colonies play a key role in adjudicating this debate. In testing Acemogul et al.'s model, Fails and Krieckhaus (2010) found that the four British settler colonies (United States, Canada, Australia and New Zealand) and the two city-states (Hong Kong and Singapore) accounted for a lion's share of the explanatory power of the model, rendering it statistically insignificant if the British settler colonies and the city-states are excluded from the analysis (Fails & Krieckhaus, 2010, pp. 500–502). We believe the results testify to the development-inducing effect of British colonialism. But given the sobering fact that the "colonial effect" disappears once the six archetypical successful British colonial stories are removed, we have to ask why British colonialism worked in these cases but not necessarily others (e.g. Nigeria). And this point leads us back to our high-definition story of Hong Kong, to see what actually happened in colonial Hong Kong. If British colonialism does not have the same effects everywhere, and also took more than one form, what was the concrete form of British colonialism in Hong Kong?

1.2   Modernization Narratives

At a certain point during his or her schooling, a locally-educated student would be exposed to a particular version of the modernization narrative about Hong Kong such as the following:

> Hong Kong was originally a fishing village. Because of its good geographical location and natural harbour, it gradually developed into a commercial cen-

[5] Lange (2009, 2004) also focused on former British colonies and basically affirmed the same argument.

tre primarily doing trades. ... Since the 1950s, massive migrants flooded into and settled in Hong Kong. To solve the unemployment problem, Hong Kong government at that time decided to develop Hong Kong's manufacturing and tourist industries, thus laying a good foundation for Hong Kong's future economic development. (New Asia Publishing House Editorial Board, 2004, p. 21)

Although coming from two different generations, the authors of this book were all introduced to a modernization narrative similar to that shown above. Like fellow students, and perhaps many Hong Kong people, we frequently took this narrative for granted. Even sceptical about it, we seldom challenged the story when it was recounted.

The same version of Hong Kong history is told elsewhere. The exhibition in the Hong Kong Museum of History (2015) starts from the early settlement period of Hong Kong with emphasis on the advantageous natural environment, and illustration of selected local Chinese customs and rituals. The museum is spatially and visually arranged and a *staged* and *linear* history is presented, similar to what is found in the primary school textbook. This image of a reconstruction of a fishing village turned modern metropolis has gradually blended with the construction of heritage emphasizing distinctive traditional Chinese characteristics after the transfer of sovereignty in 1997 (Cheung, 1999).

But there is more to the modernization narrative that was told to Hong Kong people. The last colonial governor, Chris Patten, articulated the perfect example of such a discourse in his final policy address:

Success in Hong Kong is the result of a combination of factors. This is a Chinese city. Its success is the result of the hard work and skill of its Chinese men and women. It is also a city over which, for a century and half, Britain has held stewardship. We have tried to exercise that stewardship in a way which has been true to our political values. Those values have been institutionalized in the rule of law and a meritocratic, politically neutral Civil Service ... The framework of social, legal and economic values and policies created here has given the men and women of this city the opportunity to make the most of their formidable energy and talents, to thrive, excel and prosper in a fair, ordered and orderly society. (Patten, 1996)

Patten's version praises not only what Hong Kong had achieved, but further attributed her success to the smooth and harmonious encounter between two cultures, commonly-described as "East-meets-West" (Ku,

2002). Above all, it is a narrative giving British people a celebrated role to play in history –a missionary to steward Hong Kong by laying the framework of "social, legal and economic values and policies". In other words, the British had become the agent of history propelling Hong Kong to become "a fair, ordered and orderly society" before their "glorified retreat" in 1997.

1.3   Four British Legacies

Patten's story of "missionary colonizer" has not been seriously challenged by local contemporary observers. Instead, many join the chorus to celebrate the British model of good governance (an ordered and orderly society without much conflict) and further crystalize British contributions to Hong Kong's success with reference to so-called "British colonial legacies". Four specific legacies are commonly referred to—rule of law, civil service, an open economy offering fair opportunity for all, and freedom of speech (Lau, 1997; Chan, 1997b).[6] These are still strongly supported by locals nowadays as the *core values* of Hong Kong (Wong, 2004; HKIAPS, 2014).

First, the most celebrated British "gift" to Hong Kong has been the rule of law. It is the British-style common law system with an independent and impartial judiciary, arguably the bedrock of fairness and equality for all. Most Hong Kong people consider the rule of law as the most important cornerstone of Hong Kong's success (HKIAPS, 2014).[7] It is not just a system facilitating economic transactions essential to Hong Kong as an advanced capitalist society. The system specially and significantly enables a "high degree of autonomy" that the Hong Kong Special Administrative Region (HKSAR) is supposed to enjoy after 1997 (Chan, 1997b). In the "colonial legacy" literature in institutionalist economic history, the

---

[6] Earlier enquiry on the formulation of "Hong Kong's core values" can be traced to *The Ethos of the Hong Kong Chinese* by Lau and Kuan (1988/1995). A similar discussion for the British Empire in general is found in Ferguson. The list of institutions credited to the British Empire could be much longer but here we focus only on those most commonly cited in local discussion.

[7] For example, in a 2014 survey conducted by CUHK IAPS on views on Hong Kong's core values, 92.7% of respondents agreed "rule of law" is a core value of Hong Kong, which was also the highest level among those values surveyed and was followed by "just and corruption-free" (92.3%), social stability (88.2%), and freedom (88.1%).

common law tradition has also often been singled out as the primary "agent" linking colonialism to postcolonial development. Second, besides the legal "gift", the highly capable civil service has been another British political "gift" to Hong Kong. Following the British tradition of an executive-led government and civil service, administrative officers occupied all senior positions within the administration, headed most government departments and formed the policy centre of the government (Cheung, 1997). Hong Kong's civil service has been internationally-recognized as efficient, highly professional, politically neutral and relatively free from serious corruption—the backbone of British rule in Hong Kong (Chan, 1997b). During the final transitional period, Hong Kong's team of civil servants has been widely-considered as an important political force bequeathed to the new HKSAR government to maintain political stability and good governance. Lange et al. (2006) view this legacy as a by-product of imposing direct rule in former British colonies, a relatively developed and efficient bureaucracy being put in place during and after the colonial period.

Third, Hong Kong is renowned as an open economy providing opportunity for all to get ahead. Hong Kong's economy is considered the freest in the world and very open, if not completely so, to the outside.[8] Free trade and free enterprise have become hallmarks of Hong Kong. The colonial government has often been praised for its alleged minimal intervention into the market. Again, in the institutional economics literature, the contrast between the Spanish and British colonies is also premised on the presence of mercantilist institutions in the former and market-oriented ones created in the latter (Mahoney, 2010; Lange, 2009).

Fourth, just before the handover, Hong Kong enjoyed a high degree of freedom of speech (Keller, 1992). For example, by the 1990s, political censorship over news and internet media was rare although self-censorship gradually emerged (Lau, 1997; Lee, 1998);[9] different classes and profes-

---

[8] Hong Kong has ranked number one for 25 years on the Heritage Foundation's *Index of Economic Freedom*. For instance, HK's business freedom scores a full mark in 2015. See Heritage Foundation: http://www.heritage.org/index/country/hongkong; an update of the latest development, the Heritage Foundation has excluded Hong Kong from 2021 Index of Economic Freedom, see 'Government disappointed by Hong Kong's exclusion from 2021 Index of Economic Freedom." March 4, HKSAR Press Release.

[9] As Lee (1998) pointed out, self-censorship among market-driven "information newspaper" gradually emerged as the transition in 1997 approached. Lee classified "Information paper" as those newspaper that enjoyed high credibility (e.g. Hong Kong Economic Journal,

sional groups could freely organize pressure groups to articulate their respective interests without much difficulty; public protests were tolerated. Freedom of speech has become one of the most important socio-cultural values treasured by locals. It has come to serve as a litmus test of whether "one country, two systems" could be effectively implemented and the "Hong Kong way of life" could be preserved as the *Basic Law* came into effect after Hong Kong was returned to an authoritarian China. This also connects with the institutional literature in its emphasis on inclusive institutions in British colonies while exploitative ones were consolidated in the Spanish empire based largely on plantation economies (Mahoney, 2010; Lange et al., 2006).

Although increasing cast into doubt by recent years, many observers still consider Hong Kong a remarkable example of a liberal society with a vibrant economy whose citizens enjoy a high degree of freedom and opportunity. The two modernization narratives (*fishing village turn metropolis; missionary colonizer*) and the several colonial legacies surveyed above still have great currency among local people and global observers.

1.4   Problem of the Narratives About Hong Kong's Modernization

These narratives about Hong Kong's modernization and colonial legacies share a problem: they ignore the complexity of British colonial rule and over-simplify the nature of colonialism (Ngo, 1999, p. 2). The role of mainland China in this modernization process is often also sidelined in this narrative as well—such as the supply of staples and necessities.[10] There are three ways these oversimplified narratives trapping us in a standard-definition view of colonial Hong Kong.

First, these narratives over-simplify colonial Hong Kong society by assuming it being comprised of only two socio-political groups, "the ruler" and "the ruled". We are often told the colonial ruler was a politically neutral bureaucratic administration while the ruled Chinese were politically apathetic and predominantly "economic animals" whose main

South China Morning Post, Ming Pao, Sing Tao Jih Pao etc.), compared to "story newspaper" (e.g. Apple Daily, Oriental Daily News etc.) and the "party press" (like Wen Wei Po, Ta Kung Pao etc.).

[10] Hong Kong Chronicles. Hong Kong Chronicles Institute, https://www.hkchronicles. org.hk/.

attributes were the ability to work hard and exercise entrepreneurial "skills" and "spirits" (Ngo, 1999, p. 2).[11] But in reality, colonial Hong Kong was comprised of a variety of social actors of races, classes and ethnicities alongside differences in ascribed statuses (e.g., age and sex) (Salaff, 1981);[12] The rulers, i.e., the British ruler and Chinese elites, were not that homogeneous too, and had their broader conflicting political and economic concerns. Given this complexity, our high-definition approach asks: *What was the social structure in colonial Hong Kong? Who lived in colonial Hong Kong? How did they make a living?*

Second, the aforementioned narratives also portray Hong Kong as an "ordered and orderly" society without much overt social conflict. This portrait assumes the colonial ruler invariably practiced "good governance" and could acquire legitimacy by launching and implementing "good policies" without facing resistance to its governing strategies or calling state-society relations into question. Yet in reality, Hong Kong experienced intense conflicts historically. To maintain effective colonial rule or British imperial power, the ruler co-opted local elites into the administrative structure, allowed "self-governance" of local communities by virtue of "indirect rule", and simultaneously intervened, or used force to suppress, local Chinese society occasionally in time. Hence, the effectiveness of such "indirect rule" or later coined the "administrative absorption of politics" is arguably a myth and rhetoric (Tsai, 2001).[13] This portrait also assumes *away* the agency of many social actors in Hong Kong's history, even including the British colonists.[14] Local Chinese inhabitants were far from the politically apathetic subjects portrayed (see Lau, 1982). Different groups chose in various periods to collaborate or to challenge and force the colonial regime to reformulate new social, political and economic policies.[15] From a comparative perspective, Lange et al. (2006) conclude that Hong Kong experienced more "direct" than "indirect" rule as a colony

---

[11] Lau (1982) theorized this situation using such concepts as "a minimally-integrated social-political system" and "utilitarian familism".

[12] For example, see Lazarus (2014).

[13] King (1975) helped coin this concept of "administrative absorption of politics" in Hong Kong.

[14] "*Agency*" is the capacity of an individual to act according to his or her own will. It is a sociological term in contrast to "*structure*" that limits individual choices of action.

[15] British imperialism could not succeed without non-British collaborators (mainly Chinese) facilitating in the local scene (Munn, 1998). Robinson (1972) championed this idea through his study of non-European foundations of European imperialism.

relative to many other British territories where the local elite played a far more active role in governance. *What was the nature of the state-society relationship? What were the colonial ruler's strategies of governance? What were the major social conflicts in different periods of colonial Hong Kong?*

Lastly, by emphasizing Hong Kong a "very Chinese society", the standard-definition narratives describe Hong Kong's developmental process as self-contained without involving much influence regionally from mainland China or globally from other Western or Asian countries. It downplays the contribution from other ethnic groups to the making of Hong Kong. We argue that far from being a self-contained entity, every phase of Hong Kong history was inextricably linked to the socio-political situation in mainland China and Hong Kong's fate was much shaped by the global geo-politics. *What was the position of Hong Kong in relation to the wider global and regional arenas? How did geo-political forces impinge on local inhabitants' daily lives?*

2   THE HONG KONG STORY

To provide a more balanced understanding of the multifaceted nature of Hong Kong's colonial past, we present a high-definition Hong Kong Story—first, a period of intense imperial conflicts in the nineteenth century, then the coming of decolonization and Chinese nationalism stretched before and after the Second World War, and lastly the post-war rise of Hong Kong ending with the two 1960s riots.

2.1   *The Global: The Birth of Modern Hong Kong Beyond a Harmonious Encounter (1830s–1890s)*

A barren rock with nary a house upon it. It will never be a mart for trade. (Lord Palmerston, 1841, as cited in HKSAR, 2010)

The 156 years between the raising of the British flag on the northern shore of Hong Kong Island on January 25, 1841 and the lowering of another British flag in Wan Chai on July 1, 1997 marks the beginning and the end of Hong Kong as a British colony. Although Hong Kong was no "barren rock",[16] the "Barren-Rock-Turned-Capitalist-Paradise" has

---

[16] A survey conducted by the British army documented existence of large village settlements (2000) on the Southern part (Chek-chu or Stanley) of the Hong Kong Island. The

become a legend of British colonialism (Ngo, 1999). This turning of Hong Kong into a capitalist-paradise was far from smooth and harmonious. Local Chinese *both* resisted against and collaborated with British rule during early colonization.

Rural Resistance to Colonial Rule: Coercion and Pacification
Less than a year after the British signed *the 99-Year Land Lease of New Territories* with the Qing government on 9 June 1898,[17] a "Six-Day War" took place from 14 to 19 April 1899, between the indigenous Chinese villagers and the British imperial army in the New Territories. Some 500 villagers died in this fierce battle (Hase, 2008).

Right after the "Six-Day War", the colonial government raided the commanding height of the insurgents in Ping Shan and Kam Tin and created a symbolic presence in the New Territories by taking away the iron gates of two walled-villages as trophies and establishing a police station right on top of Ping Shan Hill (Chiu & Hung, 1999)—allegedly to suppress Ping Shan's *feng shui* (Groves, 1969).

To pacify the New Territories, the colonial administration carried out a series of "land reforms". Between 1900 and 1903, it conducted an extensive land survey. Officials required local villagers to submit land deeds to the colonial authority. In return, the officials issued a Block Crown Lease for land registration. Any non-registered land would be converted into Crown Land. A "modern" system of landownership was thus instituted, and the balance of power between the Punti (本地) clans and Hakkas (客家) was greatly altered, to the advantage of the latter.[18] In retrospect, the land reform illustrates how the British colonizers skillfully exploited the Hakka-Punti rivalries to dismantle the power of the local great clans to

survey was reported in "The Hongkong Gazelle", published in the Chinese Repository [《中國叢報》]. (See https://www.thestandnews.com/culture/你可曾記起香爐/).

[17] In 1841, China was defeated in the First Opium War, which resulted in British's first occupation of Hong Kong in 1843. Conflicts over the opium trade continued after the establishment of the British crown colony and quickly escalated into the Second Opium War. This resulted in the expansion of the colony in 1860 to include the Kowloon Peninsula and Stonecutter's Island under the Convention of Peking. Conflicts between the East and West did not end with the cooling down of hostility between the two imperial powers after England backed the Qing government in suppressing the Taiping rebellion.

[18] Conflicts between the local Hakka and the Punti were cultivated by two destructive events in Qing's history: *The Great Clearance Order* (1655–1699) and the *Hakka-Punti Clan War* (1854–1867). The civil war had a profound impact on rural politics in Hong Kong and made the colonial strategy of "divide and rule" possible.

achieve rural stability in the New Territories, but it also shows how "direct" British colonial governance had been (Chiu & Hung, 1999).[19] While the British colonizers governed the New Territories with a "divide-and-rule" strategy, their system for running the urban area differed.

Administering Urban Hong Kong: Collaboration and Incorporation
The British were the most powerful group in Hong Kong. The most influential among them, next to colonial government officials, were the British merchants[20] such as the well-known Scottish businessmen, the founders of the Jardine Matheson Group, William Jardine and James Matheson.[21] To validate their social status and to promote their national tradition of horse racing, the British merchants founded the Hong Kong Jockey Club in 1884. Membership in the Happy Valley racecourse was restricted to the British initially. The Hong Kong Club was established in 1846 where "gentlemen" could spend their leisure. In this heyday of British Imperialism, "gentlemen" did not include the French or Chinese elites. Places like these were also where British merchants cultivated business networks and wealth, exchanged information and maintained their superior social and economic positions within the colony by mingling with government officials. The relationship between British merchants and government officials was actually a bilateral one—as John Rex (1974, p. 214) put it, government officials had to gain political support from the British merchants at these sites. An old saying describes the power hierarchy in Hong Kong— "Power in Hong Kong, it has been said, resides in the Jockey Club, Jardine and Matheson, the Hong Kong & Shanghai Bank, and the Governor–in that order." (Hughes, 1976, p. 23). These

---

[19] The widespread belief that the Hakkas came later to the area of Hong Kong and their relationship with the Punti was solely a "conflictual" one is disputed by Hayes (2012): Hakkas arrived as early as the first Punti (Cantonese), intermarriage between Hakka and Punti was common, mixed villages existed peacefully, and some Hakkas were Cantonese speaking Punti in Southern China before they came to Hong Kong, whereas Punti could have been Hakkas in the distant past.

[20] See "Infographic: Scots in Hong Kong" (2014).

[21] William Jardine and James Matheson set up their company first in Guangzhou on 1 July 1832, and promoted the founding of Hong Kong in 1836. The Jardine Matheson Group was the centre of trade in early colonial Hong Kong, and recorded some of the "firsts" in the modernization of Hong Kong. It purchased the first plots of land in Hong Kong at East Point for 565 pounds in 1841 Along with other British merchants, the Jardine Matheson Group cultivated a regional network and monopolized a number of industries.

networks of officials and unofficial members became "Hong Kong's power elite" (Davies, 1977). The tradition of colonial bureaucrats mingling with business elites also formed the subsequent governing framework of the post-war administrative state (Rear, 1971). Yet, the British were not a homogenous class. The British working class in early Hong Kong included prostitutes, policemen, soldiers, sailors, artisans, and low-ranking government officials who could earn more in Hong Kong than in Britain (Lethbridge, 1975).[22]

As the colonial government adhered to a segregation policy and minimizing administrative costs, it deliberately left the local Chinese society alone as long as it showed no inclination to rebel against British rule as those New Territories villagers did. Indeed, urban Chinese had little motivation to revolt, for they were seeking upward social mobility outside Qing China at the risk of being labelled as traitors by collaborating with the colonists. Both the Chinese merchants and labourers (except for forced labour) were in this sense collaborators of the colony (Law, 2015).

Chinese merchants became the second most influential class in early colonial Hong Kong after they consolidated their influence in Chinese community through establishing charity groups (Sinn, 2003). The government's disregard for the welfare of local Chinese and the incompetence of early colonial governance left a vacuum of social and political institutions serving the needs of the local Chinese society (Sinn, 2003). Excluded from the colonial judicial system, Chinese merchants developed an arbitration system to resolve local conflicts (Carroll, 2007). Man Mo Temple (文武廟) was established as early as 1847 to arbitrate, by religious rituals, local Chinese disputes. Chinese merchants stepped up to provide basic social services, like establishing the Kwong Fook I-Ts'z (廣福義祠 Kwong Fook Ancestral Hall) to temporarily store and repatriate bodies of coolies died in Hong Kong (Lethbridge, 1971). Other early attempts by the Chinese to administer their own affairs include the establishment of the District Watch Force in 1866.

In 1869, a scandalous report of emaciated patients inside the Kwong Fook I-Ts'z drove the Chinese leaders and the colonial government to

---

[22] Limited space does not allow us to describe how other Asians (e.g. Japanese), Europeans, and Eurasians pursued opportunities in Hong Kong. Europeans in early colonial Hong Kong generally lived a rather separate, if not completely segregated, life and most had minimal contacts with the local Chinese. See Carroll (2007) for a description of the lifestyles of Europeans and Eurasians in early colonial Hong Kong.

make a genuine attempt to exercise more control over local Chinese society (Lethbridge, 1971). The first hospital of the Tung Wah Group of Hospitals—the Tung Wah Hospital (東華醫院), a Chinese hospital providing Chinese medicine service to local Chinese—was officially opened in February 1872. The Hospital performed religious and social functions to control the Chinese community, alongside being a politico-judicial institution to arbitrate conflicts among local Chinese (Smith, 1976).

The founding of Tung Wah Hospital helped fill the socio-political vacuum within the local society. It signalled not only that the Chinese elites were capable of and willing to handle public affairs within Chinese society but also revealed the colonial government's ambivalence towards the emergence of a potential political rival (Sinn, 2003).[23] Certainly they did not enjoy the kind of power held by the plantation elites in the Caribbean or the Indian *Raj*, but the Chinese elite were gradually given more community responsibilities.

Still, the colonial government gradually recognized Tung Wah Group as a threat to its sovereignty and monopolization of judicial functions. It therefore incorporated the Chinese elites into the government's administrative apparatus of Boards, Councils and Committees (Sinn, 2003). After a series of diplomatic confrontations between Tung Wah Group and the Governor over a rumour concerning the outbreak of the plague in 1894, the former was forced to recognize the legitimacy of Western medicine and accepted the first Chinese practitioner of western medicine in 1896 and then progressively expanded the latter's scope (Lee, 2013). More educated Chinese elites began to distance themselves from Tung Wah Group, and were more willing to be "administratively absorbed" into the colonial state (Sinn, 2003).[24]

The Common Chinese made up the majority of the early colonial population and contributed the most economically to the colony, but stories of the common Chinese, especially the lower working class, were not well told in the colonial archives (Carroll, 2007). The identity of these migrants, betting on having a viable future in Hong Kong, as artisans, labourers,

---

[23] Only the most successful merchants with the most influential social networks would be elected into the Tung Wah Group (Sinn, 2003, p. 8). By 1881 when local Chinese merchants were the largest owners of real estate in Hong Kong and contributed 90 percent of the colony's revenue, the power of the Tung Wah Group in overseeing Chinese affairs in the colony had increased commensurately (Sinn, 2003, p. 84).

[24] This also marked the beginning of the administrative absorption of politics in Hong Kong. See King (1975) for a modern version of the process after the two 1960s riots.

security guards, smugglers, pirates, or vagabonds was often a constantly shifting one. Many would shuffle through roles within the lower stratum of the colonial social structure throughout their lives. Yet the early Chinese working class, including skilled workers like carpenters and chair makers, was far from being entirely submissive as indicated by the capacity to take collective action by going on strike for better pay or shorter work hours (Tsai, 1995).

As the majority of Chinese migrant labourers were males, a sizeable sex industry emerged in Hong Kong and overseas. By the late nineteenth century, Hong Kong had become the regional centre for trafficking women and minors. Most of these girls were kidnapped or abducted from mainland China and from the colony to be sold to brothels or for forced labour or marriage. Many Chinese in colonial Hong Kong regarded the selling of women and children by parents as *Mui Tsai* (妹仔 young female domestic helper) or to be prostitutes as legitimate, creating a direct clash between the tradition of the East and modern Western culture in terms of humanitarian values, especially in view of the international consensus on banning slavery.

No evidence suggests the colonial government (and all the men in it) were liberated from their own British patriarchal ideology during the Victorian period (Sinn, 1994, p. 165). Public outcry over exploitation of women and children originated in mainland China among the gentry class whose members urged Hong Kong to tackle these trafficking situations. This led to the setting up of Po Leung Kuk (保良局), the Society for the Protection of Women and Children, in 1878. It was an honourable move of the Chinese social elite, intertwined with British legal efforts to eradicate trafficking of women, but it also illustrated the elites' eagerness to maintain the traditional patriarchal structure by determining an acceptable legal boundary for the *mui tsai* system and concubinage (Carroll, 2007, p. 76).

Modern Hong Kong was certainly not born out of an "harmonious encounter between two cultures". Colonial government did not lead directly to stable state-society relations. Resistance and collaboration were manifested in different forms in the rural and urban areas, consequently shaping colonial governing strategies in various parts of and towards different groups of Hong Kong people. From a high-definition perspective, "indirect rule" was never a single-minded strategy employed by the colonial government, but certainly it echoed the colonial neglect of Chinese affairs and its inability to establish complete control over the local population with only a thin layer of bureaucracy. The initial attempt to self-administer their society caused a power struggle between the Chinese elites and the colonial state during social crises, e.g., the plague, followed by the marginalization of prominent Chinese organizations and the incorporation of elites into the early bureaucracy.

2.2   The Regional: Nationalism and Decolonization (1870s–1967)

Chinese Nationalism and Hong Kong
The rise of Chinese nationalism had an enormous impact on the colony's development. The nationalist wave was generated from a series of events beginning with revolutionary activities in the late nineteenth century,[25] until the leftist riots in 1967.[26]

Hong Kong had long been a sanctuary for Chinese political activists and asylum seekers. In 1895, Dr. Sun Yat-sen founded the Hong Kong Revive China Society (興中會) in the Central District, and used Hong Kong as the base for the uprising against the Qing government (Tsang, 2004). Hong Kong's connection to the Chinese diaspora in Southeast Asia, its close proximity to the long coastline of mainland China, its free port status, the relative freedom of the press and advanced publication industry (Tsang, 2004), and support from Chinese merchants in Hong Kong (such as Ho Kai) helped turn Hong Kong into the frontier of the Chinese revolution. The British colonial government was ambivalent towards the emergence of Chinese nationalism. While it maintained a tolerant attitude wishing to see political change in China, it soon prohibited Sun Yat-sen from re-entering Hong Kong in 1896 for fear of angering its Chinese neighbour (Carroll, 2007).

The birth of modern China as a nation in 1911 and the discriminatory colonial practices in Hong Kong fuelled anti-imperialist sentiments together with Chinese nationalism among the local Chinese. The failed attempt to assassinate Governor Francis May in Hong Kong by a young

---

[25] These include: The Republican Revolution in 1912, the anti-imperialist Canton-Hong Kong Strike in 1925–1926, Japan's imperialist expansion and occupation of Hong Kong in 1941–1945, the Chinese Civil War in 1946–1949, the 1950–1953 Korean War, the decolonization movement in Asia, and the Double Tenth riots by pro-Nationalist factions in 1956.

[26] After the 1967 leftist riots—a spillover from the Cultural Revolution in the mainland—politics concerning the Greater China region faded out from Hong Kong for a short period until the beginning of the Sino-British negotiations over Hong Kong's future.

Chinese in 1912 right after the Chinese Revolution could be seen as the prologue to a series of open political confrontations in Hong Kong set off by political events involving modern China. The 1912–1913 Tram Boycott was a direct consequence of the colonial government's banning of circulation of Chinese coins through discouraging tram and ferry companies from accepting the coins as fares (Chan & Young, 1994).

While the May Fourth Movement in 1919 stimulated young Chinese students in Hong Kong to call for social change, the colonial government, in line with the Chinese business elites, responded by promoting the conservative teachings of Confucianism in colonial education. Both feared weakening social control with the rising political consciousness of educated youth and the working class (Tsai, 2001) despite Governor May having already made it mandatory in 1913 for all private schools to register with the government to prevent anti-British propaganda from spreading in the colony (Carroll, 2007).

The continuing exploitation of Chinese labour led to large scale strikes by organized labour such as the Mechanics' Strike in 1920 and the Seamen's Strike in 1922 (Tsai, 2001; Carroll, 2007). The Canton-Hong Kong Strike-Boycott of 1925–1926 became a major showdown between Chinese nationalism and British imperialism in Hong Kong before the Second World War (Tsang, 2004). With Guangdong's Kuomintang (國民黨 KMT) Government supporting the strike-boycott with subsidies and accommodations, Hong Kong came to a standstill for months as students boycotted classes from 19 June 1925 onward. Shops refused to serve European customers, and around 200,000 Chinese workers left for the mainland (Carroll, 2007).

The strike-boycotts demonstrated the strong nationalistic sentiment shared between Hong Kong and Guangdong Chinese (So, 2011). The colonial government soon learned how easy it was for Chinese nationalism to spill over the border and the importance of maintaining good relations with the then conservative Guangdong government, and introduced new legislation to ban strikes for a political purpose and to sanction anti-imperialist publications (Carroll, 2007; Tsai, 2001).

Cold War Politics and Post-War Decolonization in Asia
Hong Kong's post-war development was steered by regional Cold War politics. The trade embargo imposed on China following the outbreak of the Korean War and the devastation of industrial establishments and infrastructures during the Japanese Occupation diminished Hong Kong's role

as a major entrepot connecting China and the world. Yet massive influx of Chinese refugees during and after the Chinese Civil War accelerated Hong Kong's post-war industrialization by supplying abundant labour, technology and capital for investment in the local market, and transformed Hong Kong into an industrialized city to become one of the East Asian economic miracles in the 1960s and the 1970s (see Chap. 5).

Colonial Hong Kong was vulnerable to another regional trend in Asia—decolonization. A wave of decolonization swept through Asia between 1947 and 1984. The British Empire lost nine colonies in Asia,[27] many of which had vital trade relations with Hong Kong. The rapidly shrinking British Empire compelled some British leaders to change their view towards Hong Kong, as the loss of colonies in Asia greatly reduced trade activities between the UK and Asia. Many former British colonies started to trade with the US. Hong Kong, although was still a 'colony', did the same. Keeping Hong Kong became of strategic importance for Britain's economic interests in the Far East (see Chap. 2). On the other hand, owing to the Cold War, holding on to Hong Kong had come to assume much sentimental value to the British and a pivotal point in its struggle against the spread of communism in Asia, e.g., as in Thailand and Burma, and especially against communist insurgency in Malaya during the 1950s and 1960s (Carroll, 2007).

2.3 The Local: The Rise of Hong Kong (1950s–1990s)

Influenced by the Cold War, the Young Plan, proposed by the first post-war Governor Mark Young in 1946 to introduce representative democracy to colonial Hong Kong, was shelved in 1952. Its shelving reflected British fears of communist penetration into Hong Kong and of potential harm to British economic interests. One year after the Young Plan was abandoned, a massive fire occurred on 25 December 1953 in Shek Kip Mei. This widely reported event shocked the world and forced the colonial government to intervene in the housing market on a large-scale by building resettlement estates for the fire victims. This post-war housing policy of the colonial government marked a significant departure from the

---

[27] British India (1947), British Mandate of Palestine, Burma, and Ceylon (1948), British Malaya (1957), Kingdom of Sarawak, North Borneo, and Singapore (1963), and Brunei (1984).

pre-war approach to social policy based on the "voluntarism principle" and self-governance (see Chap. 8).

Hong Kong's post-war development and its growing prominence in the international arena had strong economic roots. Its economic ascent, however, was in many ways connected to the isolation of the new China from the world economy since the early 1950s. Between the 1950s and the 1980s, rapid economic growth earned the city its fame as one of the East Asian economic miracles. Between 1968 and 1973, Hong Kong's GDP rose by 117 percent.[28] The living standards of Hong Kong residents also improved substantially. The rise of Hong Kong also witnessed the development of culture industry, fostering local film industry and many international film stars, e.g. Bruce Lee and Jackie Chan (see Chap. 6).

Fuelled by the colonial state's indifference towards local political reform and social tensions having accumulated from during the rapid post-war economic development, the local society eventually erupted in protest in the 1966 Kowloon Disturbances against a fare rise by the Star Ferry Company, followed by the 1967 leftist riots. These incidents led to a series of reforms by Governor Murray MacLehose in the "Golden Decade" in the 1970s. The 1967 leftist riots became the inflection point that dissuaded the public from engaging in politics involving mainland China while also driving Hong Kong towards a more inward-looking development phase during the *MacLehose* era (Cheung, 2009).[29]

Since the late 1960s, Hong Kong came to be viewed as more than just a political refuge. The stable environment after the Second World War encouraged many Chinese to start their families and have children. A distinct local identity and consciousness emerged among the post-war baby boomers who considered Hong Kong as their home. These post-war baby boomers transformed the city inside out, and started to demand for a more responsive and representative government in Hong Kong (see Chap. 4).

Perhaps the most consequential post-war socio-political development was the establishment of the Independent Commission Against Corruption (ICAC) in 1974 as an institutional response to clean up endemic

---

[28] See Table 1 GDP by major expenditure component (a) At current market prices in Census and Statistics Department (2017).

[29] However, Lui (2012) examined the *MacLehose Era* closely and argued many development projects had been started by the colonial government before Sir Murray MacLehose assumed his position as Governor, hence the common conception of a miraculous *MacLehose Era* was to some extent a mythical *Era* as well.

corruption in Hong Kong (see Chap. 9). The ICAC gradually made its presence felt after arresting several high-profile police officers and forcing many others to retire early. As the public's confidence in the "cleanliness" of the colonial civil service was restored, the colonial state in turn benefitted by gaining an important source of governing legitimacy.

After the 1970s, as China re-entered into the global economy, Hong Kong started to enter a post-industrial stage. After years of economic take-off, Hong Kong underwent a major structural transformation. This transformation had become obvious by the mid-1980s. Rising land rent, protectionism and keen competition from neighbouring Asian countries forced Hong Kong's manufacturing industry to relocate across the border to the Pearl River Delta where there was a large pool of docile and cheap labour (Chiu & So, 2004; Chiu et al., 2008; Chiu & Lui, 2009, followed by a rapid expansion of the financial and service sectors (see Chap. 5).

Hong Kong focused in the 1970s on economic and social affairs, but during the 1980s the issue of Hong Kong's future, the "1997 problem" overshadowed everything else. Politically, Hong Kong's democracy movement started in the 1980s. By the end of the 1980s, major social conflicts erupted as a response to the locals' worries about Hong Kong's return to an authoritarian led regime in mainland China in 1997. This conflict peaked immediately after the June Fourth Incident in 1989. Prolonged political negotiation between the Chinese and British governments in the 1990s did not result in an outcome usually seen in other former British colonies—full democracy. Rather, Hong Kong suffered from a democratic setback. The democratically elected Legislative Councillors were not permitted to board a "through-train" to automatically continue as members in the new legislature on 1 July 1997. They were replaced by a group of Beijing approved political appointees in the Provisional Legislative Council of the HKSAR. This subsequently paved the way for intense struggles over the issue of democratization in post-handover Hong Kong that persists even today.

3   THE NUANCED COLONIAL LEGACY

In light of the history reviewed above and the revived debate over the legacies of colonial modernization in Asia within the interlocking institutional framework of the economy, the system of rule and politics, and society and culture in the colonial era (Kim, 2011), we now critically re-examine the four commonly alleged "colonial legacies" discussed earlier.

3.1   Rule of Law?

The rule of law emerged from the colonial legacy of a system of rule and politics. Our review of Hong Kong's history illustrates the complexity of colonial domination of the Chinese subjects: legislation that imposed temporal and spatial restrictions on movement of early Chinese migrants, co-opting the Chinese compradors, countering resistance by local villagers during and after the Six Days War, breaking strikes initiated by the Chinese working class, and absorbing politics via bureaucratic expansion of civil servant ranks after the 1966 and 1967 riots.

The passage of a set of anti-Chinese laws in early Hong Kong, as Peter Wesley-Smith (1994) argues, demonstrates how racism once permeated the judiciary in the British colony and undermined the rule of law. For instance, the colonial system guaranteed greater "autonomy" for the British class in the early days, for "all animals are equal [before the law], but *some animals are more equal* [before the law; emphasis added] than others."[30] *Criminal trials were tailored to secure fast and efficient court processing and conviction, regardless of guilt or innocence, of the Chinese subjects, especially for those in the working class who could not speak English nor afford to hire a lawyer. Despite 95% or more of Hong Kong's population being Chinese speaking, the official court language was English, and English only, until 1974* (Munn, 1999).[31]

As Chan (1997a) *points out, a weak separation of powers between the executive and legislative branches existed in colonial Hong Kong. Legislative Council members who, before 1985, were all appointed by the government, almost always passed the bills laid on the table. One could label this type of legislature a "rubber stamp". The making of laws in colonial Hong Kong had favoured the interest of British class from the beginning—only one out of twelve Legislative Council members were Chinese in 1884, and three out of eighteen in 1923.*

Before 1997, the final adjudication of law for Hong Kong was vested in the Judicial Committee of the Privy Council in London. Meanwhile, politically motivated prosecutions were rare but still occurred in Hong Kong (Chan, 1997a). Although the legacy of the British colonial legal system was flawed by these setbacks and defects mentioned above and elsewhere (Davies, 1977; Chan, 1997a), an essential pillar of the rule of law—the

---

[30] A Quote from George Orwell (1951).
[31] See Cap 5 Official Languages Ordinance [Originally 1974, February 15].

independence of the judiciary—was in the making since the 1950s. Some argued the triggering point for this development rested on a depoliticization attempt of the colonial state, upon the complex Cold War geopolitical context, to appear impartial by resolving political incidents through independent judicial process (Choi & Lee, 2017). Barnes (1976), reviewing the local judiciary, commented, "Judicial independence in the narrow sense already exists in Hong Kong. But it needs to be expanded."

This independence of the judiciary is now fully developed, at least on paper. "The independence of judiciary is constitutionally provided for and enshrined in Article 85 of the Basic Law." It is recognized that "Judicial independence is of fundamental importance in the Hong Kong legal system, and forms a core element in the concept of the separation of powers between the Executive, the Legislature and the Judiciary with checks and balances as between them." The judiciary upholds that it should be perceived by the public to be independent and judges resolve disputes as between citizen and government impartially. (Judiciary of Hong Kong, 2004, p. 102). The former Chief Justice Andrew Li has repeatedly emphasized that the *independence of the judiciary* is the key to the effective protection of human rights and civil liberties in Hong Kong (Li, 2014) and this assessment has been upheld by second Chief Justice Geoffrey Ma during speeches in 2015, believed to be in response to controversial comments made by Chinese officials (Lau, 2015; Ng, 2015).[32]

Yet, how 'rule of law' is implemented in Hong Kong since the colonial time is often subjected to debate. For example, to stop escalating street violence of anti-government demonstration and to deal with masked protesters, on 4 October the Chief Executive Carrie Lam, invoked a law originated from colonial time —the Emergency Regulations Ordinance to impose a ban on the wearing of masks publicly. This law empowers SAR chief executive to quickly implement new law in name of maintaining social stability without having to seek prior approval from the Legislative Council. Consequently, a new law called "The Prohibition on Face Covering Regulation" came into effect.

On the other hand, Carol Jones and Jon Vagg (2017), while surveying Hong Kong's criminal justice system, argue that in early colonial era the system has been designed under a dominant narrative that "Hong Kong is essentially a stable, peaceful and safe place". With such a dominant

---

[32] In recent years, this core value has been fiercely challenged but defended by the local legal community as in the notable speech delivered by Chief Justice Geoffrey Ma in 2015.

narrative, the elements of "law, order and stability" have been emphasized in the principle of "rule of law". Hong Kong's police force, court and prison systems were designed at the outset to "maintain the status quo" and to bring law and order into practice. Anyone challenging such a premise is considered "criminal offenders" or "bad citizens" in the system.

Such version of "rule of law", a colonial 'legacy', emphasizing "law, order and stability" differs greatly form another version of "rule of law" stressing "fairness, equality, accountability, and civil and political rights" in western societies. In many western democratic societies, the former version is usually considered as "rule by law" to make explicit distinction from the latter. However, in Chinese context, both versions use the same vocabulary (法治), leaving much ambiguity and leeway to interpret what "rule of law" means in Chinese society.

Hence, contrary to many standard-definition images simply taking "rule of law" as British colonial legacy at face value, our high-definition images suggest British colonial legacy also has two faces. Undoubtedly the British installed a legal system that to a certain extent protect Hong Kong citizens' individual rights and freedom. Nonetheless, British colonizers also established a legal system consisting of many authoritarian laws for effective colonial governance. The extent these draconian laws in the legal system have been invoked to maintain control over Hong Kong, is hopefully checked by the parallel tradition of "rule of law" in shaping the city's future.[33]

3.2   An Efficient Civil Service?

The relatively "clean" and efficient civil service has a relatively short history within the colonial system of rule and politics, as syndicated corruption involving some government branches was not uncommon before the establishment of the ICAC in 1974. Yet the anti-corruption crusade started by Governor Murray MacLehose also signified the government's direct intervention into a local Chinese tradition—the exchange of mutual benefits facilitated by informal economic transactions carried out based on *guanxi* or red packets. This "meddling" into a widespread practice of the Chinese society did not take place until the British had determined to transform Hong Kong into a financial centre. This meant requiring a

---

[33] The alleged shift towards "rule by law" has been hotly debated. See Ng et al. (2017), Hollingsworth and Lau (2017).

transparent and clean transaction system. All in all, the clean civil service is an undisputed positive legacy by international standards. In 2014, the Transparency International ranked Hong Kong 17th among 175 countries in its Corruption Perceptions Index.[34] This high ranking reflects the fact that Hong Kong is widely perceived as having a clean and transparent civil service.

A legacy associated with the installation of a British style civil service is the acceptance of English as the official language. Like many other former British colonies, Hong Kong has also been given a cultural "gift"—a relatively high level of English literacy. Not only has this cultural gift provided Hong Kong with a very cosmopolitan outlook as compared to neighbouring Asian cities, it has also strengthened Hong Kong's role as a "middleman" between rising China and the West. Even after Hong Kong was returned to China in 1997, its high level of English literacy continues to be a feature that distinguishes Hong Kong as a "global Chinese city" from other "Chinese cities".

Yet, the long priority given to English also implies a slow process of localization of the civil service until it accelerated mainly in the years leading up to the signing of the Sino-British Joint Declaration. Elitist bias, institutionalized racism and expatriate domination long existed within the civil service infrastructure (Chan, 1997). For more than a hundred year top government officials were almost all expatriates. A glass ceiling was installed to prevent capable Chinese from participating in policy-making, simultaneously reinforcing the view that they were incapable as administrators of serving in that capacity.

Decisions concerning the colony were made using a top-down approach with little effort to consult the local society until 1968 when the City District Officer ("CDO") system was instituted immediately after the two large riots. Even so, the CDO was merely a "consultation" scheme lacking any system for the CDO and citizens to negotiate the city's administration (King, 1975).

---

[34] The Corruption Perceptions Index ranks countries/territories based on how corrupt a country's public sector is perceived to be. Higher rank means less perceived corruption. See Transparency International (n.d.).

3.3   *Open Economy and Fair Opportunity?*

Open economy and fair opportunity—the justification for the colonial economic system suggested by reference to its "fairness" and openness diverts our attention away from Hong Kong's economic reality. The city's economic policy was biased in favour of the British merchant class, including the Scots, and later the Shanghainese, the ally of the British merchant class, at the expense of the Cantonese speaking Chinese merchants and industrialists. From the beginning, British companies like the Hong Kong and Shanghai Bank, and Jardine, Matheson & Co. received preferential treatment from the colonial government. During post-war industrialization the Shanghainese industrialists, as compared to their Cantonese counterparts, received a larger US textile import quota. The decision by the colonial government not to upgrade local industry was in stark contrast to the sophisticated infrastructure built to groom the finance and banking sectors—a policy that also entailed at the same time a deregulation of the flow of capital in and out of the colony. As a result of its low tax base, Hong Kong's public sector was financed by a high land price policy, a policy unintendedly promoting the growth of a few conglomerates that monopolized the real-estate/ properties market from the 1980s onward.

From the early colonial days, the government's *laissez faire* policy in effect enabled the exploitation of Hong Kong in the form of welfare avoidance at the urging of the early British merchants who feared a rise in taxes would harm their businesses. On the other hand, some have considered the laissez faire doctrine to be a myth, for the colonial government did intervene, albeit selectively, in the local economy to ensure political and social stability when faced with a crisis of legitimacy (Scott, 1989).

The colonial government's non-interventionist approach resulted in weak environmental and labour regulations during post-war industrialization. This helped promote the proliferation of enterprises but ignored the occupational health and safety of the working class. In the 1960s Hong Kong was labelled a 'sweatshop' for its minimal regard for labour rights and welfare (Rosen, 2002) although some found this label to be an exaggeration (Schiffer, 1983). Environmental problems emerged as well. For example, for a while the Shing Mun River flowing through Shatin was so polluted that fish could hardly survive in it.

The government's minimal role in intervening in the housing market resulted in many people still living in squatter areas until the 1990s (Smart, 2001). Post-war living conditions were once characterized as Third World by international standards (Hambro, 1955). Investment in human capital was also low by world standards. According to the Human Development Report (1990), Hong Kong's adult illiteracy rate in 1985 was still 12% (compared to 23% in 1970), and one in five females remained illiterate (19%) despite an improvement from 36% in the 1970s (UNDP, 1990, Annex Table 4, p. 101). Even though Hong Kong later becomes a global city given its centrality in the world economic system (Sassen, 2005), opportunities for tertiary education were extremely limited until the 1980s (Hui & Poon, 1999). For a more recent period (2001–2009), Hong Kong's tertiary enrolment ratio was still low at 34.3% despite its high human development status compared to OECD countries (for comparison, the tertiary enrolment ratio in Finland was 93.8%; in South Korea 96.1%; in the United Kingdom 59.0%; and in Japan 57.9%) (UNDP, 2010).[35]

With respect to "fair opportunity", it is worth-noting that Hong Kong's Gini Coefficient in the 1990s was higher than that of all of the OECD economies. Sociologists have long qualified the portrayal of Hong Kong as a land of opportunity by pointing out the constraints to social mobility within the socioeconomic structure (Wong & Lui, 1992).

The colonial legacy in this respect is paradoxical: as an open economy having the least constraints on earth to setting up a business, Hong Kong benefits from the many positive aspects of globalization and emerges as a Chinese global city (Chiu & Lui, 2009) but at the cost of the rather extreme inequalities we see in the past and at present.

3.4 Freedom of Speech?

Another institution traceable to colonial times, also safeguarded by the rule of law, is the freedom of speech or expression. The image of Hong Kong as a liberal society enjoying a high degree of freedom of speech and expression is a colonial legacy. Few would dispute despite there actually is a speech-act offence prohibiting people to use of triad language (Bolton et al., 1996) or even to create artwork from the subculture.[36] Censorship of the publishing industry in Hong Kong peaked during the post-war era when sympathizers of the KMT and the PRC engaged in open conflicts on the streets. Such political suppression, including the prohibition of politi-

---

[35] Hong Kong ranked 22nd in terms of HDI among 148 countries in the report. See UNDP (2010, Table 13 Education, p. 192).
[36] See Lee (2007).

cal speech in schools, gradually gave way to an open society where (market) information could flow without political interference, and so that the so-called freest economy in the world could operate efficiently. Freedom of speech, in this sense, is the key to Hong Kong's global city status by turning it into an information hub.

Freedom of speech also has political consequences, for it "guarantees freedom of political debates, upon which a democratic society rests." (Chan, 2007, p. 164). Reviewing the situation of freedom of expression in Hong Kong from 1997 to 2007, Chan (2007) found that Hong Kong still had: the highest number of daily newspapers in the world, minimal threshold requirements to publish a newspaper, and a wide diversity of views and political stances presented in the media. In fact, Chan (2007) argues the major threat to this freedom of expression originated not from the Hong Kong Government's interference but from abuses by the media itself (e.g., court battles between media over defamation; the intrusion of privacy).

Yet, the obvious decoupling of the highly valued freedom of speech from a will to introduce democracy in colonial Hong Kong again highlights our concept of "Colonial Modernization". The attempt by Governor Mark Young introducing democratic reform in 1946–1947 was shelved by his successor Alexander Grantham who faced opposition to reform from the political (including Grantham himself) and economic elites, both local Chinese and British, but also from the PRC government. The allied elites feared a socialist takeover and a loss of their privileged status, whereas the PRC opposed any move possibly leading to independence for the 'colony'. Hong Kong then underwent 30 years of modernization without democracy until the first indirect election for members of the Legislative Council (LegCo) in 1985. The first direct election of LegCo only happened in 1991 and the first bill of rights was introduced in the same year, just six years before the handover. Hong Kong's lack of democratization is best attributed to the deliberate de-politicizing of the community by the colonial state rather than to the frequent claim that Chinese were culturally apathetic (Lui & Chiu, 1999).

In recent years, there has been an increasing worry from the civil society concerning the freedom of speech. Apparently, both the enactment of the National Security Law in 2020 and the threat or actual assaults towards citizens of different political views by various sides has intensified the debate surrounding the topic. As the events are still unfolding, we'll leave this to the future generation to judge.

4 Concluding Remarks: Janus-Faced Colonial Modernization

Towards the end of the British colonial rule, there was a sudden proliferation in local scholarly contributions to the field of Hong Kong studies. Two distinctive lines of inquiry dominate in these studies: (1) assessing the British legacy to Hong Kong; and (2) assessing how Hong Kong history is written.

These two lines of inquiry became the two major axes of the high-definition investigation in this chapter. First, this chapter has examined the two faces of the British colonial legacy. While acknowledging Britain's positive contributions to Hong Kong with reference to four legacies, we have also highlighted the area where the British failed Hong Kong people before they left—the failure to institutionalize a robust democracy. Second, this chapter has surveyed state-society relations in different historical periods of colonial Hong Kong, and has also challenged the dominant standard-definition image of Hong Kong—that colonial Hong Kong was largely a stable society without much conflict. In reviewing more than 150 years of the colonial history of Hong Kong, we have shown how Hong Kong people's daily lives have been influenced by global and regional social, political and economic dynamics.[37]

Our examination of Hong Kong enriches the debate over the assessment of the legacy of European colonialism and the British empire. While the common law system developed in Hong Kong certainly has its positive impacts by enabling a pro-business environment and development of the conception of the "rule of law" in the colony, the way the common law system was developed was never peaceful nor inevitable. It came side by side with a history of violent and bloody colonial domination of the colonized subjects in Hong Kong. It also developed in an imperfect form (e.g., the relative lack of juridical independence)—a major site of contention between Hong Kong people and the mainland Chinese authority in post-colonial Hong Kong history.

Notwithstanding having increasing challenges from Mainland China, the development of a clean and efficient civil service in Hong Kong and the popularization of the English language still have lasting impacts to Hong Kong's benefit in competing with other global cities after 1997.

---

[37] Some of the post-1970s social conflicts (e.g., the clash between the ICAC and police) are not highlighted here due to space limitations. They will be covered in other chapters.

Still, far from an ideal-typical liberal economic model, the British colonial government developed a "selective non-intervention" economic model in Hong Kong that favoured the interests of the capitalist class comprised of British and Chinese elites over the Hong Kong working class as reflected in substandard labour legislation and lack of welfare measures for the latter while providing the colonial government the means to actively intervene into the market when the legitimacy of the colonial regime was threatened (see Chap. 5).

As Gi-Wook Shin and Michael Robinson (1999) suggest in their seminal work on colonial Korea, any study of modern colonial history has to be conceptually grounded within a triangular field bounded by three interlocking and mutually influencing ideas: colonialism, modernity, and nationalism. Thus, instead of simply accepting the contribution by British colonialism in modernizing Hong Kong as what the standard-definition narratives suggest, we suggest that "colonial modernization" be a better notion to highlight the British's attempts to preserve their interests in the Far East and their colonial rule in Hong Kong.[38] The colonial state was far from politically and economically neutral. As soon as the Union Jack was raised on Hong Kong Island, the very first and prime concern of retaining Hong Kong as the Empire's colony was whether this "barren rock" could advance the British imperial power in China and facilitate British merchants' interests in the Far East. With this important political and historical context, the colonial ruler's many governing strategies, such as co-optation, indirect rule, and even suppression, would perhaps be justified as "good governance" in a *post hoc* manner.

While modernization theorists suggest a linear and staged history to describe the standard development pathway of many Chinese societies (Fairbank, 1992; King, 1992), our particular focus on examining the social structures and state-society relations of colonial Hong Kong has presented a more contingent and dynamic analysis that particular social conflicts and social formation can become crucial factors constraining colonial state's capacity to govern a colony, alongside altering the development pathway of a colony. "Colonial modernization" thus serves a critical lens for us to examine both the positive and negative aspects of the colonial experience encountered by the locals, not infrequently resembled those in other former colonies (Kim, 2011). Rather than a classical

---

[38] In studies of Asian colonial history, "colonial modernity" is another concept articulated to analyze the multifaceted effects of colonialism. See Barlow (1997).

"endogenous" model of modernity as seen in Western Europe, Hong Kong's pathway to modernity is closely associated with external influences with its own particularities and complexities. For example, the colonial rule of law is both repressive and progressive, while the trickle down of individual liberty has not come with democratic participation. Thus the duality and unevenness of the modernization in Hong Kong under colonialism must be reckoned with.

A final purpose in evoking the concept of colonial modernization, however, is that we should not step into the nationalist trap either. Just like there are two nationalist narratives of Korean modernity, emanated from the North and the South, on top of the colonial discourse, Hong Kong at one time was also dominated by two nationalist narratives, one espoused by the Nationalist, while the other by the Communist. This reminds us in debating against the colonial discourse, one should not simply take on the nationalist positions, as unlike after 1997, there was no single nationalist story of Hong Kong's colonial development for us to subscribe to. By questioning the colonial historiography that dominated the standard-definition image, we are not replacing it with a simple nationalist narrative of Hong Kong people struggling against colonialism. Both resistance and collaboration could be found, not all colonial legacies malicious, and not all "national" influences benign. To reread the colonial history critically does not mean that we would want to promote postcolonial nostalgia nor to endorse without caution the nationalistic version. This is particularly important when the central and SAR governments are trying to "clean up" those alleged inheritances from the colonial time. We shall come back to these issues in later chapters.

References

"Infographic: Scots in Hong Kong". (2014, September 23). *South China Morning Post.* https://www.scmp.com/infographics/article/1597861/infographic-scots-hong-kong

Acemoglu, D., Johnson, S., & Robinson, J. A. (2001). The colonial origins of comparative development: An empirical investigation. *American Economic Review, 91*(5), 1369–1401.

Barlow, T. E. (1997). *Formations of colonial modernity in East Asia.* Duke University Press.

Barnes, E. (1976). The independence of the judiciary in Hong Kong. *Hong Kong Law Journal, 6,* 7–26.

Bolton, K., Hutton, C., & Ip, P. P. (1996). The speech-act offence: Claiming and professing membership of a triad society in Hong Kong. *Language & Communication, 16*(3), 263–290.

Cap 5 Official Languages Ordinance. (Originally 1974, February 15). https:// www.elegislation.gov.hk/hk/cap5

Carroll, J. M. (2007). *A concise history of Hong Kong*. Rowman & Littlefield Publishers.

Census and Statistics Department. (2017). *2016 gross domestic product.* http:// www.statistics.gov.hk/pub/B10300022016AN16E0100.pdf

Chan, J. (2007). Freedom of the press: The first ten years in the Hong Kong Special Administrative Region. *Asia Pacific law Review, 15*(2), 163–191.

Chan, M. K. (1997a). Imperfect Legacy: Defects in the British Legal System in Colonial Hong Kong. *University of Pennsylvania Journal of International Law, 18*(1), 133–156.

Chan, M. K. (1997b). The legacy of the British administration of Hong Kong: A view from Hong Kong. *The China Quarterly, 151*, 567–582.

Chan, M. K., & Young, J. D. (Eds.). (1994). *Precarious balance: Hong Kong between China and Britain, 1842–1992*. Routledge.

Cheung, A. B. (1997). Rebureaucratization of politics in Hong Kong: Prospects after 1997. *Asian Survey, 37*, 720–737.

Cheung, G. K. (2009). *Hong Kong's watershed: The 1967 riots.* Hong Kong University Press.

Cheung, S. C. (1999). The meanings of a heritage trail in Hong Kong. *Annals of Tourism Research, 26*(3), 570–588.

Chiu, S. W., & Hung, H. (1999). State building and rural stability. In T. W. Ngo (Ed.), *Hong Kong's history: State and society under colonial rule* (pp. 74–101). Routledge.

Chiu, S. W., & Lui, T. L. (2009). *Hong Kong: Becoming a Chinese global city.* Routledge.

Chiu, S. W., & So, A. Y. (2004). Flexible production and industrial restructuring in Hong Kong: From boom to bust? In G. Gonzalez, R. Fernandez, V. Price, D. Smith, & L. T. Vo (Eds.), *Labor versus empire: Race, gender, and migration* (pp. 179–194). Routledge.

Chiu, S. W., So, A. Y., & Tam, M. Y. (2008). Flexible employment in Hong Kong: Trends and patterns in comparative perspective. *Asian Survey, 48*(4), 673–702.

Choi, S. C., & Lee, N. K. (2017). Legalization of politics: The geopolitical situations of Hong Kong and the consolidation of its rule of law in the Cold War. *Thought and Words: Journal of the Humanities and Social Science, 55*(2), 187–225. (in Chinese).

Davies, S. N. G. (1977). One brand of politics rekindled. *Hong Kong Law Journal, 7*, 44–80.

Engerman, S. L., & Sokoloff, K. L. (1997). Factor endowments, institutions, and differential paths of growth among new world economies: A view from economic historians of the United States. In S. Harber (Ed.), *How Latin America fell behind* (pp. 260–304). Stanford University Press.

Engerman, S. L., & Sokoloff, K. L. (2002). *Factor endowments, inequality, and paths of development among new world economics (No. w9259)*. National Bureau of Economic Research.

Fails, M. D., & Krieckhaus, J. (2010). Colonialism, property rights and the modern world income distribution. *British Journal of Political Science, 40*(3), 487–508.

Fairbank, J. K. (1992). *China: A new history*. Belknap Press of Harvard University Press.

Ferguson, N. (2004). *Empire: The rise and demise of the British world order and the lessons for global power*. Basic Books.

Groves, R. G. (1969). Militia, market and lineage: Chinese resistance to the occupation of Hong Kong's New Territories in 1899. *Journal of the Hong Kong Branch of the Royal Asiatic Society, 9*, 31–64.

Hambro, E. I. (1955). *The problem of Chinese refugees in Hong Kong: Report submitted to the United Nations High Commissioner for Refugees*. A.W. Sijthoff.

Hase, P. H. (2008). *The six-day war of 1899: Hong Kong in the age of imperialism*. Hong Kong University Press.

Hayes, J. (2012). *The Hong Kong region 1850–1911: Institutions and leadership in town and countryside*. Hong Kong University Press. (Original work published 1977).

HKSAR. (2010, January 20). *Speech by FS at Asian Financial Forum cocktail reception* [Press release]. https://www.info.gov.hk/gia/general/201001/20/P201001200262.htm

Hollingsworth, J., & Lau, C. (2017, August 25). Judiciary in the dock: Jailing of student activists opens door to debate. *South China Morning Post*. http://www.scmp.com/news/hong-kong/politics/article/2108186/judiciary-dock-jailing-student-activists-opens-door-debate

Hong Kong Institute of Asia-Pacific Studies, The Chinese University of Hong Kong. (2014, October 30). *CHUK releases survey findings on views on Hong Kong's core values* [Press Release]. https://www.cpr.cuhk.edu.hk/en/press_detail.php?id=1915&t=cuhk-releases-survey-findings-on-views-on-hong-kong-s-core-values

Hong Kong Museum of History. (2015). *Permanent exhibitions: The Hong Kong story*. Retrieved May 19, 2015, from http://hk.history.museum/en_US/web/mh/exhibition/permanent.html

Hughes, R. (1976). *Borrowed place borrowed time: Hong Kong and its many faces* (2nd ed.). Andre Deutsch.

Hui, P. K., & Poon, H. L. (1999). Higher education, imperialism and colonial transition. In M. Bray & R. Koo (Eds.), *Education and society in Hong Kong and Macao: Comparative perspectives on continuity and change* (2nd ed., pp. 109–126). Springer.

Jones, C., & Vagg, J. (2017). *Criminal justice in Hong Kong.* Routledge-Cavendish.

Judiciary of Hong Kong. (2004). *Hong Kong judiciary annual report 2004.* https://www.judiciary.hk/en/publications/annu_rept_2004.html

Keller, P. (1992). Freedom of the press in Hong Kong: Liberal values and sovereign interests. *Texas International Law Journal, 27*, 371–417.

Kim, N. N. (2011). A reconsideration of 'colonial modernization'. *Korean Social Sciences Review, 1*(1), 221–262.

King, A. Y. (1975). Administrative absorption of politics in Hong Kong: Emphasis on the grass roots level. *Asian Survey, 15*(5), 422–439.

King, A. Y. (1992). *From traditional to modernised.* Oxford University Press.

Ku, A. S. (2002). Postcolonial cultural trends in Hong Kong: Imagining the local, the national, and the global. In A. Y. So & M. Chan (Eds.), *Crisis and transformation in China's Hong Kong* (pp. 343–362). M. E. Sharpe.

La Porta, R., Lopez-de-Silanes, F., Shleifer, A., & Vishny, R. W. (1997). Legal determinants of external finance. *The Journal of Finance, 52*(3), 1131–1150.

La Porta, R., Lopez-de-Silanes, F., Shleifer, A., & Vishny, R. W. (1998). Law and finance. *Journal of Political Economy, 106*, 1113–1155.

Lange, M. (2009). *Lineages of despotism and development: British colonialism and state power.* University of Chicago Press.

Lange, M., Mahoney, J., & Vom Hau, M. (2006). Colonialism and development: A comparative analysis of Spanish and British colonies. *American Journal of Sociology, 111*(5), 1412–1462.

Lange, M. K. (2004). British colonial legacies and political development. *World Development, 32*(6), 905–922.

Lau, C. K. (1997). *Hong Kong's colonial legacy: A Hong Kong Chinese's view of the British heritage.* The Chinese University Press.

Lau, S. (2015, September 26). Hong Kong chief justice Geoffrey Ma sets out firm stance on rule of law and judicial independence. *South China Morning Post.* https://scmp.com/news/hong-kong/law-crime/article/1861557/hong-kong-chief-justice-geoffrey-ma-sets-out-firm-stance

Lau, S. K. (1982). *Society and politics in Hong Kong.* The Chinese University Press.

Lau, S. K., & Kuan, H. C. (1988/1995). *The ethos of the Hong Kong Chinese.* Chinese University Press.

Law, W. S. (2015). *Collaborative colonial power. The making of the Hong Kong Chinese.* Hong Kong University Press.

Lazarus, S. (2014, December 13). The role of Jews in the making of Hong Kong. *Post Magazine, SCMP.* https://www.scmp.com/magazines/post-magazine/article/1661441/role-jews-making-hong-kong

Lee, C. (2007, November 3). G.O.D. boss sorry for '14K' T-shirts. *South China Morning Post.* https://www.scmp.com/article/614170/god-boss-sorry-14k-t-shirts

Lee, C. C. (1998). Press self-censorship and political transition in Hong Kong. *Harvard International Journal of Press/Politics, 3*(2), 55–73.

Lee, P. T. (2013). Colonialism versus nationalism: The plague of Hong Kong in 1894. *Journal of Northeast Asian History, 10*(1), 97–128.

Lethbridge, H. J. (1971). A Chinese association in Hong Kong: The Tung Wah. *Contributions to Asian Studies (Journal of Developing Societies), 1*, 144–158.

Lethbridge, H. J. (1975). Condition of the European working class in nineteenth century Hong Kong. *Journal of the Hong Kong Branch of the Royal Asiatic Society, 15*, 88–112.

Li, A. (2014, August 15). Under rule of law, an independent judiciary answers to no political masters. *South China Morning Post.* https://www.scmp.com/comment/insight-opinion/article/1573656/under-rule-law-independent-judiciary-answers-no-political

Lui, T. L. (2012). 那似曾相識的七十年代 *[The familiar 1970s].* Chung Hwa Book Company.

Lui, T. L., & Chiu, S. W. (1999). Social movement and public discourse on politics. In T. W. Ngo (Ed.), *Hong Kong's history: State and society under colonial rule* (pp. 101–118). Routledge.

Lui, T. L., & Chiu, S. W. (2007). Governance crisis in post-1997 Hong Kong: A political economy perspective. *The China Review, 7*(2), 1–34.

Mahoney, J. (2010). *Colonialism and postcolonial development: Spanish America in comparative perspective.* Cambridge University Press.

Munn, C. C. (1998). *Anglo-China: Chinese people and British rule in Hong Kong, 1841–1870.* PhD Thesis, University of Toronto.

Munn, C. (1999). The criminal trial under early colonial rule. In T. W. Ngo (Ed.), *Hong Kong's history: State and society under colonial rule* (pp. 46–73). Routledge.

New Asia Publishing House Editorial Board [Xinyazhou chubanshe bianji weiyuanhui]. (2004). *General studies for primary schools, teacher book, primary 4, book 1B [Xiaoxue changshi jiaoshi yongshu sishang b].* New Asia Publishing House.

Ng, J. (2015, September 21). Hong Kong Chief Justice Geoffrey Ma transcends political debate but stands up for separation of powers. *South China Morning Post.* https://www.scmp.com/news/hong-kong/law-crime/article/1859940/profile-hong-kong-chief-justice-geoffrey-ma-transcends

Ng, J., Chung, K., & Zhao, S. (2017, July 14). Legislative Council disqualifications shift the balance of power in Hong Kong. *South China Morning Post.* http://www.scmp.com/news/hong-kong/politics/article/2102733/legislative-council-disqualifications-shift-balance-power

Ngo, T. W. (1999). Colonialism in Hong Kong revisited. In T. W. Ngo (Ed.), *Hong Kong's history: State and Society under colonial rule* (pp. 1–12). Routledge.

North, D. C. (1981). *Structure and change in economic history.* WW Norton.

North, D. C. (1990). *Institutions, institutional change and economic performance.* Cambridge University Press.

North, D. C., & Thomas, R. P. (1973). *The rise of the Western world.* Cambridge University Press.

Nunn, N. (2009). The importance of history for economic development. *Annual Review of Economics, 1*(1), 65–92.

Orwell, G. (1951). *Animal farm: A fairy story.* Penguin Books.

Patten, C. (1996). Speech of policy address. In *Official Record of Proceedings, LegCo Sitting (Hansard) 2 Oct 96.* Legislative Council, Hong Kong. https://www.legco.gov.hk/yr96-97/english/lc_sitg/hansard/han0210.htm

Pepper, S. (2008). *Keeping democracy at bay: Hong Kong and the challenge of Chinese political reform.* Rowman & Littlefield Publishers.

Rear, J. (1971). One brand of politics. In K. Hopkins (Ed.), *Hong Kong: The industrial colony: A political, social and economic survey* (pp. 55–139). Oxford University Press.

Rex, J. (1974). Capitalism, elites and the ruling class. In P. Stanworth & A. Giddens (Eds.), *Elites and power in British society* (pp. 208–220). Cambridge University Press.

Robinson, R. (1972). Non-European foundations of European imperialism: Sketch for a theory of collaboration. In E. Roger, J. Owen, & R. B. Sutcliffe (Eds.), *Studies in the theory of imperialism* (pp. 117–142). Longman.

Rosen, E. I. (2002). *The globalization of the U.S. apparel industry.* University of California Press.

Salaff, J. W. (1981). *Working daughters of Hong Kong: Filial piety or power in the family?* Columbia University Press.

Sassen, S. (2005). The global city: Introducing a concept. *Brown Journal of World Affairs, 11,* 27–43.

Schiffer, J. (1983). Urban enterprise zones: A comment on the Hong Kong model. *International Journal of Urban and Regional Research, 7*(3), 429–438.

Scott, I. (1989). *Political change and the crisis of legitimacy in Hong Kong.* University of Hawaii Press.

Shin, G. W., & Robinson, M. E. (1999). *Colonial modernity in Korea* (Vol. 184). Harvard University Asia Center.

Sinn, E. (1994). Chinese patriarchy and the protection of women in 19th-century Hong Kong. In M. Jaschok & S. Miers (Eds.), *Women and Chinese patriarchy: Submission, servitude and escape* (pp. 141–170). Hong Kong University Press.

Sinn, E. (2003). *Power and charity: A Chinese merchant elite in colonial Hong Kong.* Hong Kong University Press.

Smart, A. (2001). Unruly places: Urban governance and the persistence of illegality in Hong Kong's urban squatter areas. *American Anthropologist, 103*, 30–44.

Smith, C. (1976). Notes on Tung Wah Hospital, Hong Kong. *Journal of the Hong Kong Branch of the Royal Asiatic Society, 16*, 263–280.

So, A. (2011). Nationalism and class struggle: The making of the Hong Kong working class in the 1920s. *Hong Kong Journal of Social Sciences, 41*, 1–15.

Transparency International. (n.d.). *Country profiles*. http://www.transparency.org/country/

Tsai, J. F. (1995). *Hong Kong in Chinese history: Community and social unrest in the British Colony, 1842–1913*. Columbia University Press.

Tsai, J. F. (2001). *The Hong Kong people's history of Hong Kong, 1841–1945*. Oxford University Press. (in Chinese).

Tsang, S. (2004). *A modern history of Hong Kong*. Hong Kong University Press.

United Nations Development Programme (UNDP). (1990). *Human development report 1990*. Oxford University Press.

United Nations Development Programme (UNDP). (2010). *Human development report 2010*. Oxford University Press.

Wesley-Smith, P. (1994). Anti-Chinese legislation in Hong Kong. In M. K. Chan (Ed.), *Precarious balance. Hong Kong between China and Britain 1842–1992* (pp. 91–106). M.E. Sharpe.

Wong, T. W. (2004, September). Core values: A look from the Hong Kong social indicators findings 1988–2001. *Proceeding / Conference: International Conference on Social Orientations and Social Indicators*, Hong Kong Institute of Asia-Pacific Studies, The Chinese University of Hong Kong, Hong Kong.

Wong, T. W., & Lui, T. L. (1992). *Reinstating class: A structural and developmental study of Hong Kong society*. Social Sciences Research Centre, University of Hong Kong.

CHAPTER 2

Hong Kong as an International Hub: The Rise of Hong Kong in the Modern World-System

"Hong Kong is a free port which thrives on free trade. Its open door policy has enabled it to become one of the world's largest trading economies and an international financial and commercial centre serving the Asia-Pacific region and the Mainland of China."
—Trade and Industry Department, *2012*.
"Rice imports. Hong Kong has maintained a quota and reserve system for the import and sale of rice for more than four decades. The regime restricts which and how many businesses can participate in the market."
—Consumer Council, *1996*, p. 27.

1   INTRODUCTION

Walking around Central, Mongkok, Causeway Bay, Tsimshatsui, or in any Hong Kong shopping malls, one can easily spot a great variety of international brands on display. Indeed, the image of Hong Kong as a *shopping paradise* is not limited to tourists. It is also an image looming large in the minds of locals. The view of Hong Kong as a consumer heaven is commonly credited to the legacy of its free port status and free trade policy. With a zero-percent average tariff rate, Hong Kong has been ranked since 1995 as the freest and most open economy in the Heritage Foundation's Economic Freedom Index (The Heritage Foundation, 2018). It is a city built upon the idea of free trade stressing government should impose little to no restrictions on trade-related activities. No wonder locals looked puzzled when Korean farmers performed the *"kau tau* procession" in Causeway Bay to protest against agricultural trade liberalization policy during the 2005 World Trade Organization Ministerial Conference ("Developing countries voice", 2005). Metaphorically, "free trade" can be said to be ingrained in Hong Kong's DNA. To some, however, it is Hong Kong's *original sin.*

This metaphor is not far from how people understand Hong Kong's rise from the periphery in the British *Far East* to an international hub for global trade and finance. Lacking a sociological imagination (Mills, 1959), many locals and foreigners understand their daily life experiences simply in an individualized and common-sense way—a way without appreciation of its historical roots or connecting their local experience to global or regional happenings. A *standard-definition image* of the rise of Hong Kong typically reiterates the colonial narrative portraying "free trade" as the key to Hong Kong's prosperity. We still recall how our secondary school economics, geography and history lessons taught us about the benefits of free trade, the comparative advantage of Hong Kong's *free port* in terms of its deep water harbour and strategic location, and the patchy history of the two Opium Wars. One example is found in the first two chapters of a widely-adopted local secondary history textbook—*East Meets West: The Modern History of East Asia* (Morales, 1972).[1] The textbook starts by referring to Britain's "humble" intention to promote free trade by breaking the Chinese monopoly,[2] followed by the catastrophic Taiping Rebellion triggered *solely* by China's "internal" problems.[3] Despite the account of historical events, *East Meets West* fails to mention either English subjects selling arms to both sides of the Chinese civil war, or Britain considering the *Kingdom of Heaven* as a potential trading partner (Hendershot, 1981).

[1] Alberto C. Morales was the Principal (1968-1995) of Raimondi College, a Catholic secondary school on Robinson Road, Mid-Levels, Hong Kong. Although this textbook ceased to be the dominant textbook adopted by many local secondary schools in the 1980s and 1990s, the narrative in this textbook was still in many ways reproduced in other textbooks.

[2] The overall focus of this textbook's Chapter One was the inconvenience caused by 'heavy' tariffs and taxations, and Chinese customs on foreign trade as seen in this quote: "Since they were unable to trade freely and seek the best price for their goods, the foreigners naturally resented these restrictions." (Morales, 1972, p. 3).

[3] There was no mention of cheap foreign imports causing widespread unemployment in southern China at the time as seen in the following quote: "As Western influence before 1850 was still limited, foreign pressure could hardly be considered a major cause of China's unrest." (Morales, 1972, p. 14).

The *global dynamics* leading to British invasions of China followed by the ceding of Hong Kong were seldom explicated in these secondary school lessons. Neither was the ironic reality that the colonial state had imposed trade restrictions on strategic sectors from time to time. Conventional *East Meets West* image centring on "state-to-state" diplomacy and antagonism leaves out the agency of the Chinese compradors.[4] Many of these Chinese compradors were among the Chinese elites collaborating with the British colonizers governing Hong Kong society (see Chap. 1). Some established themselves in the colony early on through providing a helpful hand to Britain in wars and smuggling. Others gained a foothold via involvement in infamous opium and Chinese coolie trade. Our *high-definition image* of early Sino-British encounters in the section "*East Meets West and the Birth of Hong Kong*" reveals unorthodox stories of trade and early Hong Kong.

While the opium and coolie businesses between the East (China) and West dominated the early Hong Kong entrepot trade scene and demonstrated the exploitative nature of unregulated global free trade with its harm and miseries, the North-South dimension of trade between Hong Kong and Asian countries has often been overlooked. In the "*Hong Kong and the North-South Trade*" section, we reassert the importance of this North-South dimension of trade and highlight the social embeddedness of trade activities within regional networks (thus also demonstrating the "non-free" aspect of trade).[5] We start with the *standard-definition* that Hong Kong was "forced" to undergo rapid industrialization as the East-West entrepôt trade was hampered by the post-war embargo on trade with China. Reduced trade activity between China and the West certainly injured Hong Kong's economy, but our *high-definition image* shows the declining export trade between Hong Kong and the *rest*—particularly the decolonizing Southeast Asian nations. We stress the declining export trade with these Southeast Asian nations had a comparable significance determining Hong Kong's economic fate in the same period as that of the West. From stories of *Nam Pak Hong* (南北行 literally South-North Trading Association), to the legendary Shaw Brothers film production and distribution network once targeted primarily the Chinese diaspora in

---

[4] *Comprador* is a Portuguese word describing the native *buyer* who buys and sells for European employers in Macao and Canton. See Hao (2010).

[5] For one original application of the concept of social embeddedness of trade, see Polanyi (1944).

Nanyang (南洋 Cantonese word for Southeast Asia) (1920s-mid-1970s), we show how Hong Kong revitalized the thousand-year-old North-South regional network by serving as a key node within it.

The decline of North-South trade in the 1950s and 1960s was a consequence of import-substitution-industrialization (ISI) adopted by the newborn Asian nations. This global rush to nation-building, however, was a chain of events triggered by the rise of a new world hegemon, the United States. In the last section "*West Meets West in the East and the Rise of Hong Kong*", we go beyond the *standard-definition image* that Hong Kong's devotion to free trade won the support of western allies during the Cold War and it seized this precious opportunity to succeed as one of the four newly-industrialized economies in East Asia (EANIEs). Our *high-definition image* paints a more complex picture. As the United States emerged out of the wreckage of the Second World War and replaced the declining British Imperial Empire as the new hegemon, it became a stronger advocate of free trade than Britain by favouring the independence of former European colonies (Fraser, 1992). This "development period" was characterized by an unprecedented growth of capitalism (McCormick, 1989/1995). Ironically, Hong Kong at this moment had fallen into a paradoxical position as a British colony while simultaneously being disproportionately dependent on entrepôt trade with external economies. New global trade rules initiated by the dominating U.S. intertwined with regional Cold War politics and the decolonization movement in Southeast Asia to force the Hong Kong[6] to adopt export-oriented industrialization (EOI) by skipping the stage of import-substitution. As the story goes, Hong Kong rose to a semi-periphery position in the capitalist world-system, gradually being drawn into the Asian US Dollar Zone through entering the United States and its allies' markets (So, 1986; So & Chiu, 1996). Hong Kong's economic status leaped ahead as it participated in US-led financial globalization in the 1970s and 1980s and eventually became a global city for stock trading in the 1990s. American influences could also be felt in daily life with the increased import of American cultural products. Yet, was it the only foreign culture that the locals embraced? To answer this, we have to travel back in time to explore the "birth" of Hong Kong.

Similar to the discussion of Hong Kong's colonial legacies, the challenge is to avoid subscribing to the nationalist or colonialist narratives that oversimplify the city's complex developments. While highlighting the

---

[6] A direct quote from Edward Szczepanik (1958).

limitations of the colonial "East meets West" theme, we also examine the nationalist discourse in a cautious way. Our high-definition discussion would hope to reconstruct Hong Kong's trading past with a combination of local, regional and global perspectives.

2 EAST MEETS WEST AND THE BIRTH OF HONG KONG

2.1 A Long Journey to South China

Britain was not the first European nation coming to China for trade. The Chinese government has recently promoted the Belt and Road Initiative, capitalizing on the historic trade connections between the Asian and European continents via firstly the land-based Silk Road during the Han (206 BC-220), Tang (618-907) and Yuan Dynasties (1271-1368), or the "Silk Road Economic *Belt*" in the Initiative. Both the fall of the Yuan Dynasty, which had a critical role in maintaining the Euro-Asia trade route by exercising military power, and the rise of the Ottoman Empire from 1299 onwards followed by its expansion into the Southeast Europe, Western Asia and North Africa areas, had increased the cost for Europeans to trade along the original Silk Road. Seeking a new route to conduct trade with Asia, European countries began to explore the ocean route, the earliest being the Portuguese fleets reaching the South China coast around the 1510s. As diplomacy soured, the Chinese Ming Dynasty state fought and won two sea battles against the Portuguese at where is now the Tuen Mun and Lantau areas of Hong Kong in 1521 and 1522. As relations improved, the Portuguese built a permanent colony on the other side of the Pearl River mouth—Macao in 1557—to further its maritime trade relations with the region (Carroll, 2007, p. 11). Tea, silk and porcelain were then imported to Europe from Canton via sea routes following the legacy of the "Maritime Silk Road".

The Dutch East India Company followed in the Portuguese footsteps to China and dominated the East-West trade route. After the Dutch started importing tea to England in 1652 (Alexander, 2004), the British East India Company (EIC) arrived in Chinese waters around 1654 and began trading at Huangpu (Whampoa) with a base at Macao. From 1588 to 1815, Britain challenged and won major battles with successive European powers including Spain, the Netherlands and France, and became the new ocean hegemon. Though Britain lost colonies during the American Revolution between 1765 and 1783, the advent of the industrial revolution had given the British an edge in the productivity race. With an insatiable urge for new markets and a craving for trading outposts in the Far East outside those of India, Britain set her eyes on an island near the Pearl River mouth, some 35 kilometres further down from Tuen Mun where Portuguese lost their sea battles some 200 years ago—Hong Kong Island (Carroll, 2007, p. 12).

2.2   *The First Opium War: The Canton System in South China and the Helping Hands of Chinese Compradors*

The First Opium War (1839-42) was a military invasion initiated by the British Imperial State against Qing China to address two issues: complaints from its merchants concerning the *Canton System*, and more critically the potential loss of taxes from the lucrative opium trade due to the Qing government's opium ban. The *Canton System* was a trading system beginning from around 1700 and ending with China signing the first unequal treaty, the Treaty of Nanking in 1842. After the ban on sea trade was lifted by the Qing state in 1684, foreign trade activities resumed but were later restricted to the port of Canton (Guangzhou) in 1757, the largest South China city close to the mouth of the Pearl River where Arab and Persian sea traders once stayed during the Tang dynasty (the eighth century) (Perdue, 2009). Under the *Canton System*, aka the *Single Port Commerce System* in Chinese—originally designed for better surveillance on trade activities—Western traders were confined to the Thirteen Factories managed by the *Cohong* (公行 in Cantonese: *Gonghang*), a group of officially authorized *hongs* (firms operated by Chinese merchants). While the East India Company monopolized British trade outside China until 1813 and inside China until 1833,[7] the *Cohong* could be seen as a measure to protect local society from the ruthless advance of "free market".[8] All foreign trade with China had to be conducted between October and March in Canton, and the foreign traders had to return to Macau with the help of monsoon winds after the end of each trading season (Tamura et al., 1997, p. 83). Despite the restrictions, the volume

---

[7] British East India Company's monopolization over trade outside Qing China ended with Charter Act of 1813 and inside ended with The Government of India Act 1833. See Bogart (2015).

[8] See Polanyi (1944) for a discussion of trade protection as a countermovement against the advance of free market.

and value of foreign trade expanded rapidly in Canton until the late 1830s (Greenberg, 1969; Endacott, 1973).

The trade imbalance resulted in a net silver outflow to China posed the British a serious economic challenge. The British loved tea and silk products but the Chinese wanted nothing from them. A solution emerged by colonizing India where opium was cultivated as a "cash crop" and imported to China to complete a triangular trade cycle with a net outflow of silver from China to the British Empire. However, as the Chinese adage goes, "It takes two coins to make a sound." Opium imports required the collaboration of British merchants and Chinese compradors, including the Chinese merchants and the minority ethnic groups living by the sea, like the *Tanka* fishermen (蜑家 boat-dwellers) long marginalized by the dominant land-based society (Munn, 1998, p. 108). For the sea dwellers, whether to become a fisherman or a pirate or a trade facilitator really depended on the economic situation of the times.[9] Despite the Qing government's continuous ban on opium trade in the late eighteenth century, the East India Company broke it by selling the contraband to anyone capable of smuggling it into China. Deprived of proper social status and upward mobility on land, the Tanka used fast speed vessels—dragon boats or "fast crabs"—for risky deals (Carroll, 2007, p. 14).

The outflow of silver and the deleterious effects on health from smoking opium worried the Qing government even though corrupt officials tended to keep their eyes shut. In 1839, Lin Zexu (林則徐) was appointed as the Special Imperial Commissioner to launch an anti-opium campaign in Guangdong province to end the opium trade once and for all. On banning any sale of opium, aka "foreign mud", Lin commanded all opium stocks be surrendered to the authorities and destroyed the confiscated opium at Humen (虎門). In a series of Pearl River blockades first by the Qing of opium trading vessels and then by British naval forces of any foreign ship complied with the Qing's order, war eventually broke out on 3 November 1839. Again, coastal Chinese compradors, used to collaborating with the foreign merchants, involved in providing supplies to the British navy during the war. A Tanka named Lo Aqui even received a plot

---

[9] One famous Tanka fisherman who became a pirate in the South China coastal area was Cheung Po Tsai (1780s-1820s). Cheung fought numerous battles with the Qing and Portuguese Naval, one of which took place at Lantau Island near the current site of the Hong Kong Airport. Cheung Po Tsai Cave can still be found on Cheung Chau Island nowadays. After losing a major battle in 1810, Cheung capitulated with 21,000 followers and 270 junks. See Hayes (1974).

of land in Lower Bazaar of the colony of Hong Kong as a reward for his service as a supplier. The First Opium War was continued on and off until 1842 with the signing of the *Treaty of Nanking*, under which Hong Kong Island was ceded to Britain and four more ports—Xiamen, Fuzhou, Ningbo and Shanghai—of Canton were forced to open to foreigners for trade and settlements. The Canton System, originally set out as a measure to protect the Chinese society from unregulated trade, unintendedly resulted in Hong Kong being declared a free port after the opium trade was swiftly resumed.

2.3   Imperialism, Unequal Treaties, and the Planned Taking of Hong Kong, Kowloon and the New Territories

Military action required planning for effective execution. The British occupation of Hong Kong Island actually took place halfway during the First Opium War and before the signing of the *Treaty of Nanking* on 26 January 1841 under the *Convention of Chuenpi*. The Treaty was negotiated between Qing high official Qishan, and British Chief Superintendent of Trade Charles Elliot who later became the first colonial administrator (Tsang, 2009/2004, p. 16). Meeting with little to no resistance, the British navy camped on a highland, named Possession Point, in nowadays Sheung Wan (west of Hong Kong Island) and renamed the road leading from shore to it Possession Street. The possession was just the beginning, however. The Qing government was considerably weakened by the Taiping Rebellion in the subsequent years (1850-1864) and the power struggle with Western imperialism raged on with an eye on expanding the lucrative Chinese market for exports. The two processes were intertwined because foreign imports, under the banner of free trade after the First Opium War, had displaced local Chinese businesses causing widespread unemployment that fuelled the Taiping Rebellion (Chesneaux, 1973).[10]

Dissatisfied with the *Treaty of Nanking* and demanding to be treated the same as America in trade relations with China, Britain joined force with France in waging a new war against the Qing government. Following her defeat in the Second Opium War (1856 to 1860), the Qing entered into another unequal treaty with Britain, France and Russia—*The*

---

[10] "Hundreds of thousands of boatmen and porters in central and southern China were thrown out of work and it was from among this army of unemployed that several of the leaders of the Taiping rebellion emerged", Chesneaux (1973, pp. 24-25, as cited in Morgan, 1985).

Convention of Peking. The Convention required the Qing government to legalize the opium trade (which was still considered contraband after the Treaty of Nanking) and the flourishing coolie trade, to ratify the earlier Treaties of Tientsin which granted foreign traders greater freedom to travel inland and to open ten more ports (including Nanjing). Under the Convention, the Kowloon Peninsula and Stonecutters Island, opposite to Hong Kong Island and south of Boundary Street, were ceded to Britain. The occupation of Kowloon was a pre-emptive move to deter its use by other Western powers and to provide better defence for the City of Victoria while Britain was helping the Qing government in the suppression of the Taiping Rebellion (1860-64) to maintain a unified China for her expanding trade (Tsang, 2009/2004).

Qing demonstrated its weakness further by losing the First Sino-Japanese War (1894-1895), which also ended China's influence in Korea. The French then proceeded to acquire the nearby Canton Bay (21 miles southwest from Hong Kong) by a 99-year lease; Germany occupied and forced the Qing to lease Jiaozhou (in Qingdao); Lushun (Port Arthur) and Dalien were leased to Russia similarly (Tsang, 2009/2004). The growing British-Russian dispute over Afghanistan and Central Asia and the defenceless condition of Hong Kong triggered a widespread fear among the local British residents of Hong Kong of a Franco-Russian joint invasion of the colony which surfaced as fictional accounts in the local newspaper *The China Mail* in 1897 (Share, 2007, p. 27).[11] These threats turned out to be hypothetical rather than genuine, but Britain had already moved to press the Qing government into signing another unequal Treaty, *The Convention for the Extension of Hong Kong Territory* (or *Second Convention of Peking*) in 1898. Under this *Convention*, islands surrounding Hong Kong and the New Territories, South of the Shenzhen River and north of Boundary Street, were leased to Britain for 99 years and expired on 30 June 1997. The emphasis on a "lease" term could be considered a drowning British diplomatic effort to show their adherence to the "free trade" doctrine and to prevent China from becoming like the "Scrambling for Africa" (around 1880-WWI in 1914) (Carroll, 2007, p. 68). The real purpose of creating a military buffer zone in the New Territories against Western powers (rather than the Qing government) (Share, 2007, p. 28) and the bloody suppression of local villages' resistance during the Six-Day War in 1899 (Hase, 2008), however, indicated the

---

[11] The authors would like to thank Dr. Lau Siu Lun for sharing this view.

"expansion/extension" was more a realist concern than anything else. Seen in this way, the "laissez-faire" port of Hong Kong was a carefully-executed plan to maintain British influence (and, a free market) in China from the start.

2.4   Early Colonial Hong Kong: A Free Port where Commodity, People and Capital Converged

Most people are probably unaware of several stops made by the main character Fogg in Jules Verne's 1873 novel *Around the World in Eighty Days*. The locations where Fogg stopped were key ports connected to two entrepôt trades dominating the early economy of Hong Kong under the free trade policy—Bombay and Calcutta as opium trade centres in India (Trocki, 1999, p. 108), and San Francisco as the Chinese emigration centre for the US.[12] Once Hong Kong was seized as a Crown Colony and declared a free port, *hongs* (洋行 foreign firms, in Cantonese *Yeung Hong*), such as Jardine Matheson & Co. and its business rival Dent, and some Parsee firms from India soon established their warehouses there. Around 75 percent of opium from India, much of which was auctioned in Bombay and Calcutta, passed through the colony between 1845 and 1849 (Carroll, 2007, p. 34). Hong Kong thus was *de facto* an unsinkable opium vessel in the first decade powered by opium tax revenue.

Security and stability, and most relevantly the hands-off attitude guaranteed under British political control boosted the free port to become a centre for international trade, attracting Chinese merchants from the previous *Canton System* and causing its decline (Tsang, 2009/2004, p. 57). Each *hong* would be led by a *Tai-Pan* (大班), usually an expatriate familiar with Chinese customs and culture, to deal with the Chinese merchants.[13] Being a major source of government revenue and owing to objections raised by Colonial India, the *hongs* and Chinese merchants at various periods, the opium trade was not completely banned in Hong Kong until after the Second World War (Carroll, 2007, p. 35). Apart from the opium trade, the *hongs* established and competed against each other in shipping and

[12] These stops included: Suez, Bombay, Calcutta, Victoria of Hong Kong, Yokohama, San Francisco, New York City, and London. In fact, Hong Kong traded with Yokohama of Japan for dried seafood, where Chinese migrants gradually established the first and biggest Chinatown in Japan.

[13] For a fictional account in popular culture of the competition among the *Tai-Pans*, see Clavell (1966) and the movie based on it.

passenger services, insurance and banking, and dockyard related services (e.g. Swire) in Hong Kong. By the end of the nineteenth century, *hongs'* businesses, often in joint-ventures with local Chinese merchants, had expanded to include railroad systems, mining, sugar refining (e.g. Swire), and cotton factories in Hong Kong and mainland China (Fung, 2014).

The shipping and passenger service was the key to early Chinese global emigration, the infamous part of which was the coolie trade. A mass of Chinese labourers, mostly from Guangdong escaping from the Taiping Rebellion and the unemployment caused by cheap imports, either voluntarily boarded or were coerced onto coolie clippers heading towards the west coast cities like San Francisco, where the oldest Chinatown in North America locates, following the discovery of gold in California in 1849 (and later in Australia). Demand for labour and thus the profitability of transpacific passenger services was boosted by the gradual banning of slavery, making Hong Kong the key migrant labour port from China en route not only to the US, but also to South America and other British colonies in Southeast Asia. The Qing's initial ban on outmigration was not strictly enforced as it helped relieve the population pressure and remittances helped reverse the silver outflow. Chinese merchants, owning two of the largest brokers sending laborers to California, were among those exploiting the opportunities (Carroll, 2007, pp. 29–35). Chinese owners of the boarding houses frequently employed triad societies to ensure coolies stayed quiet during transhipment (Morgan, 1960). The conditions on board the ships and at the contracted work sites overseas were inhumane, especially in South America countries like Cuba and Chile where no labour treaty had been signed with the Qing government, and many coolies did not live long enough to see their homeland again (Wang, 1997; Lei, 2016).

Capital was crucial to financing the expanding trade, and the *Tai-Pans* soon felt the need for a local bank supporting the Hong Kong-based *hongs*, and for providing credit to the government to build infrastructure (Fung, 2014, pp. 35–36). On 3 March 1865 the *Hongkong and Shanghai Bank* (HSBC) was established in Hong Kong to finance British trade in the region. Founding members (shareholders) of HSBC were *Tai-Pans*, the majority of whom were of Scottish origin (eight).[14] The rest were Indian-Parsi, English and English-Jew, Danish, the American and German

---

[14] While the Scottish dominated early trade and banking in Hong Kong, the Irish had an overwhelming presence in the position of Governors. Of the 15 Governors before WWI, eight were of Irish origin (and the rest English and one English-Jew). See: The Great Scottish

(Fung, 2014, p. 36). The first branch was established in Shanghai a month later in 1865. Within 25 years, the HSBC set up offices in all major Asian cities including Yokohama (1866) and Kobe/Hyogo (1869); Calcutta (1867) and Bombay (1869); Saigon (1870); Manila (1875) and Iloilo (1883); Singapore (1877) and Penang (1884); Batavia/Jakarta (1884); Hankow (1868), Amoy (1873), Tienstsin (1881), Peking (1885); Bangkok (1888); and Rangoon (1891) (King, 1988, Table 2.1, as cited in Meyer, 2000). After capturing a significant portion of the local banking market, the HSBC was authorized to issue currency notes in Hong Kong till now (Fung, 2014, p. 37).[15] Notably, not a single Chinese *hong* was enlisted in the original HSBC board of directors.

Despite the banking industry's boom, Hong Kong's monetary systems in the early days were chaotic. China's copper, bronze and iron cash were popular in small daily transactions, uncoined silver ingots were used for large transactions of businesses, paying taxes and simply as a sign of wealth, and Spanish and Mexican silver dollars were used for international trade (Hong Kong Monetary Authority, n.d.).[16] The flow of the last two illustrates that the silver standard was practiced in Hong Kong from 1863 to

Table 2.1 World imports of sea cucumber, fresh/frozen/dried/salted/ in brine, 1995-2001 (Q=tonnes; V=US$'000)

Country		1995	1996	1997	1998	1999	2000	2001
Hong Kong	Q	5789	5020	4523	3975	2922	4759	4382
(China)	V	40,898	43,376	38,147	39,565	33,571	55,533	50,430
World total (incl.	Q	7653	6597	5630	4946	4079	6040	7299
Others)	V	48,507	49,987	44,327	44,620	39,331	61,691	56,722

India Connection. http://www.scotlandinunion.co.uk/the_great_scottish_india_connection; see also: UK Tea and Infusions Association (n.d.).

[15] A few other banks also issued notes in the early days, but only HSBC and Chartered Bank of India, Australia and China, renamed as Standard Chartered bank (1862-) have continued to do so up to the present.

[16] The flow of silver from Spanish America to China via Manila can be dated as early as the 1600s. From then on Spanish silver coins became one of the most reliable and certified means of payment in China, until the independence of nations from Spanish America which then resulted in diverse standards of minting. See Irigoin (2009).

1935 when it was converted to the Sterling standard due to the silver crisis (Greenwood, 1984).[17]

2.5 Free Trade as the Doctrine of the Colony?

Modern Hong Kong, like the rest of East Asia, was created and incorporated into the world capitalist economy by force (So & Chiu, 1996). A stylized narrative derived from this process would be: the geopolitical position of Hong Kong was so exceptional—a colony seized from Chinese territory and run by a hegemon from the Far West (Britain)—that the necessary ingredients to transform itself into a transnational city were provided by simply adhering to the doctrine of being a "free port" or the equivalent policy of "free trade" between the East and West. For now, we illustrate another high-definition image of Hong Kong—that the free trade principle (therefore, the free market) was not always followed!

An example is the highly-controlled sales of crown land for achieving financial self-sufficiency for the colony. As early as 1848 local merchants were complaining about the colonial government's "high land price policy", noting land rents contributed up to 45% of the total government revenue in 1847 (Nissim, 1998, pp. 11-12). Such a policy is still practiced today (see Chap. 8). Several strategic sectors were also not "free" as of 1996. International calls, television broadcasting, driving school, and the residential property market was either under stringent government regulations for years or dominated by one or a few service providers (Consumer Council, 1996, pp. 26-27).[18] Additionally, a quota and reserve system for the import/export and sale of rice has existed since 1955.

Rice is an essential staple in South China and Southeast Asian countries. The post-First World War period saw a limited rice supply from colonies within the region while a natural disaster in Japan had directed remaining rice exports towards its market with support from the Japanese government. On 26 July 1919 a riot took place in Hong Kong when the local

---

[17] The sudden outflow of silver from Hong Kong was a result of the US Silver Purchase Act of 1934, which drove the price of silver fourfold higher.

[18] A monopoly on international calls was granted to Hong Kong Telecommunications International (HKTI) until 2006; new licenses for television broadcasting have always been limited to a few despite keen interest from operators; only one driving school was operating in Hong Kong in 1996; restricted entry to residential property market for developers due to high cost of auctioned land; and the quota and reserve system for the import/export and sale of rice that has existed since 1955.

Chinese rice merchants withheld their stock, pushing up the price. This angered the starving laborers (coolies), then gathered in Wan Chai and started robbing nearby rice shops in groups. Soon the riot extended to major districts of Hong Kong Island and Kowloon. The government determined the riot stemmed from a lack of regulation of the rice supply, and proceeded to pass a bill to do so (Zheng & Wong, 2005, pp. 53-67). A *Rice Control Scheme* was installed in 1955 under the *Reserved Commodities Ordinance (Cap 296)* to ensure a stable supply of rice and a reserve stock sufficient for consumption in an emergency for 15 days (Trade and Industry Department, n.d.). Rice being not a "freely trade commodity" reminds us the colonial government did intervene in the market when it considered necessary to ensure political and social stability. Apart from rice, other food consumption items (e.g. fresh vegetables) were also "controlled" under the same principle (see Chap. 5).

The birth of Hong Kong was no accident but part of the plan to pro- mote one form of trade in China. Rather than seeing the *Canton System* as merely a mechanism to monopolize profits like the standard-definition image of East-West Trade frequently does, our high-definition considers it a kind of social protective measure against the uprooting effect of European capitalism. Its successor—the *Hong Kong System*—a free one, was not as natural as Morales (1972) claimed, but maintained by military means and organized violence.

3   HONG KONG EMBEDDED IN THE NORTH-SOUTH TRADE

3.1   *The Curious Case of Trade Embargo and Hong Kong*

Entrepot trade has been Hong Kong's main source of income from the beginning. During post-war reconstruction (1946-1950), the city's trade expanded by benefiting from lower import tariffs under the British Imperial / Commonwealth Preferential Tariff system. However, a signifi- cant change in the quantum and direction of the colony's trade started with the onset of the Korean War (Szczepanik, 1958, p. 45). As the sec- ond standard-definition narrative tells us, the embargo imposed on the People's Republic of China (PRC) by the US and the United Nations in 1951 for China's participation in the Korean War, had severed its trade

Fig. 2.1   Percentage import trade by countries of total import trade (Census and Statistics Department, 1969, pp. 97-104)

links, mostly via Hong Kong, to the world. Figures 2.1 and 2.2 show[19] the sudden drop in U.S. import trade in 1949-1952 coincided with the above incidents. Import trade with U.S. allies Singapore/Malaya also dropped dramatically in the same period. The impact on Hong Kong's external trade was severe. Between 1951 and 1952, earnings from entrepôt trade in Hong Kong fell from HK$644 million to HK$421 million, or by roughly 35 per cent, and was aggravated by a drop in related income from warehouses, shipping, and banking sectors (Szczepanik, 1958, p. 48). Nonetheless, a disruption in the East-West trade was not the sole factor leading to the industrialization of Hong Kong.

Although China was once the biggest market for capital goods for entrepôt trade from Hong Kong, its weight declined sharply from the first (65% of all exports from HK) in 1953 to sixth in 1955. The weight of other Southeast Asian countries in Hong Kong's entrepot trade was often understated. In 1953, the second largest export destination from Hong

[19] The graph shows the drop in Hong Kong's export trade with Indonesia, Singapore/Malaya coincided with a sudden surge of export trade with the U.S. in 1956.

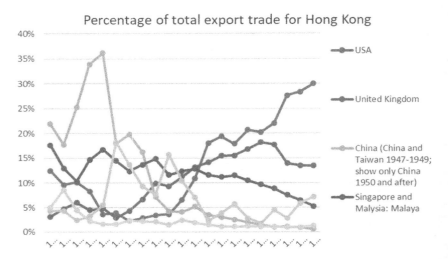

Fig. 2.2 Percentage export trade by countries of total export trade (Census and Statistics Department, 1969, pp. 97-104)

Kong was Indonesia. By 1955, Indochina, Thailand, Indonesia, Malaya and South Korea had surpassed China in Hong Kong's export destinations (Szczepanik, 1958, pp. 52-53). Nonetheless, the regional trend of decolonization and nation-building guided many newly-founded nations into adopting an import-substitution-industrialization (ISI) strategy. The Bandung Conference in 1955 triggered the anti-colonial Non-Aligned Movement and the independence of Malaysia in 1957. This development stage peaked with a series of anti-Chinese movements in Southeast Asia—1965 in Indonesia and 1969 in Malaysia—driving away the Chinese business elites and devastating Hong Kong's Nanyang trade network. Although Hong Kong had earned an edge by skipping ISI and going straight into export-oriented industrialization (EOI) in the post-War years, the decline in exports to regional developing countries should not be understated given their importance in Hong Kong's trade scene (see Fig. 2.1 and 2.2) (So & Chiu, 1995).

3.2 From Sea Cucumber to Movies: Hong Kong and North-South Trade Network

"China Hong Kong SAR, the largest direct importer of sea cucumber, re-exports half of its imports to mainland China." (Ferdouse, 2004).[20]

Hong Kong is the largest entrepôt for dried sea cucumber (88% of world trade value in 2001), a delicacy in Chinese culture. The sizable import of sea cucumber, however, demonstrates a historic trade network within the region, summarized as the oceanic trade system by Hamashita Takeshi, extending to the North East of China (north) and countries at lower latitudes (in Cantonese *Nanyang*, i.e. south) (Takeshi, 1997, pp. 35-38), hence the North-South trade. This regional trade network existed in Canton long before the British came. With the birth of Hong Kong, the network's strategic node migrated and became embedded in the local Chinese society.

As discussed earlier, the Taiping Rebellion (1850-1864) drove both business elites and coolies to Hong Kong seeking opportunities here or elsewhere. The Chinese emigration to Hong Kong contributed to the setting up as early as 1851 of *Nam Pak Hong*, literally meaning firms dealing with North South trade, and *Jin Shan Chong*, literally meaning firms catering for transpacific trade between Hong Kong and San Francisco (*Jin Shan* means gold mountain) and Australia, involving particularly the coolie trade, overseas Chinese daily necessities and remittances. The two types of firms shared one-fourth of all external trade in Hong Kong's early days (Fung, 2014, p. 27). The *Nam Pak Hongs* specialized in trading dried seafood, like sea cucumber, and daily necessities within the *Nanyang* region. These Chinese *hongs* clustered at the Sheung Wan area till today (Fig. 2.3).[21]

Early ethnic Chinese migrants (and indigenous groups) played an important role in facilitating pan-regional trade activities in each of these projected trade linkages, often as compradors. To cite some examples of their cultural influence: the Baba Nyonya (峇峇娘惹) were male and female descendants of Chinese migrants moving to Malay and intermarried with natives from as early as the Ming Dynasty (the fifteenth century). Sandakan, the second largest town in Sabah (North of Borneo), is known

---

[20] FAO FISH DAB, 2003, as cited in Ferdouse (2004).

[21] In the early period Nam Pak Hong became prominent Chinese organizations in Hong Kong responsible for the adjudication of local affairs, firefighting, and sponsoring the *District Watch Force* for fighting crime and security, as the British colonial government pursued an indirect-rule strategy.

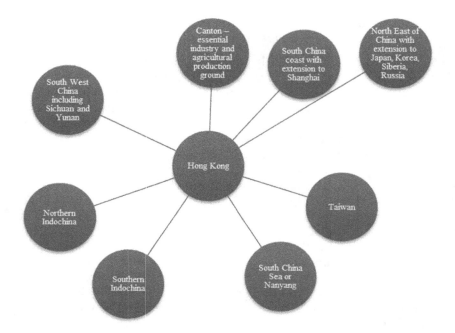

Fig. 2.3   Eight overlapping trade networks all with Hong Kong being the centre of it as identified by Hamashita Takeshi (1997)

as *Little Hong Kong* for her intimate trade and migration linkage with the Canton region. The close tie to Nanyang can also be seen from many Hong Kong movies produced from the 1950s to the 1970s targeting ethnic Chinese groups residing in Southeast Asia countries. Sir Run Run Shaw, known for his Shaw Brothers empire produced 800 films in Hong Kong alone, started his movie entrepreneurship in Singapore around 1927 marketing to the Chinese community in *Nanyang* (Chung, 2007; Fu, 2008). In high-definition, the export surge of Hong Kong's films to Nanyang in the post-war era was the outcome of the intertwining of North-South trade and Cold War politics (Mak, 2009).

In 1950, Sir Alexander Grantham, then the Governor of Hong Kong, sent a telegram to the Singapore Governor with heading "Chinese Films Made in Hong Kong" to highlight a dilemma facing the Hong Kong film industry: as a government policy, film contents would be strictly censored for any communist ideology before being released in Hong Kong but without such ideology the movies could not be shown in China (Mak, 2009, p. 1). With a small local market and to substitute for the waning China market, the Hong Kong colonial government had to help filmmakers explore film markets in Malaya, Singapore, Sarawak, and British North Borneo. To strike a win-win deal, Grantham proposed to Singapore to grant access to her distribution network and lessen her trade restrictions, to enable locals there to enjoy movies while the government need not worry about communist influence (Mak, 2009, p. 1). As decolonization and nationalist movements in Southeast Asia peaked, so did the output of Hong Kong's *Nanyang* movie production. The independence of Malaysia in 1957[22] resulted in Malay being adopted as the official film language, leaving the market for ethnic Chinese in both Malaysia and Singapore largely to Hong Kong movie producers (Mak, 2009, p. 73, 81). These movies often highlighted the Singapore-Hong Kong cultural imagination for debunking stereotypes concerning *Nanyang* (Mak, 2009, p. 99), such as the 1969 movie "The Romance of Nonya—Love with a Malaysian Girl" (娘惹之戀).[23]

4   West Meets Rest in the East and the Rise of Hong Kong[24]

4.1   *US Dollar on British/Chinese Soil*

The Second World War remade the world order. Early-industrialized nations like Britain and Japan were reduced to rubble, enabling the U.S. to become the new world hegemon with the largest gold reserves. The U.S. and its Allies established the *Bretton Woods System* to avoid repeating the chaotic monetary system during the *Great Depression* and *Beggar-Thy-Neighbor* policy that seriously hampered international trade activities and indirectly fuelled the Second World War. Under the *System* the global

---

[22] Hong Kong won the first Merdeka Tournament, a football tournament in Malaysia to honor her Independence Day, in 1957. The 1st runner-up was Indonesia, 2nd runner-up was South Vietnam.

[23] In the movie a rich Hong Kong writer (Lui Kei) visits Singapore and falls in love with a local Nyonya girl (Chan Bo Chu). Their marriage was only accepted by Lui's parents when Chan's "traditional Chinese" character was discovered—hence, restoring the diasporic linkage.

[24] The West here is the U.S. and the rest denotes the other advanced economies, including the U.K. and Japan.

monetary order was stabilized by tying the U.S. dollar to gold and all other currencies in a fixed exchange rate (though negotiable) with the dollar. With an ultimate goal to reduce trade barriers, the multilateral *General Agreement on Tariffs and Trade* (GATT), the forerunner of the World Trade Organization (WTO), was negotiated and signed in 1947 to make trade transparent and predictable. Lured by reconstruction and military aid from the U.S. (e.g., the Marshall Plan), the European metropoles were coerced into opening up their former colonies economically for U.S. investment (i.e. raw materials and markets) and politically to align new nations with the western power. Decolonization thus began with nation-building of the Third World in Asia and Africa.[25] It was under this decolonization context, and the Cold War, that Hong Kong rose from the periphery to a semi-peripheral position as a Newly Industrialized Economy (NIE) in the capitalist world-system (So & Chiu, 1996; So, 1986; So & Chiu, 1995, p. 193).

Before the birth of the PRC in 1949, the U.S. was pushing for global decolonization and had little interest in Britain keeping Hong Kong as a colony. Simultaneously Hong Kong was deliberately left by the PRC to remain a free port. As Premier Zhou Enlai stated in 1957, "Hong Kong is a free port with good connections with other parts of the world. As the purchase of equipment can be paid by instalment, production costs are low and there is a good market to train technical talents.... Aren't we mobilising all forces to turn disadvantages into advantages? Hong Kong should serve as a useful port for our economy." (quoted in Basic Law Promotion Steering Committee, 2012) The 'window display of capitalism' was sustained as Zhou Enlai reinstated in 1960 a status quo principle: "taking long-term views and taking full advantage" (長期打算, 充分利用; *Chang Qi Da Suan Chong Fen Li Yong*) in dealing with Hong Kong, despite the U.S. having moved its intelligence operations against China to Hong Kong for almost a decade. Smuggling, one of Hong Kong's traditional businesses, flourished during the Korean War and the arms embargo. Pro-PRC businessmen like Henry Fok Ying Tung broke the embargo by delivering raw materials and medical aid to the mainland under the colony's radar (Fenby, 2000, p. 120; Lo, 2009, p. 54).[26]

The so-called miraculous industrialization began with mounting population pressure caused by the influx of Chinese mainland refugees. To

[25] The number of United Nations members rose from 35 in 1946 to 127 in 1970.
[26] See also Fenby (2000); Lo (2009) for a description of the 'Black Cat' incident.

incorporate the colony (along with Japan, South Korea, Taiwan, and Singapore) into regional containment aimed at communism during the Cold War, the U.S. preferentially opened its market to Hong Kong (Law & Lee, 2004). As seen in Fig. 2.2, Hong Kong's exports to the U.S. surged from 1956 onwards and quickly surpassed its exports to the United Kingdom in 1958. Cheap labour allowed plastic flowers made in Hong Kong to flood the U.S. market, while lawsuits in U.S, courts for infringement of copyright committed by Hong Kong manufacturers were common in the 1960s.[27] Yet everything gave way to Cold War politics. Under U.S. policy, technological support and food aid were delivered to Japan making her the head of the flying geese and becoming the regional capitalist economic model (So & Chiu, 1996; So, 1986; So & Chiu, 1995, p. 193). Outsourcing and offshoring of Japanese businesses in the 1970s created a short-lived industrial upgrading opportunity for Hong Kong as it continued to serve as a window for a "capitalism paradise" with the strategic aim to destabilize communist rule in neighbouring China. Hong Kong was gradually absorbed into the Asian US Dollar Zone through specializing in flexible production of textiles, toys, and electronic products. In 1972, the Hong Kong dollar was linked briefly to the U.S. dollar as Britain's economic power continued to decline, and after a period of a floating exchange rate (1974-1983) the HKD has been linked to a fixed rate of USD till now (Kwan & Lui, 1999).

Unlike the other three Asia tigers, state building was not the driving force behind Hong Kong's development. Hong Kong's industrialization was a miracle, but a short-lived one. The institutional separation between the finance and industry sectors made it difficult for local factories to access capital like their East Asian counterparts to achieve industrial upgrading while the economic reform of China in 1978 has also slowed down the momentum of Hong Kong's export-oriented industrialization (Chiu et al., 1997, pp. 131-140). While industries rushed north to make China into the World's Factory, service sectors continued to develop and attracted global capital waiting to invest in mainland China. Hong Kong has become a key node regulating globalization within the region (Chiu & Lui, 2009). International banks and financial institutions have set up their offices and headquarters linking Queens Road of Hong Kong not

---

[27] See *Rico, Ltd. v. Hub Floral Mfg. Co.* (1962); *Florabelle Flowers, Inc. v. Joseph Markovits* (1968)

just to Wall Street in New York but also Tokyo and London,[28] and brought American culture to Hong Kong as US executives came here to work. As more people drink Starbucks than English tea, Hong Kong was drawn even closer to the core of the world capitalist system.

Notably, Hong Kong served as more than a bridge for global capital between the western countries and a developing Southeast Asia between the 1980s and 2000s. It also linked up developing countries from the South to mainland China through what Gordon Mathews (2011) has coined a process of *low-end globalization*. Hong Kong's world class port facilities and its close ties to the Greater China area has attracted merchants from South Asian, African and Latin American countries. These merchants gathered at the Chungking Mansion and conducted trades through personal connections and local compradors helping to purchase cheap products like mobile phones or clothes made mainly by the world factory. In this process of south-south trade, Hong Kong's centuries old trade networks to regions outside the western world were renewed.

4.2   *Starbucks Vs Gundam - Americanization of Hong Kong, or Japanization?*

The Hong Kong identity emerged between the 1970s and the 1980s did not challenge the onslaught of American culture arriving around the same time. Locals even embraced the American culture by equating it with a "modern" lifestyle (Watson, 2006/1997). The first McDonald's in Hong Kong was opened in 1975 on Paterson Street, Causeway Bay (Watson, 2006/1997). One after another American food chains revolutionized Hong Kong food culture: Kentucky Fried Chicken (1985),[29] Wendy's (1980s, 1991), Hardee's (1991),[30] and Hard Rock Café (1994).[31] The first 7-Eleven convenience store (by then it was a global American brand) in Hong Kong was opened in 1981 in Happy Valley and locals now intimately call it "7 *Je*" (七仔 seven son). Young men watched NBA and worn Air Jordan's on basketball courts. ER, Friends and other American TV

---

[28] In 2006, US ranked first in number of regional headquarters (295) and regional offices (594) in Hong Kong, followed by Japan (regional headquarters 212; regional offices 519), United Kingdom (114; 223), and the Mainland (112; 156). See Table 2 of Meyer (2007).

[29] See KFC Corporation (n.d.).

[30] See Apple Daily (2015).

[31] See Apple Daily (2008).

dramas swamped the local English channels, substituting American jokes for British humour.

Although local films once topped box offices by the 1980s, their market share had gradual declined from the 1990s onwards. By 2018, 19 out of the top 20 Hong Kong movie box office films were made in Hollywood, although scholars argue that local institutional change in the film industry was the main cause of the rise and decline of Hong Kong movies (Shin & Chiu, 2016; see Chap. 6). Starbucks, the American coffee company, invaded Hong Kong Central's Exchange Square in 2000, and soon locals were seen holding cups of coffee. The first coffeehouse chain in Hong Kong was Pacific Coffee, a genuine local brand with headquarters in Hong Kong, but with the founder coming from Seattle, where Starbucks was born.[32] As the story goes, as a corollary of the cultural shift, American financial products, like the high-risk junk bonds ("Thousands of Lehman cases dumped", 2012), were also traded in Hong Kong.

But is Hong Kong influenced by American trade only? In high-definition, this is certainly not the case. We have Gundam dating Hello Kitty with technological support from Doraemon here. As Japan rose in the Asian region and challenged U.S. hegemony, which has been declining since the 1970s (Wallerstein, 2000), the rise of the former's economic and cultural influence in Hong Kong has grown (Chan, 2000). In terms of economic influence, Japan (4.6%) is Hong Kong's fourth largest trading partner after mainland China (50.2%), the U.S. (6.6%) and Taiwan (5.1%) in 2017 (Trade and Industry Department, n.d.). Japan's share (5.8%) of imports to Hong Kong was the fourth largest following mainland China (46.6%), Taiwan (6.6%) and Singapore (5.8%) (Trade and Industry Department, n.d.). It was also the fourth largest export market of Hong Kong in the same year (Hong Kong Trade Development Council, n.d.; Chow, 2008; Auyeung, 2015).

The first Japanese department store, Daimaru (大丸百貨), landed in Causeway Bay in 1960. Other stores came later catering for both locals and the Japanese executives working in regional headquarters and offices in Hong Kong: Matsuzakaya (1975), Mitsukoshi (1981), Sogo (1985), Jusco (1985) and Seibu (1989) (Sharp, 2016). Leung (2002a, 2002b) identified three waves of Japanese culture in Hong Kong: the first in the 1960-70s when Japanese dramas were imported as TV became more affordable locally, the second in the 1980s with the rising number of

[32] History of Pacific Coffee, see http://www.pacificcoffee.com/eng/aboutus/index.html

department stores, and the third in the 1990s when TV dramas like *Long Vacation*, *Love Generation* and featuring Japanese idols became global hits. Unlike the Wal-Mart (U.S.), which entered Hong Kong in 1994 but left two years later (Upbin, 2004), these Japanese department stores bear cultural similarities and bring Japanese consumer culture to Hong Kong. This means relatively cheap but quality products and a ready replacement for British and U.S. made products. In those days, it is alright if one did not know who Captain America or the Avengers were, but it would be unthinkable to find a local with no idea who Hello Kitty or Doraemon were.

In this third stage of growth Hong Kong has emerged as a global city within the core of the world capitalist system. A standard-definition image would attribute Hong Kong's economic success to its free trade policy and a natural response to the global division of labour after the Second World War (Friedman, 1998). Our high-definition image shows that the U.S., due to Cold War politics, replaced the UK as the major trading partner for Hong Kong's manufacturing products since the late 1950s. This comeback East-West trade changed course as local industries moved to the Special Economic Zone of Shenzhen after China's opening, although the main export target remained the U.S. Riding on the tide of financial globalization and the associated processes of deregulation, offshoring and outsourcing, Hong Kong rose to a prominent position in the global economy by seizing the niche in service of ultra-mobile global capital, but also suffered the most should a financial crisis take place, like the 1997 Asian Financial Crisis and collapse of junk bonds in 2008. With the U.S. as the main trading partner next to mainland China, it seems American culture should have exerted a strong influence on Hong Kong right away. But the retreat of the American fast-food chains except McDonald's and Kentucky Fried Chicken shows Americanization was not always successful. A regional power like Japan exerts great economic and cultural influences on Hong Kong too. As service trading in Hong Kong expands rapidly, so has the appetite of the emerging consumption society.[33]

5   Conclusion: West Meets East

While the *standard-definition* image simplifies the explanation for the prosperity of Hong Kong, an international city dedicated to the "free trade" principle, this chapter has presented a *high-definition* image

---

[33] As in the case of the "Malling of Hong Kong", see Lui (2001).

concerning the role of trade in the rise of Hong Kong. We have begun by reviewing the global economic and political backdrops of the two Opium Wars in the late nineteenth century. Contemporary scholars often cast doubt on earlier accounts like that of British historian G. B. Endacott seeing the acquisition of Hong Kong as an accidental event while British pursuing commercial interests in China (Carroll, 2007, p. 120). Recent scholarship considers the acquisition an outcome of the expansion of capitalist world-economy from the European continent to incorporate the Far East economic system—under the flag of *free trade* (So & Chiu, 1996; So, 1986).

In the same year Adam Smith published *The Wealth of Nations* (1776), Britain lost a vast number of colonies due to the American Revolution. Thereafter, British encroachment in the Pacific region sped up—but this time working under a different logic—to economically benefit from an open market without committing to direct political control of its territory. "Free trade" was a useful rationale for stronger countries to expand their market against a competitive counterpart[34]—the way how industrialized Britain "prescribed" for the Qing Empire. As Wallerstein (1974) puts it, "the creation of 'national' barriers -generically, mercantilism- has historically been a defensive mechanism of capitalists located in states which are one level below the high point of strength in the system." In this way, Qing's action to curb the outflow of silver by suppressing opium trade was no different from the mercantilist measures England employed against the Netherlands in 1660-1715, France against England in 1715-1815, and Germany against Britain in the nineteenth century (Wallerstein, 1974).

While Hong Kong differs from Singapore, another former British colony, in terms of the government's role in the economy (Chiu et al., 1997), we have challenged the very idea that "free trade" was an all- encompassing ruling doctrine of the colonial state by recounting how a rice riot in 1919 Hong Kong has led to the Rice Control Scheme in operation from 1955 until 2003 (Cheng & Wang, 2005). For more than a hundred years, the sale and lease of (crown) land hardly followed any "free market" doctrine. Our *high-definition image* also brings to the fore the oft-neglected role of local Chinese compradors in facilitating Sino-British trade activities in the early period.

In the *standard-definition image,* Hong Kong's economic success is frequently tied to opportunities arising from the Cold War and its own

---

[34] For a contemporary debate on free trade, see Stiglitz (2002)

free trade policy. Hong Kong underwent rapid industrialization because of the post-war trade embargo on China. Our *high-definition image* points out an additional reason. Hong Kong has long played a prominent role in the regional north-south trade, as Hamashita Takeshi's (1997) study of its strategic oceanic position in South-East Asia rightly pointed out. Generations of Chinese migrants transplanted their business networks to Hong Kong (e.g. Nam Pak Hong) and other countries in Nanyang (e.g. Shaw's Nanyang film distribution). The post-War nationalist movement became one driving force that led to a declining export trade from Hong Kong to countries in South-East Asia.

U.S. hegemony grew from the Korean War. Our *high-definition image* shows how Hong Kong has benefited from this shift in world hegemony by remaining an open economy and thickening its trade ties, first involving manufacturing exports and then financial products, with the U.S. and other core countries. Japan posed a challenge to the U.S. in terms of the regional economic order in the 1970s. Since then, transnational corporations have been encouraged to offshore production lines to developing countries. This global shift was captured by China who adopted the *Open Door Policy* in 1978. Hong Kong is being drawn towards the core of the world capitalist system further by developing into a financial centre while also undergoing deindustrialization. From ET (American) to Keroro (Japanese) to *My Love from the Star* (South Korean), metropolitan Hong Kong's cultural diversity is enriched with shifting soft power of the core countries that are her main trading partners.

A *standard-definition image* of Hong Kong in becoming an international hub commonly skips many details and begins with a simplified and linear story of Britain promoting free trade first in China and then in Hong Kong, followed by how free trade facilitated Hong Kong's post-war industrialization amid China's trade embargo, and ends with Hong Kong's free economy as the key to maintaining its global financial status. Our *high-definition image* does not dispute these points but takes the story a step further by closely examining what various people or organizations did in making Hong Kong this way, and to see how macro social change has structured Hong Kong's development. In other words, our *high-definition image* has analysed Hong Kong's trade within the intersection of state-society-market of Hong Kong at different periods (early colonial to post-War to China's opening) and geographical levels (global-regional-local) towards different directions (East-South-West-North). Through this we connect the individual experience of a multicultural Hong Kong to her history and society.

What will be Hong Kong's future role in global trade amid a gradual shift of the world's economic centre from the West to the East? While China assures neighbouring countries and the developed Western world of the humble nature of her rising, the "Belt and Road Initiative" (also commonly known as One-Belt-One-Road) is nonetheless a strong indicator of its assertiveness in shaping the global trade scene. In light of history, with China's Belt-and-Road Initiative, Hong Kong's historical significance in having various types of compradors facilitate East-West and North-South trade seems to be potentially an important resource to facilitate China's bold initiative to expand its influence in Europe (and even Africa) in an attempt to contest with the United States as the world economic hegemon in the twenty-first century. As have been seen in this chapter, the rise of Hong Kong was a consequence of different global and regional geopolitical factors, giving Hong Kong opportunities to transform itself from a British outpost in the Far East to an international trade hub. In this sense, the rise of Hong Kong was very much doing the right things at the right time. That said, whether or not Hong Kong can seize new opportunities and play a role in helping China to replace the United States to become the new regional economic powerhouse depends upon the activation of different North-South and East-West trade networks over the past two centuries.

REFERENCES

Alexander, S. (2004, June 4). Tea: Still Hot After Five Thousand years. *YaleGlobal.* Retrieved May 1, 2018, from https://yaleglobal.yale.edu/tea-still-hot-after-5000-years

Apple Daily. (2008, November 22). 廣東道HardRockCafe最後一夜 [The last night of Hard Rock Café on the Canton Road]. *Apple Daily.* Retrieved June 1, 2018, from https://hk.lifestyle.appledaily.com/lifestyle/culture/daily/article/20081122/11876625

Apple Daily. (2015, December 1). 那些年的漢堡包店哈迪斯 Wendy's 相繼撤港 [Burger shops in the past: the retreat of Hardee's and Wendy's from Hong Kong]. *Apple Daily.* Retrieved June 1, 2018, from https://hk.news.appledaily.com/breaking/realtime/article/20151201/54490655

Auyeung, A. (2015, July 22). Hong Kong retains top spot for Japanese food exports because of weaker yen. *South China Morning Post.* Retrieved from https://www.scmp.com/news/hong-kong/economy/article/1842677/hong-kong-retains-top-spot-japanese-food-exports-because

Basic Law Promotion Steering Committee. (2012). *The Basic Law and Hong Kong - The 15th Anniversary of Reunification with the Motherland.* Retrieved from https://www.basiclaw.gov.hk/en/publications/book/15anniversary_reunification_ch1_1.pdf

Bogart, D. (2015). *The east Indian monopoly and the transition from limited access in England, 1600-1813 (no. w21536).* National Bureau of Economic Research.

Carroll, J. (2007). *A concise history of Hong Kong.* HKU Press.

Census and Statistics Department. (1969). *Hong Kong statistics 1947-1967.* Census and Statistics Department.

Chan, A. H. (2000). Consumption, popular culture, and cultural identity: Japan in post-colonial Hong Kong. *Studies in Popular Culture, 23*(1), 35–55.

Chesneaux, J. (1973). *Peasant Revolts in China, 1840–1949.* (C. A. Curwen, Trans.). London: Thames & Hudson.

Chiu, S. W., & Lui, T. L. (2009). *Hong Kong: Becoming a Chinese Global City.* Routledge.

Chiu, S. W., Ho, K. C., & Lui, T. L. (1997). *City-states in the global economy. Industrial restructuring in Hong Kong and Singapore.* Westview Press.

Chow, V. (2008, August 4). Hong Kong biggest importer of Japanese food products. *South China Morning Post.* Retrieved from https://www.scmp.com/article/647784/hong-kong-biggest-importer-japanese-food-products

Chung, S. P. (2007). Moguls of the Chinese cinema: The story of the Shaw brothers in Shanghai, Hong Kong and Singapore, 1924-2002. *Modern Asian Studies, 41*(4), 665–682.

Clavell, J. (1966). *Tai-pan: A novel of Hong Kong.* Atheneum.

Consumer Council. (1996). *Competition Policy: The Key to Hong Kong's Future Economic Success,* Policy & Research Study Reports. Hong Kong: Consumer Council. Retrieved April 1, 2018, from https://www.consumer.org.hk/ws_en/competition_issues/reports/19961101.html

Developing countries voice fury at farm subsidies. (2005, December 15). *The Guardian.* Retrieved from http://www.theguardian.com/world/2005/dec/15/wto.business

Endacott, G. B. (1973). *The European traders at Canton 1833-39.* Oxford University Press.

Fenby, J. (2000). *Dealing with the dragon: A year in the new Hong Kong.* Arcade publishing.

Ferdouse, F. (2004). World markets and trade flows of sea cucumber/beche-de-mer. *Advances in sea cucumber aquaculture and management* (FAO Fisheries Technical Paper 463). Rome: Food and Agriculture Organization of the United Nations. Retrieved May 1, 2018, from http://www.fao.org/docrep/007/y5501e/y5501e0f.htm

Florabelle Flowers, Inc. v. Joseph Markovits, Inc., 296 F. Supp. 304 (S.D.N.Y 1968).

Fraser, C. (1992). Understanding America towards the decolonization of European empires, 1945-64. *Diplomacy & Statecraft, 3*(1), 105–125.

Friedman, M. (1998). The Hong Kong Experiment. *Hoover Digest*, no.3. Retrieved June 1, 2018, from https://www.hoover.org/research/hong-kong-experiment [reprinted from National Review, December 31, 1997, original title 'The Real Lesson of Hong Kong'].

Fu, P. S. (2008). Introduction: The Shaw brothers diasporic cinema. In P. S. Fu (Ed.), *China forever: The Shaw brothers and diasporic cinema* (pp. 1–26). University of Illinois.

Fung, P. Y. (2014). *Transformation of Hong Kong industrial structure*. Joint Publishing (Hong Kong). (in Chinese).

Greenberg, M. (1969). *British trade and the opening of China 1800-1842*. Cambridge University Press.

Greenwood, J. (1984). The monetary framework underlying the Hong Kong Dollar stabilization scheme. *The China Quarterly, 99*, 631–636.

Hao, Z. (2010). *Macau history and society*. Hong Kong University Press.

Hase, P. (2008). *The six-day war of 1899: Hong Kong in the age of imperialism*. Hong Kong University Press.

Hayes, J. (1974). The Hong Kong region: Its place in traditional Chinese historiography and principal events since the establishment of Hsin-an county in 1573. *Journal of the Hong Kong Branch of the Royal Asiatic Society, 14*, 108–135.

Hendershot, M. E. (1981). Taiping Rebellion and Sino-British relations, 1850-1864 [Paper 3837]. Graduate Student Theses, Dissertations, & Professional Papers. Missoula: University of Montana. Retrieved from https://scholarworks.umt.edu/etd/3837

Hong Kong Monetary Authority. (n.d.). *Money Past & Present*. Retrieved May 1, 2018, from http://www.hkma.gov.hk/eng/classroom/page/notescoins/notescoins_01.htm

Hong Kong Trade Development Council. (n.d.). *Japan: Market Profile*. Retrieved June 1, 2018, from https://developed-markets-research.hktdc.com/en/article/MzIwNzY5NDc4

Irigoin, A. (2009). The end of a silver era: The consequence of the breakdown of the Spanish peso standard in China and the United States, 1780-1850s. *Journal of World History, 20*(2), 207–244.

KFC Corporation. (n.d.). *Overview of KFC HK, KFC Corporation*. Retrieved May 1, 2018, from https://www.kfchk.com/en/about/overview.html

King, F. (1988). *The Hongkong Bank in the Period of imperialism and war, 1895-1918*. Cambridge University Press.

Kwan, Y. K., & Lui, F. (1999). Hong Kong's currency board and changing monetary regimes. In T. Ito & A. O. Krueger (Eds.), *Changes in exchange rates in rapidly developing countries: Theory, practice, and policy issues (NBER-EASE volume 7)* (pp. 403–436). University of Chicago Press.

Law, K. Y., & Lee, K. M. (Eds.). (2004). *The economy of Hong Kong in non-economic perspectives.* Oxford University Press (in Chinese).

Lei, J. (2016). 末路遺民:古巴華僑訪談錄 *[the impasse of the left-behinds: Interviews with overseas Chinese in Cuba].* Oxford University Press.

Leung, F. (2002a). 西環人在八佰伴 [Sai-wan-ese at Yaohan]. In C. H. Ng & C. W. Cheung (Eds.), *Reading Hong Kong Popular Culture, 1970-2000* (pp. 371–373). Oxford University Press.

Leung, F. (2002b). 由澤田研二到木村拓哉 - 日本熱三世書 [From Kenji Sawada to Takuya Kimura]. In C. H. Ng & C. W. Cheung (Eds.), *Reading Hong Kong Popular Culture, 1970-2000* (pp. 371–373). Oxford University Press.

Lo, S. H. (2009). *The politics of cross-border crime in greater China: Case studies of mainland China, Hong Kong, and Macao.* M.E. Sharpe.

Lui, T. L. (2001). The Malling of Hong Kong. In G. Mathews & T. L. Lui (Eds.), *Consuming Hong Kong* (pp. 23–46). Hong Kong University Press.

Mak, G. Y. (2009). *Filming Nanyang: Hong Kong − Singapore Connection (1950-65)* (Doctoral thesis). National University of Singapore, Singapore.

Mathews, G. (2011). *GHETTO at the center of the world: Chungking mansions, Hong Kong.* HKU Press.

McCormick, T.J. (1989/1995) *America's Half-Century: United States Foreign Policy in the Cold War and After* (2nd ed.) Baltimore and London: Johns Hopkins University Press.

Meyer, D. (2007). *Hong Kong's Future as a Financial Centre* [Paper presentation]. Banking and Monetary History of Hong Kong: Hong Kong's Current Challenges in Historical Perspective, Hong Kong Institute for Monetary Research, Hong Kong Monetary Authority, Hong Kong. Retrieved from http://www.hkimr.org/conferences_detail-id37

Mills, C. W. (1959). *The sociological imagination.* Oxford University Press.

Morales, A. (1972). *East meets west: The modern history of East Asia.* Macmillan Hong Kong.

Morgan, G. (1985). From west to east and back again: Capitalist expansion and class formation in the nineteenth century. In H. Newby, J. Bujra, P. Littlewood, G. Rees, & T. L. Rees (Eds.), *Restructuring capital: Recession and reorganization in industrial society* (pp. 124–155). Macmillan Publishers Limited.

Morgan, W. P. (1960). *Triad societies in Hong Kong.* Government Press.

Munn, C. (1998). *Anglo-China: Chinese People and British rule in Hong Kong, 1841-1870* (PhD Thesis). University of Toronto, Toronto, Canada.

Nissim, R. (1998/2012). *Land administration and practice in Hong Kong* (3rd ed.). Hong Kong: Hong Kong University Press.

Perdue, P. (2009). *Rise & Fall of the Canton Trade System −III. Canton & Hong Kong.* MIT Visualizing Cultures, Massachusetts Institute of Technology. Retrieved June 22, 2015, from http://ocw.mit.edu/ans7870/21f/21f.027/rise_fall_canton_03/cw_essay01.html

Polanyi, K. (1944). *The great transformation: The political and economic origins of our time*. Beacon Press.

Share, M. (2007). *Where empires collided: Russian and soviet relations with Hong Kong, Taiwan and Macao*. The Chinese University Press.

Sharp, M. (2016, April 5). The rise (and occasional fall) of Hong Kong's Japanese department stores. *South China Morning Post*. Retrieved from http://www.scmp.com/lifestyle/travel-leisure/article/1932856/rise-and-occasional-fall-hong-kongs-japanese-department

Shin, V. K., & Chiu, S. W. (2016). Global distribution networks, local exhibition alliances: Hollywood's new map in Hong Kong. *Regional Studies, 50*(5), 835–847.

So, A. Y. (1986). The economic success of Hong Kong: Insights from a world-system perspective. *Sociological Perspectives, 29*(2), 241–258.

So, A. Y., & Chiu, S. W. (1995). *East Asia and the world economy*. Sage.

So, A. Y., & Chiu, S. W. (1996). Modern East Asia in world-systems analysis. *Sociological Inquiry, 66*(4), 471–485.

Stiglitz, J. (2002). *Globalization and its discontents*. W.W. Norton.

Szczepanik, E. (1958). *The economic growth of Hong Kong*. Oxford University Press.

Takeshi, H. (1997). 香港大視野:亞洲網路中心 *[a great vision for Hong Kong: The Centre of Asian Networks]*. The Commercial Press (Hong Kong) Limited.

Tamura, E., Menton, L., Lush, N., & Tsui, F. K. (1997). *China: Understanding its past*. University of Hawai'I Press.

The Heritage Foundation. (2018). *2018 Index of Economic Freedom – Hong Kong*. Retrieved December 15, 2005, from http://www.heritage.org/index/country/hongkong

Thousands of Lehman cases dumped. (2012, March 30). *South China Morning Post*. Retrieved from http://www.scmp.com/article/997044/thousands-lehman-cases-dumped

Trade and Industry Department. (2012). *Hong Kong's Trade Policy*. Retrieved April 1, 2018, from https://www.tid.gov.hk

Trocki, C. (1999). *Opium, empire and the global political economy: A study of the Asian opium trade*. Routledge.

Tsang, S. (2009). *A modern history of Hong Kong*. Hong Kong University Press. (Original work published 2004).

UK Tea & Infusions Association (n.d.). *Tea Smuggling*. Retrieved from http://www.tea.co.uk/tea-smuggling

Upbin, B. (2004, April 11). Wall-to-wall Wal-Mart. *Forbes*. Retrieved from https://www.forbes.com/forbes/2004/0412/076.html#38057be614ea

Wallerstein, I. (1974). The rise and future demise of the world capitalist system: Concepts for comparative analysis. *Comparative Studies in Society and History, 16*(4), 387–415.

Wallerstein, I. (2000). Globalization or the age of transition? A long-term view of the trajectory of the world-system. *International Sociology, 15*(2), 249–265.

Wang, G. (1997). Chinese emigrants and government policy adjustments in the late Qing — On the cases of Chinese workers in Cuba and in Peru. *The Twenty-First Century Review, 44,* 47–58. (in Chinese).

Watson, J. (2006/1997). McDonald's in Hong Kong: Consumerism, dietary change, and the rise of a Children's culture. In J. Watson (Ed.), Golden arches east: McDonald's in East Asia (pp. 77-109). : Stanford University Press.

Zheng, V., & Wong, S. L. (2005). 香港米業史 *[the history of Rice industry in Hong Kong].* Joint Publishing (Hong Kong).

CHAPTER 3

Hong Kong as a Migration Haven? Ethnic Minorities in the Global City

> As Asia's world city, Hong Kong has much to offer to you as a
> visitor, whether you are coming here on business or for pleasure: A
> city of charm: the sophistication of an international city, cultural
> diversity and cosmopolitan lifestyle [emphases added] are at the very
> core of Hong Kong's attractions.
> —*Tourism Commission (2011)*

1   THE FAÇADE OF "THE GOURMET PARADISE"

As a second-tier global city (Sassen, 1991), Hong Kong offers a cosmopolitan appeal to visitors. Assortments of "where to eat" columns in expat
magazines guide tourists to explore this "gourmet paradise"—European
cuisines in Central's SoHo area; Thai delicacy at the little Thai community
of Kowloon City; Indian curry inside Tsim Sha Tsui's Chung King
Mansion; *momo* (a kind of dumpling) in Nepalese restaurants near the
Shek Kong Barrack of Yuen Long; Vietnamese spring roll in any district.
Such a taste of cultural diversity would be impossible unless some 584,383
non-Chinese ethnic minorities (about 8.0% of the city's population) called
Hong Kong their permanent or second home (Census and Statistics
Department, 2018). Observers even dubbed the migrant city, with a pop-
ulation predominately being ethnic Chinese, multicultural (Young, 2013)
and a "cultural mosaic" (Secretary for Constitutional and Mainland
Affairs, 2007).

No wonder many people were surprised when ethnic minorities hit the headlines during the 2019 Anti-Extradition Bill Movement.[1] The protests brought ethnic tensions to the fore while fostering rare connections between ethnic groups (Lau, 2019). In July, South Asians were reportedly haunted by fears of retaliation. Rumours about their involvement in the mob attack of commuters and protestors in Yuen Long train station spread on the internet (Ting, 2019). In October, media reported several unidentified assailants appeared to be non-Chinese ethnic attacked the pro-democracy leader Jimmy Sham of the Civil Human Rights Front (Lau et al., 2019). The minority leaders promptly condemned the incident. Sham also released a statement asking protestors not to avenge him and support the ethnic minorities in Hong Kong. To show solidarity, minority communities set up a water booth for demonstrators outside Chungking Mansions on 20 October (Wan, 2019). A group of demonstrators echoed by volunteering themselves to clean the Kowloon Mosque hundreds meters away, after a police water cannon vehicle sprayed and stained the main entrance of the mosque with blue dye on the same protest day. To ease ethnic tension, the Chief Executive and the Commissioner of Police visited the Mosque the next morning to personally apologize to the Muslim community (Lum & Chan, 2019). A few days later, supporters of the movement mobilized a "thanksgiving" day or "shopping spree" in Chungking Mansions (Stand News, 2019). In response, the Hongkongers from ethnic minorities—some actively participated in the protests themselves—thanked the movement for helping them "finally" feel part of the city (Lew, 2019)—"finally", a word indicating another Hong Kong story differing from the official multicultural one.

Contrary to the official claim (Secretary for Constitutional and Mainland Affairs, 2007), the degree of institutionalization of multiculturalism in Hong Kong remains low despite Hong Kong being a migrant city (Law & Lee, 2012). In 2016, about one-fourth of the resident population (ethnic groups and foreign domestic helpers included) were born outside Hong Kong. The number of locally-born ethnic minorities doubled from 38,042 to 81,964 between 2006 and 2016 (Census and Statistics Department, 2017).[2] As ethnic minorities recently entered into the centre

[1] The full title of the Bill concerned was the Fugitive Offenders and Mutual Legal Assistance in Criminal Matters Legislation (Amendment) Bill 2019.
[2] While there was an increase in absolute numbers with place of birth being Hong Kong among all ethnic groups, *mixed with Chinese parent* was the main contributor to the percent-

of limelight, it is timely to critically reflect on how the city handle them and how the younger generation ethnic minorities struggle to identify with the evolving Hong Kong identity (Ng et al., 2019; Jackson & Nesterova, 2017).

Prejudice and discrimination are not rare experiences for ethnic minorities (Ku & Chan, 2011). NGOs serving ethnic minorities long disagree that racial discrimination is insignificant in Hong Kong (Sautman & Kneehans, 2002). They were supported in a 2009 government survey, applying the *Bogardus Social Distance Scale* to measure racial acceptance against a range of social behaviours in economic and daily social relations.[3] According to the survey, Chinese respondents accepted economic relationships more readily than daily social relationships for all ethnic groups. Unsurprisingly, in both economic and social interactions, cosmopolitan "expatriates" (Caucasian, Japanese / Korean) were more favourable in Hong Kong than other ethnic minorities whereas Arabs, Indian / Pakistani / Bangladeshi / Nepalese, and Africans were consistently ranked lowest.[4] Acceptance of the latter groups was particularly low for the social roles as tenant, family member, and child's classmate. For example, up to 43.8% of Chinese respondents were unwilling to choose for their child a *prestigious* school with a majority of students being South Asians.[5]

Chinese respondents were generally more hesitant to employ or supervise Arabs, Indian / Pakistani / Bangladeshi / Nepalese, and African as employees than other ethnic groups. Nevertheless, the level of racial acceptance seems not completely tied to economic standing. South Asians groups (Indian / Pakistani / Nepalese) had a higher median monthly

age increase. The total percentage of local born for all non-Chinese ethnic groups was 11.1% in 2006 and 14.0% in 2016 if foreign domestic helpers were included. See Census and Statistics Department (2017, Table 4.3).

[3] See Bogardus (1925).

[4] It should be noted that the Census and Statistics Department used "Arabians" to describe ethnic Arab people. We corrected the usage here.

[5] The result echoed ethnographic research showing local Chinese parents did not prefer South Asian playmate for their children due to the associated stigma (Crabtree & Wong, 2013). An interesting comparison could be made here with the city-state of Singapore. Around 1250 Singaporean Chinese were surveyed in a research asking about their racial preference for social and economic relationship—less than one-fifth would accept a Singaporean Malay or Singaporean Indian marrying into their family and around two-fifth only would accept employing the two different races to manage business (Mathews, 2016). These lower than HK figures are stunning given that the Singapore state has long institutionalized multiculturalism.

income than the Indonesian / Filipino, but the latter (along with Malaysian) were better accepted than the former (along with Bangladeshi) by Chinese respondents when considered for social and economic relationships.[6] Hong Kong might attract the global consumption class with its cosmopolitan outlook like "gourmet paradise" and "shopping paradise". As Bauman (1998) argued, however, hospitality is seldom extended to the unsung heroes behind such glorified scenes—the migrant workers or ethnic minorities working in the service or construction sectors (Reuters Staff, 2013).

Why Hong Kong, a migrant city with many ethnic cultures notwithstanding, cannot adequately become a cosmopolitan or a multicultural society? To unravel this puzzle, a series of factors contributing to the city's shifting ethnic minority policies, ethnic minorities' situations and agencies, have to be examined. Again, our multilevel (the global, regional and local) and political economy approach (by examining ethnic minorities with the dynamics of state-market-civil society relations) gives us some hints.

As will be seen, the changing formation of ethnic minority communities in Hong Kong have been shaped by various global and regional forces over the last two centuries. Locally, the situations how ethnic minorities faced changing social, economic and cultural difficulties in history were largely the consequence of the state-market-civil society interactions. With this two-pronged approach, we can identify an apparent shift in the city's ethnic minority policies (from a more multiculturalist to a more assimilationist[7]) before and after 1997. One of the important factors continuously shaping the city's ethnic minority policies has been the Chinese nationalism. In theory, both cosmopolitanism and multiculturalism[8] "reject exclusive attachments to particular culture", and "encourage cultural diversity

---

[6] Although Malaysian and Bangladeshi were included in the racial acceptance survey, their current numbers in Hong Kong remained low. Similar hierarchized racial acceptance was observed a survey conducted by Hong Kong Unison (2012). For a maximum score of 13, the mean score of general acceptance by local Chinese for: Japanese (11.40), American (11.20), Chinese (11.14), European (10.76), Filipino (7.88), Indian (7.84), Nepalese (7.63), African (7.61), Pakistani (7.56).

[7] Assimilationism is defined as a policy furthering cultural or racial process "whereby a minority group gradually adopts the customs and attitudes of the prevailing culture". See Editors of the American Heritage Dictionaries (2016a).

[8] Multiculturalism is defined as "a social or educational theory that encourages interests in many cultures in a society rather than in only a mainstream culture". See Editors of the American Heritage Dictionaries (2016b).

and appreciates multicultural mélange". Particularly, cosmopolitanism "rejects a strong nationalism."[9] That is why, when examining post-1997 educational policies, we found the younger generation of the ethnic minorities have to squarely face and bargain with the growing Chinese nationalism in Hong Kong.

Before we move on, a detour to the history of Hong Kong's ethnic minority communities is necessary. What contributes to the flows of non-Chinese migrants to, hence the rise of transnational communities in, Hong Kong? In the *first standard definition* image, transnational migration to Hong Kong is portrayed as a matter of free choice and economically motivated. For example, the Education Bureau once designed a worksheet to teach students "what attracts transnational labour to the global city". Students are first asked to reflect on the heavy workload and long working hours facing by foreign domestic workers in Hong Kong. Students then match a list of migration pull factors including: "free" passage to and from the helper's place of origin, higher wages (compared to their places of origin), rest days, "free" medical care, "free" food, and "free" accommodation (Education Bureau, 2014). The focus of the worksheet is on migrant worker's rational trade-off between income maximization and substandard work condition.[10]

Emphasizing migrants making free and individualized migration decision under market mechanism reiterated the liberal idea of universalism (Bloemraad et al., 2008). Such thought typically focused on economic gain and neglected heterogeneity of migration and historical contexts that structured migrant flow (Castles, 2004). In *high-definition image*, we outline two overlapping contexts giving rise to the transnational communities in Hong Kong—colonization and globalization. Once a jewel on the crown, Hong Kong was embedded in the former British Empire network as a key entrepôt and a migration hub in the Far East. Seeing how ethnic groups travelled within the colonial network provides us contexts and motives pushing and pulling transnational migrants to Hong Kong.

[9] See *Stanford Encyclopedia of Philosophy* for detailed explanations about history and taxonomy of cosmopolitanism and its relations with multiculturalism, access at: Kleingeld and Brown (2019).

[10] Meanwhile, the pull factors for foreigners whom work or invest in Hong Kong (i.e. the expatriates) were different according to the same worksheet: business environment, free and open society (citing especially citizens enjoy the rights and freedom which are deep-rooted in the rule of law), and being a safe city with the lowest crime rate. There is no mentioning of 'freebies' like corporate fringe benefits. See Education Bureau (2014).

After the historical detour, we examine the reality of cosmopolitanism and multiculturalism in Hong Kong in the contexts of decolonization, neoliberal globalization, and the Chinese nationalism. Hong Kong is frequently romanticized as the place where the East meets the West. In branding Hong Kong as Asia's world city, an official logo was created to blend the Chinese characters for Hong Kong with the English letters "HK". The branding exercise also describes Hong Kong's cosmopolitan "attribute" as having "a global outlook and combines the best of East and West."[11] At the end, however, "East meets West"—our *second standard definition image*—is a culturally-elitist one that does not necessarily apply to most migrant workers and ethnic minorities in Hong Kong coming from the Global South.

In our *second high-definition image*, we argue that the state and market jointly shape Hong Kong's ethnic policies and ethnic minorities' situations. Before 1997, because the colonial state did not encourage Chinese nationalism (for fear of becoming breeding ground of independence movement or Chinese communism), no explicit ethnic assimilationist policy was launched in colonial Hong Kong. As long as colonial governance was not challenged and economic growth was not disrupted, certain space of "cultural laissez-faire" was permitted. A special brand of "multiculturalism by default" was thus installed in Hong Kong, inadvertently turning the city into a cultural mosaic. Nevertheless, promoting Chinese nationalism has become a key part in China's state-building project after 1997. Under the SAR, the space of manoeuvring "cultural laissez-faire" quickly shrank, followed by overt ethnic assimilationist policies, especially in education sphere.

On the other hand, Hong Kong showcases how the market manages population flow through profit-driven calculations. In this process, different institutional barriers (legal, social and economic) have been established locally to exclude ethnic minority population from entitling various social, economic, and political rights that their Chinese counterparts can easily obtain. Citizenship in Hong Kong thus becomes a way to organize people and distribute rights and benefits according to one's marketable skills (Ong, 2006).

This chapter first deals with the global and regional contexts that gave rise to Hong Kong's migratory flows in the past two centuries. Then it

---

[11] https://www.brandhk.gov.hk/html/en/BrandHongKong/WhatIsBrand HongKong.html

examines various institutional barriers locally established in Hong Kong that sustain the city's ethnic inequalities. In the concluding part, we examine the social consequences of these inequalities, and discuss the recent visible participation of minority youths in the city's social movements as well as their identification with the city as "Hongkonger".

2   The Global and Regional Contexts: Non-Chinese Ethnic Groups in Hong Kong

Over the last two centuries, transnational migrants of different classes, ethnicities, genders and statuses came to Hong Kong under two overlapping global contexts: colonization and globalization. As for regional contexts, the Chinese diaspora, Cold War conflicts, and post-war decolonization also play significant parts.

2.1   Migration from the British Colonial Network in the Indian Subcontinent

Migrants from the Indian subcontinent were among the first non-Chinese ethnic groups coming to Hong Kong. Many of them utilized the British colonial network to make a living in the new free port. Some of them fared well while others did not. Their fates depend upon their roles and functions in the colonial network.

Indians set foot in Hong Kong with arrival of British colonial rule in 1841. In 1858, the British established Crown rule in the Indian subcontinent. Currently perceived by locals as "South Asian", Pakistani, Bangladeshi, and Indian came from different nations once administered under the same British Indian Empire.[12] The multi-ethnic nature of former British India left lasting footprints in nowadays Hong Kong. The early South Asian community mainly consisted of traders, security staffs, clerks, and seamen (Weiss, 1991).

The Parsi community, a marginalized ethnic group in India and relatively willing to absorb the foreign culture, were well-received by the early Chinese business community in Hong Kong (Plüss, 2005). Some Parsi

---

[12] The independence of India from the United Kingdom took place in 1947, followed by the independence of Pakistan in the same year, and then Bangladesh's independence from Pakistan in 1971. Nepal was once the de facto protectorate of Britain after the former's defeat in the Anglo-Nepalese War (1816) until 1923 when the protectorate was ended.

businessmen from Bombay were well-established in the colony through trading with China, e.g. Sir Hormusjee Naorojee Mody, donor and key founder of the University of Hong Kong; Dorabjee Naorojee Mithaiwala, founder of the Kowloon Ferry Company that later became the Star Ferry Co Ltd.; and Jehangir Hormusjee Ruttonjee, founder of Anti-Tuberculosis Association and Ruttonjee Sanatorium in Wan Chai.[13] They contributed to the early colony's institutional building, including the forming of the HSBC. Due to a shrinking population, however, Parsi's influential past ceases to catch local attention now (Plüss, 2005).

Apart from the Parsi merchants, other ethnic groups were initially recruited from the Indian subcontinent for security purpose, as the colonial state and British business elites did not trust local Chinese (Erni & Leung, 2014). The Jardine, Matheson & Co. employed private Indian guards to protect its warehouse at East Point against piracy (see Chap. 2). Sikhs were hired from the Punjab region to man the colonial police force (see Chap. 9). Punjab Muslims from the region now known as Pakistan served in the British Imperial Army, the colonial police force and correctional services (O'Connor, 2012). The Lascars (sailors or soldiers)—a Persian term for the South Asian and especially Indian Muslims seamen— were hired by the British merchant and military vessels. To curb regional communist insurgencies, the British Army's Brigade of Gurkhas turned Hong Kong into training base in 1969–1970. After that, Nepalese began to settle in and around the Whitfield Barracks near Jordon and the Shek Kong Barracks in Yuen Long (Sharp, 2014).

Being a symbol of political security under British colonialism, South Asians migrants were less welcomed by local Chinese (Crabtree & Wong, 2013). Similar to the post-WWII European communities in Hong Kong (Carroll, 2007), most South Asians lived an isolated life under British rule (e.g. living inside garrisons or forming own community clubs) (Erni & Leung, 2014). As Hong Kong industrialized, the second wave of South Asians came in the 1960s–1980s and filled up occupational niches vacated

---

[13] The Mody Road in Tsim Sha Tsui was named after Sir Hormusjee Naorojee Mody, known for his crucial donation towards the foundation of the University of Hong Kong in 1911. Another Parsi merchant, Dorabjee Naorojee Mithaiwala, found the 'Kowloon Ferry Company' in 1888, purchased vessels and named them after '*Star*'—hence the 'Star Ferry Co Ltd' incorporated in 1889. Jehangir Hormusjee Ruttonjee, a prominent Parsi businessman, established the Hong Kong Anti-Tuberculosis Association and Ruttonjee Sanatorium in Wan Chai for tuberculosis treatment, which was later rebuilt as the Ruttonjee Hospital in memorial of his contribution.

by the locals (Weiss, 1991; Law & Lee, 2013). Nowadays, Pakistanis, like other South Asians, continue to arrive at Hong Kong for family reunion and marriage arrangement (Ku, 2006).

British colonial state left no multicultural or ethnic-integration policy in Hong Kong but a racial hierarchy induced by colonialism. Decolonization, on the other hand, generated a surge in Hindus migrants whom was displaced by the India partition in 1947 and the ensuing religious conflicts. Quite some of the displaced eventually ended up in Hong Kong for a stable life—a migration decision which economic reasoning played a trivial role (Hemnani, 2019). Effort was spent to preserve cultural heritage and maintain ethnic tie to their homeland. The Indian Parsi, Sindhis, Sikhs and Jains are economically better off in Hong Kong for their higher social status and extensive social network achieved through century-old trading activities within the British Empire (Plüss, 2005). Comparatively, the Pakistanis and Nepalese suffered the brunt of discrimination especially during economic restructuring in recent years (Law & Lee, 2013; Crabtree & Wong, 2013; Frost, 2004). When widespread prejudice against South Asians turns into everyday racism after 1997, deprivation is the likely result (O'Connor, 2012).

2.2 Polarizations of Migration under Neo-Liberal Globalization

Back in the nineteenth century, the migration flows to Hong Kong were less polarized since a large European working class was seeking opportunities in the colony like their elite countrymen (Lethbridge, 1975). However, recent globalization since the 1980s has polarized the migration flow along the ethnic, gender, and class lines.

As western industrial production moved to a reforming China in the 1980s, transnational corporations, especially those from America, Japan, and Korea, began to set up regional headquarters and back offices in the emerging global city of Hong Kong. By "outsourcing" domestic work to developing countries, the workforce in Hong Kong continued to feminize as women joined the booming service industry (Constable, 1997; Lee, 2002). This development has created two distinct migratory flows to Hong Kong. The first one consists of professionals and managers, mostly men from the developed world, who operated the Pearl River Delta production network from Hong Kong. The other was the semi- to low skilled labours. Many of them were women from the developing countries who filled up the occupational gap left by the local Chinese. The sex ratio of ethnic minorities reflects such racializing and gendering of transnational class migration in Hong Kong. For every 1000 women from the same ethnic group, there were 1747 White men, but only 63 Filipinos men and 12 Indonesian men living in Hong Kong (Census and Statistics Department, 2017). Most of the Japanese (89.2%) / Korean (91.5%) / White (90.8%) men in Hong Kong worked at the higher end of the service sector as managers and administrators/professionals/associate professionals. Meanwhile, up to 99.0% of Indonesian women and 96.9% of Filipino women in Hong Kong worked in the elementary occupations (Census and Statistics Department, 2017).

Driven by the new international divisions of labour, polarized migrations have given Hong Kong its market-oriented cosmopolitan outlook. The image of "a shopping paradise" and "a gourmet paradise" echoed the rising consumption needs of the transnational elites. But the target of cosmopolitan treatment is highly selective (Bauman, 2000). While the transnational elites had more freedom to come, stay and form their own communities (like the Japanese in Taikoo Shing, see Sone, 2002), the migrant labours are often seen as a potential threat to the local job markets. As will be seen, migration policy is designed to exclude them from the option of settling down.

2.3   Chinese Diaspora and Thai Ethnic Enclave

People migrate for reasons other than just the economic one. For example, majority of ethnic Thais in Hong Kong were women (male to female ratio is 183 to 1000 in 2016). They came to work as domestic workers as globalization unfolded in the late twentieth century. Their migration path, however, was shaped by the historical connection between Thailand and the regional Chinese diaspora. The Thailand-Hong Kong economic and cultural ties formed part of the century-old China-Nanyang network (see Chap. 2). Hong Kong was once the export hub of Chinese labours to Thailand, and in turn Thailand was also the largest exporter of rice to Hong Kong (Hewison, 2004).

After three transnational migration waves spanning over the last 200 years, ethnic Chinese has now become the largest ethnic minority group in Thailand (Bao, 2005). Taksin the Great, a Thai King and son to a Teochew merchant, extensively strengthened Thai's trade and labour tie with the Chinese Teochew during his reign (1767–1782). Around half of the Thai Chinese nowadays can trace their origins to the coastal Guangdong region, and especially Chaozhou/Teochew (潮州). In the post-war period, a large number of Chinese migrants arrived in Hong Kong, mostly single men. Consequently, a number of Thai women married to Hong Kong as transnational brides in the 1970s—especially to Chaozhou migrants from mainland China. Many of the Chaozhous and Thais set up families and settled at the Kowloon City.

By now, the Thai community has spawned many restaurants and stores in the Kowloon City district (a.k.a. the "Little Thailand"). Due to the cultural linkage, Thai's co-ethnic businesses in Kowloon City (e.g. easier to hire Chinese as middleman or translator and targeting Chinese clients) are examples of why their ethnic economy is the most successful compared to other Southeast Asians in Hong Kong (Chan, 2015). The district has also become an anchored enclave for Thai migrant workers nowadays (Sharp & Assarasakorn, 2015), showing vividly that ethnic ties, not just economic calculation, played a role in the migration process of Hong Kong.

2.4 Cold War Conflicts and the Refugee Port: Vietnamese Boat People and Asylum Seekers in Hong Kong

Migration is not always voluntary, often easily triggered by humanitarian crisis close by or far away. Refugee and asylum seekers move involuntarily in search of a new home. In history, the colony status and its connection to the West had turned Hong Kong into a major safe haven for Chinese refugees escaping political upheaval in China (Hambro, 1957). Its refugee port status became internationalized with the arrival of the Vietnamese boat people between the 1970s and 1990s. Most escaped from the Vietnam War and the communist regime in the Cold War era.

The first significant number of Vietnamese refugees arrived in 1975 when a Danish freighter rescued 3800 of them from the South China Sea (Bousquet, 1987). Hong Kong was not a signatory party to the 1951 Refugee Convention, as the United Kingdom never extended it to the colony even though it is a signatory party. Initially, there was no legal framework to handle refugees in Hong Kong. Before 1979, Vietnamese refugees stayed with their relatives in Hong Kong or were settled in open camps where they could find jobs at nearby factories while waiting for resettlement to Western countries. With the onset of the Sino-Vietnamese War in 1979, the number of refugees from Vietnam, mostly ethnic

Chinese, surged rapidly for fear of retribution. Hong Kong soon was declared the port of first asylum and by year end there were 12 refugee camps and centres. From 1982 onward, the colonial state implemented new policy by detaining all Vietnamese refugee arrivals to closed camp operated by the Correctional Department and visits by relatives were not allowed (Bousquet, 1987). The forced repatriation of Vietnamese boat people began in 1989. Hong Kong's status of the first port of asylum officially ended in 1998.

Despite a substandard camp situation and prolonged screening process, the UN Convention Against Torture was only introduced in 1992. The boat people crisis illustrated a chapter of the largest international humanitarian action carried out (and funded) by Hong Kong people. The scale of the operation was actually comparable to the European Union's handling of the refugee crisis in the Mediterranean Sea since the Arab Spring took place in 2011. By 1999, Hong Kong had seen more than 200,000 Vietnamese refugees, resettled more than 143,000 of them and repatriated the rest. Some 1400 Vietnamese refugees remained in Hong Kong were settled locally via the "Widened Local Resettlement Scheme" in 2000 (HKSAR, 2000).

By now, the influx of Vietnamese refugee had ceased, but Hong Kong remains a hub for refugees and asylum seekers in the region. Most of the asylum seekers came from South Asia.[14] Towards the end of 2016, there were 9981 outstanding torture/non-refoulment claim cases made under the UN Convention Against Torture. These refugees, like the Vietnamese, are forced to migrate to escape political or religious prosecution. With an immigration policy forbidden to work, the asylum seekers have become the most marginalized and invisible migrant groups in Hong Kong (Carvalho, 2018). Worse still, they suffered most from racial discrimination due to a lack of local political and social support.

Economic reasons alone cannot explain migrant's decision to move to Hong Kong. Migration can be triggered by military deployment and then followed by family reunion, displacement caused by decolonization and religious conflicts, involuntary or voluntary movement of refugees and

---

[14] According to Immigration Department Statistics on non-refoulement Claim, no. of outstanding claimants in 2017: Indian 1893; Pakistani 1816; Vietnamese 1237; Bangladeshi 1179; Indonesian 918; Filipino 483; Nepalese 286; Sri Lankan 258; Gambian 129 and others 757. See Immigration Department (n.d.), last visit 1 August 2017, the figure since then has updated.

migrant labours. To recap, while the celebrated title of "gourmet paradise" is collectively written by ethnic minorities, their potential to realize cosmopolitan dream is confined by historical contexts and social position along three intersecting dimensions: race, gender, and transnational class.[15] As will be shown shortly, such intersectionality combined with local government's governance and state-building projects produced a distinctive citizenship framework in Hong Kong.

3   INSTITUTIONAL BARRIERS AND CITIZENSHIP OF ETHNIC MINORITY IN COLONIAL HONG KONG

What was the situation of ethnic minority community in pre-1997 Hong Kong? Answering this question is difficult. Scholarship concerning Hong Kong's ethnic minority in pre-1997 period is sparse and fragmented. Scarcely has "race" been a subject of study in Hong Kong's education system or public discourses. "Ethnicity" as a matter concerning Chinese ethnical differences has been taken up by some local anthropologists.[16] But for ethnicity concerning non-Chinese ethnic groups, there were only a few studies about ethnic minorities' social problems (e.g. substance uses) and language problems (see Erni & Leung, 2014; Cheung, 1993; Bilbow, 1997). Even today, academics in Hong Kong having put ethnic minority as their research focus have been mostly social scientists interested in demography, labour, migration, globalization and human rights problems (Ku, 2006; Sautman, 1995; Mathews, 2011). Outside the academia, however, a number of non-governmental organizations are actively documenting the situations of ethnic minorities aiming to reveal their experiences and needs to the government and the general public.

3.1   From "Multiculturalism by Default" to "Ethnic Nationalism"

The paucity of ethnic minority knowledge somehow reflects British colonial government's ambivalent attitude and strategy in handling ethnic minorities in pre-1997 Hong Kong. Similar to the strategy governing

---

[15] See Crenshaw (1991) for an original discussion of intersectionality concerning the marginalized.
[16] See Erni and Leung (2014) for a comprehensive review on ethnic minority research in Hong Kong, especially Chap. 7.

local Chinese before World War II, the colonial government did not want to intervene into the lives of ethnic minorities. Several examples about the building of institutions in Hong Kong's Islamic community are instructive. Today, there are five mosques in Hong Kong. Four of them are on Hong Kong Island and one in Kowloon. Despite long history of having Islamic community in Hong Kong, the colonial government did not financially support the building or reconstruct these mosques. Most of the building and reconstruction costs were donated by Indian and Pakistani Muslim communities themselves. When a local expert on Hong Kong's Islamic community interviewed the chairman of United Muslim Association of Hong Kong about government's support to build elders' homes or centres, the respondent bluntly criticized the government giving very little support and they even had to train their own social and welfare workers (Ho, 2013, pp. 33–34).

Similarly, in major education reforms in Hong Kong's colonial history, ethnic minority education received almost no attention. For instance, the first major reports on education policy (from 1965 White Paper "Education Policy to 1981 report "Hong Kong Education System") had no single word on the educational needs of ethnic minority children. Education Commission of the Hong Kong government also made no remarks on special education needs of ethnic minority students throughout the 1980s and 1990s.[17]

In colonial Hong Kong, therefore, the state-ethnic minority community relationship was consistent with its overall residualism and charities-driven nature in social welfare. The British colonial government basically left the problems of ethnic minority population to charities and community groups. Thus, the second standard-definition image that pre-1997 Hong Kong was a "multicultural" city has much to be qualified here. Undoubtedly, the multi-ethnic nature of Hong Kong society has been historically the city's social fabric, but the multi-ethnic and multi-cultural diversity was not a conscious effort propelled by the British colonial government. Very much the contrary, the colonial government adopted a cultural non-interventionism towards ethnic minority population which in

[17] See Erni and Leung (2014), chapter 5 "Education of South Asian Youth". However, we have to stress that there has been one special educational issue persisted throughout the history of Hong Kong's education system dating back to the 1960s is Hong Kong students' language proficiency and the related question of medium of instruction (MOI) in classrooms. As will be seen later in this chapter, this issue is still a hot potato for SAR government.

turn created a space for ethnic minority community to self-help, sustain and flourish their own ethnic cultures in Hong Kong. Saying pre-1997 Hong Kong was a multicultural city is a *postmortem* examination to colonial Hong Kong's default multi-ethnic and multi-cultural conditions. It should not be mistaken as a result of the colonial government's intentional actions. In short, pre-1997 Hong Kong city was in a situation of "multiculturalism by default", not "multiculturalism by policy".

However, after July 1, 1997, with Hong Kong ended its colonial era, situation and government policies concerning ethnic minority have changed drastically. Different from British colonial government, the SAR government has been active in reviving Chinese nationalist sentiment in post-handover Hong Kong. This national building sentiment shifted Hong Kong government's ethnic minority policy from "multiculturalism by default" to "ethnic nationalism". This major change has been obvious in different policy areas such as citizenship, education, and labour markets.

3.2 Changing Citizenship Models in Hong Kong

The concept of inclusionary citizenship was gradually introduced as a result of Hong Kong's modernization. However, in practice, colonial subjects—both migrants from overseas and indigenous Chinese, were treated in many shades of distinction.[18] Britain has steered its own immigration policy *towards* civic-based—immigrants access to formal membership through birthright citizenship (given at least one parent has British citizenship) and naturalization process (Asari et al., 2008; Bloemraad et al., 2008). People living in dependent territories, however, can only separately apply for British citizenship following the enactment of the British Nationality Act 1981—a policy designed to bar Hong Kong citizens from automatically getting birthright citizenship. Instead, a British National (Overseas) (BNO) nationality was introduced in 1985 for Hong Kong permanent residents in order to ease migratory tensions arising from the 1997 transition. The "one-generation only" and "voluntary registration" BNO was considered "weak-civic" nationhood base. Permanent residents of Hong Kong regardless of ethnicity, can obtain British national status

---

[18] See Go (2013) for further discussion of the concept of postcolonial cosmopolitanism, one that perhaps best captures Hong Kong's unique migration experience.

(and rights, e.g. for ease of traveling) but not British citizenship status.[19] Such an arrangement is no surprise given the highly-restrictive British immigration policy to maintain its "white" core in light of migration from multi-ethnic colonial peripheries (Joppke, 1996).[20]

After 1997, new generations of ethnic minorities who were permanent residents in Hong Kong faced a new situation. They could no longer apply for BNO (unless having born before 1997 and parents had included their names in BNO) but simultaneously their eligibility for HKSAR passport was in doubt at the beginning. Because a prerequisite for applying a HKSAR passport—possessing Chinese citizenship—is governed by the nationality law of the People's Republic of China. The naturalization process to become Chinese has been difficult for ethnic minorities. Some argued the Nationality Law of PRC does not recognize non-Chinese ethnic minorities in Hong Kong to full political citizenship right when it extended its coverage to HKSAR (Shamdasani, 2002). Local South Asian permanent residents were initially barred from naturalizing as Chinese nationals (a pre-requisite for applying the HKSAR passport for travel) amounting to denying them a basic human right. Changes have been made since then, but the naturalization process for ethnic minorities in Hong Kong to obtain Chinese citizenship was still considered non-transparent by some (Chiu, 2013).

Therefore, a new institutional barrier has been created for ethnic minorities to obtain full citizenship in Hong Kong as the shift to ethnic nationalist model intensified after 1997. This implies a lack of fertile ground to breed multiculturalism in Hong Kong. Consequently, the strong assimilation model has led to inequality in social, economic and political participation for ethnic minorities, especially for those racialized as not living up to civic competence defined by the dominant Chinese (Alexander, 2001). South Asians, such as the Nepalese Gurkhas, increasingly found themselves becoming second-class citizens in Hong Kong

---

[19] To illustrate the difficulty in applying for settlement rights, the British Gurkhas was only allowed to settle in the UK when the Labour government changed the rules in 2004. Even so, those Gurkhas retired earlier than 1997—when the brigade Headquarter moved from Hong Kong to Britain—are only allowed to settle after the UK government lost a court fight in 2009 (Sparrow, 2009).

[20] In 2020, however, the British government announced new policies over Hong Kong's BNO holders, allowing them to stay in the United Kingdom for five years and then to apply for full citizenship after China's announcement of the National Security Law over Hong Kong (BBC, 2020).

(Kochhar-George, 2010). Some politicians and local media often capitalized on the asylum seeker controversy to fuel hostility towards ethnic minorities, South Asians in particular, to undermine the legitimacy of their citizenship (Leung, 2016). The weak-civic citizenship model originated from colonial time has gradually turned into a strong-ethnic citizenship model as racialization reinforces it.

This strong-ethnic citizenship model is vividly seen in the case of migrant domestic workers in Hong Kong. Through an institutional design dated back to colonial time, migrant domestic workers are denied Hong Kong citizenship.[21] In 1971, colonial government set up requirement to become a "permanent resident"—one must live in Hong Kong for seven continuous years (Tang & Yuen, 2016). Migrant domestic workers in Hong Kong could not fulfil this seven continuous years' requirement by default, as they are required to leave the territory at the end of their two-year employment contract to have their work visa renewed. They are also required to leave Hong Kong within two weeks of termination of employment contract.

For migrant domestic workers, institutional restrictions based on "race" preclude them from being qualified for immigration, even after staying for seven years like other foreign professionals. For example, expatriates like British emigrants could easily make such cosmopolitan claim like "I'm a citizen of the world" as they settle with little difficulty in other countries (Hammerton, 2017). In 2011, Evangeline banao Vallejos and Daniel Domingo took to the court to challenge the immigration law after both had spent more than seven years working and living in Hong Kong. The High Court ruled that domestic workers should not be excluded from settling in Hong Kong in a judicial review of immigration law. Soon the government issued an exaggerated figure that 500,000 new residents

---

[21] The growth of labour exportation from Philippines since the 1970s was triggered by the first economic restructuring adjustments as required by the International Monetary Fund and the World Bank in exchange for loans to support the debt under Marcos presidency (Battistella, 1995). Despite effort to initiate export oriented industrialization, weak governance and corruption has stalled the process and remittances became a feasible option to increase Philippines' national income. Indonesian government soon followed suit and expanded its labors exportation in 1979. Meanwhile, the increase in female labor participation rate as Hong Kong industrialized and then transformed into service economy has created a demand for domestic worker from overseas. Now, more than three hundred thousands migrant domestic workers from these two countries work in Hong Kong each year. The neoliberal economy has injected one of its features—flexible labor—into policy governing the citizenship status of migrant domestic workers.

would be eligible to come and half would be applying for CSSA to stir up public sentiment (BBC, 2013).[22] At the LegCo, contradictory speeches were frequently heard from the same speakers—migrant domestic workers contributed a lot with their hard work but if they settle it would cause large social burden and unemployment among local workers (Legislative Council, 2011). The city was divided.

The High Court ruling was overturned by the Court of Appeal in 2012. For helping domestic workers to fight for the right of abode in court, the Civic Party lost their middle-class support and got one of the worst results in the subsequent District Council elections (Tsoi, 2011). These results echoed the rising "Hong Kong Chinese Orientalism" (Law & Lee, 2013), accelerating amidst the Sinicization process in postcolonial Hong Kong (Law & Lee, 2012).

Social, civil and political rights associated with citizenship are entrenched in local customs, domestic law, and institutions (Marshall, 1950).[23] When the exclusiveness of these rights is challenged, cultural processes are often invoked at the society level to reassert or redraw boundaries for insider and outsider.[24] When existing immigration law were disputed in court, cultural processes were triggered to re-racialize Hong Kong citizenship rights. Given the state has historically considered economic conditions rather than humanitarian values as the premise for immigration control (and all public policy) in Hong Kong, such cultural processes would typically highlight the potential economic burden associated with a change in the status quo (Law & Lee, 2006).[25]

---

[22] Vallejos Evangeline Banao also known as Vallejos Evangeline B. and Daniel Domingo L. v. Commissioner of Registration and Registration of Persons Tribunal (FACV 19 and 20/2012).

[23] Marshall (1950) classical definition of citizenship formulation—civil, political and social, "The civil element of citizenship is composed of the rights necessary for individual freedom—liberty of the person, freedom of speech, thought and faith, the right to own property and to conclude valid contracts, and the right to justice'; 'By the political element I mean the right to participate in the exercise of political power, as a member of a body invested with political authority or as an elector of the members of such a body'; 'By the social element I mean the whole range, from the right to a modicum of economic welfare and security to the right to share to the full in the social heritage and to live the life of a civilized being according to the standards prevailing in the society.'

[24] Such tactics include negative other presentation and scare tactics used in major media. See Flowerdew et al. (2002).

[25] See Leong (2011).

3.3   Assimilated Schooling for Ethnic Minorities in Hong Kong

In the postcolonial context, a compulsory Chinese medium instruction policy has been introduced, but has a disproportionate impact on ethnic minorities students in Hong Kong (Gao, 2017). Since 2006, ethnic minority students in Hong Kong have been institutionally channelled to the so-called "designated schools" where extra resources were supposed to be provided to accommodate their learning need, including the design of a curriculum where Chinese is learnt as a second language (Shum et al., 2016). Consequently, physical segregation of ethnic minority students in these schools and an isolated learning environment were created within Hong Kong's education system. Worse still, the designated school were often schools having inadequate student intake before and had a lower quality of teaching due to a lack of resources (Shum et al., 2016). These two challenges were reflected in academic underachievement and under-representation of ethnic minorities in postsecondary education (Gao, 2017).

To counter the trend of segregated schooling in Hong Kong, the designated school system was abolished in 2013/2014, channelling ethnic minority students into mainstream public schools and providing additional resources to schools upon admission of these students (Shum et al., 2016). Nonetheless, the chief policy objective was to focus on improving the Chinese language proficiency of ethnic minority students to allow them to compete in the same system with other local Chinese students in a meritocratic way. According to Shum et al. (2016), sociologists have already identified other institutional barriers to improving education outcomes for ethnic minority students in Hong Kong. These barriers are not necessarily language related, such as: school policy framing their pedagogical need as secondary; system structure routinely excluding them from essential education resources; process of teaching and learning lower expectations from teachers and peer Chinese students.

3.4   Glass Wall and Ceiling in the Labour Markets

To sustain a neoliberal economy, racialization is used to justify the selective cosmopolitanism in Hong Kong.[26] For example, the entitlement to Hong

---

[26] To begin with, Ong (2006) argued sovereign state actively employs zoning to create special administrative zone, to facilitate neoliberal globalization. In this process, neoliberalism intervenes in population control and shapes the citizenship formation process. Tang and Yuen (2016) reviewed the transition of colonial citizenship to postcolonial one in Hong

Table 3.1 Population and median monthly income by ethnic minority groups in Hong Kong

Ethnic group	Percentage among ethnic minorities population in Hong Kong in 2016 (number)	Median monthly income from main employment (HKD) (2016)	
		Male	Female
White (Caucasian)	10.0% (58,209)	58,000	31,000
Korean	1.2% (5209)	50,000	26,250
Japanese	1.7% (9976)	40,000	25,000
Indian	6.2% (36,462)	26,000	6750
Nepalese	4.4% (25,472)	14,500	11,000
Pakistani	3.1% (18,094)	12,800	12,000
Thai	1.7% (10,215)	15,000	8000
Indonesian	26.2% (153,299)	10,000	4210
Filipino	31.5% (184,081)	8100	4210
Whole working population	NA	16,800	12,000

Source: Census and Statistics Department (2017, Table 3.1, Table 6.5)

Kong citizenship is stratified along racial, gender and economic class lines. A glimpse of the incomes of ethnic minority groups in Hong Kong provides us hints to this (Table 3.1).[27]

At the tip are the Europeans / White, and the East Asians like Japanese and Korean, who represented the small group of the global capitalist class in Hong Kong. Collectively they contributed to only 12.9% of the local ethnic minorities' population, but their median monthly income was among the highest of all ethnic groups, and for men in particular. The median income of White men in Hong Kong was more than 13 times that of Indonesian women and Filipino women. Notably, the Indonesians and Filipinos together constituted the largest minority populations in Hong

Kong with Ong's idea, and argued state zoning has heightened struggles and contentions among Hong Kong citizens as cross border mobility of mainland Chinese citizens intensified after transfer of sovereignty. Their argument that Hong Kong citizenship is civil right based and differed from sovereign state is revealing, but their focus has been on the ethnic Chinese only, and has not touched about ethnic minorities and transnational migrant labors in their discussion. How racialization has helped to configure the neoliberal economy was neglected.

[27] Occupation would better reflect the life chance of transnational migrants. For example, considering the work autonomy of a professional vs. a domestic worker (see Table 3.2).

Kong (57.7% of all). While the majority of the Nepalese and Pakistani are Hong Kong citizens, their median income was lower than the whole working population. In some cases, the median monthly income between women and men of the same ethnic groups could differ significantly. Indian women were earning less than one-third of that of Indian men in terms of median income, since well-off Indian families tend to hire domestic workers from India (See Table 3.1) (Plüss, 2005).

Contrary to common sense, the income level of migrants is not tied to personal qualification, like educational attainment. Some 36.4% of Filipino in Hong Kong have achieved the post-secondary qualification, higher than the 32.7% of the whole population aged 15 and over (Census and Statistics Department, 2017, Table 5.2). A paradox in the market-capitalism of Hong Kong emerges - paying higher qualification persons with lower wages, or bar their shift to a job that better fit their qualification. To justify this involves creation and maintenance of racial stereotypes to legitimize existing institutional barrier and exclusionary practices (Lan, 2006).

Migratory status, race, and gender played significant roles in occupational stratification (see Table 3.2), leading to the polarized income among ethnic minorities observed earlier (see also Table 3.1 for corresponding median monthly income). The migration regime has placed stringent restriction over the type of occupations for female Filipino and Indonesian migrant workers in Hong Kong. Often, they are limited to elementary occupation like domestic work—traditionally trivialized in the Chinese society. Such stereotype was so prevalent that a local lawmaker even suggested, quite derogatorily, to reserve all "domestic servant" job to ethnic minorities with local residency (Benitez, 2018a). In contrast, among the whites in the global city—though obviously less homogenous than the classification itself implies, a vast majority of 98.8% of men and 81.6% of women were working as managers and administrators/professionals/associate professionals—jobs with greater chance of economic advancement, alongside degree of autonomy in performing work-tasks and roles (Erikson & Goldthorpe, 1992).

The majority of Indian men worked at higher end service job like managers, administrators, professionals or associate professionals (68.5%). This explained not just their salary higher than overall Hong Kong monthly median income but possibly a better life chance for their family members. Yet up to 48.2% of Indian women were working in the elementary occupations, often as domestic workers for wealthier Indian family,

Table 3.2 Proportion of working ethnic minorities by sex, ethnicity and occupation, 2016

Ethnicity	Sex	Managers and administrators	Professionals/associate professionals	Clerical support workers/service and sales workers	Craft and related workers, plant and machine operators and assemblers	Elementary occupations	Skilled agricultural and fishery workers; and occupations not classifiable	Overall	Overall Labour force participation rates
Indonesian	Male	5.6	23.3	10.5	9.9	48.6	2.2	100	60.4
	Female	0.1	0.2	0.7	0	99	Na	100	97.6
Filipino	Male	5.4	23.7	21.7	9.6	39.2	0.2	100	85.5
	Female	0.3	1	1.9	0.1	96.9	Na	100	97.5
Indian	Male	34.6	33.9	20.6	15	22.9	0	100	81.1
	Female	9	22.3	19.7	0.7	48.2	Na	100	55.3
Pakistani	Male	9.6	13.5	23.8	15	37.9	0.2	100	68.5
	Female	11.6	30.9[a]	37.3	Na	19.4	Na	100	18.5
Nepalese	Male	3.4	11.4	17.7	30.1	37.4	Na	100	84.6
	Female	2.6	5.2	55.7	5	31.2	0.3	100	63.8
Japanese	Male	51.7	37.5	9.8	0.1	0.9	Na	100	88.1
	Female	24.3	44.4	30.6	Na	0.8	Na	100	47.4
Thai	Male	6.5	13.7	40.4	16.2	23.2	Na	100	80.9
	Female	1.3	3	33.7	1.6	60.3	Na	100	61.4
Korean	Male	46.9	44.6	8.3	Na	0.2	Na	100	87.3
	Female	22	41.3	34.8	0.1	1.9	Na	100	58.1
Other Asian	Male	15.2	36.2	32.8	9.4	6.4	Na	100	67.7

White	Female	11.7	14.7	36.8	1.2	35.6	Na	100	**53.9**
	Male	42	48.8	6.4	1	1.7	0	100	84.8
Mixed overall	Female	21.5	60.1	16	0.7	1.7	Na	100	57
	Male	19.4	38.5	21.5	10.7	9.8	0.1	100	64.7
	Female	8.4	19.9	32.5	1.4	37.9	Na	100	**57.4**
	Male	13.2	30.8	23.8	18.3	13.8	0.2	100	68.4
Whole population	Female	7	24.2	39.1	1.4	28.2	0.1	100	**54.5**

Source: Census and Statistics Department (2017, Table 6.3)

[a]The high percentage of Pakistani women working as professionals/ associate professionals is likely a distorted figure because the labour force participation rates of the Pakistani women remain very low across all age groups. See Census and Statistics Department (2017, Table 6.1)

which accounted for their much lower median monthly income than their male counterparts. A majority of the Pakistani men worked in the elementary occupations (37.9%), clerical support workers/ service and sales workers (23.8%), and as craft and related workers, plant and machine operators and assemblers (15.0%). Only 23.1% of Pakistani men were working in higher end service job. Figures concerning Pakistani women must be read with care as they are likely distorted by their very low labour participation rate (18.5%). For Nepalese, while majority worked in elementary occupation (men 37.4%; women 31.2%), a significant portion of men also worked as craft and related workers, plant and machine operators and assemblers (30.1%) and women worked as clerical workers/ service and sales workers (55.7%).

Obviously, South Asians disproportionally work in elementary occupations or low-end service job compared to the whole population. This racial segmentation of the labour market further intensified due to South Asians' disadvantaged language position in the largely Sinicized education system that we talked about earlier, and the lack of recognition of their educational qualifications (Ku & Chan, 2011).

Pakistani were often denied access to jobs that they were qualified on paper (Ku & Chan, 2011; Crabtree & Wong, 2013). One main obstacle for Pakistani in finding a job, like other South Asians, was language barrier (Benitez, 2018b). This is especially so as English is gradually replaced by Chinese as the dominant language in middle to the high-end work environment. Yet "race" was sometimes the simple reason for rejecting a Pakistani candidate even if she/he could speak fluent Cantonese (Ku & Chan, 2005). Considering the low labour participation rate of Pakistani women, some would blame their patriarchy system as the main cause (So, 2010), but there were cases they were rejected from work simply for wearing their cultural attire and for not dressing like the local women in their workplace (Ku, 2006). For a long period until the 1990s, Pakistani men were preferred by banks and buildings to work as security guards. The situation changed when local Chinese experienced downward social mobility amid the post-1997 financial crisis and both ethnic groups now competed for the same security jobs which have been professionalized with higher education and language requirement under the trend of globalization (Law & Lee, 2013). Consequently, Pakistani men are also pushed to elementary occupations like recycling and construction.

The "racial imagination" of the fearless Gurkhas as a warrior clan generated both opportunities and challenges for the Nepalese in Hong Kong

(Kochhar-George, 2010). As employers and companies favoured the military-trained éx-Gurkhas to be security guards, a large number of Nepalese were hired in security business in Hong Kong.[28] Some of them worked as bouncers in pubs and bars, where they complained that police officers often showed favouritism to the expatriate customers they had troubles with (Carney, 2010). Paradoxically, the foremost stereotype associated with the second generations Nepalese and new Nepalese immigrants was that they are natural-born "security guard". For example, during the 2019 Anti-extradition law movement, Nepalese were widely employed to guard the Mass Transit Railway—pitted against protestors dissatisfied with how the MTR company handled the Yuen Long incident.

Contrary to common perception, ethnic minorities have *higher* salaried labour force participation rate than Hong Kong overall (except for Indian, Pakistani, Japanese and Korean women, and Indonesian men), and most tend to work until older age than the Hong Kong population as a whole.[29] An invisible racial glass wall and ceiling have barred them from crossing into occupations and ranks with better prospects, hence restricting their upward social mobility in general.

3.5   The Lack of Multicultural Policies and Its Social Consequences

What then are the social consequences of not having a multicultural policy in Hong Kong?

> Various measures have been introduced to help EMs adapt to life in Hong Kong, attain self-reliance, and move upwards along the social ladder. These tasks align with the goals of preventing and alleviating poverty. (Census and Statistics Department, 2018, p. vi)

The two *Hong Kong Poverty Situation Report on Ethnic Minorities* in 2014 and 2016 illustrate the social polarization consequence from the lack

---

[28] The largest of which was the British based global security corporation Group 4 Securicor (G4S). But under the globalization trend of "race to the bottom", the wage for G4S Nepalese securities was frozen for years despite huge revenue earned by the corporation and a large-scale strike eventually erupted in 2009 (Lam & Lee, 2009).

[29] "...the labour force participation rates of ethnic minority men were generally higher than the overall male average. In particular among the older segment of the population" (Census and Statistics Department, 2015, p. 10).

of proper integration policy and institutional racism in Hong Kong (Census and Statistics Department, 2015, 2018). Comparing poverty figures between 2011 and 2016, the pre-intervention poverty rate and post-intervention poverty rate for ethnic minorities in Hong Kong have both gone up together with the increase in population, from 15.8% to 19.4% in the former and 13.9% to 17.6% in the later. South Asians accounted for 40.6% of those classified as poor, whereas Pakistanis along constituted about 20.2%. Working poverty of poor ethnic minorities was common (64.7%) and higher than the overall poor population (50.3%) in Hong Kong.

However, there was a tendency in these two reports to attribute poverty to individualized traits of the now settled ethnic groups. The reports highlighted certain traits of South Asians living in poverty akin to the view of "culture of poverty" (Lewis, 1966): racialized as welfare-dependent (having larger number of children[30]), traditional (sacrificing education for family wage[31] and declining government services[32]), and blamed for failing to be assimilated due to language problems. Meanwhile, the word "discrimination" appeared only twice in each of the report, whereas the words "racism", "prejudice" or "inequality" were nowhere to be found. The institutional causes to social polarization of ethnic minorities were simply hidden from sight.

The lack of reflective multicultural policies has not just caused economic harm but physical ones in the workplace. Due to the "security guard" stereotypical assumption, public are less aware of the large amount of Nepalese construction site workers and their substandard work environment (Frost, 2004).[33] The understudy of Nepalese's (and other ethnic

---

[30] See 3.4 (ii): Family structure, "families of some ethnic groups were notably larger, whereas their numbers of working members were comparatively few. The heavy financial burden of working households still rendered it more difficult for them to move out of poverty, resulting in prevalent working poverty and poverty rates generally higher than the territory-wide average" (Census and Statistics Department, 2018, p. 16).

[31] See 2.4 (i), "...Nepalese, regardless of gender, had higher LFPR, and many of Nepalese youths even left schools early in order to join the workforce." (Census and Statistics Department, 2015, p. 10)

[32] See ES.31 Observation 6, "the degree of community involvement and usage of support services or financial assistance among SAs [South Asians] were relatively low, possibly due to language barriers" (Census and Statistics Department, 2015, p. xvii).

[33] The manifestation of discrimination for Nepalese workers at construction site is complex. The discrimination is based not just on race, but on a caste system entrenched in Nepalese culture that resulted in perpetuation of employment favoritism among the local Nepalese community (Ale, 2013).

minorities) role in construction industry resulted in their prolonged exposure to higher risk of work-related injuries than the locals—risk that can be mediated if existing language barriers are tackled, for example by providing a machine operation manual in Nepalese language (Chan et al., 2014).

As for migrant labours, the Indonesians and Philippines working in Hong Kong faced a high rate of abuse (Chiu and Asian Migrant Centre, 2005). Ban from attaining citizenship, mandatory "live-in" with the employer (Lau & Siu, 2018a), and flexible employment relation put migrant domestic workers in situation of social exclusion, rendering them vulnerable to economic and physical exploitation, such as long working hour and workplace abuse (Lau & Siu, 2018b), than majority of the South Asians working in Hong Kong as permanent resident. The abuse of Indonesian domestic worker Erwiana Sulistyaningsih suffered from her employer was a case in point (Lijas, 2014). Having someone worked for prolonged hours with low pay was economic exploitation—a characteristic of unrestrained capitalism. In these cases, racialization could be triggered to justify abuses and victims' lack of protection normally granted to citizens.

4   Concluding Remarks

This chapter has reviewed the migration regime and the situation of non-Chinese ethnic minorities in Hong Kong from colonial to post-colonial era. It has demonstrated that non-Chinese migrants came and stayed in Hong Kong through diverse networks with different purposes. In the early days, migrants from other British colonies came to this Far East frontier to "service" the colonial state. In recent neo-liberal globalization, migrants from other former Western colonies came as flexible labour to fill up the job niches that locals deemed uninterested. Feminization of the workforce in Hong Kong had induced a flow of migrant labour to fill up the domestic work left by local working women.

The consequences of ethnic immigration are far less promising than the cosmopolitan outlook Hong Kong presented to the world. Post-colonial Hong Kong has inherited the racial hierarchy from British colonialism. The government, both before and immediately after 1997, did not seem to have multicultural policies aiming at levelling the racial prejudice and discriminatory practices. On the contrary, moral panic loaded with racial imagination were periodically triggered by the government or conservatives to sway public opinions on migrant citizenship rights. The market

fundamentalism held in many locals' heart is to be blamed for the mal-
treatment against migrant labours in construction sites - for lack of safety
measures, or domestic settings.

Without proper multicultural policies, Hong Kong is therefore no
more than a cultural mosaic, a mélange of different cultures from all over
the world, but nothing more. The very thin layer of cosmopolitanism has
its own postcolonial characteristics—"distorted" acceptance of migrants
based on economic merits, not in pursuit of any humanitarian ideals. From
this perspective, Hong Kong is no better nor no worse than many other
global cities in the world. Institutional racism is no stranger in world
metropolis where migration and globalization of economic activities converge (Sassen, 1991). For one thing, relative to other Asian destination
countries, Hong Kong could rightfully present itself as offering more legal
and humane protection towards foreign domestic helpers (Sayres, 2005),[34]
though admittedly it is still far from a system that would treat migrant
workers equally as the local workers (Chiu & Levin, 1998).

Exclusion of developing country migrants from citizenship appears to be
an Asian characteristic. In some cases, like Japan, even those from the developed countries have been similarly marginalized. Capitalism requires the
creation of categories of "lower quality" but "cheap" "flexible" labour,
while Chinese (or Asian) culture amplifies it to create a migration regime
that could hardly be cosmopolitan. Recently there are activists who tended
to romanticize the colonial regime as cosmopolitan to contrast with the
Chinese ethnic nationalist policies. We doubt whether this is a legitimate
move and probably counter-productive. Certainly, the post-handover
regime has become even more assimilationist and *Han Chinese*-centric, but
that does not mean that the colonial regime had been superior in any sense.

In short, ethnic-based nationhood, assimilation as the dominant
migrant integration method, and ideologically strong liberalism are three
dominant institutional features of the migration regime in Hong Kong.

---

[34] In earlier research, Hong Kong was found to be a top destination for Filipino domestic
workers (Sayres, 2005; Semyonov & Gorodzeisky, 2005). A study classified Hong Kong as
one of the few destinations with high migration infrastructure, where migrant workers enjoy
full and equal statutory labor rights (e.g. right to unionizing) and benefits as local workers
(Ignacio & Meijia, 2009). An ILO report stated "...Hong Kong has the most developed
legal system for the protection of foreign domestic helpers" (Sayres, 2005). In spite of the
above, studies have also found that Indonesian domestic helpers in Hong Kong tended to
suffer more human right abuse than their Filipino counterparts (Chiu and Asian Migrant
Centre, 2005).

From a comparative angle, Hong Kong's migration regime is quite unique as it is shaped by two British legacies—laissez-faire ideology and (weak) multiculturalism necessitated by colonial rule, and one political reality—a shift from (weak) civic-nationhood to ethnic-based nationhood upon the return of sovereignty to China.

Despite its colonial status in the past, Hong Kong has not inherited from Britain's multicultural pluralist citizenship model, where most resident minorities have full equal social and political rights while retaining cultural difference from the majority (Koopmans & Statham, 1999). Ethnic minorities in Britain have ready access to politics through local elections. Rather, Hong Kong's postcolonial citizenship model has more in common with Germany's ethnocultural exclusionist citizenship model, where minorities are integrated into the labour market but not the political community (Koopmans & Statham, 1999). Harmony seems to exist between racial groups, but that's largely a continuation of the colonial segregated arrangement where each group ignores the life of the other. The older generation of ethnic minorities were less visible, if not absent, in participating in Hong Kong politics.

That is no longer the case as seen in visible participation of minority youths in the Umbrella Movement protest in 2014 (Walsh, 2019; Ng et al., 2019), and Anti-Extradition Movement protest in 2019. The sense of agency has been found in increasing number of cases among Hong Kong's young ethnic minorities. 'We are Hongkonger', the rise in identification with Hong Kong among minority youths has coincided with the crystallization of Hong Kong identity upon various political processes in postcolonial Hong Kong.

Scholars have found that several factors contributing to such increase in local identification. Jackson and Nesterova (2017) argued the inclusion of Liberal Studies in the last dozen years has helped to spread multicultural values and appreciation for diversity, hence reduces the level of racial discrimination among the newer generation. Ng et al. (2019) interviewed local South Asian and Filipino youths and found that those having a sense of belonging to Hong Kong are also experiencing less discrimination, achieving a higher level of sociocultural adaptation, having an inclusive conception of Hong Kong identity, and claiming to have received more social benefits like the freedom and security enjoyed in Hong Kong.

To what extent these positive remarks are result of the institutionalization of multiculturalism via legislation against discrimination and desegregation of education has yet to be studied, but one thing is certain, the ethnic minorities are active agents in the construction of identity (Ng et al., 2019). For the ethnic minorities, the formation of identity is a dynamic process. A change in institutional contexts has allowed them better identification with Hong Kong being their homeland, the more they identify with Hong Kong, the more likely they will participate in contentious politics. The more they participate in social movements, the more they identify with the Hong Kong identity.

We are Hongkongers, too.

REFERENCES

Ale, S. (2013). *Assessing the situation of Nepalese community in Hong Kong.* Outstanding Academic Papers by Students (OAPS). Retrieved from City University of Hong Kong, City U Institutional Repository.

Alexander, J. C. (2001). Theorizing the 'modes of incorporation': Assimilation, hyphenation, and multiculturalism as varieties of civil participation. *Sociological Theory, 19*(3), 237–249.

Asari, E. M., Halikiopoulou, D., & Mock, S. (2008). British national identity and the dilemmas of multiculturalism. *Nationalism and Ethnic Politics, 14*(1), 1–28.

Bao, J. (2005). *Marital acts: Gender, sexuality, and identity among the Chinese Thai diaspora.* University of Hawai'i Press.

Battistella, G. (1995). Philippine overseas labour: From export to management. *ASEAN Economic Bulletin, 12*(2), 257–273.

Bauman, Z. (1998). *Globalization: The human consequences.* Columbia University Press.

Bauman, Z. (2000). Tourists and vagabonds: Or, living in postmodern times. In J. E. Davis (Ed.), *Identity and social change* (pp. 13–26). Transaction Publishers.

BBC. (2013, March 25). Hong Kong court denies domestic workers residency. *BBC.* Retrieved from http://www.bbc.com/news/world-asia-china-21920811

BBC. (2020, July 22). UK unveils new special visa for Hong Kong's BNO holders. *BBC.* Retrieved from https://www.bbc.com/news/world-asia-china-53503338

Benitez, M. A. (2018a, July 10). Hong Kong lawmaker draws ire by suggesting up to 10,000 'domestic servant' jobs be reserved for people from ethnic minorities. *South China Morning Post.* Retrieved from https://www.scmp.com/news/hong-kong/community/article/2154608/hong-kong-lawmaker-suggests-reserving-10000-domestic

Benitez, M. A. (2018b, July 30). Hong Kong-born Nepali, 21, to speak at UN about local ethnic minorities' fight against racial discrimination. *South China Morning Post.* Retrieved from https://www.scmp.com/news/hong-kong/

community/article/2157349/hong-kong-born-nepali-21-speak-un-about-local-ethnic

Bilbow, G. T. (1997). Cross-cultural impression management in the multicultural workplace: The special case of Hong Kong. *Journal of Pragmatics, 28*(4), 461–487.

Bloemraad, I., Korteweg, A., & Yurdakul, G. (2008). Citizenship and immigration: Multiculturalism, assimilation, and challenges to the nation-state. *Annual Review of Sociology, 34*(1), 153–179.

Bogardus, E. S. (1925). Social distance and its origins. *Journal of Applied Sociology, 9*, 216–225.

Bousquet, G. (1987). 2: Living in a state of limbo: A case study of Vietnamese refugees in Hong Kong camps. *Center for Migration Studies Special Issues, 5*(2), 34–53.

Carney, J. (2010, March 14). Nepali bouncers say they lack police support. *South China Morning Post*. Retrieved from www.scmp.com/article/708596/nepali-bouncers-say-they-lack-police-support

Carroll, J. M. (2007). *A concise history of Hong Kong*. Hong Kong University Press.

Carvalho, R. (2018, July 7). Give Hong Kong's asylum seekers the right to work, NGO leader says. *South China Morning Post*. Retrieved from https://www.scmp.com/news/hong-kong/hong-kong-law-and-crime/article/2154253/give-hong-kongs-asylum-seekers-and-human

Castles, S. (2004). The factors that make and unmake migration policies. *The International Migration Review, 38*(3), 852–884.

Census and Statistics Department. (2015). *Hong Kong poverty situation. Report on ethnic minorities 2014*. Census and Statistics Department.

Census and Statistics Department. (2017). *Hong Kong 2016 population by-census–Thematic report: Ethnic minorities*. Census and Statistics Department.

Census and Statistics Department. (2018). *Hong Kong poverty situation report on ethnic minorities 2016*. Census and Statistics Department.

Chan, S. K. L. (2015). Segregation dimensions and development differentials of ethnic enclave. *International Journal of Social Economics, 42*(1), 82–96.

Chan, A. P., Javed, A. A., Wong, F. K., & Hon, C. K. (2014). Improving safety communication of ethnic minorities in the construction industry of Hong Kong. In Y. Wang, H. He, G. Shen, & Y. Bai (Eds.), *ICCREM 2014: Smart construction and management in the context of new technology* (pp. 463–474). American Society of Civil Engineers.

Cheung, Y. W. (1993). Approaches to ethnicity: Clearing roadblocks in the study of ethnicity and substance use. *International Journal of the Addictions, 28*(12), 1209–1226.

Chiu, J. (2013, April 30). Ethnic minorities make joint application for Chinese citizenship. *South China Morning Post*. Retrieved from www.scmp.com/news/

hong-kong/article/1226242/ethnic-minorities-make-joint-application-chinese-citizenship

Chiu, S. W., & Asian Migrant Centre. (2005). *A stranger in the house: Foreign domestic helpers in Hong Kong [OP162]*. Hong Kong Institute of Asia-Pacific Studies.

Chiu, S. W., & Levin, D. (1998). *Migration and regional economic integration in Asia*. Organisation for Economic Co-operation and Development.

Constable, N. (1997). *Maid to order in Hong Kong: Stories of Filipina Workers*. NCROL.

Crabtree, S. A., & Wong, H. (2013). 'Ah cha'! The racial discrimination of Pakistani minority communities in Hong Kong: An analysis of multiple, intersecting oppressions. *British Journal of Social Work, 43*(5), 945–963.

Crenshaw, K. (1991). Mapping the margins: Intersectionality, identity politics, and violence against women of color. *Stanford Law Review, 43*(6), 1241.

Editors of the American Heritage Dictionaries. (2016a). Assimilationism. In *The American heritage dictionary of English language* (5th ed.). Houghton Mifflin Harcourt Publishing Company.

Editors of the American Heritage Dictionaries. (2016b). Multicultural. In *The American heritage dictionary of English language* (5th ed.). Houghton Mifflin Harcourt Publishing Company.

Education Bureau. (2014). Core module 27: 'Global City' foundation part: Social characteristics of 'Global City' as demonstrated by Hong Kong. In *Learning and teaching resources: Current affairs cartoons worksheets*. Hong Kong: Education Bureau. Retrieved from https://www.edb.gov.hk/attachment/en/curriculum-development/kla/pshe/references-and-resources/life-and-society/Module_27_eng_s_21072016.pdf

Erikson, R., & Goldthorpe, J. H. (1992). *The constant flux: A study of class mobility in industrial societies*. Clarendon Press.

Erni, J. N., & Leung, L. Y. (2014). *Understanding south Asian minorities in Hong Kong* (Vol. 1). Hong Kong University Press.

Flowerdew, J., Li, D. C., & Tran, S. (2002). Discriminatory news discourse: Some Hong Kong data. *Discourse and Society, 13*(3), 319–345.

Frost, S. (2004). Building Hong Kong: Nepalese labour in the construction sector. *Journal of Contemporary Asia, 34*(3), 364–376.

Gao, F. (2017). Capital multiplicity and convertibility: Language minorities' multidimensional challenges to accessing postsecondary education in Hong Kong. *British Journal of Sociology of Education, 38*(8), 1165–1176.

Go, J. (2013). Fanon's postcolonial cosmopolitanism. *European Journal of Social Theory, 16*(2), 208–225.

Hammerton, A. J. (2017). Migrants of the British diaspora since the 1960s: Stories from modern nomads. Manchester University Press.

Hambro, E. (1957). Chinese refugees in Hong Kong. *The Phylon Quarterly, 18*(1), 69–81.

Hemnani, R. (2019, August 15). Hindus from Sindh who fled India for Hong Kong at Partition recall how they built a community. *South China Morning Post*. Retrieved from https://www.scmp.com/lifestyle/family-relationships/article/3022689/hindus-sindh-who-fled-india-hong-kong-partition

Hewison, K. (2004). Thai migrant workers in Hong Kong. *Journal of Contemporary Asia, 34*(3), 318–335.

HKSAR. (2000). *Plan to integrate Vietnamese refugees and migrants announced* [Press Release]. Retrieved from https://www.info.gov.hk/gia/general/200002/22/0222141.htm

Ho, W. Y. (2013). *Islam and China's Hong Kong: Ethnic identity, Muslim networks and the new silk road*. Routledge.

Hong Kong Unison. (2012). *Racial acceptance survey report*. Hong Kong Unison. Retrieved from http://www.unison.org.hk

Ignacio, E., & Meijia, Y. (2009). Managing labour migration: The case of the Filipino and Indonesian domestic helper market in Hong Kong (No. 994327253402676). International Labour Organization. Chicago.

Immigration Department. (n.d.). Enforcement. Retrieved August 1, 2017, from https://www.immd.gov.hk/eng/facts/enforcement.html

Jackson, L., & Nesterova, Y. (2017). Multicultural Hong Kong: Alternative new media representations of ethnic minorities. *Multicultural Education Review, 9*(2), 93–104.

Joppke, C. (1996). Multiculturalism and immigration: A comparison of the United States, Germany, and Great Britain. *Theory and Society, 25*, 449–500.

Kleingeld, P., & Brown, E. (2019). Cosmopolitanism. In E. N. Zalta (Ed.), *Stanford encyclopedia of philosophy* (Winter 2019 Edition). Retrieved from https://plato.stanford.edu/entries/cosmopolitanism/

Kochhar-George, C. S. (2010). Nepalese Gurkhas and their battle for equal rights. *Race and Class, 52*(2), 43–61.

Koopmans, R., & Statham, P. (1999). Challenging the liberal nation-state? Postnationalism, multiculturalism, and the collective claims making of migrants and ethnic minorities in Britain and Germany. *American Journal of Sociology, 105*(3), 652–696.

Ku, H. B. (2006). Body, dress and cultural exclusion: Experiences of Pakistani women in 'global' Hong Kong. *Asian Ethnicity, 7*(3), 285–302.

Ku, H. B., & Chan, K. W. (2011). Racism and Social Inequality: The work and employment of the South Asian Ethnic Minority. In S. W. K. Chiu & S. L. Wong (Eds.), Hong Kong divided?: Structures of social inequality in the twenty-first century (pp. 135–166). Hong Kong Institute of Asia-Pacific Studies Chinese University of Hong Kong.

Lam, A., & Lee, C. (2009, January 23). 100 Nepali security guards sacked amid strike for wage increase. *South China Morning Post*. Retrieved from www.scmp.com/article/667918/100-nepali-security-guards-sacked-amid-strike-wage-increase

Lan, P. C. (2006). *Global Cinderellas: Migrant domestics and newly rich employers in Taiwan*. Duke University Press.

Lau, J. (2019, November 7). Hong Kong's minorities face racism from police and protesters. *Foreign Policy*. Retrieved from https://foreignpolicy.com/2019/11/07/hong-kong-protests-minorities-face-violence-racism-police/

Lau, C., & Siu, J. (2018a, February 14). Judge quashes domestic helper's bid for change to 'live-in' rule in Hong Kong. *South China Morning Post*. Retrieved from https://www.scmp.com/news/hong-kong/economy/article/2133296/judge-quashes-domestic-workers-bid-change-live-out-rule-hong

Lau, C., & Siu, J. (2018b, February 15). Hong Kong's domestic workers share stories of ill-treatment, poor living conditions and rights abuses. *South China Morning Post*. Retrieved from https://www.scmp.com/news/hong-kong/community/article/2133421/hong-kongs-domestic-workers-share-stories-ill-treatment

Lau, C., Leung, C., & Lum, A. (2019). Jimmy sham, leader of Hong Kong democracy group civil human rights front, attacked on Mong Kok street. *South China Morning Post*. Retrieved from https://www.scmp.com/news/hong-kong/law-and-crime/article/3033256/jimmy-sham-leader-hong-kong-democracy-group-civil

Law, K. Y., & Lee, K. M. (2006). Citizenship, economy and social exclusion of mainland Chinese immigrants in Hong Kong. *Journal of Contemporary Asia, 36*(2), 217–242.

Law, K. Y., & Lee, K. M. (2012). The myth of multiculturalism in 'Asia's world city': Incomprehensive policies for ethnic minorities in Hong Kong. *Journal of Asian Public Policy, 5*(1), 117–134.

Law, K. Y., & Lee, K. M. (2013). Socio-political embeddings of south Asian ethnic minorities' economic situations in Hong Kong. *Journal of Contemporary China, 22*(84), 984–1005.

Lee, W. K. (2002). Gender ideology and the domestic division of labor in middle-class Chinese families in Hong Kong. *Gender, Place & Culture, 9*(3), 245–260.

Legislative Council. (2011). *Official record of proceedings—Wednesday, 9 October 2011*. Retrieved from http://www.legco.gov.hk/yr11-12/english/counmtg/hansard/cm1019-translate-e.pdf

Leong, A. K. (2011, August 10). 公民黨給自由黨主席的公開信 [An open letter from the civic party to the chairman of the Liberal party]. Civic Party. Retrieved from https://www.civicparty.hk/newspub/公民黨給自由黨主席的公開信/

Lethbridge, H. J. (1975). Condition of the European working class in nineteenth century Hong Kong. *Journal of the Hong Kong Branch of the Royal Asiatic Society, 15*, 88–112.

Leung, C. (2016, April 11). Asylum seeker controversy creating divisions, say rights groups. *South China Morning Post*. Retrieved from http://www.scmp.com/news/hong-kong/article/1935302/asylum-seeker-controversy-creating-divisions-say-rights-groups

Lew, L. (2019, October 30). The Hongkongers from ethnic minorities who thank protest movement for helping them finally feel part of the city. *South China Morning Post*. Retrieved from https://www.scmp.com/news/hong-kong/society/article/3035258/hongkongers-ethnic-minorities-who-thank-protest-movement

Lewis, O. (1966). *La Vida: A Puerto Rican family in the culture of poverty—San Juan and New York*. Random House.

Lijas, P. (2014, January 12). Beaten and exploited, Indonesian maids are Hong Kong's 'modern-day slaves'. *Time*. Retrieved from http://world.time.com/2014/01/15/beaten-and-exploited-indonesian-maids-are-hong-kongs-modern-day-slaves/

Lum, A., & Chan, H. (2019, October 21). Hong Kong protests: City leader Carrie Lam and police chief Stephen Lo apologise after water cannon sprays mosque entrance. *South China Morning Post*. Retrieved from https://www.scmp.com/news/hong-kong/politics/article/3033843/hong-kong-protests-city-leader-carrie-lam-and-police-chief

Marshall, T. H. (1950). *Citizenship and social class and other essays*. Cambridge University Press.

Mathews, G. (2011). *Ghetto at the Center of the World: Chungking mansions, Hong Kong*. Hong Kong University Press.

Mathews, M. (2016). *Key findings from the channel NewsAsia—Institute of Policy Studies Survey on race relations*. Nation University of Singapore.

Ng, H. Y., Kennedy, K. J., & Hue, M. T. (2019). What contributes to ethnic minorities' identification with Hong Kong? The cases of south Asian and Filipino youth. *Asian Ethnicity, 20*(2), 228–249.

O'Connor, P. (2012). *Islam in Hong Kong: Muslims and everyday life in China's World City*. Hong Kong University Press.

Ong, A. (2006). *Neoliberalism as exception: Mutations in citizenship and sovereignty*. Duke University Press.

Plüss, C. (2005). Constructing globalized ethnicity: Migrants from India in Hong Kong. *International Sociology, 20*(2), 201–224.

Reuters Staff. (2013, March 25). Hong Kong's foreign maids lose legal battle for residency. *Reuters*. Retrieved from https://www.reuters.com/article/us-hongkong-maids/hong-kongs-foreign-maids-lose-legal-battle-for-residency-idUSBRE92O04520130325

Sassen, S. (1991). *The Global City: New York, London, Tokyo*. Princeton University Press.

Sautman, B. (1995). *Racial identities in East Asia.* Hong Kong University of Science and Technology.

Sautman, B., & Kneehans, E. (2002). *The politics of racial discrimination in Hong Kong.* University of Maryland.

Sayres, N. J. (2005). *An analysis of the situation of Filipino domestic workers.* International Labour Organization.

Secretary for Constitutional and Mainland Affairs. (2007). *SCMA's speech at the opening ceremony of 'Culture in Motion' variety show (English only)* [Press Releases]. HKSAR. Retrieved from https://www.info.gov.hk/gia/general/200712/09/P200712090161.htm

Semyonov, M., & Gorodzeisky, A. (2005). Labor migration, remittances and household income: A comparison between Filipino and Filipina overseas workers. *The International Migration Review, 39*(1), 45–68.

Shamdasani, R. (2002, December 12). First Hong Kong Pakistani gets Chinese nationality. *South China Morning Post.*

Sharp, M. (2014, March 28). The Nepalese community in Hong Kong looks to preserve Gurkha legacy. *South China Morning Post.* Retrieved from www.scmp.com/lifestyle/article/1458561/nepalese-community-hong-kong-looks-preserve-gurkha-legacy

Sharp, M., & Assarasakorn, V. (2015). Songkran in Hong Kong: Get very wet at Thai Community's new year parade. *South China Morning Post.* Retrieved from https://www.scmp.com/lifestyle/arts-culture/article/1761830/songkran-hong-kong-get-very-wet-thai-communitys-new-year

Shum, M., Gao, F., & Wing, W. K. (2016). School desegregation in Hong Kong: Non-Chinese linguistic minority students' challenges to learning Chinese in mainstream schools. *Asia Pacific Journal of Education, 36*(4), 533–544.

So, F. H. (2010). Between two homes: The lives and identities of Pakistani women in Hong Kong. *Hong Kong Anthropologist, 4,* 86–98.

Sone, A. (2002). *'Being Japanese' in a foreign place: Cultural identities of Japanese in Hong Kong.* The Chinese University of Hong Kong.

Sparrow, A. (2009. April 29). Defeat for Gordon Brown over Gurkhas. *The Guardian.* Retrieved from https://www.theguardian.com/uk/2009/apr/29/government-loses-gurkhas-vote

Stand News. (2019, October 25). 【重慶感謝日】非裔導賞員: 等待多年盼與華人連結 如今心願成真 [African guide: Waited for years to connect with the Chinese, now wish comes true]. *Standardization News.* Retrieved from https://www.thestandnews.com/politics/重慶感謝日-非裔導賞員-等待多年盼與華人連結-如今心願成真/

Tang, G., & Yuen, R. H. (2016). Hong Kong as the 'neoliberal exception' of China: Transformation of Hong Kong citizenship before and after the transfer of sovereignty. *Journal of Chinese Political Science, 21*(4), 469–484.

Ting, V. (2019, July 30). Ethnic minority groups in Hong Kong harassed and discriminated against amid online rumours pinning blame for Yuen Long attack on them. *South China Morning Post*. Retrieved from https://www.scmp.com/news/hong-kong/society/article/3020545/ethnic-minority-groups-hong-kong-harassed-and-discriminated

Tourism Commission. (2011). *Welcome to Hong Kong and a special welcome to the tourism Commission's homepage*. Hong Kong: Tourism Commission. Retrieved from http://www.tourism.gov.hk/english/welcome/welcome.html

Tsoi, G. (2011). Democrats face defeat at this year's district council elections. *HK Magazine*. Retrieved from http://hk-magazine.com/article/8493/democrats-face-defeat-years-district-council-elections

Walsh, S. (2019). Under the umbrella: Pedagogy, knowledge production, and video from the margins of the movement. *Educational Philosophy and Theory, 51*(2), 200–211.

Wan, C. (2019, October 21). Ethnic minorities pour cold water on retaliation fears. *The Standard*. Retrieved from https://www.thestandard.com.hk/section-news/section/11/212751/Ethnic-minorities-pour-cold-water-on-retaliation-fears

Weiss, A. M. (1991). South Asian Muslims in Hong Kong: Creation of a 'local boy' identity. *Modern Asian Studies, 25*(3), 417–453.

Young, J. (2013, May 30). Hong Kong is multicultural: Don't let anyone tell you otherwise. *South China Morning Post*. Retrieved from https://www.scmp.com/comment/insight-opinion/article/1249135/hong-kong-multicultural-dont-let-anyone-tell-you-otherwise

Hong Kong as a Place of Conflict over Hearts and Minds: Identity Politics Beyond Left and Right

Eiffel Tower above clouds cannot see joyous faces, Lofty Fuji Mountain cannot hear visitors laughter, The Statue of Liberty is in the distant fog, Far away nothing can get into its embrace, The reflection of lights at the seashore of Hawaii, How can it compare to the fishing lights in the other state? Lower my head and ask softly, when? At what point? With which appearance? A light echo arrives, now, at this point and with this appearance. Why should I see and ask more? And I sing a song on the way home, Now, at this point and with this appearance, with this appearance.
—Sam Hui, "Eiffel Tower Above Clouds" (Hui et al., 1974) (Lyrics translated by Han Keat Lim. Original source from: https://lyricstranslate.com/en/鐵塔凌雲-eiffel-tower-aboveclouds.html)

1   INTRODUCTION

In the 1970s, the lyrics of a popular Cantonese song, "Eiffel Tower Above Clouds", touched the hearts of many Hong Kong people. The song was sung by an iconic legendary Canto-pop singer, Samuel Hui Koon-Kit, who popularized Cantonese pop songs in Hong Kong. The song describes bitterness and hardship experienced by overseas Hong Kong Chinese and their longing to return Hong Kong, a place they were born and belonged to.

S. W. K. Chiu, K. Y. K. Siu, *Hong Kong Society*, Hong Kong Studies Reader Series, https://doi.org/10.1007/978-981-16-5707-8_4

We use this song to open the chapter on Hong Kong identity for it reflects a shift in the 1970s in Hong Kong people's mentality—a mentality not perceiving themselves as "refugees" seeking temporary shelter from political turmoil in mainland China, but embracing Hong Kong as their home. Commonly agreed among Hong Kong studies scholars, the 1970s deems a crucial period for the birth of Hong Kong identity. The period not only represents a time when Hong Kong Chinese presented themselves as a group with a unique social, economic and cultural outlook, markedly different from their mainland Chinese counterparts. It also greatly shapes Hong Kong's socio-political conflicts in the subsequent decades, especially the emergence of radical local identity vis-à-vis conservative Chinese identity during Hong Kong's post-handover era.

Contemporary debates on local identity have great relevance to the analysis of postwar Hong Kong identity politics. Though varying in diverse theoretical positions, scholars commonly agree that individuals conceived their identities as source of meaning and life experiences (Calhoun, 1994), specific to local historical contents and contexts (Hall, 1990). Castells (1997) further argues that identities can be either self-sustaining or self-disruptive. When local identity is challenged by external forces, individuals may re-engineer themselves and reproduce certain identities that fit for survival. Conversely, local identity can also comply to subsume itself into the external force to minimize the conflict.

In the case of Hong Kong, not only did local residents conceive different identities throughout Hong Kong history to make sense of their life experiences. Intellectuals also made use of certain sojourner identity and refugee mentality to explain Hong Kong's social stability and political apathy under British colonial ruling—an explanation we consider insufficient because it ignores many social and political conflicts, as well as deep-seated political divide in postwar Hong Kong society. As we argue, one of the salient features of Hong Kong's postwar identity development is the changing forms of on-going bifurcation of identities in different segments of Hong Kong society, and the bifurcation was largely the result of external political forces (mostly from Mainland China). In response to the external forces, Hong Kong residents re-engineered and reproduced new identities fit for survival, or to minimize conflicts. As this identity bifurcation developed and the integration between Hong Kong and Mainland China deepened, forms of social and political conflicts fostered a crisis consciousness in postcolonial Hong Kong society. This crisis consciousness was transformed into an active ingredient of new political consciousness demanding Hong Kong government giving Hong Kong people's interests priority in governing Hong Kong society.

The significance of Hong Kong's postwar identity politics does not only lie in the recent emergence of radical politics that triggered large-scale social movements after 1997. As a historical case Hong Kong also presents a formidable challenge to the study of nationalism as it is remarkably different from many other societies. As such, this chapter outlines Hong Kong's identity development. It is divided into three parts. Part one examines a *standard-definition* narrative describing Hong Kong people largely composed of political refugees—having "refugee mentality" and being politically apathetic. Part two provides two *high-definition* narratives in contrast to the *standard-definition* narrative through examining shifting identity politics and the underpinning socio-political factors during postwar Hong Kong. Part three summarizes the chapter by sketching the historical transformation of Hong Kong identity vis-à-vis national identity over the past one-and-a-half century, and try to shed some light on the recent rise of radical local identity in Hong Kong.

2 SOJOURNER IDENTITY, REFUGEE MENTALITY AND POLITICAL APATHY

As discussed in previous chapters, Hong Kong's population composition has been constantly altered by regional politics from mainland China. Before the 1940s, although Hong Kong was a British colony, no border had separated the colony from mainland China. Residents required no passport to enter or leave the colony. Most (male) Hong Kong residents came to Hong Kong primarily to work without bringing their families. They never intended to stay in the colony. According to David Faure (1997), the Hong Kong Chinese at that time could be labelled as "sojourners". Hong Kong was not their home. They were oriented towards China rather than towards Hong Kong.

Entering the 1940s, mainland China was under great social and political instability and the sojourner identity of Hong Kong people changed. After the 1949 Chinese communist revolution, over a million Chinese came to Hong Kong and could not return to China anymore. To stop large influx of mainland Chinese entering Hong Kong, the colonial government swiftly set up fences along the colony's border. In turn, the communist also applied vigorous border controls, keeping the newly established communist China away from capitalist contamination. Consequently,

Hong Kong Chinese became very difficult to visit their relatives in their native villages (Chan, 1995).

"Refugee mentality" is a common way Hong Kong studies scholars describing Hong Kong identity between the 1940s and 1960s. For example, Richard Hughes (1976) sees Hong Kong people in the 1950s having refugee identity that drew on the concept of "a borrowed time, a borrowed place". Among local scholars studying Hong Kong politics and society, sociologist Lau Siu Kai's formulation of "utilitarianistic familism" has been most influential, articulating the relationship between Hong Kong people's refugee identity and state-society relations. According to Lau (1984), there are four characteristics to Hong Kong people's refugee mentality:

1. Due to their refugee status, Hong Kong people had short-term horizon. They didn't have long-term planning no matter for their career or family;
2. Because of their refugee experience, Hong Kong people considered social and political stability as their core value;
3. As Hong Kong people were mostly ethnic Chinese, they also exhibited some traditional Chinese values, placing family interests as their key priority. They would try hard to locate a "socio-political context [which] is merely the arena for the pursuit of familial interest."
4. Due to their emphasis on social and political stability and their orientation towards family interests, Hong Kong people had low participation to social and political affairs and exhibited aloofness towards society.

This kind of "refugee mentality" narrative was very prevalent, not just to academics but also to laypersons. In popular culture, some comic books published in the 1970s used this kind of narrative as their major plots. For example, one of the most popular local comic series, called "Little Rascals (小流氓)", told stories about a group of young people living in Hong Kong's old urban areas fighting with gangsters and criminals. The stories captured Hong Kong society very much close to the popular imagination of a "refugee society"—there was no police; government was irrelevant to local people's daily lives; young people were mainly immigrants and orphans, and then became sworn-brothers and formed secret society to protect themselves against gangsters.

Certainly, Lau Siu Kai was not the only scholar discussing Hong Kong people's refugee mentality, but his model was widely accepted and taken-for-granted. Notwithstanding, from a *high-definition* perspective we should critically ask: *Does Lau Siu Kai's model really reflect the social and political situation of Hong Kong of the time? More importantly, was Hong Kong really apolitical? If not, how did Hong Kong identity transform during colonial and post-colonial eras?*

In the rest of this chapter, we will mobilize our *high-definition* tools (sociological imagination and state-society-market relations) and historical evidences to critically evaluate the validity of Lau Siu Kai's model. As will be seen, Lau's claim about Hong Kong as an apolitical society is historically ungrounded and ignores numerous social and political conflicts in the colonial era. But before moving on to challenge Lau's model, let us spell out the *standard-definition* narrative we are going to debunk in this chapter, namely, postwar Hong Kong identity was characterized by refugee mentality and basically apolitical.

In order to understand how Hong Kong's identity politics developed, it is necessary to trace its historical transformation and the underpinning socio-political roots over the past seven decades.

3   Metamorphoses of Hong Kong Identities and the Socio-Political Origins

3.1   *The 1940s–1960s: From Nationalistic Chinese Identity to Ideological Chinese Identity*

As discussed in Chap. 2, the claim that Hong Kong was short of social and political conflicts is a myth. Before the 1950s, large-scale social and political conflicts, such as the Canton-Hong Kong Strike and Seamen Strike in the 1920s and 1930s, were plenty. In the immediate postwar period, these conflicts continued and mostly erupted in the form of industrial conflicts. To name a few, there were the Mechanics' Strikes (1947), Tram Union's strike (1949), and Russell Street incident (1949). Alvin So (2016) argues that these industrial conflicts featured in their highly Chinese nationalistic and anti-colonial sentiments. Most Hong Kong Chinese before the 1950s still identified themselves with Chinese nationalism and were loyal to the Chinese nation-state across the border. Hong Kong Chinese embraced Chinese nationalism as their identity, argues So, largely because the British colonial state granted few civil, political and social rights to Chinese residents in the colony, making Hong Kong Chinese resentful towards repressive colonial policies discriminating the Chinese.

Entering the 1950s, after the Chinese Communist Party (CCP) took control over mainland China and forced Kuomintang (KMT) to retreat to Taiwan, Hong Kong identity underwent a profound change, a change from *nationalistic Chinese identity* to *ideological Chinese identity*. Because the conflicts between CCP and KMT manifested as an ideological war between socialism and capitalism, Hong Kong society, an adjacent place to its motherland, was not immune to these conflicts. Beneath the surface of many industrial conflicts occurred between the 1950s and the 1960s, left-right ideological politics ("left" for supporting CCP; "right" for supporting KMT) could be identified. Most Hong Kong Chinese were drawn (consciously or unconsciously) into this ideological whirlpool, one expressed in political rivalry polarizing Hong Kong Chinese in their working, leisure and cultural spheres:

1. *Trade Union Rivalries*: Established respectively in 1947 and 1948, the pro-CCP Hong Kong Federation of Trade Unions (FTU) and the pro-KMT Hong Kong and Kowloon Trades Union Council (TUC) were the two dominant trade union federations in Hong Kong between the 1950s and 1960s. After 1949, both unions ascended and substantially changed the nature of industrial relations and industrial conflict in later years. As Leung and Chiu (1991) observe, by 31 March 1956, about 70 per cent of the workers' unions were affiliated to either one of the two federations. At the end of the 1950s, among the 245 workers' unions, 90 (38 per cent) were affiliated or friendly to the FTU, and 118 (48 per cent) to the TUC.

   The two trade union camps competed to recruit members in different sectors. The TUC was more influential in the craft occupations and trades, while the FTU had more following in the manufacturing industries. In the 1950s and 60s, both sides had built up a following in the public utilities and some civil service rank-and-file groups. Before the 1970s, the FTU and its affiliates were often the more militant ones not hesitant to adopt confrontational tactics while the TUC often took a more moderate and reconciliatory stance. Into the 1970s, independent trade unions emerged and even the FTU has gradually become more cooperative with the employers, trying not to "rock the boat" in the transition to the return to

Chinese sovereignty. Hence the TUC and the FTU would sometimes put up a "united front" in face of the challenges of the independent trade unions and the Confederation of Trade Unions.

2. *Sports Rivalries*: In the sports sector, usually there were different teams backed either by supporters of KMT or CCP. In the case of football teams, both sides have teams friendly to their cause. On the CCP side, the Happy Valley Athletic Association and Tung Sing Football Club are the best examples. Tung Sing Football Club currently (2018–2019) plays in the Hong Kong Second Division (actually the third division because of the Hong Kong Premier League). It was nicknamed the "Imperial Guards" (御林軍) because it was founded by former Hong Kong Football Association president and pro-CCP Henry Fok and wears orange as their primary colour (Tung Sing FC, n.d.). Happy Valley Athletic Association was formed in 1950 and are historically one of the most successful football clubs in Hong Kong, having won the First Division 6 times and had consistently been in the top division, until they were relegated to the Second Division after the 2009–2010 season (Happy Valley AA, n.d.). In the 1960s, they went into the Mainland to play friendly matches with clubs there in the midst of diplomatic blockade against the Communist China and in defiance of a ban by the Hong Kong Football Association (HKFA). In the aftermath of the 1967 Leftist Riot, the club protested against a HKFA statement in support of the police and withdrew from the League. A year after they re-entered through the third division, the lowest league of the time, and fought their way back to the top flight.

On the other side, we found South China Athletic Association and the Eastern Sports Club (commonly known as Eastern FC). South China is a football club which currently plays in the Hong Kong First Division, the second-level league in Hong Kong football league system. It is the football club with most honours in Hong Kong, having won a record 41 First Division titles. They have also won a record 31 Senior Shields, a record 10 FA Cups and 3 League Cups (South China AA, n.d.). On the other hand Eastern was established in 1932 and was one also one of the oldest clubs in Hong Kong (Eastern Sports Club, n.d.). Both were close to the KMT camp in Hong Kong in the 1950s and 60s, and their players were commonly selected to play for the "Republic of China" team. During the 1960s, matches featuring South China versus Happy

Valley, and Eastern versus Tung Sing are regarded as local derbies because of their contrasting allegiances, and the Eastern-Tung Sing derby was sometimes branded as the "Battle of Nationalists against the Communists" (國共大戰) (Chiu et al., 2014).

3. *Film Company Rivalries:* Similar situation also occurred in the cultural industries, the most prominent being the film industry. Most film stars and professionals were loyal to Kuomintang, partly because of the attraction of the Taiwan market at that time. An association was formed among pro-Taiwan film professionals to go between the Taiwanese government and Hong Kong film industry so that films could be exported there. Any film found to have film star or crew sympathetic to the CCP would be banned from Taiwan. On the other side, film companies (for examples, Great Wall Movie Enterprises Ltd., The Feng Huang Motion Pictures Co., and The Sun Luen Film Co.) were also found by filmmakers close to the CCP to produce movies that would arouse more sympathy to the communist cause, mainly about lives of the common people and the exploitation by capitalists and feudal landlords.

During the height of the Cold War in Hong Kong, celebrations of the respective national anniversaries (Oct 1st for the CCP, and Oct 10th for the KMT) were stages of the competition for "hearts and minds" with stars of both sides pledging their loyalties. After the 1967 Riots, film industry professionals were deported back to the mainland along "instigators" from other quarters of the community. By the 1980s, the pro-CCP companies merged into the Sil-Metropole Organisation Ltd. and began to act as mediators for Hong Kong film companies and professionals to sell their products to the gradually opening market and enter into joint ventures (co-productions) with (largely state-owned) mainland agencies (Chiu & Shin, 2014, 2018).

On top of these sectorial rivalry politics, there were also territory-wide political mobilizations between pro-CCP and pro-KMT camps. These mobilizations occasionally caused intensive militant conflicts among the two groups of highly committed supporters and the colonial state. Between the 1950s and 1960s, two territory-wide ideological mobilizations were particularly emblematic.

The 1956 Riot

Also known as "Double Tenth riot", the 1956 riot was the result of escalating provocation between pro-KMT and pro-CCP factions in Hong Kong during 10 October 1956, an important nationalist festival for pro-KMT communities. During the period of time, to mark their loyalties to Taipei's KMT government, these communities celebrated the 45th anniversary of the 1911 October Revolution, organizing a number of rallies and meetings as well as hoisting numerous red-white-and-blue KMT flags. The incident was triggered initially in a crowded resettlement estate in Kowloon, when a government officer ordered to remove some KMT flags in the estate. Shortly after the order was carried out, a disturbance between residents and officials broke out; mobs spilled out from the estate to other areas of Kowloon and the New Territories. Many shops belonged to pro-CCP sympathizers were looted and attacked. Most violence occurred in Tsuen Wan, a then new town in the New Territories, five miles from central Kowloon. A mob ransacked a clinic and welfare centre, killing four people. Some foreigners became involved, including a taxi was set fire upon on Nathan Road, resulting in the death of a Swiss national. To restore law and order, Colonial Secretary Edgeworth David had to order extra manpower from the British Forces in Hong Kong to reinforce the Hong Kong Police and disperse the rioters (Time, 1956). The riot lasted for three days. In total, fifty-nine people were killed and five hundred more were wounded.

The 1967 Riot

If we have to name the most influential social and political conflict that proves Hong Kong society was not apolitical, the 1967 Leftist Riot is the one. China's Cultural Revolution impacted directly on Hong Kong, culminating in the 1967 riot. The fuse line of the riot was an industrial dispute broken out in early May 1967 in an artificial flower factory in San Po Kong, a factory then owned by the future billionaire Li Ka-Shing (Tsang, 2007). Picketing workers with legitimate grievances were strengthened by outside demonstrators who showed their support for communist China. The dispute escalated into a clash with the factory management. Riot police were called in on 6 May to arrest 21 workers. After the arrest, the disturbances spread to other areas of Kowloon—many pro-Communist FTU representatives protested at police stations but were arrested as well. Large-scale demonstrations also erupted on the streets of Hong Kong, with many pro-CCP demonstrators carried little red books (Mao Zedong's

Quotations) in their left hands and shouted communist slogans. The police force engaged with the protesters, arrested 127 people. A curfew was imposed on 7 May.

On 16 May, pro-CCP leftists formed the "Hong Kong and Kowloon Committee for Anti-Hong Kong British Persecution Struggle". The Committee organized a series of large-scale demonstrations, with hundreds of CCP supporters rallied outside Governor's House, chanting communist slogans. By 23 May, a series of strikes began in all public transportation and utility companies, badly disrupting the city's transport services.

On 3 June and 10 June, *The People's Daily* in Beijing, a mouthpiece of CCP, ran editorials supporting the leftist struggle in Hong Kong. Rumours were circulated that the CCP was preparing to take control over Hong Kong. On 24 June, FTU organized a general strike in the city. Three days later, all leftist primary and secondary schools were also on strike. On 8 July, several hundred demonstrators from the PRC crossed the border at Sha Tau Kok and attacked the Hong Kong Police, of whom five were shot dead and eleven wounded (House of Commons, 1967).

Since the early July, the territory-wide conflict was heightened into bloody violence when leftists started to plant home-made bombs (nicknamed "pineapples") throughout the city. A seven-year-old girl and her two-year-old brother were killed by a bomb wrapped like a gift outside their residence (Wordie, 2012).

The casualties of the innocent, widely reported by the news media, quickly turned the wind of the city's public opinion towards supporting the colonial government. With these supports, the colonial government fought back and raided leftist strongholds. In one of the well-known raids, Royal Navy helicopters landed police on the roof of the Kiu Kwan Mansion (one of the leftist strongholds) in North Point and the police arrested the leftists inside the building, discovered about 8000 home-made bombs.

The waves of bombings did not subside until October 1967. Between August and October, many anti-leftist public figures were threatened or killed. On 24 August, Lam Bun, a popular anti-leftist radio commentator, was burned alive by leftists in his car. Louis Cha, the chairman of Ming Pao newspaper, were also threatened and had to leave Hong Kong for almost a year.

In December, Chinese Premier Zhou Enlai ordered the leftist groups in Hong Kong to stop all bombing and the riot came into an end. Within the 18 months of riot, in total 51 people were killed, of whom 15 were died in bomb attacks; 832 people were injured; 4979 people were arrested (Cheung, 2009). The sectorial rivalry politics and territory-wide social unrests happened in the 1950s and 1960s contrast starkly with Lau Siu Kai's politically apathetic argument about Hong Kong society. Contrary to Lau's argument, during the two decades of immediate postwar period, instead of being politically aloof, though not participating in formal institutional politics, a substantially number of Hong Kong Chinese actively participated in informal, extra-institutional and highly-volatile Chinese politics in their everyday lives. In short, we can summarize the above discussion into our first *high-definition* narrative in this chapter:

> *Hong Kong people were active in participating in Chinese politics, but not involved in colonial governance. Hong Kong politics was an extension of Chinese politics on Hong Kong soil.*

In retrospect, the type of Chinese politics extended on Hong Kong soil in the 1950s and 1960s not only changed the colonial state's governing strategies in the subsequent decade. It also haunted the minds and hearts of several generations of Hong Kong Chinese for several decades till today. As will be seen in later part of this chapter, in the 1980s when Hong Kong's 1997 problem was brought up for discussion, Hong Kong Chinese had to face squarely with the locally unpopular Chinese communist regime. New and opposite types of Chinese nationalistic identities emerged. After 1997, a radical brand of localism emerged as a powerful ideological and political force in Hong Kong society, with the extreme one demanding a complete cut of ties with mainland China.

In order to see the whole picture of how Hong Kong could develop such a radical brand of localism, the 1970s is the important piece of puzzle we cannot miss—for it is the time populist local identity was cradled.

3.2   The 1970s: The Emergence of Populist Local Identity

In the 1970s, Hong Kong society transformed rapidly. A new generation of locally born Hong Kong Chinese were coming of age in the city. This new generation, especially the university students, possessed a distinctive attitude towards Hong Kong politics, which formed the basis for a new local identity. Unlike their parents, this generation was born and raised in Hong Kong. They did not have much interaction with mainland China.

By the mid-1970s, most of these locally-born university students had graduated and became middle-class professionals such as social workers, journalists, lawyers, and environmentalists. They began to pay attention to Hong Kong's social problems and formed many concerned groups and pressure groups.

At the same time, the colonial state, after the 1967 riot, sensed the necessity to modify their public and social policies to address social problems long neglected in the colony. These include: setting up a massive public housing program, instituting labour laws to make sweatshop production more humane and consistent with international labour standards; expanding welfare expenditure to help the poor, the widowed and the elderly; and providing free education to nine years for local citizens (So, 2016). As Helen Siu (2016) succinctly points out:

> Public opinion across the ideological spectrum would agree that from the 1960s on, a distinct Hong Kong ethos emerged. It came with a generation of post-war baby boomers whose education and professional achievements had been tied to the territory at a time when China was turned inward, with Hong Kong projected to the world almost by default. This coincided with the Hong Kong Government's decision to invest heavily in the territory's future after long-neglected social issues exploded in the riots of the late 1960s. (p. 395)

More importantly, the baby boomers were not satisfied with simply showing their concerns to Hong Kong's social problems. The 1970s also witnessed the rise of local social movements. Waves of protests and social actions were organized—revealing a great desire for local people, especially baby boomers, to participate in political affairs. In contrast to the left-right politics in the 1950s and 1960s, social movements in the 1970s had many new social and political agenda. For example, while the campaign for recognizing Chinese as an official language, and Diaoyutai Island Movement continued to have great concern on national (Chinese) politics, new movements such as anti-corruption movement and urban (housing) movements had evolved around many local daily life issues in Hong Kong. Many of these young pioneers involved in these social movements later became important local politicians in Hong Kong, especially when Hong Kong began its democratization in the 1980s (Lui, 1984).

To a certain extent, the emergence of local identity in the 1970s also coincided with Hong Kong's economic development. In the 1970s, Hong

Kong already became one of the major growth engines in East Asia. In contrast to the living conditions in the 1950s and 1960s, many local Hong Kong residents were much better off. The attainment of affluence life also contributed positively to the construction of populist local Hong Kong identity, demanding more than simply bread-and-butter issues. Especially for the younger baby boomers at that time, they demanded more from the government in terms of having a more responsiveness and transparency.

Interestingly, the colonial state also launched a series of social and public relations campaigns conducive to constructing the populist local identity. These campaigns include: "I Love Hong Kong" and "Clean Up Hong Kong" campaigns, Hong Kong Festival in 1969, 1971 and 1973; Hong Kong Arts Festival since 1973; Hong Kong International Film Festival since 1977. These campaigns cultivated a sense of community among Hong Kong residents so that they would identify Hong Kong as their home (Turner, 1995, p. 15).

Similarly, local popular culture also contributed to the development of populist local identity. The most important of all in the culture industry was the development of Cantonese pop songs, films and TV dramas. Sam Hui's song that we used earlier to open this chapter is representative of these cultural products.

Yet, identity formation inevitably involves a process of boundary setting between "us" and "them". This was no different to the populist local identity emerged in Hong Kong in the 1970s. As Alvin So (2016) points out,

> It was this massive influx of new immigrants [from mainland China] in the late 1970s that finally gave birth to a new HongKonger identity. Although the coming of age of a Hong Kong-born generation and the community policies of the colonial state had laid the foundation for such an [local] identity, it was the conflict, misunderstanding, and distrust between the old and the new residents that bought the old residents together to form a new "HongKongers" identity. (p. 137)

The critical event that intensified the conflicts, misunderstanding and distrust between Hong Kong residents and mainland Chinese is the new wave of mainland Chinese immigrants in the 1970s. The colonial state relaxed border control over illegal immigrants to meet the needs of expanding Hong Kong's manufacturing sector. Before 1980, the colonial state permitted illegal immigrants succeeding to reach the urban areas of

Hong Kong to stay while the ones getting caught at the border were returned to mainland China immediately. This "touch base" policy led to an influx of about 500,000 legal and illegal immigrants into Hong Kong in the late 1970s (Lam & Liu, 1998; Burns, 1987).

In the late 1970s and early 1980s, many of the cultural products centred on constructing an identity of "we" among Hong Kong Chinese, in contrast to "other" (e.g. Mainlanders). One of the oft-cited examples is the popular 1979 TV serial, *The Good, The Bad, and The Ugly* (網中人). One of the main characters of the serial was called "Ah Chian (阿燦)", an illegal immigrant from mainland China coming to Hong Kong to join his family members. As Eric Ma (1999, pp. 66–68) argues, Ah Chian symbolized the "dirty outsiders", "ill-disciplined and lawless", had an "insatiable appetite," and always violated "the sense of good taste among the established HongKongers". Ma further argues that Hong Kong Chinese in the late 1970s defined themselves by "what is *not*", and "Hong Kong people tended to exaggerate their positive features while denigrating their mainland counterparts" (Ma, 1999, p. 66). As will be seen later, this kind of derogatory images towards mainland Chinese re-emerged in the second half of the 2000s when a wave of mainland Chinese tourists flooded into Hong Kong.

In short, in contrast to Lau's utilitarianistic familism, Hong Kong was in no sense "apolitical" not just the 1950s and 1960s, but also the 1970s. Historically, the 1970s was the time for the birth of populist local identity (facilitated by and manifested in the colonial state's community and immigration policies, new baby boomers' localistic sentiment and concerns, as well as the booming of local popular culture); the 1970s was also the time we witnessed forms of urban social movements organized by segments of Hong Kong community (e.g. locally-born university students and middle-class professionals) in the colony. Based on the above discussion, we have our second high-definition narrative in this chapter: The 1970s was not "apolitical" in any sense. Some segments of the community may be a bit more "apolitical" than others, but to say that Hong Kong as apolitical is a myth and a political construction by the establishment.

3.3   The 1980s–1997: The Co-Emergence of Democratic and Conservative Chinese Identities

After the roaring 1970s, a new era emerged between the 1980s and 1997. Hong Kong society entered its "final transition period", quickly undergoing de-colonialization, democratization and national reunification. Hong Kong again came under international spotlight, especially the political negotiation between China and UK on the city's future. The starting point of this transformation dated back to Governor Murray MacLehose's visit to mainland China in 1979. Before the visit, the British government thought that the Beijing government would have allowed the British government to extend its lease to the United Kingdom after 1997 for they had successfully managed Hong Kong and turned the city into an economic miracle. Nevertheless, to the British government's surprise, when MacLehose inquired whether the Chinese government would like to extend the lease of Hong Kong to UK, the Beijing regime gave him a blunt reply, declaring that the Chinese government was determined to resume exercising sovereignty over Hong Kong on July 1, 1997. Such a cold blow not only kicked start Hong Kong's decolonization process, it also made Hong Kong face an unclear prospect, invoking Hong Kong Chinese's fear towards Communist China that overshadowed the local identity built in the 1970s.

During the 1980s, some 20,000 Hong Kong people were leaving every year. The number soared to 40,000 in 1989, resulting in more than 1 percent of Hong Kong population emigrated during the 1980s (Task Force on Population Policy, 2003). Some tried to retain their link in Hong Kong by becoming "astronauts"—meaning that husband working in Hong Kong while having his family emigrated and living overseas. Ironically, Sam Hui's song *Eiffel Tower Above Clouds* (first broadcasted in 1973) became popular again between the late 1980s and 1997. While the song attracted many postwar baby boomers for their new populist Hong Kong identity in the 1970s, it appealed to many Hong Kong "astronauts" for their diasporic sentiment in the 1980s and 1990s. The line "far away nothing can get into its embrace" from the lyrics captured this diasporic sentiment. To these Hong Kong "astronauts", most of them still embraced Hong Kong as their home; however, they could not imagine the future of Hong Kong under CCP's ruling. More importantly, they feared that they would lose their assets, lifestyles and freedom under the ruling of a socialist government after 1997.

Even after the Sino-British Joint Declaration was signed between Margaret Thatcher and Zhao Ziyang in 1984 and codified "One Country, Two Systems"—a concept intended to mean that Hong Kong would retain its capitalist system and not be forced to adopt communism after 1997—as the institutional arrangement after 1997, Hong Kong society was still haunted by a climate of fear and anxiety. The June Fourth movement and the crackdown in Beijing further aggravated the whole political situation. About a million of Hong Kong people marched on street to protest against the Beijing government. After the June Fourth Movement, many more Hong Kong people sought emigration as a way to response to the Beijing regime. On the other hand, the June Fourth Movement also prompted a convergence of pro-democracy movements for Hong Kong and China. At that time, there was a strange convergence of Hong Kong local identity and Chinese national identity. Such a "diasporic" sentiment was vivid in a love-hate contradictory relationship and exhibited in a way widely shared by Hong Kong people at that time as "Hong Kong is part of China" but "Hong Kong is apart from China".

In order to restore Hong Kong people's confidence, the British government launched a series of political reform locally in Hong Kong in the first half of the 1990s. For example, the introduction of electoral politics at district levels in the 1990s and later expanded to the city level for election of the city's legislature. This series of political reform triggered a new pattern of identity politics. The middle-class professionals who were active in social movements in the 1970s quickly re-emerged in Hong Kong's political theatre and became professional politicians. They formed different political parties and got landslide victories in popular Legislative Council elections in 1991 and 1995. Most of these political parties positioned themselves as both the protector of Hong Kong people's interests, lifestyles and freedom, *and* the pusher for mainland China's democracy (e.g. Democratic Party). This special political orientation reflected a new identity pattern emerged—*democratic Chinese identity.*

Aside from the democratic Chinese identity, another patriotic Chinese identity—*conservative Chinese identity*—also emerged during the 1997 transition. On the one hand, because of the disastrous defeat in the legislative council elections in 1991 and 1995, many pro-CCP supporters (many of them were the leftists in the 1960s and 1970s) consolidated their political forces and formed new political parties in Hong Kong (e.g. Democratic Alliance for the Betterment and Progress of Hong Kong or DAB in short). These political parties distinguished themselves from Democratic Party by having a conservative orientation towards Hong Kong's democratic movement and promoting the Hong Kong's reunification with mainland China. On the other hand, due to rising labour costs and land rents in Hong Kong, Hong Kong manufacture massively relocated north to mainland China to seek cheap labour and rents. A new alliance between Hong

Kong's business elites and mainland Chinese officials was formed (So, 1999). These local business elites also formed new political party in Hong Kong (e.g. Liberal Party) which had similar political orientation to the conservative pro-Beijing political parties. To these local business elites, they saw the advantages of the economic opportunity outweighing the disadvantages of the fear of a socialist China, and used their economic and political influences to build good relationships with mainland Chinese officials to safeguard their interests both in Hong Kong and mainland China.

In a way, the distinctive Hong Kong identity was no more than an interlude that applied only to the 1970s and 1980s. The rise of Hong Kong identity in the 1970s was set against the backdrop of the fear of communism and China. Such a fear continued to the 1980s and the 1990s. Simultaneously, many Hong Kong people took advantage of economic opportunity of China despite their dislike of China. The co-existence of the China fear and the China opportunity then became an important ingredient for two types of identities to co-emerge, namely—pro-China VS pro-Hong Kong identities, with heavy political ideological loading (either democratic or conservative). The crossover of the two identities (e.g. Hong Kong VS China? Hong Kong in China; Hong Kong + China; anti-China VS tolerating China VS pro-China; pro-Democracy VS pro-Establishment; etc.) not only widened Hong Kong's political spectrum, but also added layers of complexity to Hong Kong's political landscape in the 1990s (Ip et al., 2014).

3.4 Post-1997: The Rise of Radical Local Identity

After the handover in 1997, Hong Kong's identity politics has undergone another round of dramatic transformation. The new political scenario as well as intense exchange between Hong Kong and Mainland China in many ways fostered a new pattern of local identity to emerge.

For over a hundred years, colonial Hong Kong was a semi-autonomous city and societally it was also a self-contained community. Hong Kong identity was largely developed and constructed in relation to China.

Often, the antagonistic sentiment against mainland China was not constructed at the abstract level as livelihoods of locals was greatly affected with increased integration. This sentiment was articulated by various newly emerged social groups into different public imageries against mainland Chinese. Among these, three frequently appeared in the public imagery, namely the derogative term "Locust"—used to stigmatized the new immigrants, "Double Non-Permanent Resident Children"—children born in Hong Kong hence acquired local residency but parents who are not permanent residents, the "People from Powerful nation"—which portray the mainland Tourists who often brag about their spending power. The former two imageries focus on the potential financial burden places on and entitlement to the local welfare system, whereas the last speaks out the negative influence from mainland tourism on local livelihoods and habits.

These public imageries and sentiments towards mainland Chinese have also fuelled increasing distrust towards Hong Kong government, as for some people the later has not actively protected, if not ruining, Hong Kong's core values and culture.

To some extent, the backlash against mainlanders can also be attributed to the great reversal of the economic positions between Hong Kong people and Mainland Chinese (Zheng & Wan, 2014). In the 1970s, while Hong Kong underwent its rapid economic development and Hong Kong people were well-off relative to Mainlanders, Hong Kong people felt a sense of superiority, and this sense of superiority also became an important core element in constructing the "populist local Hong Kong identity". In the post-handover era, however, the position gradually changed as China develops further. The resultant erosion of confidence among Hong Kong people in turn led to the fermentation of exclusionary and antagonistic attitudes towards mainlanders. At the end, a new brand of local identity gradually developed in the form of what we called *radical local Hong Kong identity*.

The emergence of this radical local identity is not a preordained process, however. Though with different material and structural factors in play, it is a "social construction" process in which many new political organizations were formed, mounting successive of social campaigns and mobilization around different conjunctures of social and political events. Consequently, the constructed public imageries and radical local identity also become an important basis of social and political actions. According to Sautman and Yan (2015), these new political organizations declared their mission to protect Hong Kong's resources and lifestyle against the "mainland invasion". Key political organizations included: "Hong Kong First", "Hong Kong Resurgence", "Hong Kong Autonomy Movement", "Population Policy Concern Group", and "Civic Passion". Alvin So (2016) argues that these new political organizations sparked a new pattern of social protests in Hong Kong. Instead of protesting against the communist party-state, anti-mainland organizations waged a series of protests targeting mainland tourists and immigrants.

More interestingly, while Hong Kong society was immersed with anti-mainland sentiment, there were obvious "generational difference" between the young, and the middle-aged and the old. According to Wan and Zheng (2016) and Chiu (2016a), after analysing longitudinal survey data on Hong Kong people's identities, they found that in 2014 about 76 per cent of the younger generation aged below 30 identified themselves as "HongKonger" while about 54 per cent of the middle-aged and older generations did so. At the same time, only about 16 per cent of the younger Hong Kong residents identified themselves as "Chinese" while about 32 per cent of the older Hong Kong residents did so in 2014. More complete data have been made available by the HKU Public Opinion Programme, and the same pattern could be found (Figs. 4.1 and 4.2). These two pieces of survey findings show that the majority of the "localists" are youngsters who were born after the mid-1980s (i.e. the post-1980s and the post-1990s generations). These younger generations commonly hold a negative attitude towards mainland Chinese government and the implementation of "One Country, Two Systems" in Hong Kong.

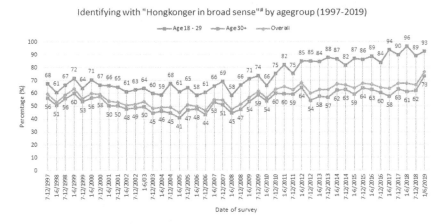

Fig. 4.1   HK Identity 1997–2019; young vs middle-aged/old (Public Opinion Programme, 2019b). #Hongkonger in broad sense = Sum of those identifying with categories "Hongkonger" and "Hongkonger in China"

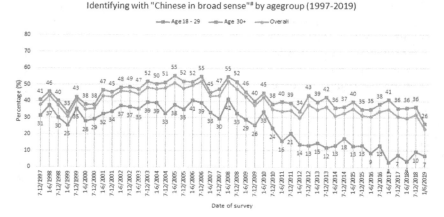

Fig. 4.2 Chinese Identity 1997–2019; young vs middle-aged/old (Public Opinion Programme, 2019a). #Chinese in broad sense = Sum of those identifying with categories "Chinese" and "Chinese in Hong Kong"

As Stephen Chiu (2016b) notes, the younger generations' localistic identification was not always the case, with the year 2008 turned out to be the turning point. Between 1998 and April 2008, there witnessed a general increasing, albeit unstable, trend of identification as "Chinese" among the younger generations and reached its peak at 41.2 per cent in June 2008 (See Fig. 4.2). After half a year, however, by December 2008 there was a great reversal. The younger generations saw an observable surge in their identification towards being "Hongkonger" and a drop in "Chinese" identification after the first half of 2008. After that point, percentage of people identifying with "Chinese" had never gone back to the 2008 level. Notably, as one of the possible explanations of the turning point, Chiu observed Hong Kong's younger generations had to face squarely with both the bright and dark sides of China in this year—the holding of the first Olympic Game in Beijing and the Xichuan earthquake that possibly heightened the Chinese belongingness feeling, but also shocked by such scandal associated with tainted baby milk powder involving corruptions. It is likely that contradictory feelings were felt by many, and possibly led to a drift towards embracing more of the "Hongkonger" identity.

In sum, this section has identified the rise of a radical localist identity in Hong Kong as key identity development in post-handover Hong Kong, coupled with the emergence of new public imageries against mainland Chinese and the establishment of many new localist political organizations. It also has identified the generational differences in patterns of Hong Kong identity vis-à-vis Chinese identity between Hong Kong residents aged below and above 30. It could be seen that the rise of radical local identity would be an important ingredient in shaping Hong Kong's political future.

4   Concluding Remarks

In this chapter, we have debunked the lasting myth of Hong Kong as "apolitical" society and explained why it is not a useful and accurate description of postwar Hong Kong. There has been complex and continued interaction between Hong Kong and mainland China, an interaction constantly shaping the development of identity politics and the forms of local and national identities in Hong Kong. To illustrate the concurrent development of local and national identities since the 1940s, we conclude this chapter by suggesting the following developmental schema (see Fig. 4.3):

In 2016, after the umbrella movement, different new political parties were formed. One distinctive feature of these new political parties is that they declared themselves as "local" political parties protecting the interests of Hong Kong people and striving for Hong Kong's democracy. These new political parties were primarily formed by the post-1980s and post-1990s generations. Compared to other pan-democratic parties in Hong Kong (e.g. Democratic Party), these new parties have less concerns over developments on the Mainland. Capitalizing on the anti-mainland sentiments, these new political forces now become a hot potato for both the Hong Kong government and the Beijing Chinese government.

While we remain sceptical if Hong Kong's local identity has ever developed into a form of "nationalisms" (Fong, 2017), a series of collective actions in protest against the Extradition Bill in the summer of 2019 has seemed to heighted a new sense of collectivity unknown before. One should also note that, at the outbreak of the protests in the early summer, responses to the identity survey conducted in mid-June have already been overwhelmingly skewed towards the "Hong Kong" side, with 92.5% and 73.3% of respondents of 18–29 years old and those 30 and above saying that they are "Hongkonger" in the broad sense (Fig. 4.1).

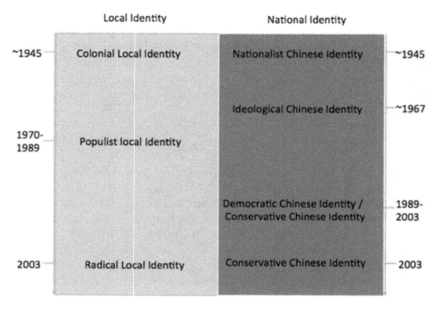

Fig. 4.3   Concurrent development of local and national identity since 1940s

Still, we want to maintain that identities are product of complex social forces, both of the long term structural and the short term conjunctural variants. The best way to understand it is to locate the heightened Hong Kong identity in the interactions between the local community, the SAR Government, and the Central Government.

Taking a longer perspective, as Greenfeld (1992, 2016, p. 35) observes in the cases of England, France, Russia and Germany, ethnic sentiments emerge out of specific cultural framework of nationalism. In Hong Kong, we similarly have observed that different postwar Hong Kong identities (colonial local vs. national Chinese; populist local vs. ideological Chinese; democratic Chinese vs. conservative Chinese; radical local vs. conservative Chinese) emerged out of different cultural frameworks of social and political identities specific to different segments and social groups of Hong Kong society. That is also why in different periods of postwar Hong Kong history, popular culture (e.g. Sam Hui's Cantonese song), colonial legacy (e.g. rule of law, freedom of speech, etc.), public imageries contrasting Hongkonger and Mainlanders, and democratic ideals towards good governance were often utilized and invoked by different social and political groups as cultural resources to draw the "us vs. them" boundary in creating different forms of identities.

In short, there is no single coherent cultural framework to allow different individuals and social groups in Hong Kong society to "imagine" themselves living in the same political communities (Anderson, 1991). Too many recent studies have emphasized the "awakening" of Hong Kong people, and especially the younger generation, in the aftermath of the Umbrella Movement (Chan & Ng, 2017; Ho, 2017). Nevertheless, our *high-definition* argument here is that there are always two lines of development in the identities of Hong Kong people. On the one side, there is the emergence of a distinctive local identity while at the same time there is another strand that always long for attachment to the mainland. Even after the Umbrella Movement, Chiu and Ye (2018) argues that another significant development is for the older age groups, hitherto less politically active, to drift towards conservative nationalism and became supporters of the pro-establishment forces. As always, there is no single trends in Hong Kong but bifurcations.

Since China's re-integration into global economy since the 1980s, just three decades of economic reform, China has already come into a position as a rising global power. Under this circumstance, Hong Kong people are also confronting the rapid rise of Chinese nationalism and the larger integrative project under the banner of "the great revival of the Chinese nation" (中華民族的偉大復興) to include various "people in frontier regions" into common interpretative framework of "the Chinese". Apparently, Hong Kong in the first decade of the new century went along with rise of Chinese nationalism, but some undercurrents have steered it away from this identification. Some argued the tightened political control and the rising social and economic conflicts between mainland and Hong Kong have hindered dramatically in local's identification process and creating new space for radical localists to advocate an exclusionary identity politics.

In many cases, Hong Kong people actually want their distinctiveness which can mark the differences from mainland Chinese. Here, we can see that Hong Kong people's appeal to Great Britain's colonial legacy in terms of political discourse is very selective. Freedom is chosen; equality is not. Historically, it makes sense: during the colonial period, the British government did not articulate any integrative project to include Hong Kong people into their Great Britain project. The only exception was in 1990.

After the 1989 June Fourth incident, in order to calm Hong Kong people from fleeing to other western countries, Governor David Wilson, with the Executive Council members, went to London to request British government to issue full British citizenship to Hong Kong people. In the end, the colonial master granted 225,000 Hong Kong people the right of abode. Other than that, political discourse on equality never took roots in Hong Kong society.

Without doubt, with more exchanges and integration between Hong Kong and Mainland China, it is safe to expect that the bifurcated development of identities will prolong, and the divide between radical local Hong Kong identity and conservative Chinese identity will still be the key tension in future Hong Kong society. This development will have long term impact on not just the future development of Hong Kong identity, but also Hong Kong's democratic future.

REFERENCES

Anderson, B. (1991). *Imagined communities: Reflections on the origin and spread of nationalism.* Verso.

Burns, J. P. (1987). Immigration from China and the future of Hong Kong. *Asian Survey, 27*(6), 661–682.

Calhoun, C. (Ed.). (1994). *Social theory and the politics of identity.* Wiley-Blackwell.

Castells, M. (1997). *The power of identity.* Blackwell.

Chan, M. K. (1995). All in the family: The Hong Kong-Guangdong link in historical perspective. In R. Kwok & A. Y. So (Eds.), *Hong Kong-Guangdong Link: Partnership in flux* (pp. 31–53). M. E. Sharpe.

Chan, K. M., & Ng, V. (2017). Localism, radicalism and cynicism in post-umbrella movement Hong Kong. *Mainland China Studies, 60*(1), 19–36. (in Chinese).

Cheung, G. K. (2009). *Hong Kong's watershed: The 1967 riots.* Hong Kong University Press.

Chiu, S. W. (2016a, April 19). 解讀港人「人心背離」之謎 [Explaining the mystery of the 'deviation of the people's heart' in Hong Kong]. *Mingpao.* Retrieved from https://news.mingpao.com/ins/文摘/article/20160419/s00022/1461030737186/解讀港人「人心背離」之謎(文-趙永佳.

Chiu, S. W. (2016b, May 17). 香港2008年, 無關痛癢還是民心轉捩點? [Hong Kong in 2008: A year of no importance or a turning point of public opinion?]. *Initium Media.* Retrieved from https://theinitium.com/article/20160517-opinion-stephenchiu-2008/

Chiu, S. W., & Shin, V. K. (2014). 兩岸三地的政治差異與文化經濟的融合—銀都在華語電影產業鏈的角色 [Political differences and cultural and economic integration in the mainland, Taiwan and Hong Kong—The role of Silmetropole in the Chinese film industry chain]. In S. W. Chiu, T. L. Lui, & S. S. Yung (Eds.), 胸懷祖國:香港「愛國左派」運動 [Caring for the motherland: Hong Kong's 'Patriotic Left' movement] (pp. 169–196). Oxford University Press.

Chiu, S. W., & Shin, V. K. (2018). Hong Kong's film industry reconstituted: Pathways to China after the Golden age. In T. L. Lui, S. W. Chiu, & R. Yep (Eds.), *Routledge handbook of contemporary Hong Kong* (pp. 365–396). Routledge.

Chiu, S. W. & Ye, J. H. (2018). 意料之外的政治覺醒:世代與港人的身份認同及政治取態 [Unintended political awakening: Generation, identity and political affiliation of Hong Kong people]. In M. K. Chang, S. P. Wan, & J. C. Chen (Eds.), 中國效應—台港民眾的觀感 [The China Effect: The public's perception in Taiwan and Hong Kong] (pp. 197–215). Hong Kong Institute of Asia-Pacific Studies.

Chiu, S. W., Lui, T. L., & Leung Y. K. (2014). 愛國足球滄桑—愉園60年 [The vicissitudes of patriotic football—60 years of Happy Valley FC]. In S. W. Chiu, T. L. Lui, & S. S. Yung (Eds.), 胸懷祖國:香港「愛國左派」運動 [Caring for the motherland: Hong Kong's 'Patriotic Left' movement] (pp. 83–113). Oxford University Press.

Eastern Sports Club. (n.d.). In *Wikipedia*. Retrieved from https://en.wikipedia.org/wiki/Eastern_Sports_Club.

Faure, D. (1997). *A documentary history of Hong Kong: Society*. University of Hong Kong Press.

Fong, B. C. (2017). One country, two nationalisms: Center-periphery relations between Mainland China and Hong Kong, 1997–2016. *Modern China, 43*(5), 523–556.

Greenfeld, L. (1992). *Nationalism: Five roads to modernity*. Harvard University Press.

Greenfeld, L. (2016). *Advanced introduction to nationalism*. Edward Elgar Publishing.

Hall, C. M. (1990). *Women and identity: Value choices in a changing world*. Taylor & Francis.

Happy Valley AA. (n.d.). In *Wikipedia*. Retrieved from https://en.wikipedia.org/wiki/Happy_Valley_AA

Ho, M. (2017). The third force and umbrella soldiers: Comparing the elections of Taiwan after the sunflower movement and Hong Kong after the umbrella movement. *Mainland China Studies, 60*(1), 59–86. (in Chinese).

House of Commons, UK. (1967). *Hong Kong (border incidents)* (HC Deb 10 July 1967 vol. 750 cc93–7). Retrieved from https://api.parliament.uk/historic-hansard/commons/1967/jul/10/hong-kong-border-incidents

Hughes, R. (1976). *Borrowed place, borrowed time: Hong Kong and its many faces.* Deutsch.

Hui, M. K., Tang, W. M., & Hui, S. K. (Lyricist). (1974). Eiffel Tower above clouds [鐵塔凌雲] [Recorded by Sam Hui] (H. K. Lim, Trans.). On *Guima Shuangxing* [鬼馬雙星]. Retrieved October 5, 2019, from https://lyricstrans-late.com/en/鐵塔凌雲-eiffel-tower-above-clouds.html

Ip, C. Y., Chiu, S. W., & Leung, Y. K. (2014). 中國意象與香港人政治身份取態 [Chinese imagery and Hong Kong people's political identity]. In H. Li (Ed.), 臺港兩地人文, 社會, 經濟發展之比較 [Comparison of humanities, social and economic development between Taiwan and Hong Kong] (pp. 56–81). Center for Hong Kong Studies, National Central University.

Lam, K. C., & Liu, P. W. (1998). *Immigration and the economy of Hong Kong* (Vol. 18). City University of Hong Kong Press.

Lau, S. K. (1984). *Society and politics in Hong Kong.* Chinese University Press.

Leung, B., & Chiu, S. W. (1991). *A social history of industrial strikes and the labour movement in Hong Kong, 1946–1989.* Social Science Research Centre, The University of Hong Kong.

Lui, T. L. (1984). *Urban protests in Hong Kong: A sociological study of Hong Kong housing conflicts* (M.Phil. dissertation, The University of Hong Kong). Retrieved from https://doi.org/10.5353/th_b3120662

Ma, E. (1999). *Culture, politics and Television in Hong Kong.* Routledge.

Public Opinion Programme, The University of Hong Kong. (2019a). Ethnic Identity—'Chinese' in broad sense (per poll, by age group). Retrieved from https://www.hkupop.hku.hk/english/popexpress/ethnic/eidentity/chi-broad/poll/datatables.html

Public Opinion Programme, The University of Hong Kong. (2019b). Ethnic Identity—Hongkonger (half-yearly average, by age group). Retrieved from https://www.hkupop.hku.hk/english/popexpress/ethnic/eidentity/hkCiti-zen/halfyr/datatables.html

Sautman, B., & Yan, H. (2015). Localists and 'locusts' in Hong Kong: Creating a yellow-red peril discourse. *Maryland Series in Contemporary Asian Studies, 2,* 1. Retrieved from https://digitalcommons.law.umaryland.edu/mscas/vol2015/iss2/1/

Siu, H. F. (2016). *Tracing China: A forty-year ethnographic journey.* Hong Kong University Press.

So, A. Y. (1999). *Hong Kong's embattled democracy.* John Hopkins University Press.

So, A. Y. (2016). The making of Hong Kong nationalism. In J. Kingston (Ed.), *Asian nationalisms reconsidered* (pp. 135–146). Routledge.

South China AA. (n.d.). In *Wikipedia*. Retrieved from https://en.wikipedia.org/wiki/South_China_AA

Task Force on Population Policy. (2003). *Report of the task force on population policy*. Retrieved April 15, 2020, from https://www.info.gov.hk/info/population/eng/

Time. (1956, October 22). HONG KONG: Trouble on the double tenth. *Time*, 68(17). Retrieved from http://content.time.com/time/magazine/article/0,9171,824497,00.html

Tsang, S. (2007). *A modern history of Hong Kong*. I.B. Tauris.

Tung Sing FC. (n.d.). In *Wikipedia*. Retrieved from https://en.wikipedia.org/wiki/Tung_Sing_FC

Turner, M. (1995). 60s/90s: Dissolving the people. In M. Turner & I. Ngan (Eds.), *Hong Kong sixties: Designing identity* (pp. 13–34). Hong Kong Arts Centre.

Wan, S. P., & Zheng, V. W. (2016). 身份認同: 對中國的「重新想像」[Ethnic identity: The 're-imagination' of China]. In S. W. Chiu, J. C. Ip, & H. Li (Eds.), 躁動青春:香港新世代處境觀察 [Restless youth: A look at the new generation in Hong Kong] (pp. 127–142). Chung Hwa Book Company.

Wordie, J. (2012, August 19). Then & now: These were our children. *Post Magazine*. Retrieved from https://www.scmp.com/magazines/post-magazine/article/1016086/then-now-these-were-our-children

Zheng, V. W., & Wan, S. P. (2014). The local consciousness of Hong Kong people: Socio-economic and political perspectives on identity. *Hong Kong and Macao Journal, 3*, 66–78. (in Chinese).

CHAPTER 5

Hong Kong as an Economic Miracle? The Myth of Laissez-Faire and Industrialization

I think there is a straightforward reason for our success … in Hong Kong, government provides the framework for a free-enterprise system to operate efficiently, while the entrepreneurial flair and hard work of a highly motivated immigrant population enable them to take full advantage of its opportunities.
—Dunn, *1996.*
If you want to see capitalism in action, go to Hong Kong.
—Friedman & Friedman, *1990,* p. 34.

1   INTRODUCTION

Hong Kong's successful transformation from an entrepot to an industrial city is now well known. The tale that Hong Kong's postwar economic miracle has been due to the colonial state's laissez-faire economic policy has also been told times and again (Friedman & Friedman, 1990; Rabushka, 1979; Riedel, 1974). The story has been so persuasive that not only did many colonial officers come to believe laissez-faire to be the secret of their success, it also convinced a Nobel laureate of economics to praise Hong Kong as a classic example of free-market capitalism.

Under such circumstances, it is easy to overlook the point that, like many other public policies, laissez-faire can also be a political product (if

S. W. K. Chiu, K. Y. K. Siu, *Hong Kong Society*, Hong Kong Studies Reader Series, https://doi.org/10.1007/978-981-16-5707-8_5

not an artifice) used to justify the colonial economic policy that often rewarded the privileged few. This chapter takes a fresh look at the "Hong Kong economic miracle", by going beyond the narrative of laissez-faireism. It does so by challenging two *standard-definition* myths, which are:

1. Hong Kong was the laboratory of a laissez-faire economy and society;
2. Laissez-faire was the basis for Hong Kong's prosperity.

We will first briefly review the laissez-faire economic doctrine, how it became associated with Hong Kong's post-war economic transformation and then the conventional way to explain her economic success. Then we will proceed to our *high-definition* investigation into Hong Kong's economic history by asking: *Was Hong Kong really a case of laissez-faire? Was laissez-faire adopted for a good reason? What really made the Hong Kong miracle?* We will conclude by assessing Hong Kong's particular mode of industrialization and its consequences for Hong Kong's post-colonial economy.

The core argument of this chapter is that laissez-faire was largely a myth created by the colonial government to justify its *political strategy* towards Hong Kong. Far from laissez-faireism, empirical evidence shows the colonial government selectively intervened in many sectors of the Hong Kong economy. Its decision to intervene in certain sectors was a product of political calculation shaped by the local governing structure and regional/ global geo-political contexts. The unique form of Hong Kong's postwar industrialization has had a lasting effect on the manufacturing industry's (in)ability to upgrade itself and remain competitive.

2   LAISSEZ-FAIRE AND THE HONG KONG EXPERIMENT

It is worth noting that the story associating Hong Kong's economic miracle with laissez-faire did not emerge when laissez-faireism was at its pinnacle in Britain between the 1840s and 1860s (Fine, 1964; Jones, 1977). Rather, it was a century later, during the early 1960s when Hong Kong was undergoing industrialization, that laissez-faire re-emerged as an influential explanation for Hong Kong's postwar prosperity. This immediately poses a puzzle: why was there a hundred-year delay in linking Hong Kong's economic miracle and laissez-faire? The answer is timing. Indeed, historical evidence shows the colonial government had mobilized laissez-faire in order to privilege trading business before World War II (Ngo,

1999, pp. 119-40). But it was not until the colonial government found laissez-faire to be a useful way to justify its political strategy to achieve social stability in Hong Kong, while at the same time neoliberal economists used the same rhetoric to discredit socialist planning during the Cold War, that the marriage between Hong Kong and laissez-faire was consummated.

2.1   Milton Friedman and the Hong Kong Experiment

As Hui (1998) suggests, the diffusion of the "free market" idea in Hong Kong could not have succeeded without the help of local neoliberal economists. While examining the connection between Hong Kong's economic miracle and laissez-faire, we also find similar rhetorical discourses advanced by foreign neoliberal economists. The most influential and well known among them was the winner of the Nobel Memorial Prize in Economic Sciences in 1976—Milton Friedman.

Milton Friedman (1912-2006) was a Jewish-American economist and statistician who taught at the University of Chicago for over three decades. He was one of the key mentors of the so-called "Chicago Boys"– a group responsible for implementing neoliberalist's doctrine, such as market deregulation, in the Latin Americas since the 1970s.[1] He spent decades campaigning on the policy known as monetarism, which was adopted by the U.S. Federal Reserve and the Bank of England in the late 1970s (Krugman, 2007). He was an economic advisor to U.S. President Ronald Reagan in the 1980s and played a key role in shaping the so-called "Washington Consensus" model of development.[2] As an economist and a policy entrepreneur, Friedman was "the great populariser of the free-market doctrine" (Krugman, 2007), by spreading the idea through his economics and public policy lectures, writings and appearance on various media.

The most influential of his writings is *Free to Choose* (Friedman & Friedman, 1990), first published in January 1980, which has been

---

[1] The Chicago Boys generally refers to a group of young male economists, whom was trained at or had come to identify with the Department of Economics of the University of Chicago under Milton Friedman and Arnold Harberger. This group of economists generally advocated free market policies such as deregulation and privatization, along other market-friendly policies.

[2] "Washington Consensus" was coined by British economist John Williamson in a presentation addressing how Latin America could deal with their debt crisis in 1989.

translated into 14 languages and was once a bestselling nonfiction book in the United States. In 1980, after decades of the Cold War and debates over the superiority of socialist planned economy vis-a-vis free-market capitalism, the winds started to shift. Starting in the late 1970s, countries within the Soviet bloc began experiencing recession; several socialist countries (including China, the Soviet Union, and Vietnam) reformed their economies to incorporate "market elements". At the same time, the Conservative Party in the U.K. won the 1979 election and its leader and free-market follower Margaret Thatcher became the Prime Minister. The timely publishing of *Free to Choose* (along with a ten-part television series broadcast) became a popular resource to promote the free-market doctrine, to provide examples of how the free market engenders prosperity, and to demonstrate how planned economies in socialist countries do not work.

Of the many countries and cities used as examples in *Free to Choose*, Hong Kong is perhaps Friedman's favourite. We have already seen the forceful and succinct statement, which praises Hong Kong as "capitalism in action", at the beginning of this chapter. Friedman used Hong Kong in many other instances to illustrate how the free market and limited government intervention can bring about prosperity:

> Hong Kong, a Crown colony of Great Britain, should be the modern exemplar of free markets and limited government... Hong Kong has no tariffs or other restraints on international trade. ... It has no government direction of economic activity, no minimum wage laws, no fixing of prices. ... Hong Kong—a speck of land next to mainland China containing less than 400 square miles with a population roughly 4.5 million people. ... Yet they enjoy one of the highest standards of living in all of Asia. (Friedman & Friedman, 1990, p. 34)

But Friedman was not satisfied making Hong Kong just "the best example" of the superiority of the free market policy. On the last day of 1997, five months after Hong Kong's colonial era had ended, Friedman proposed perhaps the most innovative "natural experiment" in social science history: "the Hong Kong experiment". The following is how Friedman described this experiment:

> Economists and social scientists complain that we are at a disadvantage compared with physical and biological scientists because we cannot conduct

controlled experiments. However, the experiments that nature throws up can be every bit as instructive as deliberately contrived experiments. Take the fifty-year experiment in economic policy provided by Hong Kong between the end of World War II and this past July, when Hong Kong reverted to China. ... In this experiment, Hong Kong represents the experimental treatment; Britain, Israel, and the United States serve as controls. ... I believe that the only plausible explanation for the different rates of growth is socialism in Britain, free enterprise and free markets in Hong Kong. Has anybody got a better explanation? I'd be grateful for any suggestions. (Friedman, 1997)

In order for the "Hong Kong experiment" to launch, Friedman needed someone to help him conduct the experiment in Hong Kong. To his great luck, he met a Scotsman in Hong Kong in 1963, a faithful follower of free-market capitalism and, above all, having the ability to steward Hong Kong's economy in line with Friedman's vision. This Scotsman was the Financial Secretary of Hong Kong between 1961 and 1971—John Cowperthwaite (1915-2006).

What exactly did Cowperthwaite do during his ten-year stint as Financial Secretary of Hong Kong? He did away with all import and export duties; levied a flat tax on corporate profits; and set the ceiling on income tax at 15 percent. In 1963, when Hong Kong suffered a severe drought, he rejected a call from industrialists to subsidize water rates. In 1970, he abolished a prostitution tax, which was expressed as a fee per dance with a "professional dance partner". When he met Friedman in 1963, he even told the economist that he kept no statistics. He said, "If I let them [government officials] compute those statistics, they'll only use them for planning" (The Times, 2006).

Milton Friedman viewed Cowperthwaite as "a real disciple of Adam Smith" and his greatest contribution to be to demonstrate the superiority of free trade and free markets over socialism. In his obituary for Cowperthwaite, he wrote:

[Cowperthwaite] proceeded to demonstrate by converting Hong Kong from one of the poorest countries in the world to one of the richest, thereby providing a striking refutation for the socialist cliché "free trade may be fine in theory but it won't work in practice". (Friedman, 2006b)

Above all, Cowperthwaite provided Friedman with a powerful example to attack the spread of socialist thinking in the UK shortly after the Second World War:

> At the very time shortly after World War II that Britain was embarking on an extreme socialist policy in the homeland, one of its last remaining colonies, Hong Kong, was embarking on an extreme free-market policy. By some accident of officialdom, the Colonial Office had assigned John Cowperthwaite to serve as the Financial Secretary of Hong Kong. The result: the home country strangled by socialism; the colonial possession converted into a showplace of free markets. (Friedman, 2006b)

Like Friedman, many observers today believe Hong Kong has a laissez-faire economy and society. For instance, Hong Kong is still ranked number one by the Heritage Foundation in the Index of Economic Freedom World Rankings. To many of these "Hong Kong fans", free trade, low taxes and a balanced budget, few state enterprises and the absence of an industrial policy are robust indicators supporting the view of Hong Kong as a laissez-faire paradise.

But was colonial Hong Kong indeed a laissez-faire economy and society as Friedman and many Western observers have contended? In the next section, we will step back and examine whether the claim that "colonial Hong Kong was a laissez-faire economy and society" can be substantiated by the historical evidence.

3   The Myth of Laissez-Faire

At first glance, the Index of Economic Freedom World Rankings appears to support the view that Hong Kong is the freest (thus most laissez-faire) economy in the world. However, a careful examination of the assessment components of the Index reveals another story. According to the Index in 2011, while Hong Kong ranked at the top by having the highest *overall score* that year, Hong Kong failed to be most competitive in some key components vis-à-vis other countries (e.g. Singapore). These components include government size, monetary freedom, freedom from corruption and labour freedom. Hong Kong only ranked the highest in six (out of ten) components, and most of them are related to trade, finance and business investment.

While Hong Kong's failure to achieve the highest rank in all components in the Index could be a moot point to make; afterall, it is still the second freest in the other indicators. But this prompts us to ask: Was Hong Kong's laissez-faire really across the board of all sectors industries or just in some? In what follows, we will answer this question by examining the banking, agricultural and manufacturing industries in colonial Hong Kong. After examining these industries in turn, we will return to another relevant question: Why and how did the colonial government abstain from interfering in the economy in such that it enabled neoliberal economists and government officials to exaggerate the state's non-action vis-à-vis the economy?

3.1 The Banking Industry

Our first case is Hong Kong's banking sector. While it is true that Hong Kong was "extremely liberal" in its financial regulatory arrangement and strongly adhered to the laissez-faire policy tradition in handling banking services in the pre-war era (Jao, 1974, p. 17), Hong Kong's post-war banking history shows quite a different picture, especially since the 1960s when banking crises erupted one after another.

There was no government regulation of Hong Kong's banking industry for its first hundred years under British rule. The Banking Ordinance passed in 1948 was the colonial state's first attempt to regulate banking activities with the aim of ensuring a sound banking system. It aimed specifically to require companies providing banking services to register as banks, to obtain official licenses, and to submit their annual balance sheets to the Financial Secretary. The passing of the Ordinance, as Leo Goodstadt (2005) notes, was largely due to intense local and overseas pressure on the colonial government that accused Hong Kong of being "the big leak in China's economy [that] bears the main responsibility for China's present economic and financial chaos."[3]

After the enactment of the Ordinance, Hong Kong's banking industry experienced a fairly stable development during the 1950s and very early

---

[3] HKRS 163-1-403 "China Trade and Commerce," (165) Letter from Chinese side, 15 August 1947 and "Memorandum of Agreement;" (289) Governor to Secretary of State for the Colonies, 10 May 1948; Colonial Secretary to Governor, 2 July 1948. The text of the treaty is reproduced in Treaty Series No. 9 (1949), Exchange of Notes...for the Prevention of Smuggling between Hong Kong and Chinese Ports (London: Cmd 7615, 1949), cited in Goodstadt (2005).

Table 5.1 Growth of Licensed Banks and Branches, 1954-2004

Year	Number of Licensed Banks	Number of Branches
1954	94	3
1959	82	13
1964	88	204
1969	73	289
1974	74	557
1979	105	906
1984	140	1407
1989	165	1377
1994	176	1464
1999	156	1490

Sources: Tai (1986, p. 2); Census and Statistics Department (various years)

1960s. The number of branches of licensed banks grew from only 3 in 1954 to 204 in 1964 (Table 5.1). Four factors accounted for this development: a) Hong Kong's attractive institutional environment to capital funds overseas, b) international banks starting to establish their representative offices in Hong Kong, c) local industrialization creating growing demand for banking services, and d) the local population's relatively high propensity to save (Jao, 1974; Chiu & Lui, 2009, p. 63). Despite enacting the Ordinance, the colonial government was reluctant to exercise its power to clean up the industry—some argued out of a political reason of not to interfere with Chinese bankers and their Chinese clients (Schenk, 2003). In some cases, even requests to use the Ordinance to close down insolvent financial institutions were rejected at the highest level of the colonial administration (Goodstadt, 2005, p. 10).

Goodstadt (2006, p.3) identified three banking clusters gradually emerged after the 1950s: the foreign-owned banks, China state-owned banks and local Chinese banks. While the China state-owned banks had a special role in Hong Kong and largely did not take part in financing the economic growth, the foreign-owned banks quickly adapted to the UN Trade Embargo by turning to finance local manufacturing industries given their prior knowledge in modern commercial banking and connections to Western markets. The local Chinese banks, operated largely as traditional family enterprises in the past with their various banking violation "tolerated" by the colonial regulators, embarked on ambitious expansion—not in the industrial sector but property development, currency and gold trade (Goodstadt, 2006).

Two discourses surrounding the unregulated expansion of the banking industry emerged in the local economics literature (Schenk, 2006). The first argued the 'over-banking' resulted in cutthroat competition among the banks and sowed the seeds of the 1961 banking crisis. Briefly, to attract more deposits, many banks offered more lucrative interest rates to depositors; simultaneously, the roaring stock market and post-war property market bubbles also fuelled the crisis. Many banks engaged in property financing and thus were being exposed to unanticipated risks. A secondary reason argued it wasn't the excessive competition, but the linkage of the bank to family and group networks, which gave rise to insider lending practice within the group, that threatened bank's liquidity and solvency as they became more vulnerable to asset market shocks (Schenk, 2006). Together these factors generated speculation to maximize short-term profits, creating a liquidity squeeze and causing many banks to overcommit their funds to real estate projects. Consequently, the first postwar banking crisis erupted in June 1961—a bank run on the Liu Chong Hing Bank.

Liu Chong Hing Bank was founded by Liu Po Shan, a Cantonese born in 1905. Because of Japanese invasion into China, Liu went from Canton to Hong Kong in 1941 and then engaged in shipping and trading businesses, mainly for rice and groceries, in Hong Kong (Leung, 2010). After World War II, Liu observed a shortage of capital in financing Hong Kong's infrastructural projects. He thus founded "Liu Chong Hing Depository Bank" in 1948 (South China Morning Post, 1977). Interest rates of the bank was attractive to depositors (especially to local citizens), and bank investment were directed to residential and development projects. In the 1950s, as land and housing prices soared, Liu's business empire expanded swiftly. Between 1955 and 1958, apart from his bank, Liu further founded three other companies in real estate, construction and insurance sectors (Cheng & Gao, 2017, p. 60).

However, in June 1961, a rumour about Liu spread, and caused a bank run to his bank (South China Morning Post, 1961a). Many depositors went to the headquarter and branches of the bank to withdraw their savings. In the end, it was until the Financial Secretary of the Hong Kong Government at that time, Cowperthwaite asked the HSBC and the Chartered Bank of India, Australia and China to support Liu's bank then the run was ended (Schenk, 2003). A joint statement was issued by the

HSBC and the Chartered Bank showing support to Liu's bank (South China Morning Post, 1961b). However, the bank run gave a heavy blow not only to the Bank but also to Liu, who died a month after the run.

After the bank run on Liu Chong Hing Bank, the colonial government commissioned H.J Tomkins, an expert from the Bank of England, to conduct a review on Hong Kong's regulatory framework. However, as Ghose (1987, pp. 69-70) notes, the recommendations made by Tomkins were largely misplaced as they emphasized more on "the need for prudential financial management rather than on any crucial dysfunction in the banking structure of the territory" (as quoted in Chiu & Lui, 2009). By 1963 the colonial government was forced to admit, in its Banking Bill 1963, that further legislation was required to handle "a number of bankers … who have conducted and still conducting their affairs in a manner completely foreign to the tradition of sound banking. The truth is that they are not really bankers, either by experience or in practice. They regard their banks as convenient channels for securing control of the public's funds for their own speculations in land, in shares and in similar ventures, without regard to banking principles" (Cowperthwaite, 1963, p. 211, quoted in Faure & Lee, 2004). However, in 1965, just before a new Banking Ordinance, which was based on the Tomkins Report, was enacted in 1966, Hong Kong experienced another banking crisis when bank runs occurred on local Chinese banks for the same problems that had triggered the earlier crisis.

Compared to the 1961 bank run, the 1965 moratorium on the establishment of new banks had far greater consequences not only for the colonial government's attitudes towards intervention in the banking industry, but also for the whole landscape of the industry. For those Chinese banks that failed, the colonial government rescued and repaid the depositors to curb the potential for serious political unrest, yet the total deposits with local Chinese banks still dropped by 30 per cent from January to September in the 1965 bank run. The largest local Chinese bank at that time, Hang Seng Bank, was taken over by its chief competitor HSBC in April 1965. As a consequence, HSBC's monopoly position in retail banking business was consolidated. Another four smaller Chinese banks survived after the Government directly injected liquidity to them. The series of intervention signalled the end of Government's benign neglect in banking industry (Goodstadt, 2006).

In the 1967 amendments to the Banking Ordinance, the colonial government introduced reforms through new and drastic measures, which can be viewed as pro-active intervention by the colonial government in the banking industry. According to Schenk (2003), among these measures, the most important two are: a) minimum capital requirement for establishing a bank was almost doubled from; b) there was a ban placed on the issuing of new bank licenses until 1974 (see Table 5.1).

Later in 1976, the government further passed the new Deposit Taking Companies (DTC) Ordinance. Under this new ordinance, a new classification system for banks and non-banking financial companies was introduced, leading to foreign and local non-banking institutions entering the market having to operate under the names of DTCs. The new DTC Ordinance further regulated interest rates agreement offered by DTCs, signalling the government's another intervention into the financial market (Schenk, 2003).

Although the amended Banking Ordinance was enacted in 1967, Hong Kong's regulatory framework still fell far short of international standards, particularly in the aspects of undercapitalized, illiquid, and even fraudulent banking activities (Schenk, 2003). Thus, following the relatively stable period of the 1970s, a new wave of banking crises erupted in the early 1980s. Between 1982 and 1985, many local and overseas banks (e.g. Hang Lung Bank in 1982, Overseas Trust Bank in 1985) experienced bank runs; some (e.g. the Hong Kong Industrial and Commercial Bank) collapsed. During the mid-1980s, the banking crisis reverberated, and consequently the colonial state had to "nationalize" the collapsed banks and revamp banking regulations by enacting a new Banking Ordinance in 1986 (Chiu & Lui, 2009, pp. 70-72).

With the enactment of the new Banking Ordinance and its subsequent amendments, Hong Kong could hardly claim to follow a laissez-faire policy in the banking industry. In particular, the new classification of banks and financial companies shows the colonial state regulated "differential access" to the banking industry.

3.2   Agricultural Industry

While the colonial state's intervention into the banking industry is a response to periodic crises, its intervention into the agricultural industry is evidently politically motivated. After the Chinese Communist Party seized power in mainland China in 1949, the colony's self-sufficiency in foodstuff production became an important political concern. At that time, the influx of immigrant farmers into the New Territories and the need to supply food for the expanding urban population also aggravated the problem. To reduce dependence on mainland China, the colonial government established two marketing organizations to solve the food supply problem.[4]

Already in the early twentieth century, the rice consumed by Hong Kong's urban population was being imported from Indo-China, Burma and Thailand rather than from mainland China. However, vegetables and marine products were still imported solely from China. In this light, it is not surprising that the colonial state would encourage local vegetable production. The Vegetable Marketing Organization (VMO) formed in 1946 was one of the marketing organizations established by the colonial state to meet this objective. VMO was later reconstituted under a VMO Ordinance in 1952 to be the centralized agency to produce, collect and transport vegetables to the urban wholesale markets. The police were also given the power to stop lorries carrying vegetables without a permit issued by the VMO.

According to Chiu and Hung (1999), apart from establishing VMO, the Agriculture Department also organized an extensive network of local vegetable marketing co-operatives. Members of the co-operatives were entitled to various benefits if they submitted their vegetables to these local organizations, for instance, low interest credit and cheap fertilizers. By 1962, over 76 percent of locally grown vegetables were handled via the co-operative network. At the same time, VMO kept vegetable imports from China at a low level, which created a large demand for local products, thereby inducing the expansion of vegetable production.[5]

After establishing the marketing co-operatives, a number of other co-operatives and voluntary associations were also founded or organized one after another under state sponsorship. These included Pig-Raising

---

[4] In June 1965, a new market was established at Cheung Sha Wan, Kowloon. Marketing services commenced with the establishment of the wholesale vegetable markets. A total of five depots manned by VMO staff and a number of collection centres were also set up in vegetable growing districts in the New Territories. As the industry became more developed, the vegetable marketing co-operative societies were formed and took over most of the collecting centres by undertaking the work of collecting, weighing vegetables, and related documentation work. Today there are twenty-six vegetable marketing co-operative societies in Hong Kong. One vegetable depot remains in operation, providing alternative services for vegetable growers who prefer not to sell through co-operative societies. Unless otherwise stated, this section is based on Chiu and Hung (1999).

[5] The history of Vegetable Marketing Organization was abstracted from the official website of Vegetable Marketing Organization of the Hong Kong SAR Government (Vegetable Marketing Organisation, 2008).

Societies, Irrigation Societies, Cooperative Building Societies, Fish Pond Societies, and Credit and Consumers' Societies in each village. The functions of these co-operatives and associations were multi-fold including granting sums of money to farmers after a bad harvest, giving loans to new vegetable farmers and pig-raisers, and sending experts to provide technical advice to farmers (e.g. new genetically modified seeds and chemical fertilizers).

The modernization effort effectively made vegetable cultivation a profitable income for new immigrants, brought close the rural-urban gap and transformed traditional rice-land into smaller plots of farmlands which also paved the way for easier land grab later the level of state intervention in the New Territories' rural agricultural economy, while being kept at a smaller scale, was still comparable to the 1970s' Saemaul Undong or the New Village Movement in the Republic of Korea. Both were politically motivated and modernizing—albeit in the case of Hong Kong there was a strong colonial concern.

3.3   Manufacturing

The foregoing discussion of the colony's banking and agricultural industries has demonstrated how the colonial state's policy towards the Hong Kong economy has been far from laissez-faire. In fact, similar state interventions are also found in other industries such as public health, housing and gambling. As a matter of fact, the colonial state was selectively intervening in much of Hong Kong's economy; the only industry in which the government effectively practiced *selective non-intervention* was manufacturing.

According to Chiu (1996), Goodstadt (2005) and others, the colonial government abstained from intervening in manufacturing (unlike in other industries) primarily in two ways: a) it limited assistance in the form of the provision of industrial land, and b) it limited credit to manufacturers.

When manufacturing began to develop in the early 1950s, industrialists soon came up against the limited supply of industrial land available in Hong Kong. From the early 1950s, leading local industrialists associated with the Chinese Manufacturing Association (CMA) repeatedly requested the colonial state to help manufacturing firms find suitable sites. However, throughout Hong Kong's industrialization process, the colonial state demonstrated a great reluctance to help the industrialists in this respect. Even after the reclamation work at Kwun Tong had commenced in 1956, and despite the strong opposition from local industrialists, new land appropriated from reclamation was sold through public auctions to industries at the *current market price* that consequently led to industrialists having to pay high rent to build or rent factory buildings or units (Chiu, 1996).

As Chiu (1996) points out, the colonial state's decision not to honour local industrialists' request was due to structural and financial reasons. Structurally, the composition of the governing coalition—by excluding local industrialists and including many financial-commercial capitalists in LegCo and Exco—enabled the colonial state to resist the demands from local industrialists. As for the financial reason, the colonial state feared that selling the newly reclaimed land below the current market price would undermine the state's ability to cover the costs of developing these areas, not to mention reaping profits from them. The Kwun Tong model of land development was originally designed to avoid the state treasury's having to incur any large-scale financial burden. But later when the lands were sold through successive public auctions, the project became lucrative, repaid more than the state's investment, and eventually justified the state's policy to sell land by public auction in the name of the financial benefits to the government.

The limited assistance to manufacturers in the form of extending credit to them reflects a similar bias against industrialists. Once again, in the early 1950s, local industrialists had already complained to the government about their precarious financial position and the inadequate support from the financial sector. Some small and medium-sized manufacturing firms could not obtain loans from banks without substantial collateral (Wah Kiu Yat Po, 1955). In 1956, industrialists proposed to the government to set up a specialized banking institution to finance industrial development at lower interest rates. The idea for an industrial bank was first proposed in connection with the Kwun Tong project. In 1958, owing to the industrialists' persistence and seeing no way to ignore manufacturers' demand, the colonial state announced that the idea of an industrial bank was under consideration, and set up a committee to investigate the possibility. Nevertheless, to the disappointment of the manufacturers, the committee recommended against the establishment of an industrial bank:

> The Committee has ... been presented with no evidence of any concrete case where an industrial development had failed to secure finance in Hong Kong but could properly have secured it from a specialized industrial bank. This, taken in conjunction with the evidence of the very considerable role

played by banks in the expansion of industry in recent years, has led us to the conclusion that the need for an industrial bank for the finance of industry in Hong Kong is not proven. (Industrial Bank Committee, 1960, p. 15)

Similar to the case of industrial land provision, the decision not to establish an industrial bank illustrates well how the configuration of state capacity in terms of the colonial state's financial concerns as well as the structural arrangement of the state-capital alliance privileged the financial-commercial capitalists. Afterwards, when the colonial state was asked to rescue ailing manufacturing industries like wig and iron smelting in the 1960s or garment in the 1990s, similar refrain was observed (Chiu, 1996).

4   THE REAL MAGIC BEHIND THE HONG KONG MIRACLE

Ironically, the colonial state's bias against industrialists notwithstanding, Hong Kong's manufacturing industry still flourished, becoming the motor for Hong Kong's rapid economic growth. According to Chiu and Lui (2009), between the 1950s and 1961, Hong Kong's manufacturing sector grew rapidly and the sector accounted for 23.6 percent of GDP and 43.0 percent of the colony's total employment by the end of this period. As such, a puzzle is presented: what was the real magic behind Hong Kong's economic miracle? In other words, what were the factors contributing to the boom of Hong Kong's manufacturing industry despite the colonial government's limited assistance to it?

Apart from the laissez-faire explanation, Hong Kong's rapid industrial growth has been commonly attributed to such several factors, including skills of emigrated Shanghaiese entrepreneurs from mainland China (Wong, 1988; Wu, 1988), the economic culture of the population (Wong, 1986), and the hard-working and flexible labour force (Lethbridge & Ng, 1984). Without denying the importance of these factors, we argue that the changing world economy, the Cold War context, and the local political and ideological conditions in the postwar era in combination also played a significant role in propelling and conditioning the particular type of industrialization undertaken in Hong Kong (Chiu & Lui, 2009, p. 27; Landsberg, 1979; Fröbel et al., 1980; Dicken, 1986; So, 1986).

As we have seen in Chap. 1, during the 1950s, the Cold War and the Korean War (thus the embargo) pushed Hong Kong to pursue export-led industrialization. To prevent East Asian states from leaning towards the Chinese Communist regime, the U.S. opened up its markets to East Asian countries. As a consequence of abundant labour supply, sufficient capital investment and a huge foreign market, manufacturing firms mushroomed in Hong Kong between the 1950s and 1960s. The number of registered factories grew from 3000 in the 1950s to 10,000 in the 1960s (Ma, 1999, pp. 26-27). These firms, once started, could tap into the extensive commercial networks established during Hong Kong's entrepot history (Chiu & So, 1996). As Chu (1988, p. 74) argues, the major factor behind Hong Kong's industrialization actually lies in the multinational trading groups or the "commercial form" of an international subcontracting system that provided Hong Kong with the opportunity to develop low-cost, labour-intensive, export-oriented industries.

Apart from the above changing global and regional geo-political factors, the rise of Hong Kong's manufacturing sector was also assisted by the colony's internal political and ideological conditions. While the colonial state's policy was biased against industrialists, the colonial state generally sided with local capitalists at the expense of working-class interests: labour protection legislation to regulate standard work hours and minimum wage laws were largely absent throughout the colonial era (Siu, 2011). Only since the 1970s serious reforms in labour laws had been put in place. Besides, Hong Kong's trade union movement was also weak and divided due to political and ideological differences between pro-Beijing trade unions and pro-Taiwan trade unions. In line with this divide, trade unions were more concerned with politics than Hong Kong workers' economic livelihood (Chiu & So, 2004; Siu, 2006).

Since the 1960s, Hong Kong's textile manufacturers had imported sophisticated machinery from overseas to upgrade their production technology. Many fashion buyers from Europe and the U.S. began to come to Hong Kong to purchase fabrics and to place orders for finished garments, thus helping to promote the subsequent boom in Hong Kong's garment industry. However, the global market soon came under threat. Quota systems were introduced by many overseas countries to restrict garment imports from Hong Kong. Facing quota restrictions on cotton garments, Hong Kong garment manufacturers then turned to producing garments made with artificial fibres like nylon and mixed yarns (Siu, 2014).

Entering into the 1970s, Hong Kong's manufacturing sector continued to thrive. Its garment industry produced mid-market ready-to-wear products from denim to woven cotton tops, shirts and trousers. In the mid-1970s, one third of the ready-to-wear products on the European market were produced in Hong Kong. At the same time, Hong Kong garment manufacturers began to recognize the importance of fashion design. The turn from producing mid-market ready-to-wear garments to up-market fashions coincided with the strong demand not only from the European and the U.S. markets but also Hong Kong markets (Chiu & Lui, 1994; Siu, 2014).

More importantly, the fast-changing foreign markets also resulted in the export-oriented industrialization of Hong Kong with a peculiar feature—most of the manufacturing firms were small-to-medium-sized firms, usually employing under 20 persons, with an average establishment size of 33 persons. The majority of the workers, particularly in garment and electronics industries, were "Hong Kong's working daughters" (Salaff, 1981). These small or medium-sized firms advocated flexible employment and "guerrilla" business strategies to cope with the rapidly changing foreign markets (Lee, 1999; Chiu & Lui, 2009).

In short, rather than laissez-faire as the *deux ex machina*, Hong Kong's postwar economic prosperity is a complex outcome of intertwining global, regional and local factors. Globally and regionally, the Cold War and the Korean War set the stage for Hong Kong to undergo export-led industrialization. But the industrialization could not succeed without Hong Kong's pre-war commercial and trading networks, which enabled local manufacturers to tap into foreign markets, especially the U.S. International competition and growing protectionism also forced local manufacturers to pursue product diversification. At the same time, local left-right politics (demonstrated in the divide in the local trade union movement), the colonial state's economic policies disfavouring the working classes' interests, and the small-and-medium-sized firm which could tap into female labour surplus in the population were also important factors contributing to Hong Kong's postwar industrialization.

4.1 A Lost Chance: Horizontal Expansion without Vertical Upgrading

Before turning to Hong Kong's post-colonial era, let us assess the consequence of the particular kind of export-led industrialization undertaken in Hong Kong. As Gereffi and Korzeniewicz (1994) suggests, the way Hong Kong's manufacturers utilized the trading and international subcontracting networks is the "buyer-driven" type in the global governance structures in global commodity chains. Local manufacturers connected to intermediate trading companies which subcontracted orders from large retailers and global brand-name buyers. This type of governance structure features in its decentralized mode of production, and is prevalent in labour-intensive and consumer goods industries, as Hong Kong's garment industry testifies.

However, one should note that this decentralized, buyer-driven, and labour-intensive manufacturing production could not have been so prolonged if there had been no steady supply of cheap and unskilled labour in the labour market. Interestingly and fortuitously, due to China's unstable political situation between the 1950s and 1970s, successive waves of immigrants from mainland China replenished the labour supply and thus enabled manufacturers to cope with labour shortages (Sit et al., 1979, p. 360, 390; England & Rear, 1981, pp. 77-80). As a result, the arrival of economically active immigrants from mainland China then produced an unintended consequence for Hong Kong of perpetuating this labour-intensive strategy.

As Greenwood (1990, p. 21) rightly points out, "the growth of Hong Kong's GDP in the 1960s and 1970s was made up, in significant degree, by the 'horizontal' expansion of the labour force, i.e. the arrival of a large number of relatively unskilled workers, rather than by the 'vertical' upgrading of skills of resident employers and employees". Other than the stable supply of unskilled labour, the lack of state support to upgrade firms' technological level for vertical expansion is yet another important reason. Furthermore, the fact that many Hong Kong manufacturers started as traders and salesmen, rather than engineers, is double-edged too: manufacturers' trader origins enabled them to have high market sensitivity and to react quickly to market signals, but limited their vision so that they lacked long-term planning for vertical upgrading. The consequence of this "horizontal expansion" without "vertical upgrading", as vividly demonstrated in Chiu and Wong's (2004) study of Hong Kong's electronics industries, is "growth without catching up". Not only did Hong Kong's manufacturing firms lack the motivation to seek product innovations, the buyer-driven and trade-led production governance structure also provided much organizational inertia for small and medium-sized firms to expand into large firms. Compared to other major East Asian competitors, such as Japan, Taiwan, Singapore and South Korea, Hong Kong's many signature industries in the 1960s and 1970s (e.g. toys, garments, electronics, plastics industries) gradually lost their competitiveness in the 1980s. If *laissez-faire* may not be the primary contributory factor for Hong Kong's industrial takeoff, it definitely was one of the key backgrounds behind the demise of manufacturing there. Relative to the intensive support offered by neighbouring states, the Hong Kong colonial state had steadfastly held firm to the non-interventionist, and hence non-supportive, stance towards manufacturing (Chiu et al., 1997). By following "pure" market logic, the only choice for This also paves the way for Hong Kong's de-industrialization since the mid-1980s (Chiu & Lui, 2001).

5   POST-COLONIAL HONG KONG: THE END OF LAISSEZ-FAIRE

One aspect of post-colonial Hong Kong that still rivets the attention of western observers is whether the new "Chinese city" is able to sustain its economic competitiveness vis-à-vis other world cities. Once again, apart from the Heritage Foundation's Index showing Hong Kong has failed to be ranked number one in all of their assessment components, in 2000 the International Monetary Foundation (IMF) also offered a new verdict on Hong Kong's economic competitiveness:

> Hong Kong is roughly as competitive as the average OECD economy ... On almost all measures, Hong Kong SAR is neither the most nor the least competitive in the 15-country sample. ... Hong Kong has become slightly less competitive in the last decade. The shift in industry mix to services has reduced economy-wide competitiveness. (Zitzewitz, 2000)

As the biggest campaigner for the principles of free trade and free markets, the IMF's verdict on post-colonial Hong Kong actually reflects a significant shift in how many neoliberalists view the Hong Kong government's economic policies. Despite various kinds of state intervention into economic activities in different industries in the colonial era, neoliberal economists and free-trade campaigning organizations still considered Hong Kong to be largely following a free market (if not completely laissez-faire) approach to the economy. However, numerous events happened in post-colonial Hong Kong disappointed many neoliberal economists to the extent that they no longer consider the city as the poster child for a free market economy.

What has Hong Kong done during its post-colonial era to disappoint its neoliberal fans? Perhaps the most important is the change in the post-colonial economic policy rhetoric. In 1998, after the Hong Kong government intervened into Hong Kong's financial markets by using public

money to buy shares of several blue chip stocks when hedge funds specu-
lated on the Hong Kong currency and attacked Hong Kong's financial
system, the Chairman of the Hong Kong Monetary Authority quoted the
former Financial Secretary of colonial Hong Kong Charles Philip Haddon-
Cave[6] to justify their interventions:

> The Government must accept such responsibilities as are necessary to ensure
> that management decisions are not frustrated by imperfections in the opera-
> tion of the market mechanism, leading to economic inefficiency or social
> distress which only the Government can remove. (Yam, 1998)

Already in the 1970s, Cowperthwaite's successor Haddon-Cave discon-
tinued his laissez-faire policy, both in practice and in rhetoric. Haddon-
Cave even invented a new term, "positive non-interventionism", to signal
a shift away Cowperthwaite's laissez-faire approach. Specifically, Haddon-
Cave stressed the importance of the need for the colonial government to
shoulder greater responsibility to correct market failures. Though the
rhetoric was being revised, many neoliberal economists, Milton Friedman
included, still considered Haddon-Cave's positive non-interventionist
approach as a modified version of laissez-faireism without deviating a lot
from the free-market principle.

In fact, the self-contradictory term "positive non-interventionism"
suggested by Haddon-Cave created great confusion for many observers.
Some (like Friedman) tried to equate laissez-faire with positive non-
interventionism. But as we argue, the two terms differ substantially in
terms of the role assigned to the government. While laissez-faire assigns
the government a passive and negative role to play in society and economy, positive non-interventionism gives the government an active and
positive role to play to "care" for the society and economy. The difference
was later re-stated by Donald Tsang (the second Chief Executive of the
Hong Kong SAR) in his policy address in 2006:

> During the colonial era in the early-1980s, the then Financial Secretary, Sir
> Philip Haddon-Cave, in addressing the prevailing needs of social develop-
> ment, broke away from the laissez-faire doctrine and put forward the view
> that the Government should carefully weigh all relevant factors before
> deciding to intervene. (Tsang, 2006)

---

[6] Charles Philip Haddon-Cave (1925-1999) succeeded Cowperthwaite as the Financial
Secretary of Hong Kong between 1971 and 1981.

Once Tsang made the above statement to declare the end of laissez-faire in Hong Kong, he quickly suggested another new term to defend the Hong Kong SAR government's new approach to the economy— "big market, small government"—under his administration.

Reflecting on the first fifteen years of post-colonial Hong Kong, one can say that Tsang's new term is an attempt by him and the SAR government to justify the many conflicting government policies launched in post-handover Hong Kong. On the one hand, we see more government intervention into many industries in the post-handover era. Apart from the intervention in the stock market in 1997, the SAR government has introduced new stamp duties on the sale of property, set a poverty line, and, above all, promulgated minimum wage law. All these policies, in the eyes of many neoliberalists, represent a significant departure from free-market principles.

Yet, on the other hand, we should not lose sight of the fact that more de-regulation and the introduction of market elements into public services. For instance, the SAR government privatized most of its previously managed shopping malls in public housing estates by transferring them to a newly listed company called "The Link". The government also allocated many social enterprise projects and lump-sum grants to the social services and welfare sector in the name of boosting service efficiency. Again, we argue, similar to the laissez-faire policy we have examined above, no matter whether it is labelled "positive non-interventionism" or "big market, small government", both are simply rhetorical expressions that did not emerge from academic or ideological beliefs. Rather, these policy vocabularies should be considered as a product of consciously pragmatic political strategies in order for the (post-)colonial state to justify both its intervention and non-intervention when deemed necessary.

6 Concluding Remarks: Hong Kong as an Exemplar of Crony Capitalism?

On 6 October 2006, a month after Donald Tsang declared the "big market, small government" approach to Hong Kong's economy and about a month before Milton Friedman's death,[7] the once-biggest fan of Hong Kong wrote a commentary for the Wall Street Journal entitled, "*Hong*

[7] Milton Friedman died on 16 November 2006, same year as John Cowperthwaite (21 January 2006).

Kong Wrong: What would Cowperthwaite say?" In the commentary, Friedman denounced Tsang's new approach which would destroy the foundation of Hong Kong's prosperity laid down by Cowperthwaite (Friedman, 2006a). To a large extent, the story of Hong Kong's economic miracle and the myth of laissez-faire start with Friedman but also end with Friedman. After Friedman's death, global observers have gradually removed the association of the banner of laissez-faire with Hong Kong. But locally, many people, especially government officials and capitalists, still help circulate the laissez-faire myth to justify their policies and sustain their class interests whenever the public clamours for the SAR government to adopt such measures as increasing corporate taxes, building more public housing to solve housing problems, and introducing standard working-hour legislation. In this respect, as we have repeatedly argued in this chapter, the changing rhetoric of economic policy (from "laissez-faire", to "positive non-interventionism", then to "big market, small government") is best viewed as the product of political calculation and a means to justify colonial and post-colonial government policies.

However, despite the changing rhetoric, perhaps the most persistent phenomenon we have found in this chapter, no matter whether it is in the colonial or post-colonial era, is the strong "state-business alliance" in the city. This has been demonstrated in some historical studies (e.g. Ngo, 1999) and our survey of Hong Kong's banking and manufacturing industries. Recently, this strong alliance has been so obvious that it has led Hong Kong to earn a new image as an exemplar of "crony capitalism" when Hong Kong ranked at the top in *The Economist*'s crony-capitalism index in 2014 (The Economist, 2014).

To sum up, based on the examination of the banking, agricultural and manufacturing industries, we conclude that Hong Kong's colonial economic policy resembled more a type of "selective non-intervention" than laissez-faireism. While there is no doubt that colonial Hong Kong state done the least in promoting manufacturing industries especially in comparison to the other "Little Dragons" (Haggard, 1990), it had not shied from getting its hands dirty in the other sectors. We also find there was a political logic underlining the selective non-intervention approach. It was not ideological or academic beliefs that impelled the colonial state to abstain from intervening in the economy. Rather, it is the result of political calculation. This political logic is clear when we examine the colonial state's limited assistance to industrialists in terms of land provision and setting up of an industrial bank in the 1950s. The composition of the governing coalition that privileged financial-commercial capitalists, as well as the colonial state's financial stringency together shaped the colonial state's decision whether or not to intervene in a particular industry.

To the question, "What really made the Hong Kong postwar miracle?", we have revealed that the rapid growth of Hong Kong's manufacturing industry, despite limited help from the colonial government, stemmed from a number of factors. To name a few, these factors include: international trading and commercial networks developed in the pre-World War II era, global and regional geo-politics and protectionism, as well as the local politico-ideological divide and manufacturers' business strategies. But we have also seen the perversity in Hong Kong's export-led industrialization: Hong Kong's special way of industrialization— "horizontal expansion" without "vertical upgrading"—very much paves the way for Hong Kong's manufacturing industries to lose their competitiveness vis-à-vis other countries. This detailed and multi-level analysis has provided a new angle for assessing the nature of Hong Kong's economic miracle and its negative consequences, which goes beyond the *standard-definition* laissez-faire narrative.

By the end of the second decade of the twenty-first century, the laissez-faire story is becoming as hollow as ever. Save for a few die-hard neoliberals who blamed Hong Kong's economic stagnation on government meddling that goes wrong, even many conservatives are reviewing their stand on the subject. In the recent debate over the intensification of social movements, and especially among the younger generation, government inaction has been singled out has a prime cause by commentators even from the establishment camp. The role of the state in fermenting the socioeconomic contradictions in Hong Kong SAR will be the subject in later chapters.

References

Cheng, T. H., & Gao, H. (2017). 可繼之道:華人家族發展挑戰與出路 [ways for carrying on: Developmental challenges and breakthroughs to Chinese family businesses]. Chung Hwa Book Company (Hong Kong) Limited.

Chiu, S. W. (1996). Unravelling Hong Kong's exceptionalism: The politics of laissez-faire in the industrial Takeoff. *Political Power and Social Theory*, *10*, 229–256.

Chiu, S. W., & Lui, T. L. (1994). A tale of two industries: The restructuring of Hong Kong's garment-making and electronics industries. *Environment and Planning A: Economy and Space, 26*(1), 53–70.

Chiu, S. W., & Lui, T. L. (2001). Flexibility under unorganized industrialism? The experience of industrial restructuring in Hong Kong. In F. C. Deyo, R. F. Doner, & E. Hershberg (Eds.), *Economic governance and the challenge of flexibility in East Asia* (pp. 55–78). Rowman & Littlefield.

Chiu, S. W., & Lui, T. L. (2009). *Hong Kong: Becoming a Chinese global city.* Routledge.

Chiu, S. W., Ho, K. C., & Lui, T. L. (1997). *City-states in the global economy: Industrial restructuring in Hong Kong and Singapore.* Routledge.

Chiu, S. W., & Hung, H. (1999). State building and rural stability. In T. W. Ngo (Ed.), *Hong Kong's history: State and society under colonial rule* (pp. 74–101). Routledge.

Chiu, S. W., & So, A. Y. (1996). *East Asia and the world economy.* SAGE Publishing.

Chiu, S. W., & So, A. Y. (2004). Flexible production and industrial restructuring in Hong Kong: From boom to bust. In G. G. Gonzalez, R. A. Fernandez, V. Price, D. Smith, & L. T. Võ (Eds.), *Labor versus empire race, gender, migration.* Taylor & Francis.

Chiu, S. W., & Wong, K. C. (2004). The hollowing-out of Hong Kong electronics: Organizational inertia and industrial restructuring in the 1990s. *Comparative Sociology, 3*(2), 199–234.

Chu, Y. W. (1988). *Dependent industrialization: the case of the Hong Kong garment industry* (Master's thesis, University of Hong Kong, Hong Kong). Retrieved from doi:https://doi.org/10.5353/th_b3025263.

Cowperthwaite, J. J. (1963). The Banking Bill 1963. *Hong Kong Hansard.* 19 June. Hong Kong Government. Cited in Faure, D., & Lee, P. T. (Eds.). (2004). *Economy.* Hong Kong: Hong Kong University Press.

Dicken, P. (1986). *Global Shift.* Harper & Row.

Dunn, L. (1996). The way are. In *Hong Kong annual report 1996: A review of 1995 and a pictorial review of the past fifty years.* Government Information Services Department.

England, J., & Rear, J. (1981). *Industrial relations and law in Hong Kong* (2nd ed.). Oxford University Press.

Fine, S. (1964). *Laissez faire and the general-welfare state.* University of Michigan Press.

Friedman, M. (1997, December 31). The Real Lesson of Hong Kong. *National Review.*

Friedman, M. (2006a, October 6). Hong Kong Wrong. *Wall Street Journal.* Retrieved from https://www.wsj.com/articles/SB116009800068684505

Friedman, M. (2006b). Cowperthwaite and the free market in practice. In J. Gwartney, R. Lawson, & W. Easterly (Eds.), *Economic freedom of the world 2006: Annual report*. Academic Foundation.

Friedman, M., & Friedman, R. (1990). *Free to choose: A personal statement*. Harvest Press.

Fröbel, F., Heinrichs, J., & Kreye, O. (1980). *The new international division of labour*. Cambridge University Press.

Gereffi, G., & Korzeniewicz, M. (1994). *Commodity chains and global capitalism*. Praeger.

Ghose, T. K. (1987). *The banking system of Hong Kong*. Singapore: Butterworths.

Goodstadt, L. F. (2005). Crisis and Challenge: The Changing Role of the Hongkong & Shanghai Bank, 1950-2000 (HKIMR Working Paper No. 13/2005). Retrieved from doi:https://doi.org/10.2139/ssrn.1009002.

Goodstadt, L. F. (2006). Painful Transitions: The Impact of Economic Growth and Government Policies on Hong Kong's' Chinese'Banks, 1945-70 (HKIMR Working Paper No. 16/2006). Retrieved from doi:https://doi.org/10.2139/ssrn.1008733.

Greenwood, J. (1990). The changing structure and competitiveness of the Hong Kong economy. *Asian Monetary Monitor, 14*, 21–31.

Haggard, S. (1990). *Pathways from the periphery: The politics of growth in the newly industrializing countries*. Cornell University Press.

Hui, P. K. (1998). Rhetoric and translation—The diffusion of Liberal economic ideology in Hong Kong. *Hong Kong Journal of Social Sciences, 13*, 69–90.

Industrial Bank Committee. (1960). *Report of the Industrial Bank Committee*. Public Records Office Hong Kong.

Jao, Y. C. (1974). *Banking and currency in Hong Kong: A study of postwar financial development*. Springer.

Jones, G. G. (1977). The British government and the oil companies 1912–1924: The search for an oil policy. *The Historical Journal, 20*(3), 647–672.

Krugman, P. (2007). Who was Milton Friedman? *New York Review of Books, 54*(2), 27.

Landsberg, M. (1979). Export-led industrialization in the third world: Manufacturing imperialism. *Review of Radical Political Economics, 11*(4), 50–63.

Lee, K. M. (1999). Flexible manufacturing in a colonial economy. In T. W. Ngo (Ed.), *Hong Kong's history: State and society under colonial rule* (pp. 162–179). Routledge.

Lethbridge, D., & Ng, S. H. (1984). The business environment and employment. In D. Lethbridge (Ed.), *The business environment in Hong Kong* (2nd ed., pp. 52–69). Oxford University Press.

Leung, P. W. (2010, February 11). 香港早年的銀號銀行業 [Early banking industry in Hong Kong]. *Takungpao*, p. B11.

Ma, C. W. (1999). Culture, politics, and television in Hong Kong. In *Culture, politics, and television in Hong Kong* (pp. 26–27). Routledge.

Ngo, T. W. (1999). Industrial history and the artifice of the laissez-faire colonialism. In T. W. Ngo (Ed.), *Hong Kong's history: State and society under colonial rule* (pp. 119–140). Routledge.

Rabushka, A. (1979). *Hong Kong: A study in economic freedom*. University of Chicago.

Riedel, J. (1974). *The industrialization of Hong Kong*. J.C.B. Mohr.

Salaff, J. (1981). *Working daughters of Hong Kong: Filial piety or power in the family?* Columbia University Press.

Schenk, C. R. (2003). Banking crises and the evolution of the regulatory framework in Hong Kong 1945-1970. *Australian Economic History Review, 43*(2), 140–154.

Schenk, C. R. (2006). *The Origins of Anti-Competitive Regulation: Was Hong Kong 'Over-Banked' in the 1960s?* (HKIMR Working Paper No. 9/2006). Retrieved from doi:https://doi.org/10.2139/ssrn.1008230.

Sit, V. F., Wong, S. L., & Kiang, T. S. (1979). *Small scale industry in a laissez-faire economy: a Hong Kong case study*. Centre of Asian Studies, University of Hong Kong.

Siu, Y. K. (2006). New labour protest movements in Hong Kong: The experience of the student-worker mutual aid campaign. In S. Dasgupta & R. Kiely (Eds.), *Globalization and after*. SAGE Publishing.

Siu, Y. K. (2011). A brief history of the struggle for standard work hours legislation in Hong Kong. *Hong Kong Journal of Social Sciences, 41*, 17–40.

Siu, Y. K. (2014). *The work, lifestyles and domination of chinese migrant garment workers, in comparative perspective* (Doctoral dissertation, Australian National University, Canberra, Australia). Retrieved from http://hdl.handle.net/1885/156361

So, A. Y. (1986). The economic success of Hong Kong. *Sociological Perspectives, 29*(2), 241–258.

South China Morning Post. (1961a, June 16). Another Heavy Run on Local Chinese Bank. *South China Morning Post.*

South China Morning Post. (1961b, June 20). Another Heavy Run on Local Chinese Bank. *South China Morning Post.*

South China Morning Post. (1977, April 4). Liu Chong Hing Bank Computerises. *South China Morning Post.*

Yam, J. (1998, August 24). Intervention True to Guiding Policy. *South China Morning Post.*

Tai, L. S. (1986). Commercial banking. In R. H. Scott, K. A. Wong, & Y. K. Ho (Eds.), *Hong Kong's financial institutions and markets* (pp. 1–18). Oxford University Press.

The Economist. (2014, March 15). Planet Plutocrat. *The Economist*. Retrieved from http://www.economist.com/news/international/21599041-countries-where-politically-connected-businessmen-are-most-likely-prosper-planet

The Times. (2006, February 3). Obituaries for Sir John Cowperthwaite. *The Times*.

Tsang, D. (2006). *Policy address of 2006*. Hong Kong Government.

Vegetable Marketing Organisation. (2008). *V.M.O's History*. Retrieved from http://www.vmo.org/en/index/page_about/item_history/.

Wah Kiu Yat Po. (1955, February 16). 外商銀行工業貸款放寬對本港工業發展漸有行動加以支持 [Industrial lending relaxation by foreign banks to support industrial development in Hong Kong]. *Wah Kiu Yat Po*.

Wong, S. L. (1986). Modernization and Chinese culture in Hong Kong. *The China Quarterly, 106*, 306–325.

Wong, S. L. (1988). *Emigrant Entrepreneur*. Oxford University Press.

Wu, J. (1988). Entrepreneurship. In H. C. Y. Ho & L. C. Chau (Eds.), *The economic system of Hong Kong* (pp. 155–168). Hong Kong: Asian Research Service.

Zitzewitz, E. (2000). *Domestic competition, cyclical fluctuations, and long-run growth in Hong Kong SAR* (Working Paper No. 00/142). International Monetary Fund. Retrieved from https://www.imf.org/en/Publications/WP/Issues/2016/12/30/Domestic-Competition-Cyclical-Fluctuations-and-Long-Run-Growth-in-Hong-Kong-Sar-3723

Hong Kong as Asian Hollywood? Hong Kong's Film Industry in the Golden Age and After

> For decades, Hong Kong was Asia's movie capital, dubbed time and again as the 'Hollywood of the East'. Recently, however, tales of Hong Kong's once thriving motion picture industry are sombre stories explaining its decline.
> —Hana Davis (2019), Journalist

1 INTRODUCTION

Over much of the past century, Hong Kong had been well-known for its motion picture industry. As many of the films it produced, there are dramatic twists and turns in the history of the industry. To begin with, although the city's film industry was deemed the "Hollywood of the East"

This chapter is based on a larger project on the Hong Kong and China film industries that was supported by the General Research Fund (GRF) from the Research Grants Council (RGC) of the University Grants Committee (UGC) in Hong Kong (Ref No. 442312). Some parts of it previously appeared in Shin and Chiu (2016) and Chiu and Shin (2013, 2019). We are grateful for the permission of Victor Shin to use materials from the chapters.

or the "Asian Hollywood" (Stokes, 2007; Hammond, 2000; Stokes & Hoover, 1999, p. 17; Dannen & Long, 1997), its box-office grosses had been dominated by imported movies for several decades prior to 1982 (see Fig. 6.1 and Appendix for the overall trend in HK film box office takings). Despite the famed Chinese martial-arts pictures produced by Golden Harvest and starring Bruce Lee in the early 1970s, the output of Hong Kong film companies accounted for only around forty per cent of the total box-office revenue throughout the 1970s. The rebound of Hong Kong movies[1] did not occur until the early 1980s. For the first time in the history of Hong Kong cinema, the box-office grosses of Hong Kong movies outweighed those of the imported films in 1982, announcing the arrival of

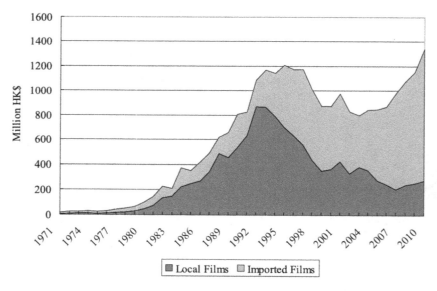

Fig. 6.1 Box office grosses of local versus imported films, 1971–2010 (million HK$). (Source: Appendix)

[1] According to the definition given by the Hong Kong Motion Picture Industry Association Limited (MPIA), "Hong Kong movies" refer to the films produced by any registered companies in Hong Kong (Hong Kong Motion Picture Industry Association Limited [MPIA], n.d.). Fifty per cent or above of the "listed effective post(s)" in the movie should also be taken up by Hong Kong permanent residents (MPIA, n.d.). These posts include "film producer, director, script writer, actor or actress" (MPIA, n.d.). Movies that fulfil these criteria are regarded as "Hong Kong movies".

the industry's golden age. The output of Hong Kong movies subsequently surged to 120 in 1990, and reached its peak of 186 in 1993 (Appendix). Nevertheless, the industry's heyday lasted for only one and a half decades. The film outputs and box-office revenue for Hong Kong movies began to plunge from their peak after 1993 (Fig. 6.1). The preponderance of Hong Kong movies in the domestic market was increasingly eroded by imported, mainly Hollywood, films. Only four years later, in 1997, foreign movies once again surpassed Hong Kong movies in box-office performance. The difference in theatrical receipts between imported films and local movies widened even further after that.

While not the largest industry, the film industry offered a useful lens to apply a sociological perspective on how the economy operates in Hong Kong. Why Hong Kong's film industry was able to survive and even prosper in the 1980s amid the challenge from Hollywood in the 1980s? How did the industry react to the challenge of the Hollywood blockbusters at that time? Why did Hong Kong's major film companies fail to retain their power and dominance over the film market in the 1990s? How was the commodity chain of Hong Kong movies restructured during the late 1990s and how has the restructuring impacted on the Hong Kong film industry throughout the 2000s? To address these questions systematically, we start from the standard-definition explanations of the rather abrupt reversal of the fortunes in the local film industry from the boom of the 1980s to the bust since the mid-1990s. Arguably, these standard-definition accounts have not provided a complete explanation for the decline of Hong Kong films. Instead, we have to apply a broader institutional perspective focusing on the industry's organizational structure to find a high-definition picture.

The beginning of the industry's downfall, notes Teo (2008), can be traced back to 1993—the year when Steven Spielberg's *Jurassic Park* set a new record for the highest box-office grosses in Hong Kong. From that time onwards, Hollywood movies began to gain a firm grip over the Hong Kong film market. From 1993 to 2006, the market share of imported films, mainly from Hollywood, skyrocketed from 26.4 per cent to 71.8 per cent. The latest figure we have was from 2010, when imported films dominated the box offices with a 79.4% share (Fig. 6.2 and Appendix). The blockbuster of the year was a Hollywood picture most of the time. In 1997, James Cameron's *Titanic* became the first movie to earn more than 100 million HK dollars in the Hong Kong box office. This record stood

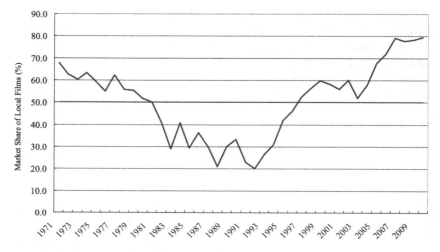

Fig. 6.2   Percentage share of imported films in Hong Kong market, 1971–2010. (Source: Appendix)

until *Avatar*, another Hollywood science-fiction epic film directed again by James Cameron, surpassed it in 2009.

1.1   Standard-Definition Explanations to the Downfall of Hong Kong Film Industry

The decline of Hong Kong's film industry has attracted considerable attention from local observers.[2] We can identify five groups of factors

---

[2] Chan et al. (2010) mention in their review of the rise and fall of Hong Kong's film industry five major reasons for the industry's downfall: the changing consumption pattern of cinemagoers because of the proliferation of alternative entertainment media, the repetitive formulae used in film production which undermined the quality of Hong Kong movies, the withdrawal of foreign capital from Southeast Asia, the declining demand for Hong Kong movies in overseas markets, and the spread of illegal downloading of movies. These reasons largely overlap with the six factors highlighted by Teo (2008) for the industry's downfall. They include the growth of Hollywood's market share in Hong Kong, video piracy, the poor quality of Hong Kong movie screenplays, the underdeveloped market in China which was not ready at that time to serve as an outlet for the movies exported from Hong Kong, as well as the rise of other Asian film industries in the 1990s which undercut the traditional Asian markets for Hong Kong movies (Teo, 2008, pp. 342–343).

constituting the standard-definition images commonly taken to be responsible for the decline of Hong Kong's film industry. These narratives are:

1. *Diminishing cultural resistance*: Given the backdrop of Hollywood's return to the Asian film market in the 1990s, some observers attributed the industry's decline to the growth of Hollywood's market share in Hong Kong. In Lee's (2006a, 2009) analyses of cinemagoers' acceptance of U.S. movies in East Asia, he observes that Hollywood's blockbusters, particularly those receiving Academy Awards in visual, audio, and technical effects, are more likely to overcome cultural barriers, and to achieve better box-office results abroad. Producers of these pictures, notes Oh (2001), intentionally choose to focus on the "less culturally resistant genres and more internationally appealing content in order to diminish the cultural discount effect" (p. 42).[3] Examining the acceptance of foreign movies in Hong Kong, Lee (2006b) finds that less culturally specific movies from Hollywood, such as science-fiction and action films produced with big budgets, are more acceptable to Hong Kong cinemagoers as compared with American comedies containing more culturally specific contents. In this respect, Hollywood's advanced filmmaking technologies would help its movies to overcome cultural barriers abroad and attract overseas audiences when traversing cultural borders (Noam, 1993). Hong Kong's film industry with less capital resources than Hollywood is expected to be less capable of competing with the big-budget productions from the U.S. Hollywood's blockbusters thus inevitably came to dominate the Hong Kong film market.

2. *Spread of video piracy*: Besides the competitive advantages of Hollywood movies in virtue of their capital resources and advanced filmmaking technologies, there are other, more local, factors that have been highlighted in the conventional discussion. Some commentators, for example, consider the spread of video piracy as the key factor that exacerbated the decline of Hong Kong's film industry

---

[3] This claim assumes that the cultural products distributed abroad may suffer a "cultural discount" (Hoskins & Mirus, 1988) because the products may lose their appeal if the consumers in other markets do not share the same socio-demographic characteristics, such as "to have the same background knowledge, linguistic competence, and other forms of cultural capital to fully appreciate them" (Lee, 2008, p. 119).

(Lim, 2006). Curtin (2002) stresses that the rising demand for pirated copies of movies reflected the "continuing popularity of the industry's output, yet ... [the cinemagoers] are now more willing to buy and rent video copies than to buy theatre tickets" (p. 238). Film distributors were also said to hesitate about purchasing the rights to Hong Kong movies lest pirated copies could be released before the movies were launched officially (Symonds, 2007). Instead, they would prefer distributing Hollywood movies more likely to draw in cinemagoers rather than distributing Hong Kong movies. Given this situation, a Hong Kong film director, Chan Hing-kai, claims piracy to be the biggest challenge for the Hong Kong film industry before 1997 (Ma et al:, 2007).

3. *Proliferation of alternative entertainment media*: Some studies consider the industry's decline to be a consequence of the proliferation of alternative entertainment media which changed the consumption pattern of cinemagoers in Hong Kong. Zhang (1998) stresses that the youngsters, as the largest audience for Hong Kong movies, have access to a variety of entertainments, such as television, pop music and electronic games, apart from cinema-going (see also Leung, 1999). This view suggests that the rising popularity of alternative entertainments might have dampened Hong Kong's youngsters' interest in cinema-going thereby lowering the box-office grosses of Hong Kong movies.

4. *Changing regional film production structure*: Some observers attributed the Hong Kong film industry's decline to the changing structure of the regional production complex of motion pictures in Asia. There are two variants of this argument. First, for a long time, many critics claimed that the overreliance on presales of distribution rights to overseas film markets, Taiwan in particular, had undermined the quality of Hong Kong movies (Chung, 2007). Between the late 1980s and the early 1990s, film investors from Taiwan poured their capital into Hong Kong's film market because Hong Kong acted as a "stepping stone" for Taiwan film investors eager to take advantage of the co-production partnership with film companies in China (Liang, 1998). Taiwan capital covered as much as one-third of the production costs during this period (Chung, 2007, p. 361). To cope with the surging demand for films, many filmmakers in Hong Kong shortened the production time by using repetitive formulae such as typical casts and plots (Lim, 2006). Many critics thus repeatedly

used the phrase "hasty and unpolished productions" (*cu zhi lan zao*, 粗製濫造) to describe the quality of most Hong Kong movies throughout the 1990s (Chan et al., 2010). This drop in the quality of local movies led to the desertion of cinemagoers. Second, a variant of the "Taiwan factor" attributes the Hong Kong film industry's decline to the slump in exports of its film products. Following a regulatory change in China in 1993 that excluded many co-productions from the Chinese market, Taiwan capital withdrew as quickly as it came (Chung, 2007, p. 363). Because of this abrupt drying up of foreign investment, the industry experienced a sharp turn during the latter half of the 1990s.

5. *Small domestic film market*: While the slump in exports contributes to the industry's downfall, some studies cite Hong Kong's small-scale domestic film market as a reason for the sag in foreign sales. Lee (2006b, p. 265) stresses that Hong Kong's domestic market is too small to support its film industry to compete effectively with other rising movie industries in East Asia. In a similar vein, Fu and Sim (2010) view Hong Kong as a case illustrating how a small domestic film market limits its film companies' ability to make movies that are "culturally transmissible". This is why, they stress, most of the films exported from Hong Kong are "kung-fu and gangster movies" as film companies rarely pursue "innovation beyond duplicating such themes … [and develop] more broad-appeal programs" (Fu & Sim, 2010, p. 138). Hence, the demand for Hong Kong movies in overseas markets stumbled.

These standard-definition explanations, advanced mostly by industry insiders and film critics, offer insights into the industry's decline. Yet, it remains unclear which of them are crucial in shaping its fate. For instance, one key fact about the downfall of Hong Kong's film industry is its suddenness. Except perhaps for the "Taiwan factor", none of these purported causes for its fall could account satisfactorily for the sudden reversal of the industry's fortunes. Relative to the plunge of Hong Kong movies in terms of their output and the box office from their 1993 peak, the challenge posed by Hollywood movies was actually more a consistent but relentless climb in the box-office shares. Likewise, piracy had already afflicted Hong Kong's film industry for some time during the 1980s (Booth, 2000). Changes in consumer tastes cannot be a key causal factor in explaining the sharp decline because tastes normally change slowly over time. Moreover, during the golden age of the industry over the 1980s, film critics had frequently levelled the charge of "hasty and unpolished productions" on Hong Kong movies (Teo, 2008).

The following section will address this puzzle by laying out the wrenching change in the Hong Kong film industry's fortunes during the early 1990s. Then it will delve into the relationships between the global distribution networks of the Hollywood majors and their local alliances in Hong Kong who availed imported movies to dominate the Hong Kong film market. Empirical evidence shows that the standard-definition narratives could not account satisfactorily for the rise and fall of Hollywood's and Hong Kong movies respectively. To forge a high-definition story, we argue further that it should be the larger institutional change in the film market leading to the downfall of the film industry.

2   REVISITING THE GOLDEN DECADE: THE RISE OF DISTRIBUTOR-LED PRODUCTION SYSTEM

The downfall of Hong Kong's film industry occurred in the early 1990s, but the "seeds" of this event were sowed back in the 1980s, the period most scholars recognize as a "golden age" for Hong Kong cinema. Before we delve into the industry's decline since the mid-1990s, we revisit the 1980s by delineating the institutional contours of the industry and film market setting the stage for the dramatic demise that followed. The boom decade in the industry corresponded with the emergence of what we call the "distributor-led production system" organized around several major film companies. Unlike their American counterparts, no legal regulation in Hong Kong prohibits film companies from integrating the processes of production, distribution, and exhibition "under one roof". The "majors" are commonly regarded as film companies dominating the industry through investing in and distributing movies on one hand, and operating or possessing their own theatre chains on the other (Chan, 2000).

Some scholars attribute the success of the 1980s to various "indigenous" factors, including both the supply of and the demand for local film products (Cheuk, 2008; Zhao, 2007). On the supply side, the rise of a "new wave" of young directors, many of whom received tertiary education in Hong Kong or in overseas film schools, and were trained in the television sector, resulted in a burst of local movies that resonated with the taste, or the quest for self-identity of Hong Kong cinema-goers during the 1970s and the 1980s (Fu & Desser, 2000; Teo, 1997).

On the demand side, as the baby-boom generation with its rising consumption power reached adolescence in the 1980s, a surging demand for entertainment, including cinema-going, boosted the box-office receipts of Hong Kong movies (Sui, 2009, p. 109). Due to this emergence of the "new wave" of directors along with the rising demand from the baby-boom generation for entertainment, the industry achieved remarkable success not only in its domestic market, but it also reaped prodigious profits from its distribution network in the region (Leung, 1993; Leung & Chan, 1997). With the highest per capita production in the world, and the second largest number of films exported in the early 1990s, the Hong Kong film industry was coined the "Hollywood of the East" or the "Asian Hollywood" (Stokes, 2007; Lam, 2007, pp. 60–61; Hammond, 2000; Stokes & Hoover, 1999, p. 17; Dannen & Long, 1997).

Although the spurt in both the supply of and the demand for local film products signify the commercial success of Hong Kong cinema, less attention has been devoted to why those "new-wave" directors had the chance to prove their worth during the 1970s and the 1980s. The structural factors, on the supply side, enabling those directors to make a successful ascent, are often overlooked in existing literature. Hence, this chapter proposes that the accession of the "new-wave" directors attested not only to their talent and ability but was also related to the conversion of the dominant mode of production in the Hong Kong film industry, thus giving these "new-wave" filmmakers an opportunity to prove their talents in a less-restricted environment, and leading to a new institutional model throughout the 1970s and the 1980s.

Besides, on the demand side, even though the baby-boom cohort would have boosted the rate of theatrical attendance, these potential audiences might not necessarily prefer to watch Hong Kong movies. Since the baby-boom generation, in general, has attained a higher level of education than their parents, they could be expected to show a higher degree of interest in imported movies in a foreign language (Leung, 1993, p. 61). As Curtin (2007) puts it:

> [T]his generation was more experienced with Western popular culture than with traditional Chinese culture and politics. Consequently, Hollywood movies and American music became quite popular in Hong Kong during the 1960s. (p. 43)

In this sense, "the quest for identity" might not be adequate for why the baby-boom cohort favoured local productions over foreign movies. This pinpoints that the inadequacy of the aforementioned "indigenous" factors in accounting for the success of the Hong Kong film industry in the 1970s and the 1980s. Thus, here we suggest a high-definition picture to situate the industry in a proper context. To this end, we will apply a sociological approach to elucidate the historical and institutional context of the Hong Kong film market and the interactions among film companies having shaped the path by which the local film industry travelled.

The *Hollywood studio system* (adopted by, among others, Warner Brothers, Twentieth-Century Fox and Paramount) was once a prevailing model in the movie business before the late 1940s. In a studio system, film production, distribution, and exhibition (screening) are all carried out in-house within the major film companies. By contrast, in a *distributor-driven model*, these tasks are performed by separate companies occupying different roles in an independent production system. While some film companies would forge alliances with one another, the distributors were central to the coalition in most cases. The major distributors of Hong Kong movies until the mid-1990s operated their own theatre chain by acquiring or allying with several theatres or cinemas. Those that did not follow a film studio system—almost all distributors except Shaw Brothers and Sil-Metropole—would look for producers and directors, or invest in some production companies, to shoot movies for them. In this fashion, besides carrying out the sales and marketing of the film products, the Hong Kong movie distributors were also the chief investors in most productions in the 1970s and the 1980s. The movies produced in this system would be screened in the theatre chains controlled by the distributors. Revenue received from the box office was used to cover the accrued expenses involved in the production, distribution, and exhibition of the movies.

Three major film companies dominated the Hong Kong film market over the 1980s, namely, Golden Harvest, Golden Princess, and D&B. Golden Harvest, established in 1971, was the first company that carried out this "distributor-led production system" in Hong Kong. The company started its business in film distribution and later operated its own chain of cinemas. Golden Harvest invested in several film production companies which in return supplied Golden Harvest with movies regularly. These movies were then shown in the theatre chain of Golden Harvest. Under the umbrella of Golden Harvest, many independent production companies sprouted throughout the 1970s and the 1980s. These included Hui's Film Production Co., Ltd., a production company directed by the renowned comedic actor and director Michael Hui (Xu Guan-wen, 許冠文); Bo Ho Films Co., Ltd., headed by a well-known martial-arts actor and director Samo Hung Kam-bo (Hong Jin-bao, 洪金寶); Golden

Way Films Ltd., led by a famous martial-arts actor and director Jackie Chan (Cheng Long, 成龍); Film Workshop Company Ltd., founded by famed director Tsui Hark (Xu Ke, 徐克) and his wife; and many others. These satellite production houses had made over four hundred movies for Golden Harvest, many of which were blockbusters and reaped huge profits for their parent company.

After the success of Golden Harvest, the distributor-led production system became the dominant practice in the Hong Kong film industry. Film companies entering the field during the 1980s also followed this system. Two of these companies, Golden Princess and D&B, rose to prominence by financing their own flock of independent production companies and screening their products. Golden Princess was the second largest film company with its market share slightly smaller than Golden Harvest's. It was established in 1980 and backed up by its parent company, Kowloon Development Company Ltd., a conglomerate with big investments in a vast range of infrastructural projects and public transport in Hong Kong, including The Kowloon Motor Bus Co. Ltd. (KMB). Similar to Golden Harvest, the company financed a bunch of independent production houses as its satellites, including Cinema City Enterprises Ltd., Always Good Film Company Ltd. Magnum Films Ltd., and many others (Chan, 2000, p. 643; Stokes, 2007, p. 155).

In line with Golden Harvest and Golden Princess, D&B also followed the "distributor-led production system". The company was set up in 1984 by Dickson Poon (Pan Di-sheng, 潘迪生), a businessman embarking on various trading businesses, including jewelleries, watches, and wearing apparels. D&B employed some directors to shoot movies in the first few years. However, the company stopped employing directors directly in the late 1980s; instead, it contracted with several independent directors for film production on a project basis. D&B hired its own producers to monitor all of its productions. Under the supervisions of these producers at the top, the company contracted with several independent directors for film production. Although D&B was engaged in the film business for only nine years (1984–1992), the shortest among the major film companies established from the 1970s to the 1980s, it produced and distributed over a hundred pictures, some of which turned out to be the yearly blockbusters. For instance, two of the company's productions in 1988 were the top two blockbusters of the year (*It's a Mad Mad World II* and *Heart to Hearts*) (Hong Kong Film Archive [HKFA], 2012a).

During the late 1980s these three major film companies dominated the Hong Kong film market not by actually owning the cinemas but by controlling them with exclusive exhibition deals. The "majors" requested the exhibitors who were scouting for movies to sign an exhibition contract. Each exhibition contract typically lasted for one to two years (Curtin, 2007, p. 53). The contract resembles an "exclusive deal" entailing that the exhibitors, or the cinema owners, screen exclusively the films provided by a major distributor within a certain period of time (Chan, 1985). Once it was signed, not only did the distributors acquire the "booking rights"[4] to control the exhibition blocks (the period in which each movie is screened), they also forbade the exhibitors to shop freely among other distributors for movies to screen (Leng et al., 1985). In this respect, the theatres could screen only the movies released by their "major" partners. Most cinema owners at the time accepted either willingly or reluctantly the exclusive exhibition deals offered by the "majors". Since most cinemas in Hong Kong over the 1980s were traditional theatres with only one to two screens, they could not screen a small number of movies at each turn. The theatrical setting as such blunted the bargaining power of the cinema owners for their exhibition blocks could be easily filled up by a major distributor. Consequently, the "majors" took advantage of the setting of traditional theatres and controlled the exhibition sector until the 1990s.

As shown in Table 6.1, Golden Princess allied with 47 theatres in 1984, controlling almost half (49.5 per cent) of the theatres in the market. This

Table 6.1 Theatrical possession of Golden Harvest, Golden Princess, and D&B, 1984–1989

Year	Golden Harvest		Golden Princess		D&B	
	Theatres allied	%[a]	Theatres allied	%[a]	Theatres allied	%[a]
1984	31	32.63	47	49.47	5	5.26
1985	37	35.58	32	30.77	22	21.15
1986	20	19.05	43	40.95	25	23.81
1987	27	23.48	48	41.74	24	20.87
1988	27	20.30	40	30.08	25	18.80
1989	23	19.66	38	32.48	21	17.95

Sources: Tabulations from cinematic advertisements in *Singtao* daily and *MingPao* daily, 1984–1989; Economic Information & Agency [EIA] (various years); Hong Kong Motion Picture Industry Association Limited [MPIA] (various years)

[a]Percentage share of theatres under their corresponding theatre chain in the total number of theatres of the year

---

[4] "Booking rights" refer to the right to control how often and how long a movie will be put on screen.

is followed by Golden Harvest possessing around one-third (32.6 per cent) of the theatres in the same year. When D&B was established in 1984, the company aligned with only five theatres. A year later, D&B expanded its theatre chain by co-opting over twenty theatres. In 1986, the theatrical possession of the company peaked at 23.8 per cent. On the whole, the three companies controlled approximately three-fourth of the theatres over the late 1980s. This made them the three major theatre chains in Hong Kong.

As each theatre chain requires at least 30 movies to put on screen each year (EIA, 1989, p. 168), there was a huge demand for films to fill up the exhibition blocks of each theatre chain. In this regard, after Golden Harvest entered the market and engaged in film production, the number of movies produced and released in Hong Kong climbed from 94 in 1971 to 103 in 1974 (HKFA, 2012b). When Golden Princess joined the competition, the total film outputs in Hong Kong spurted upwards by 8.3 per cent, climbing from 109 in 1979 to 118 in 1980. At the time D&B set up its theatre chain, the number rose moderately from 87 in 1984 to 89 in 1985, and reached a high of 116 in 1989. The three companies altogether produced over 50 movies each year and reaped around 40 per cent of the total box-office grosses during the late 1980s (HKFA, 2012a).

While these three major film companies gained a lion's share of the market, the film companies without any alliance with the "majors" could barely scrape by. They included the film companies that distributed and exhibited foreign movies. As Hong Kong's movies occupied most of the screens available in the market, the number of theatres exhibiting local movies exclusively climbed from 23 in 1970 to 27 in 1980, and even increased to 33 in 1982 after Golden Princess came into operation (Table 6.2). In this very year, the domestic box-office revenue for local movies exceeded that for foreign movies for the first time in the history of Hong Kong's cinema (see Fig. 6.1).

With fewer theatres exhibiting foreign movies, the box-office sales of imported films nose-dived while Hong Kong's movies outperformed the Hollywood blockbusters in their home market. The box-office grosses of imported films plunged from 1.1 billion H.K. dollars in 1971 to 855 million in 1979, and dipped further to 811 million in 1982 at constant prices (Table 6.3). By contrast, the box office of local movies surged during the same period, reaching a high of 1.6 billion in 1988 at constant prices. The

Table 6.2   Theatres in Hong Kong by exhibition of local movies or imported films, and both, 1970–1985

Year	Exhibited local movies exclusively		Exhibited imported movies exclusively		Exhibited both		Total number of theatres
	Number of theatres	%[a]	Number of theatres	%[a]	Number of theatres	%[a]	
1970	23	22.33	28	27.18	26	25.24	103
1971	14	N.A.	31	N.A.	32	N.A.	N.A.
1972	11	11.34	40	41.24	29	29.90	97
1973	34	N.A.	22	N.A.	14	N.A.	N.A.
1974	23	29.63	30	37.04	10	12.35	81
1975	22	26.19	32	38.10	8	9.52	84
1976	34	40.96	26	31.33	15	18.07	83
1977	23	N.A.	29	N.A.	16	N.A.	N.A.
1978	14	18.67	24	32.00	24	32.00	75
1979	16	20.00	18	22.50	26	32.50	80
1980	27	32.53	30	36.14	5	6.02	83
1981	29	35.37	24	29.27	23	28.05	82
1982	33	37.08	19	21.35	28	31.46	89
1983	48	53.33	14	15.56	22	24.44	90
1984	56	58.95	17	17.89	14	14.74	95
1985	39	37.50	14	13.46	45	43.27	104

Sources: Tabulations from cinematic advertisements in *Singtao* daily and *Mingpao* daily, 1970–1985; EIA (various years); MPIA (various years)

Notes: "N. A." denotes data are not available because of the deficient information on the total number of theatres in the corresponding years

Data reflect only the theatrical composition on June 30 and December 31 of each corresponding year

[a]The sum of the data in these three columns may be less than a hundred since there could be some theatres that were not open to business in the corresponding year

dominance of Hong Kong's movies in their domestic market is shown to have persisted throughout the 1980s, which signified the boom in the Hong Kong film industry.

3   THE FALL OF HONG KONG'S FILM INDUSTRY

The Hong Kong film industry fell from its peak since 1993, and the film market was dominated by imported movies thereafter. The reversal of fortune of Hong Kong's film industry and the return of imported films' dominance over Hong Kong was largely a result of the fall of the major film companies of the 1980s. In the following section we delineate how the restructuring of the cinema sector and the expansion of

Table 6.3 Screening and box-office grosses of local movies and imported films in Hong Kong, selected years

Year	Local movies		Imported films	
	Number of movies	Weighted box-office grosses[a] (in million HK$)	Number of films	Weighted box-office grosses[a] (in million HK$)
1971	94	535	441	1134
1973	96	610	335	924
1975	98	451	300	653
1977	88	573	321	947
1979	109	692	293	855
1982	99	1183	265	811
1984	87	1252	232	860
1986	86	1169	279	668
1988	115	1626	234	429

Sources: Chan (2000); Hong Kong Film Archive [HKFA] (2012a); MPIA (various years)

Notes: [a] Figures are weighted by the ticket price in each corresponding year, and are at constant 1997 prices

multiplex-cinema[5] circuits in Hong Kong led to the collapse of the "majors" and then fostered the conditions for Hollywood's distributors to align with the movie exhibitors in Hong Kong. This transformation was completed in three stages.

3.1   Stage One: The Rise of Newport

The restructuring of the Hong Kong cinema sector began in the late 1980s when a new film company, Newport, was established. The liberalization of China's film market since the late 1970s along with the lifting of martial law in Taiwan in 1987 hastened the flow of financial capital from film investors in Taiwan to China via Hong Kong.[6] The capital inflow

[5] Multiplex cinemas are different from the traditional theatres described earlier. Multiplex cinema is equipped with at least three screens or houses, with each house contains less than a thousand seats.

[6] Following China's economic reform in 1979, the Chinese government has gradually relaxed its tight control over the film industry. The government permitted foreign film companies to forge co-production partnerships with the Chinese film studios. When the Taiwan government lifted its martial law in 1987, there was an influx of financial capital from Taiwan to China via Hong Kong. By the early 1990s, co-production deals between film companies from Hong Kong, Taiwan, and China were exceptionally active. The movies produced in this way brought together capital from Taiwan, the film personnel from Hong Kong, and the sites or locations in and the manpower for film production from China. For instance, although Cinema City was a satellite production company of Golden Princess, many of its

from Taiwan gave birth to Newport Entertainment Co. Ltd. in 1988. Newport served as a "middleman" between foreign investors, mainly from Taiwan, and the independent production companies in Hong Kong (Lam, 2007, p. 60). Overseas investors wanting to invest in Hong Kong movies might pass their money to Newport. The company would then lend money to the production companies in Hong Kong.

The rise of Newport cut into the income stream of the pre-existing "majors". The owner of Newport was Chan Wing-mei (Chen Rong-mei, 陳榮美), a theatre owner whose cinemas were formerly allied with the pre-existing major film companies. When Chan established his theatre chain in the late 1980s, he wrested several theatres from the existing "majors". Six of the 21 theatres in Newport's theatre chain were formerly allied with D&B, four were tied-up with Golden Princess, and three with Golden Harvest (Chan, 1988).

While the establishment of Newport entailed the wresting of a considerable number of theatres from the "majors", each theatre chain in the market was comprised of fewer theatres than before. Assuming that a movie that is shown in more cinemas, on more screens, and for more days is more available for the public to know about, and *ceteris paribus*, has higher box-office sales, the cutback of the "majors'" theatrical possession would inevitably result in a sharp slump to their revenue. Before Newport was established, at least 20 theatres screened exclusively the movies Golden Harvest, Golden Princess, and D&B distributed in 1987.[7] After Newport came on the scene, however, only Golden Harvest could maintain the same number of theatres for the screening of its movies whereas the number of theatres allied exclusively with Golden Princess dropped approximately one-third (30.8 per cent) from 26 to 18. D&B faced a similar challenge. In 1987 D&B controlled 21 theatres but the number dipped to 15 in 1989. Although Golden Harvest still possessed around 20 theatres in the early 1990s, the number dropped gradually over the years. This provides clues as to why the box-office revenues of the three "majors" plummeted.

productions were financed by Long Shong Group, a film distributor in Taiwan (Liang, 1998, p. 124). Another Taiwan film distribution company, Scholar, had also invested in the movies produced by Win's Movie Production Company in Hong Kong. Several other film companies in Taiwan, such as New Ship, Hua Liang, Feng Ming, Chang Hong, and Upland Films Co. Ltd., also funded the film production companies in Hong Kong (Liang, 1998, p. 125).

[7] This information is drawn from the cinematic advertisements in *Singtao* daily and *Mingpao* daily. We compile the data from a sample of the two movies from each company that received the highest and the lowest box-office grosses in the respective year.

With fewer theatres under the "majors'" control, their income stream was trimmed. The revenues of Golden Harvest, Golden Princess, and D&B slumped by 27.8 per cent, 15.5 per cent, and 45.2 per cent respectively from 1987 to 1989 (Table 6.4). Before Newport's entry, Golden Harvest had 21.2 per cent of the market share, followed by Golden Princess (19.1 per cent), and D&B (12.7 per cent). After Newport entered the market, however, the market share of Golden Harvest plunged to 16.7 per cent, while Golden Princess's and D&B's market shares shrank to 17.6 per cent and 7.6 per cent respectively. In the early 1990s, the theatrical receipts as well as the market share of the three "majors" continued to fall significantly. The revenue for these "majors" was just slightly over half of what they earned before Newport was established.

Table 6.4 Theatrical receipts and market share of Golden Harvest, Golden Princess, D&B, and Newport, 1985–1995

Year	Golden Harvest (since 1971)		Golden Princess (1980–1995)		D&B (1984–1992)		Newport (since 1988)	
	At constant 1997 prices (in million HK$)	Market share %[a]	At constant 1997 prices (in million HK$)	Market share %[a]	At constant 1997 prices (in million HK$)	Market share %[a]	At constant 1997 prices (in million HK$)	Market share %[a]
1985	359.5	20.01	270.8	15.07	95.2	5.30	–	–
1986	355.2	19.34	274.0	14.92	224.2	12.21	–	–
1987	424.5	21.22	382.0	19.09	254.8	12.73	–	–
1988	454.3	22.10	258.8	12.59	204.8	9.97	28.5	1.38
1989	306.3	16.67	322.9	17.58	139.6	7.60	38.7	2.11
1990	261.2	14.51	258.4	14.36	119.7	6.65	166.3	9.24
1991	382.6	22.84	220.7	13.17	95.6	5.71	135.4	8.08
1992	329.1	19.12	240.9	13.99	12.0	0.70	170.6	9.91
1993	269.1	16.74	18.8	1.17	–	–	250.3	15.58
1994	203.3	16.43	39.5	3.19	–	–	22.2	1.79
1995	133.6	12.27	19.9	1.83	–	–	55.7	5.12

Sources: Chan (2000); HKFA (2012a); MPIA (various years)

Notes: The company's theatrical receipts are weighted by the ticket price in each corresponding year, and are at constant 1997 prices

[a]The company's share in total box-office grosses of both local movies and imported films

Given the much reduced profit gained from theatrical receipts, the major film companies had to make strenuous efforts to maintain their operations. When these "majors" could no longer afford the cost of maintaining a certain volume of movies for their theatre chains, some of them closed down their movie business while others changed their company's strategies.[8]

After D&B had shut down, the Louey family, the owners of Golden Princess, wound up their theatre chain in 1993 and ceased investing in film production. In the subsequent years, Golden Princess distributed only three movies before it shut down completely in 1996. Peter Yuk Wah Lam (Lin Xu-hua, 林旭華), a council member of the Hong Kong Motion Picture Industry Association Limited (MPIA), noted that the restructuring of the cinema sector followed by the establishment of Newport struck a nerve with the Louey family.[9] Before Newport came on the scene, Golden Princess controlled a considerable number of theatres allowing the company to maintain its profit margin during the 1980s. The owners bestowed a high degree of autonomy on the film directors and did not monitor closely how the filmmakers spent the money in their film projects as long as the movies turned out to be box-office successes. When Newport came into operation and wrenched some of the theatres from Golden Princess, however, Lam argued that the reduction of theatres in the company's theatre chains cut into its income stream. The owners then became frustrated with the way the filmmakers handled their books. One Louey family member who was an accountant even admitted that he found the bookkeeping practice of the filmmakers very confusing. As the core business of the family was running KMB, an anonymous industry executive stressed that movie business was not that important for them (Curtin,

---

[8] Stephen Shin (Xian Qi-ran, 冼杞然), the Executive Director of D&B, informed us during an interview that the company's owner, Dickson Poon (Pan Di-sheng, 潘迪生), planned to leave the film industry in 1992. As he put it, "One afternoon, Dickson called for a meeting with me. He told me in all seriousness that if the company could not control as many theatres as before, we won't be able to recoup film production costs. This is the first time I realized that the company might be shut down." When we asked whether this led the company to close down, he replied, "The company folded up abruptly at the end of 1992 mainly because we lost our theatre chain to Regal. D&B did not own the theatres; the theatres belonged to separate owners. In mid-1992 we noticed that the theatre owners who formerly allied with us refused to renew our contract because they turned to Regal … As we could not control the theatrical screening of our movies, Dickson said there was no point to keep investing such a large sum of money in this industry. He then made up his mind to close down the company" (Personal interview, 12 April 2012).

[9] Personal interview, conducted on 25 August 2011.

2007, pp. 64–65). Consequently, when the Louey family could no longer put up with "the industry's inability to institute transparent practices that might regularize production, distribution, and financing" (Curtin, 2007, p. 7), they folded Golden Princess in the mid-1990s.

3.2 Stage Two: The Mass Closure of Traditional Theatres[10]

After Golden Princess and D&B ceased operating, Golden Harvest became the last and the only major film company dominating the Hong Kong film market during the 1980s that still managed to survive. Although Golden Harvest has continued to carry on its business up to the present, in the late 1990s it rearranged its core business from investing in film production to distributing and showing foreign movies in Hong Kong. The company made this adjustment largely because the rising price of retail space in Hong Kong drove many traditional theatres formerly controlled by Golden Harvest to close down during the 1990s.

Since the 1980s, the price of retail space in Hong Kong had shot sky-high. Theatrical rents grew as much as 40 to 50 per cent per year in the 1980s (EIA, 1987, p. 165). The rent for some theatres was even 2.5 times that of the previous years' rent. As most of the major distributors of Hong Kong movies rented rather than bought a group of cinemas to build their theatre chain, they had to bear a huge rental cost in their exhibition business. Although some major distributors could afford the rent, fewer cinemas were available in the market. This is because in the 1990s the rising price of retail space drove many cinema owners to redevelop their properties for alternative uses and thus over 100 theatres closed down. The total number of theatres in Hong Kong shrank from 120 in 1990 to 79 in 1998, or by 34.2 per cent (MPIA, 1970–2007). Almost half (45.6 per cent) of the theatres were demolished and converted into shopping malls, commercial buildings, and private apartments (Cinema Treasures, n.d.; Lie, 2007). As the movie business became less lucrative than setting up shopping malls, commercial buildings, and private apartments, a lot of theatre owners took their curtain calls during the 1990s (Zheng, 1987).

Since most of the theatres controlled by Golden Harvest were demolished in the 1990s owing to the rising price of retail space, the theatrical receipts it received were hardly sufficient to recoup the cost of its film productions. In the mid-1990s, the number of theatres allied exclusively

---

[10] As noted earlier, in Hong Kong a theatre in traditional settings has only one to two screen(s) or house(s) with more than a thousand seats installed in each theatre.

with Golden Harvest was halved, plummeting from 21 to 11 between 1991 and 1995 (Fig. 6.3). In this period, the company's theatrical receipts shrank accordingly, diving from 382.6 million H.K. dollars to 133.6 million at constant prices (see Table 6.4).

Not only did the mass closure of traditional theatres affect Golden Harvest, it also brought about a restructuring of theatre chains in the Hong Kong film market. In 1992 Regal Films Co. Ltd. took over some of the theatres previously allied with D&B. In 1993 the Regal Circuit was divided into two by Raymond Wong, a partner of Regal who then founded Mandarin Films Limited. While the theatre chain of D&B was succeeded by Regal and Mandarin, the theatres under Golden Princess were merged

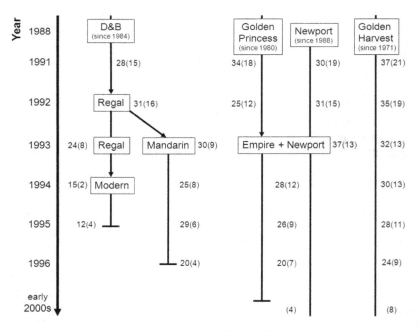

Fig. 6.3 Composition of theatre chains of major film companies since the 1990s. (Notes: Numbers with parentheses are the number of theatres that screened only the movies released by a major film company in the respective year. Numbers without parentheses refer to the number of theatres which each major film company mobilized for the screening of its movies in the year. The sum of numbers without parentheses should exceed the total number of theatres in the year because some theatres might have screened the movies released by different "majors" in the same year. Sources: Dannen & Long, 1997)

with Newport. When Golden Princess wound up its theatrical business in 1993, Chan Wing-mei, the owner of Newport, regained some of the theatres from Golden Princess (Chan, 1992), and set up the Empire Circuit, another theatre chain separated from the Newport Circuit.

The restructuring of theatre chains, however, did not make the "newcomers" (such as Regal, Mandarin, and Empire who took the place of the past "majors") better off but caught them in a vicious cycle. As the soaring price of retail space drove many theatre owners to close down their theatres and to redevelop their properties for alternative uses, the total number of theatres in the market fell noticeably. In this situation, the more "newcomers" tried to set up their theatre chain, the fewer theatres each film company controlled, and the more difficult they could achieve the economy of scale necessary for cost recovery. Consequently the number of theatres these companies possessed was much smaller than the "majors" did in the 1980s.

As shown in Fig. 6.3, when the Regal Circuit was established in 1992 it allied exclusively with 16 theatres while 31 theatres in total screened its movies. In that year, the company released 20 movies and earned 167 million H.K. dollars at constant prices from the box office (Table 6.5). After the split, however, half of its theatres joined Mandarin. The number of theatres fully controlled by Regal dropped from 16 to eight. With fewer theatres under its control, the total theatrical receipts from the Regal Circuit in 1993 slumped by 43.8 per cent to 93.9 million H.K. dollars at constant prices. When its owner, Steven Kit-sing Lo (Luo Jie-cheng 羅傑承), faced difficulty in recouping the huge cost involved (EIA, 1995, p. 155), he folded up his film business in May 1994.

Although another "newcomer", Modern Films Co. Ltd. (新一代), undertook Steven Lo's exhibition business after he relinquished his control over Regal Circuit (Fig. 6.3), the box-office performance of Modern's theatre chain was even worse than that of Regal's. In the second-half of 1994, only two theatres were allied exclusively with Modern while just 15 theatres in total were showing Modern's movies, a lot fewer than its competitors. With the fewest theatres among all theatre chains, Modern earned in 1994 only less than half (45.4 per cent) of the box-office revenue for Regal in the previous year (Table 6.5). In 1995 Modern's theatrical receipts dived a further 44 per cent. The financial situation of Modern was so precarious that the company lasted for only two years, shutting down in 1995 (EIA, 1996, p. 139).

Even though Mandarin's theatre chain surpassed Regal and Modern in the box office, the company faced the same problem. The number of

Table 6.5   Film outputs and box-office grosses of Regal, Mandarin, and Modern, 1992–1996

Year	Regal (1992–1994)		Mandarin (1993–1996)		Modern (1994–1995)	
	Film outputs	Box office at constant 1997 prices[a] (in million HK$)	Film outputs	Box office at constant 1997 prices[a] (in million HK$)	Film outputs	Box office at constant 1997 prices[a] (in million HK$)
1992	20	167.0	–	–	–	–
1993	19	93.9	23	154.6	–	–
1994	7	32.3	16	128.8	13	42.6
1995	–	–	17	70.1	13	23.8
1996	–	–	11	41.8	–	–

Sources: Chan (2000); HKFA (2012a); MPIA (various years)

[a]Figures are weighted by the ticket price in each corresponding year, and are at constant 1997 prices

theatres under Mandarin was much smaller than those under its competitors. While Newport and Empire, the largest-scale theatre chain at the time, allied exclusively with 13 theatres in 1993, Mandarin had only nine theatres (Fig. 6.3). In 1996 the number of theatres controlled fully by Mandarin was further reduced to four, leading to a box-office revenue that was about only a quarter (27 per cent) of that in 1993 (Table 6.5). As Mandarin could not afford the operational cost of its exhibition business (EIA, 1997, p. 96), it closed down its theatre chain in late 1996 albeit the company still engaged in film production in subsequent years.

The rising price of retail space stymied not only Golden Harvest and the foregoing "newcomers"; it also stunted the development of Newport. As discussed earlier, in 1993 Chan Wing-mei, the owner of Newport, regained some theatres from Golden Princess after the latter petered out, and set up the Empire Circuit (Fig. 6.3), a sister company of Newport (Chan, 1992, p. 42). Although Chan's two Circuits comprised the largest number of theatres, the soaring price of retail space drove many of his allied theatres to shut down. While there were around 12 theatres knocked down every year during the 1990s (MPIA, 1970–2007), the total number of theatres in the Newport and Empire Circuits plunged from 37 to 20 in just three years after Chan took over Golden Princess's theatre chain in 1993. With fewer theatres, its box-office revenue dropped sharply by 81.6 per cent between 1993 and 1996.[11]

[11] Same data sources as Table 6.4.

The number of cinemas under Newport fell from 21 at its inception (Chan, 1988, p. 4) to just four in 2009 (Fig. 6.3). In brief, owing to the rising price of retail space, many distributors of Hong Kong movies controlled fewer cinemas than before so that they could hardly achieve the economy of scale necessary for cost recovery. While some film company owners, including those of Golden Princess, D&B, Regal, and Modern, wound up their movie business, others such as Golden Harvest stopped engaging in film production. The collapse and restructuring of the major film companies that had dominated the Hong Kong film market during the 1980s marked the demise of the "distributor-led production system" in Hong Kong.

3.3   Stage Three: The Rise of Multiplex Cinemas

The alliances between the film exhibitors in Hong Kong and the distributors of foreign movies hastened the downfall of Hong Kong movies. As noted earlier, some major distributors of Hong Kong movies left the field by the mid-1990s. Other film companies curtailed their investment in film productions because of the soaring price of retail space that drove the theatres they controlled to vanish throughout the 1990s. As a result, traditional theatre (with only one to two screens per establishment) chains vanished during the 1990s, multiplex-cinema circuits with multiple screens within a single complex mushroomed concurrently in Hong Kong.

Multiplex-cinema circuits have come to occupy a lion's share of the Hong Kong film market. The four circuits that have dominated the film market since the mid-1990s are the Broadway circuit,[12] UA cinemas,[13] Golden Harvest,[14] and the Multiplex Cinema Limited (MCL).[15] They

---

[12] Broadway's first theatre was established in 1949. The company converted its theatre to a multiplex cinema in 1987.

[13] UA is the first among the four major multiplex circuits to set up multiplex cinema in Hong Kong. The first UA cinema was set up in 1985 in Shatin, a suburb in Hong Kong. It contained six screens and houses.

[14] From the early 2000s, Golden Harvest withdrew from film production and focused on its distribution and exhibition business. The company made this adjustment largely because its theatrical possession was not large enough to achieve the economy of scale needed for cost recovery once some multiplex exhibitors, such as Broadway and UA, have grabbed a lion's share of the cinemas in Hong Kong since the late 1990s. In this case, the company converted its theatre chain into multiplex-cinema circuit, and began to screen the movies released by any film companies.

[15] The parent company of MCL is Intercontinental Film Distributors (HK) Ltd. (IFDL). IFDL distributes foreign movies in Hong Kong. Before the establishment of MCL, IFDL rented several traditional theatres for movie screenings.

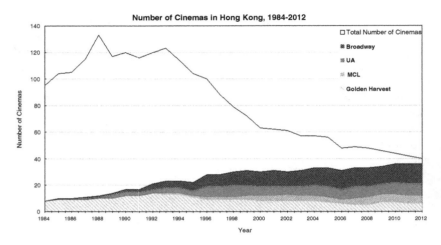

Fig. 6.4 Number of cinemas in Hong Kong, 1984–2012. (Sources: Booth, 2000; Buck, 1992)

reaped altogether almost 80 per cent of the box office in the late 2000s (Ming Pao, 2007). Broadway is one of these cinema circuits that had expanded rapidly during the 1990s. The number of cinemas and screens in the Broadway circuit soared from five cinemas with 16 screens in 1993 to 11 cinemas with 49 screens in 1999, whereas UA, the second-largest cinema circuit in Hong Kong, had eight cinemas with 36 screens in 1999 (Fig. 6.4). In the late 2000s, the two circuits dominated the exhibition sector by owning over 20 cinemas and about 100 screens in all. They are followed by Multiplex Cinema Limited (MCL) which expanded from one cinema with two screens at its inception in 1993 to six cinemas with 38 screens in 2012. Golden Harvest came forth as it began to convert its theatre chain into a multiplex-cinema circuit from the mid-1990s. In the late 1990s, almost half of its cinemas were converted into multiplex. In 2012 Golden Harvest had 26 screens in its circuit, with five of its six cinemas in multiplex settings.

While multiplex cinemas have become the standard in most film markets, the transformation of Hong Kong's cinema sector provided an opportunity for the distributors of foreign movies to co-opt the exhibitors in Hong Kong and make a comeback into the Hong Kong film market. While multiplex cinemas had gradually replaced the theatre chains of the distributors of Hong Kong movies, most of the multiplex exhibitors at the time faced difficulty in finding movies to screen. Although the theatrical setting of multiplex cinemas allows the exhibitors to put a variety of movies on the screens at a turn, the exhibitors could suffer a huge loss if they do not have enough movies to fill their exhibition blocks. The multiplex exhibitors thus have to cope with the shortage of movies. They could not rely on the distributors of Hong Kong movies because most of the major distributors had already ceased investing in film productions or had even wound up their movie business for the reasons presented earlier.

Under this circumstance, the distributors of Hollywood movies took advantage of the transformation in the Hong Kong film industry and successfully co-opted the multiplex exhibitors in Hong Kong. Columbia TriStar, for example, cooperated with EDKO, the distribution arm of Broadway circuit since the 1990s. Buena Vista, the distribution arm of Walt Disney, allied with Intercontinental Film Distributors (HK) Ltd. (IFDL), the parent company of Multiplex Cinema Limited (MCL). In 2006 IFDL acquired the "Hong Kong distributorship for UIP's[16] Paramount Pictures and Dreamworks Animation products".[17] Although UA does not ally with any Hollywood studio, it has its own distribution arm, Lark Films Distribution, to arrange screenings of imported films in its circuit.[18] When Golden Harvest ceased to invest in film production during the 2000s, it made use of its distribution arm, Panasia, to acquire the distribution rights of foreign movies. These movies would then be shown in Golden Harvest's cinemas.

Unlike the old theatre owners, the multiplex exhibitors are omnivores relying on both the distributors of Hollywood movies and the local film companies for their film supply. Also, they are no longer controlled by the major distributors of Hong Kong movies. Before multiplex cinemas became popular in Hong Kong during the 1990s, the major distributors of Hong Kong movies were able to control the cinema sector owing to the setting of the theatres discussed earlier. The restructuring of Hong Kong's cinema sector has however changed the relations of power between the movie exhibitors and the distributors of locally-made movies. As the number of screens in a cinema determines how many movies it can show at

---

[16] United International Pictures (UIP) is a joint venture that handles the overseas distribution of movies from several Hollywood studios, such as Paramount, Metro-Goldwyn-Mayer (MGM), United Artists, Universal, and DreamWorks.

[17] See Intercontinental Film Distributors (HK) Limited (n.d.).

[18] See Lark Group (n.d.).

each turn and thus the capacity of the exhibitor, cinemas with more screens are more flexible in arranging their movie screenings. Since the multiplex cinemas in Hong Kong are equipped with at least three screens or houses, these cinemas could show a relatively large number of movies from different film distributors at each turn. Multiplex exhibitors are therefore more capable of negotiating with the film distributors for better terms in making the exhibition deals. For this reason, multiplex exhibitors differ from traditional theatre owners in that they have a great deal of bargaining power over the film distributors in Hong Kong, and they did not agree to comply with any "exclusive exhibition deals". The distributors of Hong Kong movies, henceforth, could no longer control the movie screenings.

While the exhibition blocks[19] were previously controlled by the major distributors of local movies, now it is the multiplex companies that decide when and what movie(s) is/are screened in which house(s) of their circuits, and the multiplex exhibitors are not constrained by the major distributors of Hong Kong movies. These exhibitors could reserve favourable exhibition blocks for the imported films distributed by their allies, whereas the production companies of Hong Kong movies no longer benefit from the block-booking preferential treatment offered by the exhibitors. Foreign movies hence came to dominate the Hong Kong film market after 1997 (see Fig. 6.1). The multiplex exhibitors together with their distribution arms have released and screened more and more imported films in Hong Kong. In 2006, the theatrical release of foreign movies was three times higher than that of the local movies in the Hong Kong film market.[20] Of the 226 movies screened in Hong Kong in 2006, 172 were imported films while only 54 were locally produced (HKFA, 2012b). The number of local movies exhibited in 2006 was just one-third (33.1 per cent) of the number exhibited in 1999.

The surge of imported films shown in Hong Kong also resulted in their rising box-office share of the market. The theatrical receipts of imported films have outperformed those of Hong Kong movies since 1997, a trend that has continued up to the present. From 2003 to 2006, imported films recorded a 40 per cent growth in their box-office grosses, climbing from 485.9 million H.K. dollars to 685.8 million, whereas the box-office grosses of Hong Kong movies dropped from 417.8 million H.K. dollars to 290.3

[19] As noted earlier, exhibition blocks refer to the period in which each movie is screened in a cinema.
[20] Same data sources as Fig. 6.1.

million, or by 30.5 per cent.[21] No wonder film critics and commentators, and even industry insiders, claim that the Hong Kong film industry is already a "sunset" industry (Chan, 2006; Chung, 2007; Lee, 2006a).

4 HOLLYWOOD OF THE EAST NO MORE? REFLECTIONS ON THE STANDARD-DEFINITION EXPLANATIONS

So far, we have identified a series of changes taken place in the cinema sector that altered the market order of Hong Kong's film industry in the early 1990s, namely, the rise of Newport, a challenger for the major film companies, and the mass closure of traditional theatres, to be replaced by multiplex cinemas. These changes triggered off a restructuring in the exhibition sector and led to the decline of the domestic film industry. In the following, we shall evaluate the relative importance of the standard-definition explanations for the industry's decline and incorporate them into our analysis to reconstitute a narrative of the vicissitudes of Hong Kong's film industry.

While some studies contend that the inflow of foreign capital investment from Taiwan resulted in the overreliance on pre-sales in the Hong Kong film industry, we hold a different view. Foreign capital was a significant source of finance for Hong Kong movies, yet it led to a paradoxical result that plunged the industry into a sharp decline through spawning Newport, a new and significant challenger for the existing major film companies in the late 1980s since it wrested a considerable number of theatres from the "majors". Each theatre chain in the market henceforth comprised fewer theatres than before. With fewer theatres under their control, the "majors" were hard pressed to recoup their film production costs. This led to the winding up of two "majors", namely, Golden Princess and D&B, and gave rise to the entry of other "newcomers" who set off the cinema sector's second wave of restructuring. Hence, foreign capital was an exogenous shock to the field as it altered the power relations among the film companies in Hong Kong; its role is not necessarily the one described in the conventional accounts.

As noted earlier, some studies attribute the decline of Hong Kong's film industry to the slump in exports of its film products and also to the small size of the domestic film market. We found this claim doubtful on several grounds. Despite the small-scale domestic market, Hong Kong's film industry experienced its heyday in the 1970s and the 1980s. Its film

---

[21] Same data sources as Fig. 6.1.

outputs climbed steadily and even out-grossed the imported movies from Hollywood at the domestic box office. It was coined as the "Hollywood of the East" since its market share in some countries even matched with that of Hollywood (Dannen & Long, 1997; Stokes & Hoover, 1999; Hammond, 2000; Stokes, 2007). It would be grossly "unfair" to blame the small scale of Hong Kong's film market for its fateful decline.

While triad intrusion and video piracy are oft-cited explanations for the industry's decline, the distraction they purportedly caused to the industry might be overstated. We do not intend to claim triad intrusion and video piracy were innocuous, but we suggest that they did not account for the downfall of Hong Kong's film industry for two reasons. First, as pointed out by experts in triad studies, the triads sometimes perform a "service" to an industry or the local economy (Gambetta, 1993; Chu, 2000). Most film projects in Hong Kong depended heavily on private equity and angel capital, namely, affluent individuals who provide capital for a film business. This pattern of film finance is understandable given that the Hong Kong government had no policy to support the financing of film projects until the late 1990s (Lie, 2007) while most commercial banks in Hong Kong concentrate on trade finance and are notoriously conservative (Chiu et al., 1997). Even the industrialists who enjoyed their golden days in the 1960s constantly complained about the reluctance of the banks to finance their production and expansion (Chiu, 1994). The same situation is evident in the Hong Kong film industry. Given this situation, some anonymous insiders contend that the triads were actually the "dark knights" financing many film projects in Hong Kong throughout the 1980s and the 1990s. Since triads are always seeking places for money-laundering, film production houses with "casual" accounting practices could be an ideal place for triads to invest (Curtin, 2007, p. 74). Moreover, the triads provided "location services" for filmmakers shooting movies in public areas. These "services" included an effort to ensure the "cooperation of the shopkeepers and the people who live" in the area (Curtin, 2007, p. 72). In these respects, triads could have "contributed" to the Hong Kong film industry.

Second, the decline of the industry should not be attributed to the "piracy problem" as piracy existed almost a decade prior to the decline of Hong Kong movies circa the mid-1990s. Since the late 1980s, the widespread distribution of pirated copies of movies in the form of video cassettes or Video Home System (VHS) in Asia has already menaced the worldwide distribution of Hollywood movies (Buck, 1992; Darlin, 1992). In Hong Kong, even industry insiders acknowledge that piracy has been a problem ever since video copies of Hong Kong movies became available for rental around the 1980s (Booth, 2000). This period, however, was the "golden age" of the Hong Kong film industry as the film outputs in Hong Kong climbed steadily and even surpassed the imported movies from Hollywood in the domestic box office. Besides, as video piracy of Hong Kong movies and imported films existed during the 1990s, piracy should have affected Hollywood's and Hong Kong movies more or less equally in the film market. If this is the case, why then did Hong Kong movies lose turf to Hollywood and why could the latter achieve a remarkable success in the Hong Kong film market? It follows that piracy should not be taken as the root cause of the industry's decline although it could have harmed the film market to some degree (Wang, 2003; De Vany & Walls, 2007; Dejean, 2009).

Changes in consumption patterns as a result of the proliferation of alternative entertainment media have often been mentioned as a cause of the calamity experienced by the Hong Kong film industry during the 1990s. These changes, however, did not lead directly to the decline of the industry. Although Leung (1999) found cinema-going to be a less popular choice of media consumption among young people in Hong Kong, she herself highlighted that over the 1990s, "[s]urprisingly, young people ... visited cinema more frequently than before". Leung's findings are supported by the box-office figures. As shown earlier in Fig. 6.1, the total theatrical receipts in the Hong Kong film market dived steeply over the 1990s. In the midst of the freefall, the box-office revenue of locally-made movies shrank at a much faster pace than that of the imported films. While the box-office grosses of Hong Kong movies plummeted monotonically from 1993 onwards, the box office of foreign movies grew steadily.

An implication is: even if the proliferation of alternative entertainment media changed the consumption pattern of some Hong Kong cinemagoers, many people still visited cinemas yet few of them watched Hong Kong movies. This points to a key question about the root causes of the decline of Hong Kong's film industry, particularly why cinemagoers "preferred" to watch imported films rather than locally-made movies after 1993. We address this puzzle in the following.

Some studies contend that imported films, notably Hollywood's movies, have dominated the Hong Kong film market because of their advanced filmmaking technologies. This helps the movies to overcome cultural barriers abroad and attract overseas audiences. Despite Hollywood's comparative advantage, we have showed that it is the institutional settings of the film industries in receiving countries determining whether Hollywood could expand its dominance over foreign film markets. Hollywood's successful invasion of the Hong Kong market since the 1990s largely depended on the re-alignment between the local multiplex exhibitors and the distributors of foreign movies. As early as the 1980s when the old market order prevailed such that most theatres were controlled by the major distributors of Hong Kong movies, the market share of Hollywood's movies was much smaller than that of the local movies. In the 1990s, however, the rising price of retail space in Hong Kong drove many cinema owners to redevelop their properties for alternative uses, for example, to build shopping malls, commercial buildings, or private apartments. Having fewer cinemas, the major distributors could hardly achieve the economy of scale necessary for cost recovery. The owners of some major distribution companies therefore wound up their movie business and left the industry by the mid-1990s.

The downfall of the major distributors of Hong Kong movies provided an opportunity for the distributors of foreign movies to co-opt the exhibitors in Hong Kong. After multiplex cinemas had replaced traditional theatres, the multiplex exhibitors controlled the exhibition blocks, namely, when and what movies could be screened in the cinema. This restructuring in the cinema sector provided the distributors of foreign movies an opportunity to ally with the multiplex exhibitors. But for the rising price of retail space driving most traditional theatres to go bust, multiplex exhibitors might not be able to seize control of the exhibition blocks of Hong Kong movies and Hollywood's film companies could not co-opt a majority of exhibitors in Hong Kong. Owing to these alliances, Hollywood's blockbusters came to be widely screened in Hong Kong since the 1990s. In this vein, it was the alignment between the multiplex exhibitors in Hong Kong and the distributors of imported films, including the Hollywood film companies, on the one hand, and the rising price of retail space, on the other, that led to the mass closure of traditional theatres and the restructuring of the Hong Kong cinema sector. Figure 6.5 summarizes the situation where imported films have dominated the retail space whereas most Hong Kong movies were pulled from the screen after a short period of time or did not have a chance of theatrical release thereafter.

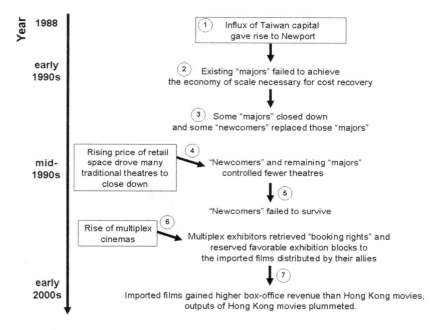

Fig. 6.5 Key incidents leading to the downfall of Hong Kong's Film Industry during the 1990s

5 CONCLUSION

Hong Kong was once one of the world's largest movie exporters. It was a production hub of movies in Asia prior to its decline in the 1990s (Leung & Chan, 1997). As noted earlier, Hong Kong's film industry was coined as the "Hollywood of the East" since its market share in some countries even matched with that of Hollywood. However that may be, our analysis shows that the industry became enfeebled after 1993. Its revenue from exports plummeted from one billion HK dollars in 1991 to 507.4 million in 1998 (Chan, 2000, p. 92; Hong Kong Trade Development Council [HKTDC], 2001, p. 10; Census and Statistics Department, n.d., various years). In 2010, its overseas sales remained at its nadir at 125 million HK dollars (Census and Statistics Department, n.d., various years), testifying to the closing of Hong Kong's "Asian Hollywood" eminence.

To cope with the industry's downfall, many Hong Kong's filmmakers expanded into the Chinese market by engaging in co-productions with the Mainland. Chan and Fung (2011) refer to the co-productions as a form of "structural hybridization" that can be understood as the collaboration between Hong Kong's and China's film companies and personnel in various domains, such as "management, investment, scriptwriting, shooting, artists and talent composition, organization of the filming crew, post-production, marketing efforts and strategies" (p. 80). Co-production deals seem to have provided a short respite for the Hong Kong film industry because according to CEPA, the movies that are jointly produced by Hong Kong and the Mainland are treated equally in terms of distribution as the movies made in the Mainland. While the Chinese government imposed an import quota of 34 films per year, Mainland-Hong Kong co-productions are exempted from the quota restrictions. They were shielded from competitions with foreign movies, including Hollywood's blockbusters, for distribution in China. Practitioners from Hong Kong, in particular film directors, producers, actors and actresses, thus sought to gain wider market access and to approach potential investors for their movies in the Mainland by means of co-production.

Understanding the division of labour between Hong Kong and China in co-production, Fung and Erni (2013) identifies three modes of cooperation characterizing the power relations among the personnel. He refers to China's role in first model as a "controller" of the co-production. Companies in the Mainland possess a great deal of power in the project as they take charge of the production and distribution. Hong Kong's actors and actresses are cast but producers from Hong Kong do not involve in the production. Hence, these projects just benefited the Hong Kong performers who may gain popularity among the Chinese audience. Hong Kong's producers play a leading role in the second type of co-production. They oversee the production whereas their Chinese partners become an "abettor" assisting them in gaining permission from the Chinese authorities for access to the Chinese market. These movies and TV programmes are usually shot in China, but they involve actors and actresses from both sides of the border. In the third form of co-production, Hong Kong and China are both the "co-producers" who take part in the production equally. They also share the profits from sales on a more or less equal basis.

The advent of Mainland-Hong Kong co-productions, however, did not come as a panacea for the Hong Kong film industry. Despite the preferential treatments under CEPA, the role of Hong Kong's filmmakers has turned gradually to be of subordinate importance in the production process. As Yu Dong—the CEO of a leading movie distribution company in China—put it, nowadays Hong Kong plays a less significant role in the Chinese film industry as many of its filmmakers are just assisting the film directors from the Mainland to make movies. Most of the movies are based on stories written by the Mainland scriptwriters whereas the Hong Kong personnel's involvement in the project is minimal (see Chu, 2015, p. 111). Chu (2013) describes this trend as a situation where Hong Kong's filmmakers are no longer an essential player; they are just "commissioned to produce films of Mainland themes and stories" (p. 111) and thus do not have much of the authority to control the project. This suggests that the model characterizing China as a "controller" in the co-production, as discussed earlier, has become prominent in the field.

While Hong Kong's filmmakers seem to be losing out on their control of the co-production, the dwindling of Hong Kong's film industry has attracted considerable attention from scholars. Many studies have shed light on how Hong Kong's filmmakers sought to secure support from the Mainland investors by striking a balance between compliance with China's censorship regulations and the freedom of expression in film production (see Teo, 2008; Yeh, 2010; Pang, 2011; Szeto & Chen, 2011; Chan, 2013). Central to their observation is the dilemma between the preservation of some features of Hong Kong movies that might have contravened China's film censors and the filmmakers' compliance with the censorship in order to gain access to the Chinese market. This dilemma, as Szeto and Chen (2012) argue, led to the vanishing of Hong Kong's "localness" in its film products, as most of which are co-productions that aimed at the Mainland audiences.

Film critics and commentators have raised a similar concern about the decline of Hong Kong cinema (see Wong, 2008; Zhang, 2008). Guangzhou's *The South Metropolis Daily*, for example, made a cover story in 2010 to mourn for the absent of Hong Kong's characteristics in co-productions. In a review published by the Hong Kong Film Critics Society (2013) of the Hong Kong movies made in 2012, the critics claimed that Hong Kong's film directors are too concerned about the box-office returns in China that are ten times of the Hong Kong box office (p. 248). This provides clues as to why most of the co-productions became less attractive to Hong Kong's moviegoers as they are catered to the Mainland audiences. The result is that the Hong Kong film industry has become increasingly concentrated with a large number of movies targeted at mainland China whereas the Hong Kong film market are of less concern to the filmmakers.

Is there a solution for reviving the Hong Kong film industry? *Bloomberg Businessweek* seeks to answer this question through interviews with two Hong Kong film directors—Chun-chun Wong (黃真真) and Johnnie To (杜琪峰) (Lee & Yue, 2015). The article explores the ways Hong Kong's filmmakers could cope with the Chinese censors without compromising much on the movie content and removing the elements they wanted to incorporate into the film. Its observation is more or less concurrent with Chu's (2015) argument—the cooperation between Hong Kong and China cannot be characterized by the dichotomy between the "big-budget Mainlandized inauthentic co-productions" and the "small-budget local authentic Hong Kong movies." Instead, these studies suggest that Mainland-Hong Kong co-productions can actually "both be making money and culturally significant" (p. 119).

The recommendations offered in the past studies are highly suggestive but they focus mainly on film production, in particular how the Hong Kong filmmakers could overcome the Chinese censorship and tap the Mainland film market. The Chinese market undeniably has great potential. It is explicable that most Hong Kong's film companies have shifted their market focus to China, giving priority to the Mainland audiences. However, as Chan and his colleagues (2010) point out, "does this mean that all future hopes for the Hong Kong film industry rest with the China market?" (p. 78). Not necessarily. Chan et al. (2010) highlight the risk factors that remained in entering the Chinese film market, such as the "unpredictable changes in policy, government intervention, and censorship". These factors still caused reservation for Hong Kong's filmmakers to rely solely on advancing into the Chinese market.

Given this circumstance, a possible way to revitalize the Hong Kong film industry is to capitalize on what the industry has already achieved and to develop its competitive edge on a new platform. Without doubt, China's film market is one such platform. Yet helping Chinese movies to penetrate overseas market through international film trade could be an alternative way out of an impasse. After shedding much of its production side, therefore, further studies are encouraged to delve into the expertise of Hong Kong's film industry practitioners in international distribution and networking in order to explore in greater depth the competitive edge of Hong

Kong's film industry in globalization. For instance, among the best-selling co-productions, such as *Hero* (2002), *House of Flying Daggers* (2004), *Curse of the Golden Flowers* (2006), *Lust, Caution* (2007), and *True Legend* (2010), Hong Kong's EDKO Films Ltd. contributed to these projects by promoting international sales and drawing in support from overseas investors, whereas its Mainland partners took charge of the production.

Besides, Hong Kong's talents have proven their competitive edge in China of having high market sensitivity and rich experiences in film distribution and international marketing. For example, veterans from Hong Kong, such as Nansun Shi (施南生), Jeffrey Chan (陳永雄), Yam-chi Chu (朱任之) and many others, are senior executives of the distribution arm of the leading film companies in China. This suggests that Hong Kong's film companies and practitioners have assumed a brokerage role in film distribution and financing that fuelled growth of China's film industry. Hong Kong's competitive advantage in international trade, film promotion and networking enabling Chinese movies to tap into global exhibition outlets are areas that Hong Kong remains competitive. Further studies are thus encouraged not to stick exclusively to an analysis of the "revival" of local Hong Kong film production but take a broader view of the possibilities by which the industry can flesh out its role as a key broker for China's film distribution. This area of research deserves greater scrutiny than it has received thus far.

All in all, the development of Hong Kong's film industry presents a noteworthy case of how regional and national politics are pertinent to the restructuring of Hong Kong economy. The opening of China's film market and the lifting of martial law in Taiwan during the early 1990s constituted a structural condition that allowed market players to develop new practices and conventions. This led to a new market order that allowed Hollywood exporters to capitalize on their competitive advantages and made a successful return to Hong Kong. This case study thus contributes to the economic sociology of Hong Kong studies in two aspects: first, it illustrates how economic restructuring can be driven by exogenous forces at the global or regional level and mediated by the interactions among market players at the national level. Second, it accentuates the importance of the interplay between globally-oriented actors, namely, the Hollywood exporters in this study, and the locally-embedded actors—the film distributors and exhibitors in Hong Kong, to our understanding of market transformations. By putting Hong Kong studies in a sociological perspective, we could develop a high-definition understanding of the history of Hong Kong society that goes beyond the most common-sense narratives and conventional accounts.

Similar to the larger economy, the Hong Kong story in films is one of fast boom and slow demise. A combination of favourable global and regional conditions with local institutional settings contributed to a golden period in the 1980s. Nevertheless, internal crisis of the 1990s coupled with the opening up of the mainland market caused the Hong Kong film industry to mutate into a mainland-oriented form. Very much the same as the local manufacturing industry, the result is an up-rooted sector that catered primarily for the need of the mainland market. Although the logic of cultural production may be different from material ones, what we observe in Hong Kong is the stagnation of both sectors and further dis-embededdness from the local context. As in many other aspects of Hong Kong life, the gradual integration with the mainland has led to many challenges that both the governments and the community have struggled to keep up with.

APPENDIX

Table 6.6 Screening, box-office grosses, and market share of imported films in Hong Kong, 1971–2010

Year	Local movies		Imported films		Market share of imported films
	Number	Box office[a]	Number	Box office[a]	
		(in million HK$)		(in million HK$)	(%)
1971	94	5.7	441	12.2	68
1972	99	9.2	422	15.4	62.6
1973	96	11.2	335	17	60.2
1974	103	11.8	285	20.2	63.2
1975	98	10.2	300	14.8	59.2
1976	95	13.9	283	17.1	55
1977	88	16.2	321	26.8	62.3
1978	99	22.9	301	28.8	55.7
1979	109	30.1	293	37.2	55.3
1980	118	48.1	278	51.3	51.6
1981	108	72.5	289	72.6	50.1
1982	99	133.8	265	91.7	40.7
1983	95	149.7	176	61.2	29
1984	87	221.4	232	152	40.7
1985	89	248.7	226	103.6	29.4
1986	86	269.9	279	154.4	36.4
1987	76	345	290	147.1	29.9
1988	115	488.5	234	129	20.9
1989	116	459.4	351	197	30

Year	Local movies		Imported films		Market share of imported films
	Number	Box office[a]	Number	Box office[a]	
		(in million HK$)		(in million HK$)	(%)
1990	120	537.3	222	268.6	33.3
1991	135	634.3	384	187.6	22.8
1992	175	867.5	294	218.3	20.1
1993	187	861.7	273	308.8	26.4
1994	143	790.5	318	352.7	30.9
1995	143	700	337	507.8	42
1996	108	632.4	312	540.2	46.1
1997	86	556.3	383	617.3	52.6
1998	85	440.4	370	567.7	56.3
1999	163	351.1	281	520.2	59.7
2000	144	366.1	195	507.5	58.1
2001	119	427.9	190	544.6	56
2002	91	331	195	496.5	60
2003	77	384	169	414.1	51.9
2004	84	355.6	170	485.3	57.7
2005	66	274.5	177	569.4	67.5
2006	54	244.8	172	624.2	71.8
2007	67	204.6	N.A.	772.7	79.1
2008	67	240.2	N.A.	838.4	77.7
2009	65	251.2	N.A.	900.3	78.2
2010	77	276	N.A.	1063	79.4

Sources:1. 1971–1999 number of movies imported into Hong Kong: Chan (2000, p. 91)

2. 2000–2006 number of movies imported into Hong Kong and 2001–2002 box-office takings: MPIA (1970–2007)

3. 1971–2010 Number of film outputs in Hong Kong: HKFA (2012b)

4. 1971–1989 box-office takings: Chan (2000, p. 92)

5. 1990–2000 box-office takings: HKTDC (2001, p. 10)

6. 2003–2010 box-office takings: Census and Statistics Department (n.d.) (various years)

Notes: [a] Box-office figures are weighted by the Consumer Price Index (CPI) in each corresponding year, and are at constant 2010 prices. This study used General Consumer Price Index in 1971–1974 and CPI(B) in 1975–2010. [c.f. Census and Statistics Department, 1971–2011]

"N.A." denotes data that are not available

Local movies refer to the films produced by any registered companies in Hong Kong. According to the definition given by the Hong Kong Motion Picture Industry Association Limited (MPIA, n.d.), 50 per cent or above of the "listed effective post(s)" in the movie should be taken up by Hong Kong permanent residents. These posts include "film producer, director, script writer, actor or actress." Movies that fulfil these criteria are regarded as "Hong Kong movies". Imported films refer to non-local movies imported into Hong Kong from other places

REFERENCES

Booth, M. (2000). *The dragon syndicates: The global phenomenon of the triads.* Bantam Books.

Buck, E. B. (1992). Asia and the global film industry. *East-West Film Journal, 6*(2), 116–133.

Census and Statistics Department. (1971–2011). *Consumer Price Index and its movements.* Census and Statistics Department.

Census and Statistics Department. (n.d.). (Various years). *Statistical digest of the services sector.* Census and Statistics Department.

Chan, C. W. (1985). 院線最新形勢分析 [Movie magic: Coming soon]. *City Entertainment Magazine* [電影雙周刊], *166*, 11–12.

Chan, C. W. (1988). 「新寶」院線成立對香港電影市場影響的研究 [A study of the impact of the establishment of 'Newport' circuit on the Hong Kong film market]. *City Entertainment Magazine* [電影雙周刊], *245*, 2–5.

Chan, C. W. (1992). 「形勢所迫」，另開新線，陳榮美專訪 ['Having no alternative in the given situation', Setting up a new theatre chain, an interview with Chan Wing-mei]. *City Entertainment Magazine* [電影雙周刊], *354*, 42–43.

Chan, C. W. (2000). 香港電影工業結構及市場分析 [The structure and marketing analysis of the Hong Kong film industry]. *City Entertainment Magazine* [電影雙周刊].

Chan, K. (2006). 王晶:電影作為生意 [Jing Wong: Movie as a business]. *Hong Kong Economic Times*, 1 February, C01.

Chan, K. M. (2013). 開放與局限:中港合拍影片的過去與今天 [Opening and constraints: Mainland-Hong Kong co-productions in the past and today]. In S. K. Cheung, K. C. Leung, & K. M. Chan (Eds.), 香港‧論述‧傳媒 [*Hong Kong, discourse, media*] (pp. 91–115). Oxford University Press.

Chan, J. M., & Fung, A. Y. (2011). Structural hybridization in film and television production in Hong Kong. *Visual Anthropology, 24*(1–2), 77–89.

Chan, J. M., Fung, A. Y., & Ng, C. H. (2010). *Policies for the sustainable development of the Hong Kong film industry.* Hong Kong Institute of Asia-Pacific Studies, The Chinese University of Hong Kong.

Cheuk, P. (2008). *Hong Kong new wave cinema 1978–2000.* Intellect.

Chiu, S. W. (1994). *The politics of Laissez-Faire: Hong Kong's strategy of industrialization in historical perspective* (Occasion Paper No. 40). Hong Kong Institute of Asia-Pacific Studies, The Chinese University of Hong Kong.

Chiu, S. W. & Shin, V. K. (2013). *The fall of Hong Kong movies: A post-mortem investigative report* (Occasion Paper No. 225). Hong Kong Institute of Asian Pacific Studies.

Chiu, S. W., & Shin, V. K. (2019). Hong Kong's film industry reconstituted: Pathways to China after the Golden age. In T. L. Lui, S. W. Chiu, & R. Yep (Eds.), *Routledge handbook of contemporary Hong Kong* (pp. 365–396). Taylor & Francis.

Chiu, S. W., Ho, K. C., & Lui, T. L. (1997). *City-states in the global economy: Industrial restructuring in Hong Kong and Singapore.* Westview Press.

Chu, Y. K. (2000). *The triads as business.* Routledge.

Chu, Y. W. (2013). *Lost in transition: Hong Kong culture in the age of China.* State University of New York Press.

Chu, Y. W. (2015). Toward a new Hong Kong cinema: Beyond Mainland–Hong Kong co-productions. *Journal of Chinese Cinemas, 9*(2), 111–124.

Chung, S. P. (2007). 香港影視業百年 [*100 years of Hong Kong film and television industry*]. Joint Publishing.

Cinema Treasures. (n.d.). *About us.* Retrieved May 3, 2010, from http://cinema-treasures.org/about

Curtin, M. (2002). Hong Kong meets Hollywood in the Extranational arena of the cultural industries. In K. Tam, W. Dissanayake, & T. S. Yip (Eds.), *Sights of contestation: Localism, globalism and cultural production in Asia and the Pacific* (pp. 79–10). The Chinese University Press.

Curtin, M. (2007). *Playing to the world's biggest audience: The globalization of Chinese film and TV.* University of California Press.

Dannen, F., & Long, B. (1997). *Hong Kong Babylon: An insider's guide to the Hollywood of the east.* Miramax Books.

Darlin, D. (1992, January 28). Copycat crime: Video pirates abroad face a swash-buckler worthy of Hollywood—Richard O'Neill goes to Korea to fight Filmdom's war against bootleg taping—Protecting a key U.S. Export. *Wall Street Journal*, p. A1.

Davis, H. (2019, June 8). Opera, gangsters and swordplay: The rise and fall of Hong Kong cinema. *South China Morning Post.* Retrieved from https://www.scmp.com/news/hong-kong/society/article/3013205/opera-gangsters-and-swordplay-rise-and-fall-hong-kong-cinema

De Vany, A. S., & Walls, W. D. (2007). Estimating the effects of movie piracy on box-office revenue. *Review of Industrial Organization, 30*(4), 291–301.

Dejean, S. (2009). What can we learn from empirical studies about piracy? *CESifo Economic Studies, 55*(2), 326–352.

Economic Information & Agency. (1970–1997). *Hong Kong economy yearbook.* Economic Information & Agency.

Fu, P., & Desser, D. (Eds.). (2000). *The cinema of Hong Kong: History, arts, identity.* Cambridge University Press.

Fu, W. W., & Sim, C. (2010). Examining international country-to-country flow of theatrical films. *Journal of Communication, 60*(1), 120–143.

Fung, A. Y., & Erni, J. N. (2013). Cultural clusters and cultural industries in China. *Inter-Asia Cultural Studies, 14*(4), 644–656.

Gambetta, D. (1993). *The Sicilian mafia: The business of private protection.* Harvard University Press.

Hammond, S. (2000). *Hollywood east: Hong Kong movies and the people who made them*. McGraw-Hill.

Hong Kong Film Archive. (2012a). Basic search. Retrieved August 5, 2012, from http://ipac.hkfa.lcsd.gov.hk

Hong Kong Film Archive. (2012b). *Hong Kong filmography (1913–2010)*. Hong Kong Film Archive.

Hong Kong Film Critics Society. (2013). 2012香港電影回顧 [*2012 Hong Kong cinema in retrospect*]. Hong Kong Film Critics Society.

Hong Kong Motion Picture Industry Association Limited [MPIA]. (1970–2007). Hong Kong films: Annual review. *City Entertainment Magazine* [電影雙周刊].

Hong Kong Trade Development Council. (2001). *The north American market for Hong Kong film*. Research Department, HKTDC.

Hoskins, C., & Mirus, R. (1988). Reasons for the U.S. dominance of the international trade in television Programmes. *Media, Culture & Society, 10*(4), 499–504.

Intercontinental Film Distributors (HK) Limited. (n.d.). *About us*. Intercontinental Film Distributors (HK) Limited. Retrieved May 3, 2010, from http://www.intercontinental.com.hk/about_us/ifdl_about_us_index.htm

Lam, K. (2007). 電影發展局成立的前因初探─從香港電影工業結構談起 [Probing into the cause of the establishment of Hong Kong film development council─Starting from the structure of the Hong Kong film industry]. In N. Zhou (Ed.), *2006 香港電影回顧* [2006 Hong Kong cinema in retrospect] (pp. 58–68). Hong Kong Film Critics Society.

Lark Group. (n.d.). *UA CineHub*. Lark Group. Retrieved May 29, 2010, from http://www.lark.com.hk/en/uacinehub/index.html

Lee, F. L. (2006a). Audience taste divergence over time: An analysis of U.S. movies' box office in Hong Kong, 1989–2004. *Journalism and Mass Communication Quarterly, 83*(4), 883–900.

Lee, F. L. (2006b). Cultural discount and cross-culture predictability: Examining the box office performance of American movies in Hong Kong. *Journal of Media Economics, 19*(4), 259–278.

Lee, F. L. (2008). Hollywood movies in East Asia: Examining cultural discount and performance predictability at the box office. *Asian Journal of Communication, 18*(2), 117–136.

Lee, F. L. (2009). Cultural discount of cinematic achievement: The academy awards and U.S. movies' East Asian box office. *Journal of Cultural Economics, 33*(4), 239–263.

Lee, Y. C., & Yue, X. (2015, March). 回歸本土:新合拍片年代 [Return to the local: A new era of co-productions]. *Bloomberg Businessweek, 11–24*, 42–29.

Leng, X., Ji, E., & Mu, M. (1985). 德寶:電影神話另一章 [D&B: Another chapter of the myth of cinema]. *City Entertainment Magazine* [電影雙周刊], *176*, 3–9.

Leung, G. L. (1993). *The evolution of Hong Kong as a regional movie production and export Centre*. Unpublished M.Phil. Thesis. Hong Kong: Division of Communication, Graduate School, The Chinese University of Hong Kong.

Leung, G. L. (1999). *Study on the influence of media on youth: A secondary analysis report submitted to the working group on the influence of media on youth, commission on youth*. Commission on Youth.

Leung, G. L., & Chan, J. M. (1997). The Hong Kong cinema and its overseas market: A historical review 1950–1995. In *Fifty years of electric shadows: Hong Kong cinema retrospective* (pp. 143–151). Urban Council.

Liang, L. (1998). 論兩岸三地電影 [A discussion on the mainland China, Taiwan, and Hong Kong cinema]. Mulin Publishing.

Lie, F. (2007). 單邊主義讓香港電影故步自封 [Unilateralism makes Hong Kong's film production rests on its laurels]. In N. Zhuo (Ed.), *2006 Xianggang dianying huigu* [2006 Hong Kong cinema in retrospect] (pp. 48–57). Hong Kong Film Critics Society.

Lim, K. F. (2006). Transnational collaborations, local competitiveness: Mapping the geographies of filmmaking in/through Hong Kong. *Geografiska Annaler, 88*(B), 337–357.

Ma, K. F., Chan H., & Shum, L. T. (2007). 談笑論香港電影十年與香港回歸的關係 [A discussion on the relationship between Hong Kong cinema in a decade and Hong Kong's hand-over]. In N. Zhuo (Ed.), *2006香港電影回顧* [2006 Hong Kong cinema in retrospect] (pp. 30–45). Hong Kong Film Critics Society.

Ming Pao. (2007, December 11). 院線逐個捉 [Mapping each cinema circuit]. *Ming Pao Daily News*. Retrieved December 28, 2009, from http://www.mingpaovan.com/htm/News/20071211/HK-gca2.htm

Noam, E. M. (1993). The international market in film and television programs. In E. M. Noam & J. C. Millonzi (Eds.), *The international market in film and television programs* (pp. 41–58). Ablex Pub. Corp.

Oh, J. (2001). International trade in film and the self-sufficiency ratio. *The Journal of Media Economics, 14*(1), 31–44.

Pang, L. (2011). The state against ghosts: A genealogy of China's film censorship policy. *Screen, 52*(4), 461–476.

Hong Kong Motion Picture Industry Association Limited [MPIA]. (n.d.). Definition of HK movie. Retrieved October 6, 2015, from http://www.mpia.org.hk/content/about_definition.php

Shin, V. K., & Chiu, S. W. (2016). Global distribution networks, local exhibition alliances: Hollywood's new map in Hong Kong. *Regional Studies, 50*(5), 835–847.

South Metropolis Daily. (2010, May 15). 地道港片回潮的幕後因由探尋 [Reasons behind the comeback of local Hong Kong movies]. *South Metropolis Daily*. Retrieved November 22, 2015, from http://dailynews.sina.com/gb/ent/film/sinacn/m/2010-05-15/ba2959091.html

Stokes, L. O. (2007). *Historical dictionary of Hong Kong cinema*. Scarecrow Press.

Stokes, L. O., & Hoover, M. (1999). *City on fire: Hong Kong cinema*. Verso.

Sui, A. (2009). 香港電影百年: 1971–1994 [Hong Kong films in a century: 1971–1994]. 環球首映:香港電影 [Movie: Hong Kong Film], *3*, 100–116.

Symonds, S. (2007). Mainland measures: Fighting piracy in China poses special challenges. *Film Journal International*. Retrieved from http://www.filmjournal. com/filmjournal/esearch/article_display.jsp?vnu_content_id=1003557337

Szeto, M. M., & Chen, Y. (2011). Mainlandization and neoliberalism with postcolonial and Chinese characteristics: Challenges for the Hong Kong film industry. In J. Kapur & K. B. Wagner (Eds.), *Neoliberalism and global cinema: Capital, culture, and Marxist critique* (pp. 239–260). Routledge.

Szeto, M. M., & Chen, Y. (2012). Mainlandization or Sinophone translocality? Challenges for Hong Kong SAR new wave cinema. *Journal of Chinese Cinemas*, *6*(2), 115–134.

Teo, S. (1997). *Hong Kong cinema: The extra dimensions*. British Film Institute.

Teo, S. (2008). Promise and perhaps love: Pan-Asian production and the Hong Kong-China interrelationship. *Inter-Asia Cultural Studies*, *9*(3), 341–358.

Wang, S. (2003). *Framing piracy: Globalization and film distribution in greater China*. Rowman & Littlefield.

Wong, R. (2008). 2007香港電影及其於中國電影文化新格局中的因素 [The Hong Kong film and the facts in new pattern of Chinese film culture in 2007]. *Contemporary Cinema* [當代電影], *3*, 54–57.

Yeh, E. Y. (2010). 一個市場化視角的分析-後回歸時期香港電影的產業與內容變化 [An analysis from a marketization perspective—Changes in the industry and content of Hong Kong films in the post-handover period]. *Contemporary Cinema* [當代電影], *4*, 131–136.

Zhang, J. (1998). 九十年代港產片工業一瞥:困景的探討及出路 [*A glimpse at Hong Kong films in the 1990s: An analysis of the crisis and solutions*]. Society for the Concern of Hong Kong Film Industry Development.

Zhang, Y. (2008). 一'拍'漸'合'有'融'乃'大':改革開放30年區域合作策略下的內地與香港合拍片 [The cooperative movies between mainland and Hong Kong in 30 years]. *Contemporary Cinema* [當代電影], *11*, 59–64.

Zhao, W. (2007). *1897–2006 the history of Hong Kong film*. China Radio and Television Publishing.

Zheng, B. (1987). 曝光/捉影:戲院跟進地產業 [Exposure/capture: Cinemas move forward with the real estate sector]. 電影雙周刊 [City Entertainment Magazine], *214*, 13–14.

CHAPTER 7

Hong Kong as a Land of Opportunity? Social Mobility and Inequality in a Divided Society

"Hong Kong is a fair and open society. It is full of opportunities for those who are prepared to capture them."
Young people should ask themselves: "Why can't I become the next Li Ka-shing?"
—Former HKSAR Chief Secretary Henry Tang, as quoted in *SCMP*, 2011. (See "The road to" (2011)).

1 INTRODUCTION

Henry Tang's speech touches on a contentious debate about contemporary Hong Kong society: whether it is (still) a *land of opportunity*. Tang comes from a family taking refuge and establishing textile businesses in Hong Kong after the Chinese Civil War. Like other successful second generations (Lui, 2007), Tang saw ample opportunities in the industrializing city, experienced its growth from an underdeveloped area into an affluent society, and occupied key political and economic positions. Yet, Tang's audience stood at the opposite end of the spectrum—the so-called fourth (born after the 1980s) and fifth (born after the 1990s) generations. It is not uncommon to hear the younger and generally better-educated generations protest over blocked opportunities. One frequently cited root of the problem is the real estate hegemony installed by tycoons of earlier generations—like Li Ka-shing. This chapter aims to shed light in this

S. W. K. Chiu, K. Y. K. Siu, *Hong Kong Society*, Hong Kong Studies Reader Series, https://doi.org/10.1007/978-981-16-5707-8_7

debate by reviewing key empirical research on Hong Kong's social mobility and inequality.

We identify three standard-definition images of Hong Kong's social mobility debate. The *first standard-definition image* was raised in the 1980s as a retrospective review of how locals, the first and second generations of the post-War migrants from Mainland China, took advantage of Hong Kong's industrializing opportunities to move up the social ladder. In the *high-definition image*, however, the view post-War Hong Kong provided "a level playing field" is imprecise and somehow misleading (Wong & Lui, 1992). Specifically, it fails to acknowledge and study how "class" affects people's life-course experiences and their subsequent courses of action. Wong and Lui (1992) thus introduced John Goldthorpe's class schema to study Hong Kong's mobility structure, demonstrating the co-existence of both opportunities and inequalities during its post-War period of development.[1]

Since the 1980s, globalization and China's economic reforms have impacted on Hong Kong social class structure. As factories were relocated north to Shenzhen, Hong Kong deindustrialized into a regional hub providing professional services to manufacturers and transnational businesses. The China opportunity was often seen as key to expanding the service sectors in the global city. The *second standard-definition image* concerned two contradictory scenarios the middle class in the late globalization period. Pessimists claim suggested deindustrialization causes disappearing middle class, while optimists predicts that professional middle classes should "look north" and benefit from the new opportunities on the Mainland.[2] In the *second high-definition image*, however, we found a lack of conclusive evidence to support either of the two claims.

The debate over whether the newer generations are facing diminished opportunities has intensified since the 2000s. Observers noted that radical activists of the "post-80s" generations grew in numbers with young people increasingly frustrated with their career prospects (Cheng, 2014). The HKSAR government soon joined the chorus and professed "young people protest due to blocked mobility". The *third standard-definition image*

---

[1] Goldthorpe's class schema was first developed in the 1970s to study Western industrialized society. The concept was modified over time. Updated social mobility studies include: Erikson et al. (1983) or Erikson and Goldthorpe (1992).

[2] See the recent speech by National People's Congress Deputy Andrew Yao Cho-fai and Director of the Liaison Office of the Central people's Government in Hong Kong. See Liu (2017); RTHK (2017).

assumes a frustration-aggression view on how social inequality has motivated young people to participate in popular movements. Our *third high-definition image* seeks to debunk several myths in the frustration-aggression link.

Two questions are unavoidable in this debate: whether opportunities to move upward are expanding or shrinking? Whether individuals have equal chances to take advantage of these opportunities? (Wong & Koo, 2016; Wong & Lui, 1992). Since the macro environment and local institutions change over time, the analysis of the emerging class structure and occupational mobility of Hong Kong requires a dynamic model.

Answering the first question entails a focus on the changing dynamics of the macro environment, and how Hong Kong's social class structure was shaped by post-War industrialization, recent globalization and regional development such as China's opening. The second question addresses how transformation of local institutions, such as education and the family, have created or disrupted a level playing field for those trying to move up the social ladder.

2 HONG KONG UNDER INDUSTRIALIZATION: A LAND OF OPPORTUNITY OR INEQUALITY?

2.1 *The Refugee Society as the Land of Opportunity*

There were four waves of political and economic refugees from Mainland China during the post-War period (Chen, 2013).[3] Hong Kong's population grew rapidly from 2.2 million to 5.1 million between 1950 and 1981. Not surprisingly, these migrants considered the industrializing Hong Kong as a land of opportunity compared to the socialist society back home.[4]

---

[3] Roughly, the first wave in 1957 after Hong Kong's Double Tenth Riot in 1956; the second in 1962 after the end of the Great Famine in Mainland; the third in 1972 after Murray MacLehose became Governor in 1971; and the last in 1979 after the beginning of China's Open Door Policy in 1978 (Chen, 2013).

[4] Since the earliest social mobility debate centred on the thesis of post-War Hong Kong as a refugee society, some background about the government's border policy and Chinese immigration is warranted here. Before the establishment of the PRC in 1949, mainland Chinese could enter Hong Kong without much restrictions. The colonial government set up the Frontier Closed Area along the Shenzhen border in 1951 as immigration activities intensified. In response to the Sha Tau Kok Police Station shooting incident in 1967, the border was completely sealed off. In 1974, the Touch Base Policy (抵壘政策) was introduced to

In Lau's (1982) view, post-War Hong Kong was a refugee society where Chinese migrants, an inherited Confucian culture and a "don't rock the boat" refugee mentality, opted for political stability and pursued family-oriented economic goals. Economically, people could compete on equal grounds because their socioeconomic status had hit the "reset" button. Politically, the policy-making process was dominated by colonial techno-bureaucrats and not much could be done by the local Chinese. He concluded Hong Kong's stability amidst rapid modernization was the result of a structurally-atomized society of families that was not culturally disposed to collective political action. Hong Kong's social structure thus resembled a "minimally-integrated socio-political system", and its political culture was dominated by "utilitarian familism".

From a liberal perspective, the land of opportunity was made possible by capitalism and (colonial) modernization. The logic of industrialism turned society into one of social openness, rendering class of little significance. Individuals could change their class position through personal ability and hard work (Wong & Koo, 2016). During modernization, individuals disembedded from traditional society were reattached to modern institutions. Meritocratic system (e.g. education) became key to achieve upward mobility instead of nepotism. Such equality of opportunity fostered social harmony in Hong Kong despite hardships endured by migrants.

2.2   Class Does Matter

In response, other sociologists quickly pointed out three alternative views. First, expanding opportunities do not necessarily imply an open system where people have a fair chance to advance regardless of their class backgrounds. Second, the absence of explicit class action in Hong Kong does not mean the non-existence of class realities, because class positions still structured people's life chances and consciousness. Third, studies excluding class from their agenda often resort to normative and cultural explanations (e.g. Confucian culture in Lau's study), thereby underestimating the

control immigration by awarding permanent residency to those successfully reaching the urban centre. Those arrested at the Closed Area faced immediate repatriation. The Touch Base Policy ended on 24 October 1980—coincidently just a few months after the Chinese government" established the Special Economic Zone in Shenzhen.

effects of other non-cultural factors, such as education credentials (Wong & Koo, 2016; Wong & Lui, 1992). Regarding the first alternative, it is demonstrated that social fluidity did not necessarily increase with expanded opportunities for social mobility in Western European industrial societies (Erikson & Goldthorpe, 1992). In a dialogue with the Marxian class model, the CASMIN (Comparative Study of Social Mobility in Industrial Nations) team under the Oxford sociologist John Goldthorpe's lead developed a Weberian class schema that defines class positions by individuals' positions in the social division of labour via their occupations in the labour market.[5] Occupations formed the basis for a seven or threefold class schema (Table 7.1). Each class is

Table 7.1 The Hong Kong class structure

7-folded class	Description	3-folded class
I	Upper service class: higher-grade professionals, administrators and officials, managers in large establishments, larger proprietors	Service
II	Lower service class: lower-grade professionals, administrators and officials, higher-grade technicians, managers in small business and industrial establishments, supervisors of non-manual employees	
III (IIIa+IIIb)	Routine non-manual employees in commerce and administration, personal service workers and shop sales personnel	Intermediate
IV (IVa+IVb)	Petty bourgeoisie: small proprietors, artisans, contractors, with or without employees	
V	Lower-grade technicians, supervisors of manual workers	
VI	Skilled manual workers	Working
VII (VIIa+VIIb)	Semi-skilled and unskilled workers, agricultural workers	(Labour)

Reproduced from Wong and Lui (1992, p. 30); adapted from the CASMIN class schema

[5] Crompton and Scott (1999) summarized the post-war development of class analysis as follow: The development was driven by two political debate at the time: "openness" and "embourgeoisement". Openness, and level of meritocracy, was central to debates over impact of educational policy on social mobility. Embourgeoisement—the phenomenon of workers becoming middle class, led to questions about the shape of the class structure, political outlook and action in Britain. This resulted in two sociological traditions of class analysis: the Marxist analysis of relations of domination and exploitation in employment by Erik Wright;

represented by members who commanding different resources vis-à-vis other classes and sharing similar "life chances" as others located in a similar class. Members of a class tend to share similar experiences towards social structural fluctuation (e.g. mass unemployment due to the economic downturn) and hold class-specific interests (Bergman & Joye, 2005). It should be noted that the occupation-based class scheme excludes the capitalist class—for example Li Ka Shing—and the most marginalized, like homeless people.[6]

Applying the CASMIN class map, Wong and Lui (1992) interviewed male household respondents for their class background and their fathers' (occupation of the father when the son was 14 years old).[7] Let's consider absolute mobility first, followed by relative mobility.[8] Total mobility, defined as total rate of movements of respondents moving away from the grey shaded area (the diagonal cells) in a 7-folded class map (Table 7.2), is 76.4% (42.4% for upward mobility, i.e. son moved left from the shaded area; 34.0% for downward mobility, i.e. son moved right from the shaded area).[9]

The high absolute mobility rate of Hong Kong society, or a high degree of openness, was similar to other developed economies at the time (Wong & Lui, 1992). There was a great expansion of the upper service class (I), if one compares the figures of *total fathers' class* with *total sons' class*. Only 5.2% of fathers were in class (I), but 10.1% of all sons. A similar pattern holds for Class (II) as well.

and Goldthorpe's occupational classification, which was informed by Max Weber's theorization of class.

[6] These two groups are excluded due to their relatively low numbers, which makes it difficult to derive meaningful interpretation in macro class analysis.

[7] This was common practice of class surveys at the time when women's labour force participation rate was low and typically temporary until marriage.

[8] Erikson and Goldthorpe (1992) identified two types of social mobility: absolute mobility—defined as that resulting from structural changes like economic expansion, measured as the proportion of people in each class position compared to that of their parents; and relative mobility—defined as the extent to which one's class origins determine one's class destinations, measured as the odds an individual from each class origin fell into each of the other class destinations. See Wong and Koo (2016) for further discussion.

[9] Figures shown here are original ones from Wong and Lui's (1992) paper. Authors of this chapter recalculated with data from Wong and Lui's (1992) table and found for a 7-folded class map: upward mobility 41.4%, downward mobility 35.2%. The slight discrepancies might be a result of rounding up of figures.

Table 7.2 Intergenerational mobility matrix (reproduced from Wong & Lui, 1992, p.41)

	Son's (respondent) class in 1989							
	Service		Intermediate			Working		
Father's class	I	II	III	IV	V	VI	VII	Total fathers (%)
I (%)	**12**	6	3	4	6	2	6	39
	-30.8	-15.4	-7.7	-10.3	-15.4	-5.1	-15.4	-5.2
II (%)	7	**13**	4	5	9	4	3	45
	-15.6	**-28.9**	-8.9	-11.1	-20	-8.9	-6.7	-6
III (%)	8	15	**15**	8	10	9	7	72
	-11.1	-16.7	-20.9	-11.1	-13.9	-12.5	-9.7	-9.6
IV (%)	28	27	21	**43**	37	35	60	251
	-11.2	-10.8	-8.4	-17.1	-14.7	-14	-24	-33.4
V (%)	8	11	7	7	**12**	16	6	67
	-12	-16.4	-10.4	-10.4	-18	-23.9	-9	-8.9
VI (%)	6	7	12	9	11	**20**	25	90
	-6.7	-7.8	-13.3	-10	-12.2	-22.2	-27.8	-12
VII (%)	7	15	13	22	38	32	**61**	188
	-3.7	-8	-7	-11.7	-20.2	-17	-32.4	-25
Total sons (%)	76	94	75	98	123	118	168	752
	-10.1	-12.5	-10	-13	-16.4	-15.7	-22.3	-100

The bold figures are on the diagonal of the table with identical father and respondent's class positions. The underlined figures are those on the "lower" half of the diagonal indicating "upward" mobility of the son relative to the father

The higher percentage of self-recruitment in the upper service class (I, 30.8%) and unskilled manual class (VII, 32.4%) suggested a stronger degree of succession or inheritance[10] in these two classes. At the top class I the situation paralleled a high inflow rate, i.e. increased "room at the top", while class VII at the bottom was actually shrinking with low inflow rates. The great flux or mobility was mostly experienced in the intermediate classes (III, IV, V), where only one-fifth or less of the sons in each stayed in the same class (Wong & Lui, 1992).

Relative mobility was calculated as the "odds" of one class arriving at a class destination relative to another.[11] Members from each class position

[10] Inheritance effect is defined as the persistence of class membership across generations.

[11] a concept traceable to the English origin of the CASMIN school by using the terminology of odds being used in bookmakers that accepts and pays off bets on sporting events based on an estimated odds or chance by which a certain team or horse won.

classified by their class origins are matched against another class, and then their relative odds of moving (either up or down) towards another class were estimated. Without exception, the service classes (in Table 7.1) invariably had an advantage over the lower (intermediate and working) classes. Similar intermediate classes also enjoyed superior, albeit smaller, odds against the working class. In Wong and Lui's survey, sons from the service classes (I, II collapsed) had an advantage of as great as 10.2 times over sons from the working class (VI, VII collapsed) in arriving at the service class destination than at the working class destination. Even though total mobility had increased, with everyone has a higher chance of upward mobility, those from a higher class background have an advantage in getting ahead or keeping their current position. This suggests class inequality still existed despite a rather open class structure in post-war Hong Kong (Wong & Liu, 1992).

For the second alternative, Wong and Lui (1992) examined if there were enough differences among classes to warrant class formation. Among the service class, those "promoted" from the working class tended coming from the Mainland with fathers working as employees rather than employers compared to the immobile one. Those service class members experiencing no change in class position tended to have better education as did their fathers. Although the service class composition exhibited some heterogeneity, members shared similar socio-political attitudes towards work (tended to perceive it as meaningful), politics (tended not to feel politically powerless) and social justice (tended to be conservative: perceived the employment relationship not exploitative in nature). Their views were in slight contrast to those of the working classes in the 3-folded class schema.

Wong and Lui (1992) further explored to what extent education determined one's class destination. While the relationship between educational qualifications and membership of the service classes was empirically strong, social origins still mattered if qualifications were controlled. For people with similar education levels, those with fathers from the service class were more likely to be found in the service class than those from working class origins. In sum, class has altered people's life chances along with of Hong Kong's presumed meritocratic system.

For the third alternative perspective, comparative studies have demonstrated that normative and cultural explanations cannot account adequately for similarities of mobility structure observed across societies (Chan et al., 1995). As a newly industrialized economy in the 1980s and one of the four little dragons/tigers, Hong Kong was used as a case to see if its social fluidity[12] conformed to an exceptional "East Asian Model". The model suggests that the East Asian region was characterized by strong developmentalist states, fast economic growth, export-oriented industrialization and relatively egalitarian income distribution, but also repressive labour regimes and policy that were skewed towards industries at the expense of rural income (Deyo, 1989). Similar to other normative and cultural explanations, the East Asian Model assumes that common cultural heritage among East Asia states could explain why their social fluidity could resemble each other more than that of the Western market-driven economies.

Nevertheless, Chan et al. (1995) found no evidence for the presence of the East Asia model in Hong Kong when they fit Hong Kong's social mobility data with that of the CASMIN project. Intriguingly, Hong Kong's social fluidity was closer to that of Sweden than Japan. In Hong Kong, there was an absence of sectoral barriers, weak *inheritance* effects (defined as persistence of class membership across generations) but the coexistence of strong *hierarchy* effects against long-range mobility. It is relatively easier for individuals to leave their class origin in Hong Kong than Japan (lower inheritance effect), but once having left they travelled a shorter class distance (less likely to reach Class I, II) than equivalent groups in Japan. The social class structure should be regarded as rather different for the two places.

Hong Kong's strong hierarchy effects, Chan et al. (1995) then argued, was caused by the underdevelopment of its higher education system during colonial times. Before 1984, the average percentage of the population aged 17–20 enrolled in first-year first-degree places in government-funded programs never exceeded 2.8% and rose to only 17.2% in 1994 (Fig. 7.1). For comparison, the gross enrolment ratio for tertiary education for both sexes in HK and Japan in 1984 was 12.2% versus 29.5% respectively, and 21.5% versus 38.7% respectively in 1994.[13] The manual-non-manual gap was wider in Hong Kong because of a credential divide between the requirements for recruitment to occupations in the English-speaking

---

[12] Social fluidity refers to "the inequality between individuals from different classes in their chances of coming to occupy one rather than another destination class" (Breen, 2007).

[13] Gross enrolment ratio, tertiary, both sexes (%) is derived from total enrolment in tertiary education, regardless of age, expressed as a percentage of the total population of the five-year age group following on from secondary school leaving (UNESCO Institute for Statistics. See The World Bank: http://data.worldbank.org/indicator/SE.TER.ENRR).

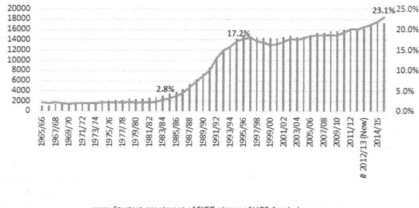

Student enrolment of FYFD places of UGC-funded programmes (full-time equivalent)

Fig. 7.1 Student Enrolment of First-year first degree (FYFD) places of UGC-funded program 1965/66 to 2015/16. (#To tie in with the implementation of the new academic structure, UGC-funded institutions have admitted two cohorts of students under the old and new academic structures in the 2012/13 academic year (University Grants Committee, 2019))

white-collar world of commerce and the Cantonese-speaking world of manufacturing and manual personal service.

Historically, those rising to middle class positions took one of the two paths; either through the elitist education system and competition for academic qualifications, or through the non-credential path where opportunities were widely available due to structural changes in the economy (Lui, 2003). In both cases, the middle class succeeded through competing in the high growth economy. As an unintended consequence of the openness in social mobility, the newly-emergent middle class embarked on the "politics of the rearguard" because its members subscribed to an "instrumental mentality" by attributing their success to individualized efforts.[14] With their belief that the capitalist system worked to their advantage, the middle class became politically conservative and refrained from participating in the 1990s democratic movement in Hong Kong (Lui, 2003). Lui further

[14] Here Lui (2003) tried to explain why the middle class in Hong Kong failed to become the vanguard of political reform despite the expanding opportunity for democratic participation during this period.

argued that, as part of the decolonization process in the 1990s, the Chinese middle class in Hong Kong has already been absorbed into the establishment and found ways to promote its interests, hence there was little need to create their own political groups. While the middle class members behaved like the alleged refugees in retraining from rocking the boat, class interests rather than "refugee mentality" should be the better explanation.

3   SOCIAL INEQUALITY IN THE GLOBAL CITY

3.1   *Social Polarization*

Globalization has done far more than deindustrialized Hong Kong and transformed it into service-driven economy. Income disparity became more pronounced during the post-industrial era, with Gini Coefficient increased from 0.430 in 1971 to 0.539 in 2016 (Census and Statistics Department, 2017).[15] Like other global cities, occupational polarization and widening income inequality have happened in Hong Kong. To illustrate the extent of social polarization, we follow and update Chiu and Lui (2004)'s work with 2011 census data on employment and occupational changes.

Hong Kong's deindustrialization process had started from the late 1980s, as the working population in manufacturing decreased by 82%, from 768,121 in 1991 to 138,400 persons in 2011. Meanwhile, workforce in the service sectors expanded spectacularly between 1991 and 2011: a 128.5% increase for "Financing, insurance, real estate and business services" (employing 18.6% of the total workforce), an 80.1% increase for "Wholesale, retail and import/export trades, restaurants" (31.2% of total), and a 71.3% increase in "Community, social and personal services" (26.1% of total).

Consequently, deindustrialization drastically changed in Hong Kong's occupational structure (Table 7.3). The number of "Plant and machine, operators and assemblers" and "craft and related workers" dropped by 50.4% and 37.6% respectively between 1991 and 2011. On the other hand, there was a considerable expansion in the workforce at the higher end of the service sector as professionals (a 144.7% increase), associate

---

[15] Calculated with monthly household income from main employment; there is no data on wealth distribution in Hong Kong.

Table 7.3 Working population by occupation, 1991, 2001 and 2011

| | 1991[a] | | 2001[a] | | 2011[b] | | | 1991–2011 | |
	No. of persons	% share	No. of persons	% share	No. of persons	% share	Absolute change	% change	% point change
Managers and administrators	249,247	9.20%	349,637	10.70%	369,700	10.50%	120,453	48.30%	1.30%
Professionals	99,331	3.70%	179,825	5.50%	243,100	6.90%	143,769	144.70%	3.20%
Associate professionals	279,909	10.30%	498,671	15.30%	699,700	19.80%	419,791	150.00%	9.50%
Clerical support workers	431,651	15.90%	529,992	16.30%	510,400	14.40%	78,749	18.20%	-1.50%
Service and sales workers	359,319	13.20%	488,961	15.00%	582,100	16.50%	222,781	62.00%	3.20%
Craft and related workers	397,992	14.70%	321,000	9.90%	248,200	7.00%	-149,792	-37.60%	-7.60%
Plant and machine, operators and assemblers	365,826	13.50%	238,666	7.30%	181,400	5.10%	-184,426	-50.40%	-8.30%
Elementary occupations	503,832	18.60%	635,393	19.50%	696,800	19.70%	192,968	38.30%	1.20%
Others[c]	27,996	1.00%	10,561	0.30%	2700	0.10%	-25,296	-90.40%	-1.00%
Total	2,715,103	100%	3,252,706	100%	3,534,200	100%	819,097	30.20%	–

[a]Secondary data from Chiu and Lui (2004)—Table 1. Working population by industry, 1991 and 2001

[b]Census and Statistics Department—Table E003: Number of employed persons by industry and occupation (First Quarter 2011) (Census and Statistics Department, 2011c)

[c]Others (Skilled agricultural and fishery workers; and occupations not classifiable)

professionals (a 150% increase), and managers and administrators (a 48.3% increase) but also at lower end as service and sales workers (62.0%). The increase in elementary occupations was less dramatic (38.3%) but the sheer number of persons employed suggests the change was indeed substantial.

As Chiu and Lui (2004) argued, the resulting occupational polarization is both relative (in terms of share) and absolute (in terms of the numbers). Evidence from the relative income differentials further supports the presence of polarization among occupational groups. While overall median monthly income measured at current prices increased by 112.8% between 1991 and 2011, that for elementary occupations increased by just 42.9%, and for service and sales workers by only 80.0%. In contrast, the increases in the median monthly income of the high-end service sectors were much higher and above the increase in the overall median monthly income: for managers and administrators (202.1%), professionals (114.4%) and associate professionals (125.0%) between 1991 and 2011. The growth in the professional sectors, thus also indicating the expansion of the middle class, apparently could not compensate for the sluggish growth of income experienced by those working in the lower service sectors. Echoing Chiu and Lui (2004), social polarization appears to have worsened in recent years (Table 7.4).

Table 7.4 Median monthly income from main employment (HK$)

Occupation	Median monthly income from main employment (HK$)			Percentage change	
	1991[a]	2001[a]	2011[b]	1991–2001	1991–2011
Managers and administrators	12,000	26,000	36,250	116.7	202.1
Professionals	15,000	30,000	32,160	100	114.4
Associate professionals	8000	16,000	18,000	100	125
Clerical support workers	5000	10,000	10,000	100	100
Service and sales workers	5000	9110	9000	82.2	80
Craft and related workers	5000	10,000	10,500	100	110
Plant and machine operators and assemblers	4500	10,000	10,000	122.2	122.2
Elementary occupations	3500	5300	5000	51.4	42.9
Overall	5170	10,000	11,000	93.4	112.8

[a]Secondary data from Chiu and Lui (2004)—Table 3. Median monthly income from main employment of working population by occupation, 1991 and 2001. Original data from census and Statistics Department

[b]Census and Statistics Department—Table 2.10 Median monthly income from main employment of working population by occupation, 2001, 2006 and 2011 (Census and Statistics Department, 2011a)

The widening gap in median monthly income between the top and bottom of the occupational hierarchy was not the sole cause for the increase in overall income inequality. By contrasting the interdecile ratio of monthly median income of various sectors, it appears that the downsizing of manufacturing potentially shifted the labour force from a relatively equal (in terms of income) industrial sector, to the relatively less equal sectors of financing, insurance, real estate, business services, community, social and personal services, thus exacerbating the overall income polarization (Chiu & Lui, 2004). Lee et al. (2007) suggest Hong Kong is comparable to other post-industrial societies in that a closure of professional and semi-professional labour markets from the rest of economy has made it difficult for people laid off from the manufacturing sector to achieve upward mobility by finding a job in the service sector where acquisition of credentials is strongly favoured. The once skilled manufacturing workers become unskilled in the knowledge-based society and could only find manual jobs in the expanding lower end service sector (or become unemployed), which accommodates the consumption need from the expanding transnational capitalist class, e.g., the professionals. A low-income poverty trap thus was created for the less fortunate.

The impact of the sectorial shift on income polarization is mediated by other local institutional contexts, such as gender, migration and also family (Chiu, 2008; Chiu et al., 2005; Chiu & Lui, 2004; Chiu & Lui, 2009). The occupational polarization was gendered (Chiu & Lui, 2004). While the percentage of women working as plant and machine operators and assemblers dropped significantly between 1991 and 2011, there was a substantial increase of women working in top service jobs as managers and administrators, and professionals (14.9% and 11.2% respectively). That said, more women turned to work in elementary occupations (465,856) and as service workers and shop sales workers (306,288) in 2011 (772,144 women total).

Two social processes associated with this feminization of the workforce in Hong Kong—migration and marriage homogamy in families—have impacted on income polarization in Hong Kong. The expanding middle class, one that serves mainly the transnational capitalist class, has allowed upward social mobility for local women (also for men), but their departure from the traditional domestic role has also created a service sector demand for transnational workers—female migrant domestic helpers.[16] The demand is especially strong among dual-earner families which can could now afford to purchase household services instead of doing the work themselves (Lee et al., 2007). With no buffering regulation in the form of a minimum wage before 2011 (except for foreign domestic helpers) a race-to-the-bottom ensued, causing a downward spiral in wages for low-end service work.

Immigrants from Mainland China were negatively affected by the economic restructuring in Hong Kong too.[17] In a 1994–6 survey that used Goldthorpe's class schema to compare the social mobility of immigrants with the locally born, Chinese immigrants (excluding those living less than ten years in HK) were found to be three times less likely than locally born Hong Kong residents to hold jobs in the service class and the routine non-manual class, but were twice as likely to work in manual jobs (Chiu et al., 2005). The drop in manufacturing employment has benefited the locally born Hong Kong residents more than the immigrants by increasing the former's chance of gaining access to the service class while reducing the chance of the latter. The disadvantage is still present even when controlled for educational qualifications, with immigrants having only 54% chance compared to that of locally born Hong Kong residents to gain a job at the top of the class hierarchy (since Mainland-earned credentials generated a lower return compared to the local ones). The lower transferability of premigration human capital also hindered the opportunities for immigrants for general upward promotion (Chiu et al., 2005). In short, the existence of the "ethnic penalty" apparently prevented the closing of the initial labour market disadvantage experienced by Chinese immigrants in Hong Kong. This occupational polarization among migration lines has largely been sustained in recent years, with disproportionally more new arrivals from Mainland (defined here as those residing in HK for less than 7 years) compared to the whole population working as service workers and shop sales workers (38.1% vs. 17.5%) or in elementary occupations (27.3% vs. 13.3%) in 2011, despite small percentage increases in new migrants

---

[16] The expansion of the middle class also allowed upward mobility for men, thus male migrant workers have also been imported to work in the typical 3-D jobs as in other global cities, for example construction. See chapter on migration.

[17] Naming the population settling in Hong Kong from the Mainland is a political process in itself. During colonial period, they were called "immigrants", but in the SAR, the official label has been "new arrivals" from Mainland China.

Table 7.5   Proportion of working new migrants aged 15 and over by occupation, 1991, 2001 and 2011

	Percentage of working population					
	1991[a]		2001[a]		2011[c]	
Occupation	New arrivals[b]	Whole population	New arrivals	Whole population	New arrivals	Whole population
Managers and administrators	4.9	9.2	3	10.7	3.6	10.9
Professionals	0.9	3.7	0.9	5.5	2.7	7
Associate professionals	3.2	10.3	4.1	15.3	6.9	21.1
Clerks	10.3	15.9	10.9	16.3	9.9	16.8
Service workers and shop sales workers	15.2	13.2	30.7	15	38.1	17.5
Craft and related workers	15.7	14.7	11	9.9	91	7.9
Plant and machine operators and assemblers	24	13.5	4.1	7.3	2.2	5.4
Elementary occupations	25.4	18.6	34.9	19.5	27.3	13.3
Others	0.5	1	0.3	0.3	0.1	0.1
Total	100	100	100	100	100	100

[a]Secondary data from Chiu and Lui (2004)—Table 8. Proportion of working new migrants aged 15 and over by occupation, 1991 and 2001

[b]Defined as new immigrants from Mainland China who had been in Hong Kong for less than 7 years

[c]Census and Statistics Department—Table 6.4 Proportion of working PMRs aged 15 and over by occupation, 2011 (Census and Statistics Department, 2011b)

observed in the professionals and associate professionals occupational groups (Table 7.5).

The occupational polarization has widened the overall household income gap—not just directly but also through social processes within the family. Chiu (2011) observes that the expansion in tertiary education amid the growth in high-end service jobs has resulted in an increasing number of women becoming highly-educated professionals. Simultaneously, a large number of women, often middle-aged and relatively less educated due to past circumstances, were pushed into the low-end service sector—where jobs are more likely to be casualized and informalized as well. Meanwhile, due to homogamy, the highly-educated professionals and the lowly-educated service workers tend to marry people from similar backgrounds. Comparing the husband's birth cohort from 1936 or earlier until 1982–1986, Chiu (2011) found that more couples were increasingly having similar educational attainment—therefore a similar level of income. Between 1991 and 2001, those wives married to husbands at higher income quintiles have a higher and increasing labour force participation rate than do wives married to husbands in lower income quintiles, and the labour force participation rate of the latter was actually decreasing. This means that income inequality intensified because dual-earner families are also likely to be professional couples with higher income in Hong Kong. Since the higher income groups are likely to have dual-earner households while the lower income groups are less likely to, and higher income men are marrying higher income women and vice versa, overall household income inequality (the basis for calculating the Gini Coefficient) had increased.

So far, we have focused on the winners and losers as Hong Kong transformed into a global city. The middle class seems to have fared pretty well—or has it?

3.2 The M-Shaped Society Debate

As globalization continued, the loss of mid-level managerial jobs in industrialized countries coupled with emerging highly-paid knowledge-based work has led to a debate in the West over the formation of the *M-Shaped Society*.[18] A similar debate in Hong Kong has intensified in the context of a depressed economy, an increasing number of residential mortgage loans in negative equity following the 1997 Financial Crisis, and the bursting of the housing bubble. Middle class expansion "seemed" to have come to a halt with the rising unemployment rate and shrinking personal wealth. Lui (2010) summarized three general views of the impact of economic changes on the social structure at the time: (a) the size of the middle class was decreasing *relative* to the economically active population—in terms of the

---

[18] The term "M-shape Society" originated from Kenichi Ohmae's 2006 book *The Threats and Opportunities Arising from the Disappearance of Middle class* (M型社會). The concept first appeared in William Ouchi's (1984) book *The M-Form Society: how American Teamwork Can Recapture the Competitive Edge*. In response to the debate in Hong Kong, the Census and Statistics Department (2006) published an appendix chapter with the title "Has Hong Kong Developed into an "M-shape Society"?" in the 2006 Population By-census Report.

pace of growth; (b) the middle class was disappearing—declining in absolute numbers; (c) That points (a) and (b) are symptomatic of broader
changes in the social structure of Hong Kong—as the economy matures,
the opportunities for social mobility dry up.

Based on a comparison of three separate surveys conducted in 1989,
1992, and 2006, Lui (2010) observed that Hong Kong's class map had
changed slowly over the years. As seen in Lui's table, the middle class continued to account for around one-fifth of the total sample in each survey,
whereas skilled, semi-skilled and unskilled workers continued to shrink
during this period (40.6%→30.4%). The middle class was not disappearing, but its growth had slowed down (Table 7.6).

In terms of intergenerational mobility of a 7-folded class map (tables
not replicated here), Lui (2010) estimated upward social mobility at
44.4%, downward mobility at 18.6% and immobility at 23.1% in 2006.
This suggested up to 76.9% of respondents in 2006 moved to different
class positions from those of their fathers during childhood. This is comparable to Wong and Lui (1992)'s 7-folded class map we discussed earlier
(in that case, 76.4% changed class positions, with 42.4% moving upward
and 34.0% moving downward). Social mobility pattern remained open in
Hong Kong and there was no evidence of a drastic reduction in mobility
opportunities (Lui, 2010). Despite the open structure, inheritance effects

Table 7.6   Class maps of Hong Kong, 1989, 1992 and 2006

7-folded Class	Brief description	1989 (%)	1992 (%)	2006 (%)	3-folded Class
I	Upper service class	8.6	10	7.5	Service class
II	Lower service class	11.3	10.5	13.4	
III	Routine non-manual employees	9.5	24.9	16.9	Intermediate class
IVa	Small employers	9.5	24.9	16.9	
IVb	Petty bourgeoisie	14	11.5	8.2	
V	Technicians and supervisors	15.9	7.3	20.4	
VI+VII	Manual workers (VI—skilled; VII—semi and unskilled)	40.6	35.7	30.4	Working class
Total		N = 943	N = 590	N = 1157	

Original source: Table 1. Class Maps of Hong Kong, 1989, 1992 and 2006 (Lui, 2010). Table 2.
Distribution of class origins and class destinations for men in the labour force in Hong Kong. (Wong &
Koo, 2016, as cited in Lui, 2010)

impact differently for different classes. Those located at the two poles— Classes I and II, and V, VI and VII—experienced some sort of inheritance effects whereas Class III and IV are least likely to constrain the respondents from leaving their original class positions. Respondents from Class I were able to avoid downward mobility by staying or moving to Class IV and becoming small employers/self-employed. The working class would find it more difficult to leave their original class positions. Still, according to Lui (2010), opportunities for short-range upward mobility are present for most of the classes.

Despite rising income inequality in Hong Kong, the M-Shaped Society thesis of a shrinking middle class in the global city was not evidently supported in Lui's (2010) study. Some might attribute the middle class's fortune to their benefitting from opportunities created by China. In fact, the situation is more complicated. The anxiety over mobility opportunities is related to the new developments in China over the past two decades: unevenness of the China opportunities in Hong Kong, and second, new opportunities in the Mainland itself not fully materializing (Lui, 2010, 2014).

3.3   Blessed with the China Opportunities?

As Lui (2010) put it, the middle class is "splitting up" as Hong Kong's dependence on the Mainland's economic growth and development has increased. As a key international hub adjacent to China, Hong Kong's economy naturally would benefit from its spectacular economic growth. However, the impacts were not evenly spread but concentrated on some selected sectors. Table 7.3 shows that managers and administrators accounted for 10.5% of the overall working population in 2011, not that different from the comparable figure in 1991 (9.2%). From 1996 to 2001 the absolute numbers working as managers and administrators actually dropped. On the other hand, the percentage working as professionals and associate professionals had increased significantly (Lui, 2010). Those working as administrators and managers were usually promoted based on the accumulation of work experience instead of acquiring specialist knowledge like professionals. These two occupational groups thus experienced different career development as China was opening up.

Administrators and managers' experience was initially useful when factories were first relocated to the Mainland, but not later. Financial services require more specialized knowledge, and is, unlike a factory job, not easily transferrable to another region. Thus, the local financial sectors continued to enjoy the benefit of high-speed growth in the Mainland. This is seen in the change in the main industry employing Hong Kong residents working in China from manufacturing to other sectors. According to Lui (2010), in the period of 1995–2005, professionals and associate professionals have surpassed managers and administrators to become the leading occupation of Hong Kong residents working in the Mainland. In addition, the middle class was split within the local economy. The service sectors serving primarily the local community have not benefited much from the China opportunities as their qualifications were not readily transferrable. Similarly, professionals working in public and/or non-profit organizations (which mainly provide services to the local community) were less enthusiastic about economic integration than people from the same class working in the business sectors (Lui, 2010).

The horizontal restructuring of Hong Kong industries by relocating and scaling up production in China from the 1980s onward (see Chap. 5), has fostered a honeymoon period until the 2000s for Hong Kong residents who wishing to work in the Mainland (Lui, 2014). The failure to pursue industrial upgrading has led to a shrinking number of factories in Hong Kong so that the only opportunities in the manufacturing sector for local residents would be to work on the Mainland. Hong Kong workers were eventually replaced by workers recruited from China; however, it became difficult for the local working class to get promotion via accumulation of job experience.

Lui (2014) highlights two trends among Hong Kong residents working in the Mainland: first, education credentials have become more important to obtain a job in China; second, there is increasing emphasis on experience and seniority. Hong Kong residents working in the Mainland are significantly older than the median age of the local working population. This means that the more senior professionals, managers and administrators are enjoying the China opportunities more than their junior colleagues. The average person in Hong Kong would find it difficult to compete directly with others in the Mainland due to the segmented labour market. Rather, those working in the Mainland are mostly attached to Hong Kong-based companies looking for China opportunities rather than creating jobs for their staff. In short, China opportunities have yet to fully materialize.

4 INEQUALITY AND ITS SOCIO-POLITICAL CONSEQUENCES OF INEQUALITY: RADICAL POLITICAL AND SOCIAL MOVEMENTS ARISING FROM STALLED YOUTH SOCIAL MOBILITY?[19]

Political scientists have long perceived deteriorating living standards and the widening of the gap between rich and poor as root causes of radical politics in Hong Kong (Cheng, 2014). The government even adopted this frustration-aggression logic to account for the outbreak of the Umbrella Movement in 2014. For instance, Jeffrey Lam, a Legislative Council member from the establishment camp who also sat on the Executive Council, twice raised the youth social mobility issue for discussion in LegCo meetings as a follow-up to the 2014 movement (Legislative Council, 2014). The government's position on the issue was further reflected in a LegCo Research Brief (Issue No.2) released later with this concluding note: "Social mobility is essential to the creation of social harmony" (Legislative Council Secretariat, 2015). Paradoxically, many local studies have argued that a gradual shift from materialistic to postmaterialistic values among younger generations—though among only a relatively small percentage of them—was indicative to the flourishing of new social movements, such as the conservation protests by the Post-80s in the early 2000s (Ma, 2011; Wong & Wan, 2009). These two seemingly contradictory views form the basis of our third standard and high-definition images concerning the recent debate about social mobility in Hong Kong.

The third standard-definition image states that *youth's negative experience of social mobility has led to the radicalized political action in Hong Kong*. As we shall demonstrate, the relationship between political action and mobility experience is more complex. It involves three issues. First, is overall social mobility really shrinking for the younger generations in recent years? Second, further to our earlier discussion concerning the credential path to success (which argued youth are enjoying better mobility opportunities with the expansion of government-funded university degree programs), are youth becoming "frustrated" because counter-intuitively: (1) a university degree earns them less than expected and/or (2) the credential path creates a new barrier for children of less educated parents for they possess less cultural capital? Third, does a negative "social mobility"

---

[19] This line of academic investigation is still unfolding in recent years so this is our humble attempt to summarize key research findings concerned.

experience of individuals really increase the likelihood that youth will participate in radical forms of political action? This chapter will tackle the first two questions but leave the third one about the direct linkages between mobility, discontents and protests to Chap. 10.

4.1   Are Younger Generations Experiencing Shrinking Opportunities for Upward Social Mobility?

To answer this question, Wong and Koo (2016) contrasted Hong Kong's social mobility patterns in 1989 and 2007, employing Goldthorpe's class scheme. They found that the total mobility rate in 2007 was 73.9%, comparable to 74.6% in the earlier study conducted in 1989 (Wong & Lui, 1992). They also observed three major changes in class structure over the period: first, the categories of professionals, managers or administrators and routine non-manual workers (Class I, II and III) have expanded rapidly. Second, the non-agricultural self-employed sector (Class IVab) has been declining. Third, the manual sector has continued to contract. One-third of respondents in 1989 were technicians, supervisors or skilled manual workers but only one in eight worked in these occupations in 2007. Wong and Koo (2016) argued that structurally upward mobility via employment should be more feasible for youth, with the expansion in the socially desirable middle-class occupations and the shrinking of undesirable working-class jobs by 2007.

Contrary to the popular belief that mobility opportunity was shrinking, there was actually an increasing level of social fluidity with much more long-range upward and downward occupational mobility by 2007 compared to 1989, although the distribution of these opportunities remained influenced by one's class origin (Wong & Koo, 2016). Comparing relative mobility between 1989 and 2007, Wong and Koo (2016) concluded that it has become easier for people to move across a level boundary, but at the same time, each class was also more likely to retain its own members in 2007. Thus recent economic growth in Hong Kong has led to weaker hierarchy effects (easier to cross class boundaries) but a stronger inheritance effect (more likely to stay behind). Apparently, social mobility and class inequality have continued to co-exist in present-day Hong Kong (Wong & Koo, 2016).

When comparing across Chinese societies, the intra-generational occupational mobility of the younger generation in Hong Kong in 2016 even fares a bit better. In a recent report (Hong Kong Institute of Asia-Pacific

Studies, 2016) submitted to the HKSAR Central Policy Unit that compared how social mobility has impacted on youth[20] political attitudes and action, it was found that 48.5% of young people in Hong Kong have experienced social mobility, compared to 41.2% in Taiwan and 30.9% in Macau.[21] The percentage of young people experiencing upward social mobility was also highest in Hong Kong (35.9%), compared to Taiwan (24.0%) and Macau (19.5%), even though most did not reach the highest occupational class (only 6.6% reaching the highest Class 1 in HK). On the other hand, around 8.6% of young people in Hong Kong experienced downward mobility, which was comparable to Macau (8.5%) but lower than Taiwan (11.6%). The difference among these societies in intragenerational occupational mobility in HKIAPS' report was mainly due to the fact that up to 44.0% of the 30–35 age-group in Hong Kong sample has experienced upward mobility (and 10.3% has reached the highest level), compared to Taiwan (27.8% & 5.4%) and Macau (27.9% & 4.7%). Even for the 18–29 age-group, Hong Kong still fares better (28.4%) in terms of upward mobility than Taiwan (20.9%) or Macau (13.0%).

Considering inter-generational occupational mobility, young people with fathers who were employers or administrators of large institutions, or who were professionals at their age of 15, had a much higher chance to remain in upper classes relative to those whose fathers were farmers or manual workers (see Table 5.2 in HKIAPS, 2016). This finding was comparable to another study that showed a strengthening inheritance effect in upper occupational classes (Wong & Koo, 2016). Yet, the HKIAPS report also indicated children of farmers or manual workers fare much better than children of routine non-manual employees, service workers and petty bourgeoisie (the intermediate class) in terms of "upward mobility without reaching the top". This difference in mobility matches the deindustrialization process in Hong Kong, which has led to a "natural" upward flow of the lowest occupational class (Lui, 2010; Wong & Koo, 2016). Contrary

---

[20] Youth here were defined as those 18–35 years old.
[21] Stephen Chiu is part of the research team behind the CUHK HKIAPS 2016 report (HKIAPS, 2016). It employed Erikson, Goldthorpe and Portocrarero 1979 (EGP) class scheme, but collapsed agricultural workers, semi-skilled and unskilled workers, and skilled manual workers into one class (5); routine non-manual employees, service workers and petty bourgeoisie into one class (4); lower-grade professionals, administrators and officials into one class (3); lower salaried higher-grade professionals, administrators and officials into one class (2); and higher salaried higher-grade professionals, administrators and officials into one class (1).

to common sense, those at the bottom were actually better able to escape their class origin.

The same conclusion was drawn from a new report released in 2020, using updated data of far better quality than previous studies. Chiu et al. (2020) collaborated with the Census and Statistics Department to conduct a Thematic Household Survey (No. 65) in late 2017 to survey the inter- and intra-generational mobility experiences of about 10,000 respondents of 22 to 47 years of age (Census and Statistics Department, 2019). The reason that an official survey is necessary was because of the practical difficulties of conducting a household survey in Hong Kong ever since the new century. As discussed in the Chap. 9, the development of private housing estates as heavily guarded (and gated) communities basically rendered any academic surveys in households residing there impossible. While telephone surveys were sometimes conducted to collect socioeconomic statuses, their short duration of interview make it difficult to collect detailed mobility histories. The Thematic Household Survey overcome most of these difficulties and resulted in one of the most reliable and comprehensive data on the recent mobility patterns. Furthermore, if we are further confining our analysis to the younger cohorts, a larger sample size would be even more desirable.

Selecting the 4940 younger respondents (aged 22–35) from the full sample, Chiu et al. (2020) then compared the 2017 findings with another large-scale survey executed around 1995 by Stephen Chiu and Lui Tai Lok.[22] Although not quite as large as the Thematic Household Survey, the 1995 survey collected information from 1743 respondents from 23 to 55 years old, making it one of the largest survey of this kind until Wu (2010)'s survey in 2007.[23] As the Thematic Household Survey employed a simpler class scheme based on occupational categories classified into Class I (managers and professionals), Class II (associate professionals), Class III (clerical, services and sales, and manual employees), and Class IV (elementary occupations and agricultural and fishery employees), the

---

[22] Both of them were at the Chinese University of Hong Kong at the time. The 1995 survey was in some sense of better quality than Wong and Lui (1992) because the former had a larger sample size and also surveyed both men and women rather than just men.

[23] The "Social Inequality and Mobility in Hong Kong" survey was conducted in 2007, which included a successful household interview of 4013 persons born between 1946 and 1989. See Wu (2010). But it also faced the same sampling hurdles as mentioned earlier.

1995 data (the survey adopted the Goldthorpe scheme) were recoded to make it comparable.[24]

The headline findings were reported in Fig. 7.2. For the two waves, overall mobility patterns were remarkably similar. In 1995, 18.9% of all youth between 22 and 35 years old experienced downward mobility relative to their parents, 40.5% had upward mobility, and 40.7% had no change in occupational class positions. In 2017, the rates of downward and upward mobility, and immobility were 17.3%, 39.3% and 43.4% respectively. If anything, downward mobility appeared to be lower for all classes, resulting a lower overall downward mobility rate. Differences in upward mobility across the two waves was most visible for those coming from Class II households, with 22.1% in 1995, but 29% in 2017. Even those from Class III also saw significant improvement in upward mobility rates from 36.7% to 40.9%. Although for those from the more advantaged Class I origin, the possibility for maintaining their position was also higher across the two periods, but if "fear of falling" has also been alleged as the source of youth discontent, this finding could also be construed as not conducive to discontents.

From a high-definition perspective, there seems to be a lack of compelling evidence to support the recent view that youth occupational social

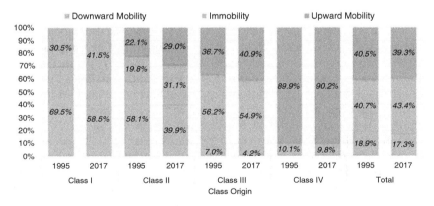

Fig. 7.2 Mobility Patterns by Class Origin: 1995 versus 2017. (Source: Chiu et al. (2020))

---

[24] 667 respondents between 23 and 35 years old were selected from the 1995 survey for the comparative analysis.

mobility in Hong Kong has been shrinking (comparing the 1990s, 2000s, and the most recent 2017). In addition, young people in Hong Kong are currently experiencing better chances for upward occupational mobility than those in Taiwan and Macau. This is the case even though a stronger 'inheritance' effect has been found with respect to father's occupational class, namely, the higher occupation class status of parents tends to benefit their children by keeping them in a higher class position. With this conclusion on the long term trends in social mobility in Hong Kong, we will come back to the more direct linkage between mobility experiences and propensity to protest among young people in Chap. 10.

This brings us to the second issue: it has been argued a university degree earns little in return for young people nowadays, and the expanding credential path has actually created a new barrier for those coming from more disadvantaged families. Given that parent's class background has an impact on young people's intergenerational mobility, would this be "reflected" in differentiation of education experience—which then strengthens rather than weakens the inheritance effect of class?

4.2   The University Dream: Does Obtaining a University Degree Enhance One's Upward Social Mobility in Hong Kong?

There is no simple answer to this question since it depends on how one approaches the issue. The cross-sectional view—one based on comparing youths of different educational background within the same time frame—suggests acquiring a degree enhances one's social mobility prospects. For instance, the HKIAPS (2016) report found that youth obtaining a tertiary or higher educational qualification were more likely to remain in the top occupational class or to experience upward mobility.[25] Likewise, Chiu and Leung (2014) examined the relationship between income and educational level among Hong Kong youth aged 25 years old or below by predicting each level's income with 2011 Census data. Using the "Form Five qualification" as the reference group, they discovered youths acquiring a university degree would have a 164% increase in income, with the percentage earnings increase greater for females than males. The Government's study on earnings mobility (Financial Secretary's Office, 2016) lends further support to the "university dream". Within a generation (10 years' time), more than 90% of individuals with "sub-degree or below but above

---

[25] See point 5.17 p. 55 of the HKIAPS (2016) report.

secondary education" (both self-financing and publicly funded), and individuals with publicly funded first degrees experienced upward mobility (see Table 2: Individual Earnings Mobility of 2001/02 Graduates (2003/04 to 2013/14)). Given the higher income level earned by all degree and sub-degree holders of the same cohort, it is no wonder that most youths and their parents would devote their resources to chasing the "university dream".

Although degree holders managed to maintain their advantage over youth with lower level qualifications, there seems to be a general decrease in earning potential of those aged 15–29 across all educational qualifications when comparing 2001 and 2011 census data (Chiu & Ip, 2014). Accordingly, the median income of youths (15–29) acquiring a degree qualification or above has dropped from HKD17,313 in 2001 to HKD15,500 in 2011. Compared to the median income of the entire Hong Kong working population aged 15 or above (2001: HKD12,287; 2011: HKD12,000), the income ratio for degree holders aged 15–29 has dropped from 1.41 in 2001 to 1.29 in 2011. This drop in the income ratio was particularly noticeable for youths achieving qualifications from "higher than form five to non-degree programme", which has come even closer to that obtained by those with only a Form Five or lower qualification.

In addition, Chiu and Ip (2014) discovered that young people aged 15–29 found it increasingly difficult to gain entry to certain occupations upon graduation. Despite the increase in university degree holders, comparing 2001 and 2011 data, the proportion of professionals and associate professionals among the 15–29 age group have both dropped, but that of clerks has increased. This implies that more university graduates would likely end up working in intermediate service jobs than upper-level ones. Overall, young people are facing a deteriorating labour market condition in Hong Kong, with those associate degree holders—who fell into the "university dream trap" but who were unable to obtain a degree—eventually suffering relatively more (Chiu & Ip, 2014).

How can we reconcile the seemingly contradictory findings that, on one hand, the opportunity for occupational mobility remains open, yet on the other, young people are increasingly experiencing deteriorating labour market conditions even as tertiary education has expanded? We offer two explanations here. First, the recent massification of higher education in Hong Kong has skewed towards market mechanism (Mok, 2016). The student enrolment in first-year first degree (FYFD) places of UGC-funded programs increased by only 5.5% from 17.6% in 2003/04 to 23.1% in

2014/15 (see earlier chart). The Government has been unwilling to expand public spending on higher education and has been constrained to do so by political and economic elites (Lee, 2015). According to Lee (2015), the massification, which accelerated during the two financial crises of 1997–2003 and 2007–2008, turns out to be partially-privatized and has aggravated rather than reduced social inequality by creating a bunch of self-financed sub-degree programs with low social recognition. This ends up producing graduates with low labour market employability. In addition, the upward mobility potential of higher education further worsens as the increasing rate of growth in the number of graduates outcompeted the increasing rate of growth of higher status occupations like managerial or professional jobs, resulting in intensified "positional competition" (Wu, 2010; Mok, 2016).

Our second explanation elaborates further on the inheritance effect of class (Wong & Koo, 2016). This "inertia against movement" is likely created by the social stratification function of education itself, since in a knowledge economy higher educational qualifications can be considered a proxy for upper occupational class. For instance, Vere (2010) has found that in Hong Kong the probability for a son to obtain a degree if his father also has one is 74%, compared to only 20% for the son whose father had only primary or less education.[26] There are multiple causes for this "degree inheritance".

We consider first the education path to gain entry to local degree programs. Chiu and Ho (2006) found that investment in home educational resources and social and cultural communication, often associated with higher socioeconomic status (SES) parents, actually played a part in raising students' reading test scores (rather than the socioeconomic status itself). Ho (2010) also found that students from higher SES families and those who studied in schools with a higher average SES level tended to achieve significantly better academic results and exhibit higher self-efficacy than their counterparts in scientific literacy. Again, it was argued that parental investment in cultural resources and involvement in organizing science learning activities at an early age, a phenomenon associated with higher SES, actually had an important part to play in the higher scientific literacy performance of the student (rather than the SES itself).[27] In a similar vein,

---

[26] See point 2.47 (Vere, 2010).
[27] Hence, by controlling the parenting type, the effect of SES on academic achievement would actually disappear (Chiu & Ho, 2006; Ho, 2010).

Lee and Chiu (2016) explored the impact of social class on students' achievement under the new senior secondary curriculum. They found that parents with a tertiary level of education was a significant determinant of success in the HKDSE examination for most of the core subjects. Family-based resources, extracurricular reading activities in particular, were found to be beneficial for achieving better results across subjects. In short, the difference in the parenting approach adopted by parents with higher and lower educational levels (i.e., a proxy for different occupational classes) could be associated with "degree inheritance".

In short, the more youth cherishes a university dream, the more intensified the competition becomes along the credential path. The deteriorating job market—lagged growth in higher-end service jobs and declining earnings mobility—has made the situation even worse. Again, class background determines whether the university dream materializes and shapes mobility outcomes in Hong Kong.

5   Conclusions

The "Hong Kong Story" is one that is not easy to tell, commented sociologist Lui Tai Lok. The same could be said of the subject of social mobility and social inequality in this place.

In Hong Kong, social fluidity and inequality go hand in hand. As Hong Kong was transformed from an industrial society to a post-industrial one, new occupational opportunities flourished at the expense of manufacturing positions. Those in the middle continue to leave their class of origin with relative ease, but those who already reached the top are also more likely to stay there. China opportunities offered a special treatment effect that buffered some of the negative impacts of deindustrialization, but it also resulted in polarized income inequality not just between high and low-end service jobs, but also between those that serve China's capitalism, and those jobs that are locally embedded. Most youth dream of obtaining a university degree—and should if they wish for upward mobility. But not every university dream can be achieved under the semi-privatized massification trend in higher education.

Understanding of the extent local and pattern of mobility have so far been hampered by a lack of solid data, although sociologists are trying their best to fill the gap in official data with their own research. The closest approximations so far proposed by the academic community suggested that while class structure still mattered and inequality became exacerbated, the middle class was not disappearing but neither did it boosted tremendously by the so-called "China opportunities". Further from the truth is also that young people are now being pushed to radical politics as a result of their declining mobility opportunities, as there seems no compelling evidence that there has been a decline in mobility opportunities for the younger generations.

REFERENCES

Bergman, M. M., & Joye, D. (2005). *Comparing Social Stratification Schemata: CAMSIS, CSP-CH, Goldthorpe, ISCO-88, Treiman, and Wright.* Cambridge Studies in Social Research, No. 10. Social and Political Science.

Breen, R. (2007). *Intergenerational mobility: Core model of social fluidity.* The Blackwell Encyclopedia of Sociology.

Census and Statistics Department. (2006). *Hong Kong 2006 Population By-census – Thematic Report: Household Income Distribution in Hong Kong.* Census and Statistics Department.

Census and Statistics Department. (2011a). *Hong Kong 2011 population census – Thematic report: Household income distribution in Hong Kong.* Census and Statistics Department.

Census and Statistics Department. (2011b). *Hong Kong 2011 population census – Thematic report: Persons from the mainland of China having resided in Hong Kong for less than 7 years.* Census and Statistics Department.

Census and Statistics Department. (2011c). *Table E003: Number of employed persons by industry and occupation (First Quarter 2011).* Census and Statistics Department.

Census and Statistics Department. (2017). *Table E305: Gini Coefficient by household size, 2006, 2011 and 2016.* Census and Statistics Department.

Census and Statistics Department, & Kong, H. (2019). *Thematic Household Survey Report No. 65: Education and employment trajectories of young and middle-aged persons.* Census and Statistics Department.

Chan, T. W., Lui, T. L., & Wong, T. W. (1995). A comparative analysis of social mobility in Hong Kong. *European Sociological Review, 11*(2), 135–155.

Chen, B. (2013). 大逃港(修訂本) [Escaping to Hong Kong (Rev. ed.)]. Hong Kong Open Page.

Cheng, J. Y. (2014). The emergence of radical politics in Hong Kong: Causes and impact. *China Review, 14*(1), 199–232.

Chiu, M. M., & Ho, E. S. (2006). Family effects on student achievement in Hong Kong. *Asia Pacific Journal of Education, 26*(1), 21.

Chiu, S. W. (2008). *Family changes and income inequality under globalization: The case of HK [Presentation].* Central Policy Unit, HKSAR Government.

Chiu, S. W. (2011). Family changes and income inequality under globalization. In S. W. Chiu & S. L. Wong (Eds.), *Hong Kong divided? Structures of social inequality in the twenty-first century* (pp. 201–242). Hong Kong Institute of Asia-Pacific Studies, CUHK.

Chiu, S. W., Choi, S. Y., & Ting, K. F. (2005). Getting ahead in the capitalist paradise: Migration from China and socioeconomic attainment in Colonial Hong Kong. *International Migration Review, 39*(1), 203–227.

Chiu, S. W., & Ip, C. Y. (2014, December 5). 青年「下流」問題的虛與實 [The fiction and reality of the issues of "downward mobility" of the youth]. *Mingpao*, p. A44.

Chiu, S. W., Jiang, N., & Yu, H. (2020). *Blocked youth social mobility in Hong Kong: Myth or reality?* Academy of Hong Kong Studies, The Education University of Hong Kong.

Chiu, S. W., & Leung, Y. K. (2014, December 17). 青年「下流」= 讀書無用? ["Downward mobility" of the youth = studying is useless?]. *Mingpao*, p. A31.

Chiu, S. W., & Lui, T. L. (2004). Testing the global city-social polarisation thesis: Hong Kong since the 1990s. *Urban Studies, 41*(10), 1863–1888.

Chiu, S. W., & Lui, T. L. (2009). *Hong Kong: Becoming a Chinese global city*. Routledge.

Crompton, R., & Scott, J. (1999). Introduction: The state of class analysis. *The Sociological Review, 47*(S2), 1–15.

Deyo, F. C. (1989). *Beneath the miracle: Labor subordination in the new Asian industrialism*. University of California Press.

Erikson, R., & Goldthorpe, J. (1992). *The constant flux: A study of class mobility in industrial societies*. Clarendon Press.

Erikson, R., Goldthorpe, J., & Portocarero, L. (1983). Intergenerational class mobility and the Convergence Thesis: England, France and Sweden. *British Journal of Sociology, 34*(3), 303–343.

Financial Secretary's Office. (2016). *2015 study on earnings mobility (Information Paper)*. Hong Kong SAR Government.

Ho, E. S. (2010). Family influences on science learning among Hong Kong adolescents: What we learned from PISA. *International Journal of Science and Mathematics Education, 8*(3), 409–428.

Hong Kong Institute of Asia-Pacific Studies. (2016). *Impact of social mobility on the political attitudes and behaviours of young people: A comparative study of Hong Kong, Taiwan, and Macao (2015.A4.011.15C)*. Hong Kong Institute of Asia-Pacific Studies, CUHK (in Chinese).

Lau, S. K. (1982). *Society and politics in Hong Kong*. The Chinese University Press.

Lee, K. M., Wong, H., & Law, K. Y. (2007). Social polarization and poverty in the global city: The case of Hong Kong. *China Report, 43*(1), 1–30.

Lee, S. Y. (2015). Massification without equalisation: The politics of higher education, graduate employment and social mobility in Hong Kong. *Journal of
Education and Work, 29*(1), 13–31.
Lee, T. T., & Chiu, S. W. (2016). Curriculum reform and the social class achieve-
ment gap. *Social Transformations in Chinese Societies, 12*(2), 148–165.
Legislative Council. (2014). Members' Motion – Hon Jeffrey LAM's motion on
"Increasing upward mobility opportunities for young people" (Council meetings of 17 December 2014 and 7 January 2015). https://www.legco.gov.hk/
yr14-15/english/counmtg/motion/cm20141217m-lkf.htm
Legislative Council Secretariat. (2015). *Social Mobility in Hong Kong* (Research
Brief Issue No.2 2014–2015). Hong Kong: Legislative Council Secretariat.
https://www.legco.gov.hk/research-publications/english/1415rb02-social-
mobility-in-hong-kong-20150112-e.pdf
Liu, L. (2017, March 14). Look north, HK youths told. *China Daily.* http://
www.chinadaily.com.cn/hkedition/2017-03/14/content_28544705.htm
Lui, T. L. (2003). Rearguard politics: Hong Kong's Middle Class. *The Developing
Economies, 41*(2), 161–183.
Lui, T. L. (2007). 四代香港人 *[Four Generations of Hongkongers].* Step Forward
Multi Media.
Lui, T. L. (2010). Hong Kong's changing opportunity structures: Political con-
cerns and sociological observations. In K. B. Chan, A. S. Ku, & Y. W. Chu
(Eds.), *Social stratification in Chinese societies* (pp. 141–164). Brill.
Lui, T. L. (2014). Fading opportunities. Hong Kong in the context of regional
integration. *China Perspectives, 2014*(1), 35–42.
Ma, N. (2011). Value changes and legitimacy crisis in post-industrial Hong Kong.
Asian Survey, 51(4), 683–712.
Mok, K. H. (2016). Massification of higher education, graduate employment and
social mobility in the Greater China region. *British Journal of Sociology of
Education, 37*(1), 51–71.
Ouchi, W. G. (1984). *The M-Form society: How American teamwork can recapture
the competitive edge.* Addison-Wesley.
RTHK. (2017, June 6). Look north if you want to succeed: Zhang
Xiaoming. *RTHK.* http://news.rthk.hk/rthk/en/component/k2/1334442-
20170606.htm
South China Morning Post. (2011, May 23). The road to rich pickings. *South
China Morning Post.* https://www.scmp.com/article/968546/road-rich-
pickings
University Grants Committee. (2019). *CDCF Data Mart – Statistics.* http://cdcf.
ugc.edu.hk/cdcf/searchStatSiteReport.do
Vere, J. P. (2010, March 5–6). Special topic enquiry on earnings mobility [Paper
presentation]. The 26th International Conference of the American Committee

for Asian Economic Studies (ACAES), Doshisha University, Kyoto, Japan. https://hub.hku.hk/bitstream/10722/127842/1/Content.pdf?accept=1

Wong, K. Y., & Wan, P. S. (2009). New evidence of the postmaterialist shift: The experience of Hong Kong. *Social Indicators Research, 92*(3), 497–515.

Wong, T. W., & Lui, T. L. (1992). *Reinstating class: A structural and developmental study of Hong Kong Society*. Social Sciences Research Centre Occasional Paper 10. Social Sciences Rseach Centre, the University of Hong Kong (in association with the Department of Sociology, The University of Hong Kong).

Wong, Y. L., & Koo, A. (2016). Is Hong Kong no longer a land of opportunities after the 1997 handover? *Asian Journal of Social Science, 44*(4–5), 516–545.

Wu, X. (2010). *Hong Kong's Post-80s generation: Profiles and predicaments (Commissioned Report)*. Central Policy Unit, HKSAR Government.

CHAPTER 8

Hong Kong as a Battlefield for Shelter: Hong Kong's Housing Problem and a Dual Land Regime

"With a population of nearly 7.5 million and almost no developable land remaining, these people get by in illegally subdivided apartments so small that they're called 'coffin cubicles',"
—Stacke, *2017.*
"Feudalism, not overpopulation or land shortage, is to blame for Hong Kong's housing problems,"
—Kilpatrick, *2018.*

1   SETTING THE STAGE: THE HOUSING CRISIS

Living in Hong Kong has become like a Battle-Royale for shelter. The community has been clamouring for a housing crisis and recent governments have been scrambling for a solution. The crisis appeared in many forms, but the haphazard living conditions of subdivided units,[1] has actually riveted global attention (Lam, 2017). According to the 2016 population by-census, up to 91,787 households or 209,700 people resided in subdivided flats (or cubicle to be more precise, 75 sq. ft. to 140 sq. ft) (Census and Statistics Department, 2001 & 2017). Hong Kong is also the least affordable city to buy an apartment in the world. According to a

---

[1] A common definition of subdivided units is a flat being divided into two or more subunits for rental purpose.

S. W. K. Chiu, K. Y. K. Siu, *Hong Kong Society*, Hong Kong Studies Reader Series, https://doi.org/10.1007/978-981-16-5707-8_8

2019 survey (Demographia, 2019), Hong Kong has a median ratio of 20.9 for the median property price to the median household income, implying an average household have to take more than two decades to buy an apartment even without spending on anything else. The National Geographic report attributed the housing crisis to the commonsense of overpopulation and a scarcity of land, but the rebuttal by Ryan Kilpatrick in the *Free Press* points perhaps to something more profound. What indeed is the "feudalism" that he is referring to?

In her second policy address, the fourth Chief Executive Mrs. Carrie Lam laid out one of the most controversial reclamation projects in Hong Kong history—the "Lantau Tomorrow Vision" project. Reclaiming 1700-hectare of land to build artificial islands near the waters of East Lantau, the project is predicted to cost about HK$400 to HK$500 billion (US$64 billion), and is said to provide about 260,000 to 400,000 homes to 1.1 million people. Seventy per cent of these homes would be public housing. The government argues the reclamation is necessary as *housing problems in Hong Kong are caused by a land shortage.*[2] The ever-increasing waiting time for obtaining a public housing unit, notably from 2.7 years in 2012 to 5.4 years in 2020, is also tied to the land shortage.[3]

Since the late 2000s, public dissatisfaction of the housing situation has been mounting. A series of surveys commissioned by the Radio Television Hong Kong, the local public broadcast station, lends testimony to the rising discontent towards the government's housing policy after 2009 (Chiu et al., 2018; Chiu, 2019b; Hong Kong Connection, 2018) (Fig. 8.1). A catchy phrase, *the real estate hegemony* (地產霸權), aka the collusion of the big developers and political elites, has been popularized in anti-neoliberalists critique of the housing problems in Hong Kong since then. The argument is not complicated—the privatization trend and the financial logic working under neoliberalism's free market ideology has encroached on the daily life of Hong Kong people, transforming the city fundamentally.

---

[2] As illustrated by the report of the Task Force on Land Supply (TFLS) in 2018: "Land shortage has been plaguing Hong Kong in recent years. The society at large is suffering from multi-faceted problems with "pricy", "tiny" and "cramped" living conditions, characterized by soaring property prices and rents; the difficulties in purchasing the first home; and all sorts of problems associated with overcrowded living space, inadequate community facilities, and high business operating costs." (TFLS, 2018a).

[3] Data Source from a series of surveys commissioned by the Radio Television Hong Kong Television Department and conducted by the Hong Kong Institute of Asia-Pacific Studies, The Chinese University of Hong Kong

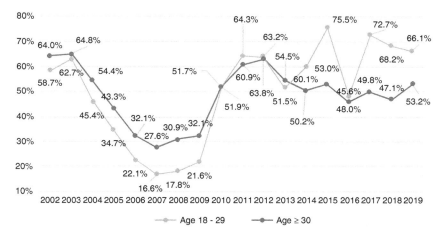

Fig. 8.1 Popular dissatisfaction over housing policy, 2002–2019 (% of respondents dissatisfied). Source: Chiu (2019a)

While the skyrocketed housing price and rent, and left-wing critique of real estate hegemony conveniently capture the still images of Hong Kong's urban housing problems, the origin, development of and the proposed solution to these phenomena is less than clear. The government has not made this situation better by tying its deficiency in housing policy to the malfunctioning of the land market, as stated in the beginning paragraph, therefore complicating the argument.

Can the government's mega reclamation project solve Hong Kong's land supply and housing problem once and for all? A group of economists signed an open letter in support of the project by arguing reclamation is more cost effective than developing the New Territories, for the government could recover the cost through land sale instead of having to purchase land from existing landowners (Sung & Wong, 2018). As a government report suggests, Hong Kong is actually not short of land, with only 24.3% of the total land area of 1111 km² (111,100 hectares) is built-up and the rest are actually various types of vegetated area such as grassland and woodland (see Fig. 8.2). Besides, a civic organization also suggests that there were 1521 hectares of brownfields in the New Territories that could be made available for building purposes (Liber

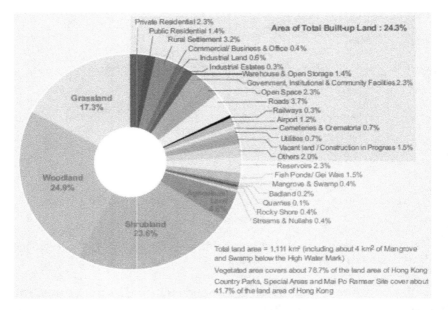

Fig. 8.2 Land Utilisation in Hong Kong. Source: Task Force on Land Supply (2018b)

Research Community, 2018a, 2018b).[4] Where are these lands and why were they not utilized—apart from economic reasons? Why is there an urgency to launch the costly reclamation project while arguably the big developers are holding a substantial amount of lands in the New Territories? Some puzzles remain unexplained.

Apart from this introduction, this chapter has three parts. The second gives a brief history of housing policy in Hong Kong and outlines three main logics governing interventions to the housing market. The third discusses myths surrounding the "lack of land" discourse and recent land policy development. The fourth is the conclusion.

The origins of the current housing crisis are often framed in opposing way by the "two sides of the aisle"—the economic liberals, and those who follow the legacy of Henri Lefebvre's Marxist urban sociology. On the one

---

[4] The Legislative Council identified 1300 hectares. See LC Paper No. CB(1)160/19–20 (07). Panel on Development. Meeting on 26 November 2019. Background brief on developing brownfield sites as a land supply option.

side, supporters of the free market argue that housing crisis emerges because market is not "free" enough as the government intervenes too much. They also propose to unleash the market forces by privatizing public housing. On the other side, critics argue government intervention is either too limited, or is done in favour of the capitalist system that could be extracted to the colonial period (Lee & Tang, 2017). At the centre of these discussions is the role of the state and its interventions in the land and housing market. One problem in these discussions is that often the market (either the good or bad side) is being enshrined as the primary explanation of the housing crisis. Is the shortage of land the cause of the housing crisis? Commonsense suggests so, but others found either no causal relationship between land supply and housing prices (Tse, 1998), or that new housing supply in Hong Kong is independent of land supply by the government (Lai & Wang, 1999; Huang et al., 2015). Simply put, while developers have land and the government wants to build more houses, why was land not extensively developed in the New Territories according to the supply and demand market principle?

To fill this gap, we would tap on urban planning literatures to highlight an institutionalist perspective on what leads to stability or change in land and housing policy (Kim, 2012; Taylor, 2013; Sorensen, 2017). A sizable literature touches on the historical diffusion of British zoning culture (e.g. green belt) and the isomorphic development of town planning institutions in Hong Kong that play a crucial role in regulating land use (Lai, 1998, 1999, 2000, 2004, 2011; Lai & Yu, 2001; Lai & Ho, 2001; Hui & Ho, 2003; Tang et al., 2005; Tang et al., 2007; Tang & Wong, 2008; Lai et al., 2009; Lai & Kwong, 2012; Yu & Hui, 2018). These studies consistently demonstrated a strained relationship between town planners (e.g. via zoning) and the free market over land use (Lai & Yu, 2001; Lai, 2004; Lai & Kwong, 2012), and how "town planning as an institutionalized control of spatial manifestations of human activities in a market economy" since the colonial time (Lai, 2005, p.11). Tang et al. (2005) examined green belt planning policy and illustrated the peculiar flexibility of the Town Planning Board in accommodating (or, privileging) applications of small village house construction in the green belt zone. We highlight how town planning institutionally worked against the market force, and reintroduce a perspective other than that of the neoliberal market fundamentalism or one that attributed a land shortage solely to a high land price policy.

In the concluding part, we revisit some reasons why the ruling elites in post-colonial Hong Kong failed to articulate a united front to resolve the growing worries about Hong Kong's "property hegemony" and high housing prices. The government claims that the Lantau Tomorrow Vision project will resolve the so-called land scarcity issue through massive reclamation in several outer islands. Why is there such a *new framing of an old social problem?* Is it merely a new attempt to tackle a long existing social problem, or does it signal the start of a reconfiguration of political economy through resolving urban and rural development issues once and for all?

2   FRAMING THE HOUSING PROBLEMS: THE LOGICS
OF INTERVENTION

2.1   *Government Intervention in Hong Kong Housing in Hong Kong: A Quick Sketch*

Hong Kong's history of urban housing development can be roughly divided into four periods according to level of government intervention (Chan, 1999):

Pre-1954: Laissez-Faire

Before 1954, the Hong Kong government seldom intervened in urban planning, not to mention the housing market. Several fragmented ordinances regulating housing and urban environment existed but were rarely enforced seriously. The only exceptions were the discriminatory zoning ordinances (Lai & Yu, 2001, see also Chap. 2) and public health related building ordinances that addressed the colonial state's "sanitary syndrome" (Ip, 2011). Still, both ordinances regulated housing not out of welfare need. Large-scale interventions occurred whenever there were acute social crises during this period, such as the demolition of houses during the plague outbreak between 1894 and 1906 (Chan, 1999). The concept of public housing was first introduced in 1938 by a government commission to investigate housing difficulties in Hong Kong (Ip, 2011). Again, the true concern of the 1938 commission was to solve the public health crisis due to a spread of tuberculosis in the overcrowded living environment (Jones, 2003). No institutional arrangement was made after this commission. Nor were any attempts to set out any long-term strategy to deal with the deteriorating housing conditions.

After the Second World War and the establishment of new regime by the Chinese Communist Party, Hong Kong's housing environment further worsened with the influx of political refugees from mainland China. In 1947, the colonial government launched a rent control policy chiefly to control the rents of all pre-WWII premises (Cheung, 1979). Some land under the Lion Rock and Kowloon Bay in Kowloon was reserved to allow residents to build temporary houses for shelter, to which the government later regulated and licensed in 1964. The Hong Kong Housing Society was established as pilot schemes for public housing in 1952. These better-quality model units were equipped with independent kitchen and toilet, but was abandoned by the Financial Secretary and the Chief Building Surveyor for being low cost-effective in living density ratio (Ip, 2011).

There are two conventional explanations to the government's *laissez-faire* attitude towards housing need. First, colonial ruler perceived Hong Kong merely as a trade port with no apparent incentive to improve local's daily lives. Second, the postwar refugee community carried a mentality that satisfied with "a roof to shelter" and did not demand much from the government (Lau, 1984).

1954–1972: Large-Scale Intervention
Hong Kong's population rapidly increased due to migration from the mainland and the postwar baby boom in this period. Most people considered the public housing projects in Hong Kong were triggered by the 1953 Christmas Shek Kip Mei squatter area fire, which left some 53,000 people homeless. The government was forced to intervene for fear that the situation would turn into a territory-wide social instability. Resettlement estates were built on the areas where the burnt-down buildings originally located.

Some argued that Shek Kip Mei fire was just a *trigger*, rather than the origin to the government large-scale intervention into public housing (Jones, 2003; Faure, 2003; Smart, 2006). Jones argued there was a public housing policy transfer from the UK to Hong Kong (recalled the setting up of the Housing Commission in 1938), albeit a slower one compared to other former British colonies. After a fire broke out in Kowloon Walled City in January 1950, the Hong Kong government had already embarked on a gradual learning curve in handling squatter problems in Hong Kong.[5]

---

[5] For example, a housing plan to build five-story public housing buildings was submitted by the Chief Architect, Stanley Feltham, to the Public Works Department of the Government

Eventually, the seven-story Mark I type public housing, with only communal bathroom and facilities, were adopted.

In any case, the year 1954 was a landmark. Two new departments were established— the Housing Authority and the Resettlement Department, with the former played a key role in postwar public housing development. In 1964, the colonial government introduced the means-tested "Low-cost Public Rental Housing" to the working classes. Just a decade between 1954 and 1964, the percentage of public housing increased from 4% to around 45 per cent of the total population (Lin et al., 1979).

1972–1985: Consolidation

In early 1972, the government announced an ambitious "Ten Year Public Housing Plan", to provide 1.8 million people with "satisfactory accommodation", or permanent, self-contained housing, and rebuild the earliest Mark I and II types public housing estates in 15 years. This was the so-called "Golden Era of MacLehose". The Housing Authority was restructured and assigned to carry out the plan, which also ended the resettlement policy in Hong Kong (Leung, 1999). Since 1973, the Housing Authority became a self-supporting statutory body responsible for building and managing of public housing estates. The government supported it with free land and low interest rate loan. However, only 119,117 housing units were built between 1973 and 1980, accommodating 713,935 residents or 40 per cent of the original target. In 1982, the Ten Year Public Housing Plan was extended to 1987 (Leung, 1999).

As Hong Kong's population grew rapidly, the public housing development was expanded to new towns in the New Territories. In the early 1970s, several "satellite cities" was developed in full speed, including Tsuen Wan, Tuen Mun, and Shatin. Between 1961 and 1991, proportion of population in the New Territories increased from 14 to 43 per cent (Chan, 1999). To cater for the rising middle-class population, the "Home Ownership Housing Program" (HOS) was launched in 1976. In 1978, the government further invited private developers to involve in the Program.

1985–2000: Privatization

The idea to privatized public housing was diffused from the British "Right to Buy" policy passed in the Housing Act 1980 under British Prime

in 1950 (Public Records Office, HKRS 155-1-1899).

Minister Margaret Thatcher's rule.[6] The Housing Authority in Hong Kong launched a "Long-term Housing Development Strategy" (1987), pursuing the privatization direction. The major changes included expansion of redevelopment program, moving public rental housing tenants to assisted home purchase flats, balancing the provision of rental flats and Home Ownership Scheme flats, redevelopment sites into Home Ownership Scheme flats and introduction of a home purchase loan scheme (Hong Kong Housing Authority, 1994). The gist of the strategy was to gradually substitute the public sector with the private market as the primary supplier of housing.

The Hong Kong government set out a series of policies in line with the Housing Authority's Development Strategy (1987). Examples included a reduction in public rental housing provision, encouraging "wealthy tenants" to participate in private housing market, and providing loan schemes to first-time buyers. In 1991, the Housing Authority launched the short-lived Sale of Flats to Sitting Tenants Scheme (SFSTS), providing an opportunity for sitting tenants of public rental housing to buy their units (La Grange & Pretorius, 2000). In 1997, the scheme was modified as the Tenants Purchase Scheme to allow public housing tenants to purchase their occupied units in a very low price (e.g. HKD300,000).

Nevertheless, the Housing Authority's 1987 Long Term Housing Strategy failed to solve Hong Kong's housing problem due to persistent shortage and continual high demand for public rental housing. The strategy tried to encourage homeownership among wealthy tenants so that the turnover rate of public housing units can be increased, but the rapid development of private housing market in Hong Kong was overlooked. By the 1990s, housing prices grew dramatically to a level that was not even affordable by the new middle classes.

The New Millennium: The Two U-Turns in Public Housing Policy and the Look for "New" Land
After the retrocession, a new Ten-Year Housing Plan was announced in 1998. The Plan, dubbed the 85,000 plan for setting an annual target to build 50,000 public units and 35,000 private units and to achieve 70%

---

[6]The Right to Buy policy was passed in the Housing Act 1980, a year after Margaret Thatcher became Britain's Prime Minister. The legislation granted tenants of council house the right to buy their residence at a discounted value. The ultimate purpose of the housing privatization was to cut back state's involvement in the market.

housing ownership, resulted in many controversies when the Tung Government admitted having abandoned the goal during the Asia Financial Crisis. The financial crisis ended the 1990s housing price speculation and turned many properties into negative equity. Secretary for Housing, Planning and Lands, Suen Ming Yeung then announced nine strategic policies to stabilize the housing market, among them were the immediate halt of the land auction, stopping of production and sale of HOS, stopping of Tenants Purchase Scheme, and a change to demand-driven production of public rental housing. This was a U-turn in public housing policy.

In 2014 the SAR Government made another U-turn in housing policy and introduced a new Long Term Housing Strategy, which has set a rolling housing supply target to build 200,000 PRH units and 80,000 subsidised sale flats within a ten years-time (see Table 8.1).[7] The Strategy also outlined, along with other long- and short-term measures, developing Lantau and reclamations outside Victoria Harbour as a possible way to boost land supply for housing. In 2018, Chief Executive Carrie Lam formally launched the Lantau Tomorrow Vision development project.

2.2   Logics of Government Intervention: Existing Images

Why did the Hong Kong Government (Colonial and SAR) intervene into the housing market? In this section, we highlight extant images of the three logics of state intervention to the housing since the 1950s. These three logics are the collective consumption logic, political logic, and financial logic. While not exclusionary to each other, the three logics identify different key factors behind housing intervention. No single logic can explain the institutional responses for all periods since each logic accounted for a small part of the state's action towards macro changes in the local, regional and global context in conjunction with Hong Kong's socio-economic and political development.

---

[7] The timeline of development of housing policy is consolidated from the facts mentioned in this chapter and the following references: HKHA (1996); Legco Panel on Planning, Lands and Works (1996); Leung (1999); Nissim (2012); Wong (1998).

Table 8.1 Development of housing policy in Hong Kong

Year	Events
1947	Rental control policy was enacted.
1948	The Hong Kong housing society was established as a voluntary organization. Originally, it was formed as a branch of the Council of the Social Services in 1948.
1950	Kowloon Walled City fire occurred.
1950–1953	Stanley Feltham submitted a housing plan to the public works Department of the Government.
1951	The housing society was incorporated and became a statutory body.
1951	The Tung tau squatter fire occurred.
1953	The Shek kip Mei fire happened and led to more than 50,000 residents lost their shelters.
1954	Resettlement estates were built on the areas where the burnt-down buildings originally located.
1954	The resettlement department and the Hong Kong housing authority were established.
1960	A land exchange system began.
1964	The low-cost housing programme was launched.
1966–1967	Riots happened in Hong Kong.
1972	Ten year public housing plan was launched.
1973	The housing authority was restructured and the new housing department was formed.
1976	The home ownership plan was launched.
1978	Flats of the home ownership scheme (HOS) were sold.
1978	The private sector participation scheme was launched.
1982	The ten year public housing plan was extended to 1987 as the targets of it were not fulfilled.
1983	The land exchange system was brought to an end.
1984	The letters A/B program was replaced with a "monetized scheme".
1986	The housing subsidy policy was endorsed by the housing authority.
1987	It was the end of the ten-year building plan and the beginning of the long-term housing policy
1987	The housing subsidy policy (i.e., double rent policy) was implemented on "well-off families" of the public rental housing.
1988	The home purchase loan scheme was launched.
1991	The Sale of flats to sitting tenants scheme was launched.
1993	The housing subsidy policy was reformulated.
1997	The secondary market scheme of the HOS was implemented.
1998	The 1998 Long-term Housing Policy was announced with annual target to build 85,000 units.
1998	Tenants purchase scheme was started.

(*continued*)

Table 8.1 (continued)

Year	Events
2014	The 2014 Long-term Housing Policy was announced with a target to build 200,000 PRH units and 80,000 subsidized sale flats in 10 years
2018	Lantau tomorrow vision development project was announced.

Public Housing: The Logic of Collective Consumption for Social Stability and Economic Development of Local Hong Kong Society

The first logic focused on public housing as collective consumption in furthering social stability and economic development of the local Hong Kong society (Castells et al., 1990, p.4). The concept of collective consumption was developed by Castells, a Marxist urban sociologist, in his 1977 book *The Urban Question*. Briefly, to ensure the long-term interest of the capitalist economy, the state intervenes to provide collective means of consumption, such as education and in our case, housing, to reproduce a labour force that fits capitalist productive activity. In this way, collective consumption is differentiated from individual consumption with the potential to mobilize consumers for political purposes.

The massive public housing project after the Shek Kip Mei fire was nothing out of *charity or welfare right*, which was secondary to developmental concern (Castells et al., 1990). Transforming Hong Kong from an entrepôt to a manufacturing centre was the top administration priority. Facing successive waves of Chinese refugees from mainland between 1950s and 1960s, the colonial state never directed enough public resources to improve the livelihoods of the population, making public housing program always falling behind its minimum targets (Castells et al., 1990).

Castells et al. (1990) summarized four main reasons why the colonial state intervened in the housing market in this period. For the first two, land clearance and social containment were means to social control and economic growth between 1950s–1960s. Apart from a restoration of public order and hygiene in a city that was swiftly becoming entirely made up of slums and squatters, the colonial state acquired land near or in the urban area for industrial development.

The third reason concerned social stability and political legitimacy after the two territory-wide riots in 1966 and 1967 (Scott, 1989). There was a dramatic shift in colonial social and welfare policies to address the housing need. For example, the Report of the Commission of Inquiry on Kowloon

Disturbance 1966 purportedly showed an official reflection on the relationship between dense living environment and social stability (Hong Kong: Government Printer, 1967). It was also observed that the densely populated resettlement estates of Tung Tau Tsuen and Wong Tai Sin were hot spots for mob sabotage during the 1967 riot. By contrast, things were far more peaceful in the low-cost housing estates where living conditions were generally better (Leung, 1999, p.142). As a response, the government planned for more and better living quarters and development of the new towns.

For the last reason, through subsidizing wages (i.e. providing cheap housing and water) and improving the stability of the labour force (i.e. building public housing estates near factory zones), the whole capitalist system benefitted without incurring fiscal pressure on the business community and the manufacturers. In this way, a consensus was reached among the economic and the political elites of Hong Kong towards state intervention in the housing market (Castells et al., 1990).

The public housing programs transformed the concepts of welfare in Hong Kong. By the 1970s, people considered being placed on the public housing waiting list as the symbol of "becoming" a Hong Kong citizen (Castells et al., 1990). As a social stabilizer, public housing was a key means of urban governance to advance living conditions, thereby easing the tendency of residents to pursue extra-institutional means to pressure the government to improve their livelihoods. By pacifying the working class and indirectly subsidizing the manufacturers, the accumulation of capitals continued as industrialization sped up in post-War Hong Kong.

The Political Logic: Regional Political Threat on Internal Security
Castells et al.'s neo-Marxist interpretation of public housing policy in Hong Kong defined the Shek Kip Mei squatter fire as the pivotal point where economic policy shifted from *laissez-faire* to active state intervention in collective consumption. However, it was challenged as a functionalist[8] argument for not providing enough empirical evidence to support such claim (Smart, 2006, p.15). While Castells et al. (1990) maintained that the public housing policies catered mainly the social and economic development of Hong Kong, Smart (2006) argued that they were

---

[8] Though, Castell was considered a Marxist urban sociologist for developing the concept of collective consumption. Smart's critique is still valid on the ground that Marxism focuses on the logic of economic determinism and often functionalism does the same.

responses to a larger regional political concern in the 1950s and the 1960s, especially when facing the threat of the newly established Communist regime in mainland China.

Smart (2006) argued the significance of other squatter fires in the 1950s was ignored. Between 1950 and 1953, at least 12 fires occurred in squatter areas, including the Tung Tau Squatter Fires in 1950 and 1951 and later the Shek Kip Mei Squatter Fire in 1953. These fires led to more than 100,000 homeless victims (Leung, 1999). Squatter villages were problematic because they lacked planning and were difficult to police and control. Whenever there were fires broken out in squatter areas, the colonial government's fragile position was exposed as fire victims often refused to be resettled in other "tolerated squatter areas", which was exactly the aftermath of Tung Tau Squatter Fire in 1951. (Smart, 2006). Failed resettlement plan alerted the colonial authority about the seriousness of the squatter problem and kicked start resettlement plans before the Shek Kip Mei fire.

Most importantly, the 1951 Tung Tau fire raised a concern about the security and the position of the colony with the Chinese Government (Smart, 2006). The fire triggered a "comfort mission" from mainland China, which was considered a political threat to internal security by the colonial state. For fear that the mission could become a source of subversive activities, the colonial authority denied its entry. This did not end peacefully. Student riots erupted in Kowloon areas, coupled with denouncements by leaders of Communist China over how fire victims were maltreated, further heightened a political concern over the loyalty and unreliability of the Chinese population.[9]

The Shek Kip Mei fire merely enabled earlier ideas to be put in place (Smart, 2006). It was the regional political factors from mainland China that affected the context and decisions made by the colonial administration in handling squatter problems. This political logic contrasts sharply with Castells et al. (1990)'s collective consumption argument, which sees the colonial government's social policies being an objective condition in service of Hong Kong's capitalist system. There was, in fact, no grand

---

[9] After the riots, the colonial government filed a report and asserted that: No single factor in the Colony has so much bearing on the crime situation as the squatter problem. Because of the geographical nature of the squatter settlements, the complete lack of planning and the absence of lighting of any kind, no proper police supervision can be exercised and patrol work is almost impossible at night in these areas...these areas provide shelter and meeting places for *political agents of all kinds*. (Smart, 2006)

social policy on housing but a trial-and-error experimentation triggered by an anxiety over political security beyond the border. The purposive housing act of the colonial state was not always guided by, if not sometimes independent from, society demand for ontological security.

The Financial Logic: Neoliberal Globalization and the Privatization of Public Housing
To begin with, let us define "financialization". It describes the process of the growing dominance of global finance and short-term flows of investments over the contemporary world economy (Williams, 2000, as cited in Smart & Lee, 2003). There is a reduction of the distance between high finance and every life and a lowered barrier between global banking and household finance (Finlayson, 2009), that means home ownership is also affected. Under financial globalization, credit (e.g. financing through stock market and mortgage) has become more accessible through integrated markets.

In Hong Kong, "financialization" process happened in the same period of the rise of the class-monopoly rent in the urbanized area, which is defined as "the rate of return to a class of providers of an urban resource (such as housing) is set by the outcome of conflict with a class of consumers of that resource." (Harvey, 1974, p. 239). Between the end of the 1970s and 1990s, Hong Kong gradually transformed into a service economy and deindustrialized. The new middle class apparently could better afford private apartments in the housing markets. This echoes Henri Lefebvre's earlier observation that "a 'secondary circuit of capital' is supplanting 'the primary circuit of capital in production'" in highly urbanized area (Harvey, 1974, p. 239). In Smart and Lee's (2003) word, "a finance-led regime of accumulation and a property-based model of regulation" emerged from this period in Hong Kong.

1983 was a remarkable year. In response to the escalating crisis of confidence over Hong Kong's future, the Government announced Hong Kong dollar was pegged to the US dollar at the fixed rate of HKD7.8 to one USD. Some blamed this for the city's soaring property prices in recent years, as Hong Kong has to follow US's interest rate—which makes cheap credits easily accessible (Li, 2013). The rapid growth of the stock market and the skyrocketing valuations of real estate between 1984 and 1997 turned Hong Kong into a finance-led growth regime candidate (Smart & Lee, 2003). As housing prices were driven up by export and interest rates, so did domestic expenditures in Hong Kong (Ho & Wong, 2006). This regime, once started, pushed Hong Kong's housing market down the speculative spiral, projecting another housing myth that *Hong Kong's high housing price as a normal situation.*

While private housing developed swiftly in parallel with centralization and concentration of capital by real estate developers (Tang, 2008), there was also a change in the role of the Housing Authority in response to financialization. By 1983, MacLehose's ambitious ten years public housing program failed by missing 50 per cent of its original target. The subsidized Home Ownership Scheme (HOS) was expanded to absorb well-off tenants from the public housing rental units so as to increase their turnover rate. The restrictive income limit for buying subsidized housing under the HOS pushed the more well-off tenants towards the private market. The Housing Subsidy Policy was also implemented to reduce the subsidy to "well-off families" of the public rental housing by having them to pay double of the rent. All these signalled an intensified attempt to privatize public housing in Hong Kong. The rate of ownership in the public sector increased from 5 per cent in 1982/3 to 22.9 per cent in 1984/5 and that in the private sector increased from 56.8 per cent in 1982/3 to 74.4 per cent in 1984/5. (La Grange, 1997).

Then came the 1997 Asian Financial Crisis. Towards the end of the same year, the Housing Authority implemented a new privatization policy—Tenant Purchase Scheme (TPS). Sitting tenants in designated public housing estates could purchase their own flats at up to an 88% discount off the estimated market price (Ho & Wong, 2006, p. 264). It seems that the original purpose of TPS and the 35,000 private units target outlined in Tung Government's 1998 Ten-Year Housing Plan was to strengthen an asset-based social policy through achieving 70% housing ownership.[10]

This shift to asset-based welfare in Hong Kong was in line with global welfare state retrenchment and reduced public welfare funding under financial logics of neoliberalism (Hacker, 2004; Doling & Ronald, 2010). Home ownership has become increasingly central to the debate of asset-based welfare amid the restructuring of the welfare states (Watson, 2009). The major difference from cash-based welfare is that in asset-based welfare "a person builds up a portfolio of assets out of current savings so that

---

[10] The timing to mimic the Singapore model was a bad one. According to Ho and Wong (2006), the privatization of public rental housing broke the housing ladder by drawing away potential buyers of the Home Ownership Scheme, which in turn drew away would be buyers in the "sinking" private housing market.

foregone consumption possibilities in the present can be translated into future consumption of welfare-enhancing services." (Watson, 2009, p.44). It is said that asset, or home ownership, helps to cushion the adverse effect of crises experienced by an individual throughout the life course, such as sudden unemployment and retirement. A similar argument was made by local economist Richard Wong (1998): privatization benefits Hong Kong's economic growth by releasing an additional 0.5% to 1%, eliminating the distortions of consumption patterns such as a decision to participate in the labour market and schooling opportunities for children, removing the failed redistribution of income by public housing program, providing assets for self-support and stabilize society.

In *high-definition* image, appraising Hong Kong's privatization of public housing policy as asset-based welfare would miss several important details. Adrienne La Grange (1997) found that Hong Kong's privatization policy was too ambitious and consisted of a large scale of public rental housing. The focus of the Housing Authority on the highly demanded public rental housing did not allow the policy to achieve the reorientation on the sectoral distribution of Hong Kong housing stock. (La Grange, 1997). Contrary to the deteriorating condition of social housing in overseas like Britain due to a cut in public funding, the quality of public rental housing has been improving a lot in Hong Kong. Sitting tenants of the public rental housing preferred to retain access to their units regardless of subsidies provided by the government. The considerable demand for assisted home ownership was still unsolved; and neither the Housing Authority has attained the redistribution of housing resources to the degree that it anticipated (La Grange, 1997). The privatization movement was, in La Grange's view, not that successful before 1997.

Second, Hong Kong is not the only East Asian economy that promotes home ownership in building the asset-based welfare (Lee, 2013). Singapore has one of the highest home ownership rates at around 91 per cent of the population in 2018. Some 92% per cent of these homeowners purchased their unit built by the Singaporean Housing Development Board (HDB). The difference between Singapore and Hong Kong perhaps lies at the extent the privatization movement is institutionalized. Hong Kong case was very weakly institutionalized. There was NO privatization, notably describing a transforming process rather than a status, since Secretary for Housing, Planning and Lands, Suen Ming Yeung announced the nine strategic policies to stabilize the housing market. There was a *complete* reliance on the private market to achieve homeownership in Hong Kong between 2002 and 2014. Both HOS and TPS was halted under the pressure of local developers and of those private flat owners experiencing negative equity (Chen & Pun, 2007). In contrast, home ownership is highly institutionalized in Singapore (Lee, 2013). There was a strong government will to socialize the housing risk, as the public housing was part of a national project to stabilize the society since Singapore's independence in 1965.

One consequence was the polarization of housing needs. The swift recovery of the housing market in the mid-2000s indicated a new speculation trend that is sustained not only by local buyers but also increasingly by newly well-off mainland Chinese. Unfortunately, housing is NOT quite seen as a citizenship right in Hong Kong society, with public housing tenants periodically being demoralized and stigmatized. Despite this, more young people—some 18 years old, single and highly educated people are on waiting list for public housing now, as they do not expect a chance to purchase even a tiny private apartment (Ng, 2018). Some went further to argue housing crisis has become a deep-seated source of social conflict in Hong Kong society, directly threatening the political legitimacy of the post-colonial state.

Is the Housing Crisis Caused by a Shortage in Land Supply?

Unfortunately, it is beyond the scope of this chapter to empirically test the causal link as described in the section title. What we could do, is to summarize major arguments that targeted the second part of the statement—*is there a shortage in land supply in Hong Kong, and if yes, what cause it?* Due to historical circumstances, two land use regimes existed in Hong Kong: the high-density urban development on the two sides of Victoria Harbour, and the low-density rural and village development in the New Territories (Ng, 2006). Under the dual land regimes there are four most discussed development issues in which political economy has impacted directly on land supply: (a) harbour reclamation, (b) urban renewal in the urban area, (c) village land development, and (d) green zoning in the (mostly) rural area. Viewing this way, the land shortage problem nowadays is a unique result of a long path of structuration of institution governing land use from the colonial era. This is what made Hong Kong's highly contested land shortage problem unique.

2.3 Reclamation—A Room with a (Sea)View and the Harbor Protection Movement

In 2017, the Our Hong Kong Foundation made a strong statement for reclamation in its second Land and Housing Policy Advocacy Series by comparing regional (e.g. Singapore and Macau) and colonial reclamation policy (Wong et al., 2017). The main point, which is also embraced by the recent government, is that the land shortage was caused by a halt of reclamation. Specifically, the government has made it explicit to look for reclamations "outside the Victoria Harbour". Why?

To start with, we need to understand the background of reclamation in Hong Kong. The tendency of the metropole to choose islands as colonial trade post to avoid conflicts over land boundaries resulted in land reclamation being a standard way to expand these island cities in the past (Hudson, 1970; Lai, 1999; Grydehøj, 2015). By 1991, 5% of total land surfaces in Hong Kong comprised land reclaimed from the sea, compared to 10% in Singapore and 33% in Macau (Glaser et al., 1991)—all being former colonies and having a similar geographical limitation in development like that of Hong Kong at the beginning.

In fact, the East Lantau reclamation was no new proposal from the government. Back in 1794, Lantau was once considered the prime site for British settlement after a survey of the area (Hudson, 1970). As early as in 1961, R.C. Clarke and J.E. Jackson proposed a reclamation plan very similar to the Lantau Tomorrow one around the islands near east Lantau, which could provide 5540 acres of land for industrial development (Hudson, 1970). Hudson further noted the abandoned 1961 proposal reflected no pressing need on mere land space for urban expansion but deep-water port development, as *extensive undeveloped land existed north of the urban area*. We revisit this later when discussing what is limiting land use in the rural area.

Nonetheless, the relatively low reclamation rate of Hong Kong was a stark contrast to the way British Empire viewed reclamation in colonies— such as in Bombay—as glorifying projects in the nineteenth century (Riding, 2018). It was not infrequent for colonial urban planning to meet with political resistance. Government plans of land reclamation along the praya on Northern Hong Kong Island were often opposed by the European capitalist class owning the marine lot, and sometimes even by the military department until British acquisition of Kowloon (Hudson, 1970). Before that, unplanned reclamations were carried out privately by the European trading firms to expand their docks for entrepot trade along the coastline. By 1881, both the marine lot-holders and government realized the financial benefits from rising rent and land sales—rather than an altruistic concern of public health—in the reclamation area (Hudson, 1970). Notably, London always mandated Hong Kong to finance its own growth and infrastructure. Since the reaching of a consensus, resistance against harbour reclamation as a way of city expansion seldom surfaced—until the rise of protect the harbour movement in the 1990s (Lai, 1999; Ng, 2006, 2011).

Starting from the 1990s, reclamation (and development) proposal along the Victoria Harbour coast was subjected to new environmental regulation due to maturation of the global environmental regime, and the rise of the civil society in Hong Kong (Ng, 2006, 2011; Lam & Chan, 2017). In 1995, with strong support from the business community (especially those who had a vast interest at the waterfront) and environment-conscious professionals, the Society for Protection of the Harbour was established and lobbied against excessive reclamation in the Victoria Harbour.[11]

The Society drafted the Protection of the Harbour Ordinance that was passed by the Legislative Council on 27 June 1997—three days before the handover. To some, this Ordinance signalled the emergence of a new kind of environmental rationality, in contrast to the state's technical rationality, that began to shape land policy from bottom-up in Hong Kong (Ng, 2006, 2011). In 2003, the Society for Protection of the Harbour won a Judicial Review against the Government's reclamation proposal at the Wan Chai waterfront with the Ordinance. The Society also conducted a fund-raising activity at Central that was supported and attended by Legislative Council member Shek Lai-him—representative of the Real Estate and Construction constituency. Reclamation dropped to 84 hectares between 2005–2009, compared to a total of 2291 hectare between 1985 and 2004 (Research Office Information Services Division, 2016). In 2019, when interviewed over Government's Lantau Tomorrow plan, the founder of the Protection of the Harbour Society—Winston Chu

---

[11] The founder of the Society for Protection of the Harbour, Winston Chu—a London trained solicitor and served on the Town Planning Board from 1988–1996, claimed the idea to protect the Victoria Harbor originated from his mother who complained about the deteriorating sea view from her home. Chu was also found to have business connections to one of the largest property developers in Hong Kong (Apple Daily, 2003a, 2003b, 2003c; Lam, 2018).

reiterated his view that reclamation would drive up housing price, and that developing the New Territories was the *only* way to solve the housing problem (Cheng, 2019).

The series of events highlighted that reclamation no longer enjoyed the same level of support from key developers in Hong Kong. Two exceptions that voiced out their support of the Lantau Tomorrow plan were The Wharf (Holdings) Limited, whose subsidiaries reportedly had housing interest in Tung Chung area at northern Lantau (Tang, 2016), and the pro-Beijing Hong Kong Chinese Importers' & Exporters' Association (Lam, 2018). The failure of the state to rally mass support from economic elites seems to highlight a disintegrating state-business order as decolonization continued (Lui & Chiu, 2007). The postwar colonial government, with the arbitrating power of the executive branch, faced less resistance from the British dominated business sectors towards pro-growth infrastructural construction like reclamation that helped to create the land reserve (note: but they had a different stance towards developing the countryside as we shall discuss later).[12]

While attempts to preserve the sea view of Grade A offices were rational act just like those trading firms protecting their pier along the praya a hundred years ago, it is intriguing why most, if not all, local property developers favour the development of the New Territories as an alternative in this land debate (i.e. outside the Victoria Harbour yet also not the coast in outer islands)? Why is there still a shortage of land (and space)?

2.4 From Letters AB to Brownfields: When Tradition (Land Right) Meets Modern (Law System)

There are multiple reasons why "undeveloped land up north", as observed by Hudson (1970), continues to be so. One puzzle we mentioned earlier is why the big developers wish, but fail to develop the northern part of Hong Kong. By 2019, the major developers are believed to be holding no less than 1000 hectares of agricultural land in the New Territories (Task Force on Land Supply, 2018a).[13] This amounted to one-fourth of all built-

---

[12] There are, of course, various environmental groups such as the Greenpeace objected treating reclamation as the best way to create land in Hong Kong. The civil society involvement, however, is not our focus in this chapter. Please refer to Chap. 10 on social movement.

[13] Short to Medium Term Option: Tapping into the Private Agricultural Land Reserve in the New Territories. https://www.landforhongkong.hk/en/supply_analysis/private_land.php

up area for residential flats. How did they get hold of these lands and why they were not utilized?

Unlike in Hong Kong Island and Kowloon where much land was soon declared crown land after colonization, the New Territories was leased under the Convention for the Extension of Hong Kong Territory.[14] After the bloody Six-Day War of 1899, the colonial state decided to pacify rural resistance by preserving indigenous inhabitants' land rights and traditions (See Chap. 1). As Hong Kong industrialized and urbanized in the 1960s, the colonial government began to tap on those land held by the rural landlords. The "Letters A/B" system (1960–1983) was introduced as a land exchange entitlements system to replace the original cash compensation. The system monetized rural land, reduced village resistance amid development, and incentivized the local Chinese private developers to accumulate land in the New Territories. On the other hand, the British capitals were not interested in this Letters A/B System, for it involved uncertain land right in a leased part of Hong Kong that would soon end in 1997.

The issued Letter B (the Land exchange entitlement document), "would offer the land owner of the piece of private land to be resumed by government a choice of either a cash payment or a future grant of building land in any new town development area in the New Territories at an unspecified future time" (Poon, 2011, p. 73)[15] The major local developers soon recognized the Letters represented a future land grant liability on the part of the government and actively purchased them through own network, hence drove up the price of Letters A/B. The colonial government stopped the policy in 1983 after realizing its potential impact on future land supply (Poon, 2011, p. 74).

With the agreement of the two governments who signed the Sino-British Joint Declaration in 1984, the colonial government set out to absorb the Letters A/B by monetizing them (Poon, 2011, p. 74). To put it simply, many New Territories land sales were allocated to Letter A/B tender—as if the Letters were cash offer, thus channelling land supply away from public auction. In this process, those new and smaller

---

[14] As a geo-historical reminder, the New Territories makes up 86.2% of Hong Kong's territory and was leased to the Britain under the Convention for the Extension of Hong Kong Territory. Land in this area remained largely untapped by the government.

[15] "Letter A" was issued when "a landowner voluntarily surrendered his land with vacant passion for public purpose without going through the statutory resumption process. Other redemption terms were the same as those of 'Letter B'" (Poon, 2011).

developers with no Letters A/B in stock were pushed out of the land market, whereas the four major Letters A/B holders enjoyed extraordinary profit margins from the development of such sites (Poon, 2011, p. 75).

In 1996, the colonial government introduced the New Territories Land Exchange Entitlement (Redemption) Bill seeking to enable the Government to redeem New Territories land exchange entitlements with cash and to extinguish all other rights against the Government under those entitlements (Cap.495). It was, however, too late. The Consumer Council issued a report in 1996 confirming the residential property market was no longer freely competitive due to unidentified large amount of land held by developing conglomerates and recommended the government to intervene to remove market entry barrier (Consumer Council, 1996, p. 28).[16] So the first limitation to rural land use, was that a large amount have already been taken over by large developers, but for some reasons they cannot use it.

A second limitation to rural land use concerned the Small House Policy. The Policy was introduced in 1972 to allow a male indigenous villager aged 18 or above descended through the male line from one of the recognized villages in the New Territories to apply for building a small house for once in his lifetime. By 2012, 932 out of the 1300 hectares of idle land in the New Territories had been zoned for "Village Type Development" and mainly for development of small houses by indigenous villagers.[17] This "ding" (丁 literally descents) right is protected by the Article 40 of Basic Law, which states that the lawful traditional rights and interest of the indigenous inhabitants of the New Territories shall be protected. The debate has heightened, as the government appealed against the Court of First Instance's rule that the "ding" right should no longer be extended to land granted by, or exchanged with, the government, finding those scenarios unconstitutional and unlawful (Lau & Ng, 2019). Government's appeal to sustaining its policy to zone rural land use for small houses is

[16] "f) residential property. The Consumer Council's report revealed that new entrants were deterred by the high cost (HK$2–5 billion) of lots of residential land in Government land auctions and unfamiliarity with the development control process. Incumbent players were able to reduce their land costs over all because of land banks built up in earlier periods. Government could remove impediments to small developers by providing more lots of 'manageable size' in a way which would satisfy town planning requirements and streamline the development control process, making it more transparent." (Consumer Council, 1996, p. 28)

[17] Reply by the Secretary for Development to question by the Hon Dennis Kwok in the Legislative Council (HKSAR Government, 2015).

intriguing, as they may not exceed three storeys or be of a height of more than 8.23 metres (27 feet) and their roofed-over area generally should not exceed 65.03 square metres (700 square feet). A third limitation to rural land use concerns the brownfields controversy, which also echoes the first limitation that involves the big developers. Several land research conducted by the Liber Research Community (LRC) warranted our attention here. With the moto of "*The rich have a thousand hectares of land while the poor have no place to stand*", the LRC[18] strongly advocated for the optimal use of brownfield sites in Hong Kong.[19] In 2018, LRC published the report *Brownfields in Time: Tracing the Course of Brownfields Expansion in the New Territories*, which was, notably, supported by the WYNG Foundation despite LRC's typical crowd-funding model.

Incidentally the Board of Trustee of the WYNG Foundation, formed in 2011, has a strong connection to a web of environmentally conscious political and economic elites in Hong Kong.[20] The WYNG Foundation, along with Hongkong Land, Rockefeller Brothers Fund, Swire Properties, and Sun Hung Kai & Co. Ltd. was some of the business funder organizations for Civic Exchange, of which the founder is Christine Loh—also the Chairperson of the Society for Protection of the Harbour from 2003. Another key funding project of the WYNG Foundation is TrailWatch,

---

[18] According to its website, the Liber Research Community is committed, through land research, to uncover vested interest in development projects, make hidden information public, help the public to reconceptualize land systems and follow up on major development controversies (Liber Research Community, n.d.).

[19] Some notable publication directly related to the development of brownfield sites are: Liber Research Community (2015, 2018a, 2018b).

[20] The Board of Trustee included Dr. Anthony Ng and Ms. Anna Wu—both being the founding members of the Hong Kong Observers, a middle class-based pressure group that was active between the 1970s and 1980s. Two notable founding members of the Hong Kong Observers were former Chief Executive Leung Chun Ying and Christine Loh, who, together with Anna Wu, was recruited by Leung to become Under Secretary for the Environment and the Executive Council respectively. Essentially, Christine Loh was the Chairperson of the Society for Protection of the Harbour from 2003, and established the influential independent and non-partisan think tank Civic Exchange since 2000—of which one of the early directors and individual funder of projects was Winston Chu—the lawyer that found the Society for Protection of the Harbour and challenged the government reclamation projects in Victoria Harbor with three judicial reviews we mentioned earlier (Civic Exchange, n.d., 2010; Lu, 2005).

which strongly advocates the protection of Hong Kong's country parks through organizing hiking activities.[21]

What we try to illustrate here is that by 2018, both the government and the developers have recognized the brownfield advocacy from LRC, and private business funding, at least for one time, was being channelled to this progressive NGO. Certainly, the government and developers approach the brownfield land issues quite differently, and their approaches were not consistent as time goes by. The 2018 LRC report considered 2008 the watershed for "legalization" of unauthorized brownfields (p.27–29). Applications for brownfield operations skyrocketed since 2002, and the number of approved applications by the Town Planning Board has drastically increased (Fig. 14 of the report). The year 2008 was a watershed because half of the brownfield operations applications before that would be rejected, whereas after that year more than 90% got approved (Fig. 16 of the report). Lee and Tang (2017) attempted to make a similar point by attributing the rise to town planners and illustrating an increase in approval rates (from 67.5% to 89.2%) for planning applications for whole-site redevelopment within government, institution or community sites upon comparing the period of 1990–1998 to 1999–2015.

LRC pushes for the use of "Land Resumption Ordinance" to cope with brownfields and private developers' farmland reserves for public housing.[22] Nonetheless, private developers long preferred a different approach. In the heat of the land debate, two researchers from the Public Policy Institute of Our Hong Kong Foundation, a think tank that focused on housing and land issues and was found by former Chief Executive Tung Chee Hwa, published an article detailing the problems behind (Ip & Sat, 2018). In summary, this article argued that if "Land Resumption Ordinance" was to be widely used to capture the brownfields, it would conflict with the right of private ownership of property judicially protected under the Basic Law. It was expected the government would have to fight judicial reviews initiated by private developers should the "Land Resumption Ordinance" be invoked, and then possibly faced the

[21] In the home page—"Enjoy your hiking more, Share your trekking experience, Protect our country parks" (TrailWatch, n.d.).

[22] Research Highlights 2019 of Liber Rresearch Community, point 1. "Actively advocating the use of "Land Resumption Ordinance" to cope with brownfields and private developers' farmland reserves for public housing. This advocacy has become part of the official housing and land policies already." https://liber-research.com/en/report-archive/

long-term legal repercussion that extended into the future land planning should the later win a case in the court.

In short, there is plenty of land in rural New Territories, the developers have some, the government wants to keep some for the village houses, and fears to fight a legal battle against the developers and villagers for both traditional land right now protected as private property right under a modern legal system. But that is not the end of the story. The majority of land in the New Territories are country parks and green belt, yet we need to explore why they are not considered.

2.5   A Missing Angle: Land Shortage as an Unintended Consequence of a British Colonial Legacy—Green Zoning?

Of all the causes to land shortage that we have discussed there seems to be a purposive action of the political and economic elites, or, the civil society. Despite the escalating protests, the eventual passing of the NENT Planning in 2014 suggested the government has little regards, if any, towards the civil society. Thus, it is unlikely the civil society could be considered a cause to the land shortage in Hong Kong. Reviewing literatures, the land shortage could be an unintended consequence of a British colonial legacy—the green zoning in town planning.

In 2018, the Task Force on Land Supply (TFLS) recommended to the Government to shelve any development of the periphery of country parks given its low public support. This periphery area, coined as the Green Belt (GB) and country parks in Hong Kong have remained relatively untouched over the years. These conservation related zoning concepts originated from the Britain in the 1950s, and have left many to think of the country park as one of the British legacy. It remains a puzzle, though, that as MacLehose's Ten Year Public Housing Program in the 1970s aggravated the urban land shortage problem, why was the other 75% of land in the countryside remained undeveloped?

A review of the Abercrombie Report (Hong Kong Preliminary Planning Report)—a strategic plan drafted in 1948—suggested the conventional idea that the colonial state did not have long term plan over urban development had been changing by the time of the Report's publication (Lai, 1999). According to Lai, many of the report's physical planning proposals including the allocation of the population to the Kowloon area and construction of first-generation new towns in the New Territories (Kwun Tong and Tsuen Wan) had been implemented later. Reclamation, in Lai's view, was not just an economical alternative to acquiring private rural land in the New Territories, it was crucial to the development of the second or third generation new towns (like Tai Po) in a very short period.

In terms of rural development, the Abercrombie Report maintained a very conservative stance towards sub-urbanization and agricultural uses, a view that echoed the European "green belt" town planning movement at that time. This resulted in the restriction over the extensive urbanization of the New Territories in the next 40 years except for the new town area (Lai, 1999). The "Conservation of the Hong Kong Countryside" Government Report submitted by Lee Talbot in 1965 reinforced such a view. In such case, a partial cause of the "lack of land" for housing development could be attributed to historic town planning policy of the colonial state—zoning, as a deliberate attempt to un-develop rural land rather than simply abiding by the *Laissez-faire* ideology.[23]

The Abercrombie Report (1948) was the first to lay out that Green Belt was to create "wider open spaces" to support passive recreation in urban territory in Hong Kong (Tang et al., 2005, p.233). Planning touches on Green Belt near urban area and new towns (1960s onward) were different, with lax attitude towards development in the former but much wider land area defined as a physical boundary to urban expansion in the later (Tang et al., 2005). Two events that happened around the 1960s, both indicating the spread of environmental rationality (Meyer et al., 1997), transformed how land was regulated in the New Territories by institutionalizing zoning for conservancy. Together they could be seen as the colonial state's major intervention in rural land use after the conversion of all New Territories land to either Block Crown Lease or Crown Land (Chiu & Hung, 1997).

The first event happened in 1965, Professor Lee Talbot, a former US marine, a pilot and a world-famous conservationist was invited by Governor David Trench to conduct an aerial survey of Hong Kong. Later he duly submitted the government report titled "Conservation of the Hong Kong Countryside", with a map of proposed parks included (Wong, 2013). While the pressing concern of the overpopulated city was searching for

---

[23] Another reason not to develop the rural land was to create a military buffer zone for the British army. This can be dated back to one of the original purposes to obtain the New Territories in 1899 (see Chap. 2 on history). Notably, the famous MacLehose trail covered all defensive fighting positions in the New Territories from east to west and the fastest runners up until 1980s were, of course, the Gurkhas (Agnew, 2018).

land to build more affordable housing and cheap land for industrialization, the Report suggested keeping the 75% land in the countryside as
rural mass recreation areas for people to enjoy birdwatch and nature—
which, in retrospect, often considered a British legacy nowadays. That left
a large proportion of land untouched in the form of zoning for conservation, with uncertainty over rural land use due to the leasing status of the
New Territories greatly reduced.

The second event happened two years after the release of the first
report, a group of University Professors and Doctors, and most importantly, British elite merchants and bankers got together to establish the
first green group in Hong Kong, the Conservancy Association, to lobby
for a slowdown of urbanization and industrialization process in the New
Territories. Some prominent founding members of the Association
included: Jeremy Brown of Jardine Matheson (later the management
director), Mr. and Mrs. John Marden, former president of Wheelock and
Company, Sir Quo-wei Lee, Chairman of Hang Seng Bank, Richard
Charles Lee, later Chairman of Hysan Development Company Limited,
Mr. H Kadoorie of the Kadoorie Family, Mr. Lam Chik Ho of Lam Woo
& Company Limited, Mr. Robert Steer Huthart, Managing Director of
Lane Crawford Limited.

It is quite obvious that these initial members of the Conservancy
Association represented a network of British business elites, had a vast
interest in the urban area of Hong Kong Island and the Kowloon Peninsula,
but no interest in the rural land that rests on leasing terms under the
Convention for the Extension of Hong Kong. Apart from reforestation
through planting trees around the New Territories, the Conservancy
Association successfully opposed the construction of a petrochemical
complex on Lamma island in the 1970s billed as a major step towards
industrial upgrading. No wonder almost no local Chinese industrialists
joined the Association.

The institutionalization of the environmental regime through Green
Belt zoning, legislation of Country Parks Ordinance in 1976, and the
cultural diffusion of environmental values to the public by the Conservancy
Association, has kept a large part of the rural land from major development. This happened in a time when environmental consciousness was
rising and a growing number of organizations and spontaneous protest
actions press for environment regulation within a context of expanding
political opportunities in Hong Kong (Chiu et al., 1999).

In 1991, the Green Belt Zone was specifically added to the amended Town Planning Ordinance to institutionalize "a general presumption against development" within the defined area (Tang et al., 2005). The main planning functions of the widely scattered GB zone, which amounted to 25% of all 55,040 hectares of land covered by statutory land-use plans, are: "To conserve existing landscape features, areas of scenic value and areas of recognized 'feng shui' importance; to define the outer limits of urbanized districts; and to serve as a buffer between and within urban areas; to provide additional outlets for passive recreational uses." (Tang et al., 2005, p. 233–234).

Nonetheless, Tang et al. (2005, 2007) also argued the rhetoric of describing the green belt for conservation and environmental protection was only established by early 1990s. Rather than being a zone for conservation, analysis of statutory land-use zoning plans by Tang et al. has found that Hong Kong green belt was a transition zone that helped to accommodate the "small house" (or "Village-type house") policy. While the Country Park was well managed by the Country and Marine Parks Authority, development in the Green Belt zones—for example in the case of applying for small scale "Village-type house"—has a success rate as high as 60% (Lai & Fong, 2000; Lai & Ho, 2001). In face of local rural politics, the town planners were more likely or flexible to give way to applications by individual villager than when the applicants for rezoning were developers who were bounded by the logic of economy of scale (Tang et al., 2005, 2007). There seems to be a decoupling of formal policies and organizational practices of the Town Planning Board concerning Green Belt zoning (Meyer & Rowan, 1977).

In short, the town planners, as a professional group working with some degree of autonomy in the polity, has not been totally accommodating towards the onslaught of the market force in their assessment of rezoning applications (Lai & Ho, 2001; Tang et al., 2005). Zoning often privileges those that are socially or economically embedded in the local social network, for example in the UK residents welcome the Green Belt zoning for preserving their community and landscape view, against those benefiting from unrestricted urban sprawling such as developers and people looking for housing with cheaper price. That's why economists often blame Green Belt zoning for causing housing shortage (The Economist, 2015, 2017). In colonial Hong Kong, zoning was frequently used to socially stratify land use based on racial/ethnic line in the Peak, Shek O and Cheung Chau Island, which often hampered, rather than maximized, economic benefits from land use (Lai & Yu, 2001; Lai, 2011).[24] More recent and relevant example would be the zoning for "Village Type Development" we mentioned earlier.

Perhaps one consequence for the approval of village house in scattered, isolated and discontinuous patches of Green Belt, is that it has become more difficult for developers, who own various lands in the New Territories through the A/B Letter scheme, to achieve economy of scale to initiate development. The relocation of Tsoi Yuen Village due to construction of high-speed railway illustrated our point. Access to the new Tsoi Yuen Village (菜園村) was blocked by a neighbouring Pat Heung village, who owned the road with a private company (Wong & Lee, 2013). On one hand, the fragmented property right and their proximity to nearby villages was one barrier for housing development. On the other hand, town planners could not bear the political cost of explicitly deviating from the Green Belt concept in approving rezoning applications—a point echoed by Government's shelving of the idea to develop the peripheral area of country park after the land debate in 2018. The transaction cost to change is simply too high (Taylor, 2013).

To say that zoning requirements and the protection of Green Belts is at least partially related to the alleged land shortage in Hong Kong should not be construed as a yes to developing them for properties. The "shortage" must be understood as the result of complex and multiple causes as sketched in this chapter. A balance between the environment and the need for shelters should indeed be struck and delicate weighting of costs and benefits has to be executed. This is something that the colonial and SAR governments have not done, not least successfully, for a long time. In the concluding section we will turn to a new political impetus towards the quest for a solution.

3   CONCLUSION: A TRIUMPH OF THE POLITICAL LOGIC?

Housing is always a social problem in Hong Kong. The timing it entered the public arena and becomes a focal point of debate, however, is more often politically driven (Chiu, 2019c, 2020). The official discourse has gradually changed as the government proclaims housing problems as the

---

[24] "Government has also been seen to be active by developers in rejecting major development proposals in statutory green belt zones." (Lai & Ho, 2001, p. 325)

social source of "deep-rooted contradictions" that allegedly mobilize numerous social movements in recent years.

Back in 2005 December, Premier Wen Jiabao told former Chief Executive Donald Tsang Yam-kuen to focus on solving the "deep-rooted contradictions and problems" persisted in Hong Kong. Interpretation of what were these contradictions differed. At that time, some observers argued it means the social consequence (e.g. inequality, hallowing out of the industry) resulting from the economic restructuring as Hong Kong integrated with China's globalizing economy. Others pointed to the confrontations between the executive authorities and the legislature in Tung's era (SCMP Reporter, 2005). In the second decade of the SAR, on top of social mobilizations over political developments, protests also broke out over land and conservation issues related to the construction of the high-speed rail-link and later the North East New Territories New Development Areas Planning (2007-now). In 2010, Chinese Premier Wen Jiabao repeated his warning to Tsang to deal with the "deep-rooted contradictions"—as Donald Tsang's approval ratings in public opinion survey dropped to a low level similar to Tung's final year in the administration.

While Tsang sidestepped the housing problems by downscaling public housing developments and suspending land auctions, his successor Leung Chun-ying embraced the "deep-rooted contradictions" discourse and announced the new Long Term Housing Strategy (LTHS)—the first since 1998—on the day after the Umbrella Movement protests came to an end. Ever since then housing issues have become a focal concern in successive Budget report and Policy Address of the SAR Government.[25]

The climax of this new *political project*, a comparison we draw in parallel with Lethbridge's (1985, p. 105) analysis of anti-corruption moral crusade by the former governor Maclehose in the 1970s, was the "Big Land Debate" orchestrated by the government's Task Force on Land Supply in

---

[25] For example, the first two chapters of the Chief Executive's 2019 Policy Address was II. Housing and III. Land Supply. Under Land Supply, it reads, "1. about 450 hectares of brownfield sites in the New Territories may have development potential but have not been covered by new development areas (NDAs) or other development projects. These sites are mostly private land larger in size and located nearer to existing new towns and major highways, including brownfield sites in Ping Shan and Lam Tei. The Planning Department will accord priority to the study of 160 hectares brownfield sites that are closer to existing infrastructure and assess their suitability for public housing development, with a view to commencing follow-up technical assessment by the end of this year. ..." (HKSAR Government, 2019, 2020).

2018. In 2017, the Task Force on Land Supply (TFLS) was established by Leung's successor Carrie Lam to review the sources of land supply, to evaluate land supply options, and to engage the public to deliberate on these options. The aim of TFLS was to achieve a broad consensus among the community on the priority, pros and cons, trade-offs of various land supply options (Task Force on Land Supply, 2019). The Task Force successfully caught the public's eyeballs by attributing all housing problems to one of the root causes— "Insufficient Land Supply" and by including the Fanling golf course in the land debate. The Task Force pointed out the land development has halted since 2005, reclamation has decreased by 80%, a lack of new town completion since 2000, a severe shortage of completed residential unit, and the almost complete halt of subsidised sale flats, resulting in long and growing average waiting time or 4.7 years for general applicants for public rental housing and the world's highest rental cost and proliferation of subdivided units.

On 20 February 2019, the government announced it would adopt all the short-to-medium term options and medium-to-long term options to provide land supply as recommended by the TFLS (Development Bureau, 2019). In the first land supply strategy the government implicitly implied Suen Ming Yeung's nine measures to stabilize housing market (hence, the heart of the middle class) would no longer be reconsidered,

"land shortage is the root cause of many problems besetting Hong Kong, including not only housing but *many other issues* (note: not specified, emphasis by authors), and must be addressed by the entire community without delay. Hence, the Government's core strategy in this regard is to increase land supply on a sustained basis. We should uphold and follow through this policy position *regardless of short-term economic changes or fluctuations in property prices* (emphasis by authors)." (Development Bureau, 2019, p.5)

Government responses to the short-to-medium term options are expediting brownfield development, unleashing development potential of private agricultural land in the New Territories and developing 32 hectares of land of Fangling Golf Course for housing purpose. Medium-to-long term options, on the other hand, include expediting studies on the East Lantau Metropolis through construction of artificial islands in the Central Waters, expediting studies on near-shore reclamation outside Victoria Harbour, continuing to develop and study caverns and underground space, developing more new development areas in the New Territories, and commencing studies on the river trade terminal site and Tuen Mun West. The Government agreed with the TFLS to put aside the opinion of developing the periphery of country parks given its low public support. For a short period until the outbreak of the 2019 Anti-Extradition Bill protests, the government seems to enjoy a rare applause at least from some on the public housing wait list.

The framing of the housing and land problems as the "deep-rooted contradiction" behind political mobilization came to a new level when several mainland media agencies engaged in agenda setting during the height of the 2019 Anti-Extradition Bill protests. The Xinhua News Agency published an article on the 4th of September describing the unaffordable housing, along with social inequality and stagnated social mobility, being the key to all sorts of social and political problems in Hong Kong (Hwang et al., 2019). In the same article, those who owned properties were pit against those who do not, and those suffering from social inequality were pit against those demanding for democracy. In another Xinhua article dated 12 September, the housing problem is not just defined as the entry point to resolve the "deep-rooted contradictions", but also urged the government to use the Cap.124 Land Resumption Ordinance "extensively" to obtain land in the New Territories (Xinhua News Agency, 2019). Two days before, the Democratic Alliance for the Betterment and Progress of Hong Kong (DAB) also published in all major newspaper that they demanded the Government to seize private developers' land via invoking the Land Resumption Ordinance—one approach that the political party and the Government formerly strongly opposed to (Ng & Wong, 2019; Lam, 2019a). Carrie Lam was quick to respond to DAB's new request, but the Heung Yee Kuk was also quick to give a defiant message to her in responding to this rising "land seizure movement"— "Don't take our support for granted" (K. C. Ng, 2019). But yet, the prevailing political logic of housing has arisen once again from political influences from outside of the SAR's border (Smart, 2006).

Brownfield sites are now prioritized in land supply option (Legislative Council, 2019). After the 2019 Anti-extradition Law Amendment Bill movement, the real estate developers began to donate or lease their farmland reserve—most of which are brownfield sites—to the government to build public houses (Reuters Staff, 2019). Weelock Properties, New World and Henderson, have offered to donate their land to the government to mitigate the housing crisis (Kwan, 2019). For instance, New World has donated almost one-fifth or 3 million square feet of its land bank—mostly farmland—to Hong Kong government and charity for the building of social housing (Lam, 2019b). Henderson soon follows suit and expressed it was ready to cooperate with the government if it invokes the Lands Resumption Ordinance to take back some 7.3 million square feet of private farmland in the New Territories (Lee, 2019). That happened after the Chinese state media published three commentaries highlighting a "root cause" of social conflicts were unaffordable housing and pressured the local developers (J. Ng, 2019). The political logic seems to prevail over the industrial capital accumulation logics (Castells et al., 1990), which has long declined in importance as Hong Kong deindustrialized, and the neoliberal financial logic that centred on urban capital accumulation (Chen & Pun, 2007; Harvey, 1974, 1982), in time of big political change.

In this chapter, we tell the story of the housing crisis in Hong Kong, a saga that has been playing on for most of the postwar years and has long been a captivated story to many western observers. It is not without reason. On the one hand, the legendary Christmas tale of 1953 as a "syndrome" that kicked off different large-scale public housing programs in a recognized free-market economy already constituted an interesting puzzle for sociologists, economists and policymakers to explore. On the other hand, the skyrocketed housing price that turns Hong Kong as the world's most expensive city in the world also attracts investors from various places in the globe to reap profits from this tiny city.

To recap, through our *high-definition* analysis, we would like to put forward the following HD arguments to Hong Kong's housing problems:

(a) Hong Kong's housing problem is not simply a structural problem about land supply and large population. It is a by-product and unintended consequences of Hong Kong government's land policies between the 1960s and 1980s. The power struggle between the government and the property developer (British), and then later (the local Chinese one), underpinning Hong Kong government's various intervention logics (collective consumption, political, and financial logics) during different historical periods.

(b) Against the neoliberal argument that promotes privatization as the most desirable way to solve the housing demand in Hong Kong, it is not only that privatization cannot achieve an equitable allocation of housing and land resources. It is also that a large part of Hong Kong's housing problems, especially housing demand from the lower classes, have to rely on *more* government interventions into the housing market in order to secure them to get access to basic and decent sheltering in Hong Kong.

(c) Nevertheless, the timing to initiate a break from past hands-off government practice has less to do with the rising grassroots resistance against housing inequality, but more to do with the political crisis intensified by the quest for democracy and fear of further integration of the two systems, namely the socialist system and the capitalist system, under the one country. Such development has implications in terms of the reconfiguration of the political economy in Hong Kong.

As have hinted at the beginning of this chapter, Hong Kong's postcolonial government's inability to resolve Hong Kong's housing problem can be seen as a classic "growth *vs.* legitimacy" dilemma confronted by a capitalist state in pursuit of accumulation through uneven urban development. As have been seen, the role of the Hong Kong state in relation to the market has been swinging like a pendulum acting as between a housing provider and a market facilitator. As both housing prices go on skyrocketing and urban poverty become prevalent, this dilemma becomes increasingly obvious and further exposes the Hong Kong state's undecidedness to position herself in relation to the housing market.

Due to the promotion of property ownership since the 1980s, private property ownership has played a key role in Hong Kong people's "ontological security" and a type of Lockean social contract has been established. The skyrocketing housing prices making most of the Hong Kong people unable to purchase has directly challenged this social contract in Hong Kong society, thus threatening the Hong Kong state's legitimacy. But at the same time, the historical legacy in the New Territories and the unholy alliance between property developers and Hong Kong government in using speculative real estate projects as the key driver of growth also put the government in a very difficult position to choose between economic growth and political legitimacy. A repositioning of the Hong Kong state in relation to the market should be the key to the predicament. Indeed the "feudalism" that Ryan Kilpatrick alluded to in his rebuttal of National Geographic's repeating of the old clichés of too many people on too little land, is nothing more than the combined weight of capitalism, weak governance, and perhaps genuine feudalism in the right for male original inhabitants to construct their own houses.

In this chapter, we have summarized the major themes and debates of the land and housing questions in Hong Kong. While we could not exhaust all the outstanding issues (for example on urban redevelopment), we have also pointed to a few puzzles that have yet to be tackled substantially by experts in the field. We are not saying that there is anything wrong in preserving our country parks and rural landscapes, but the fact remains that build-up land accounts for only a small portion of all land in Hong Kong and in the New Territories many lands are being left idle. If the Government is so keen to solve the housing crisis, why would it spare most of the Fanling Golf course from the bulldozer? But if capitalist interests are indeed supreme in Hong Kong, why would the rural land banks of the major developers still could not be turned into valuable assets? And if the government, both under colonialism and the SAR, has little regard for the environment and conservation, would not touch the green belts?

The elevation of land and housing as the "deep-rooted contradictions" appeared to have signalled the reposition amidst the heat of the Anti-Extradition Law Movement protest. Yet the pandemic and the cooling off of the protest might have the paradoxically effect of easing the urgency to search for new land and houses by the government. If the housing question ceased to serve any political function to the local government and the establishment, would they still show the same sense of urgency as in 2019? No wonder repeated reminders are heard from time to time.

References

Agnew, M. (2018, July 25). Why David Wilson started the Wilson Trail: former Governor 'absolutely astonished' at pace runners today are completing his trail. *South China Morning Post.* Retrieved from https://www.scmp.com/sport/outdoor/trail-running/article/2156738/why-david-wilson-started-wilson-trail-former-governor

Apple Daily. (2003a, September 26). 徐嘉慎入稟禁填海 [Winston Chu filed for ban on reclamation]. *Apple Daily.* Retrieved from https://hk.appledaily.com/local/20030926/L7CGPUAFYBKK4LDO6OJBDATWUA/

Apple Daily. (2003b, October 9). Involving Li Ka-shing's interests, cards in 'Hero of Victoria Harbour's hand revealed. *Apple Daily.* Retrieved from https://hk.lifestyle.appledaily.com/nextplus/magazine/article/20031009/2_3587255/

Apple Daily. (2003c, October 12). 母親一言鬧醒徐嘉慎 [Winston Chu was waked up by his mother's word]. *Apple Daily.* Retrieved from https://hk.appledaily.com/local/20031012/NWPM7N7WLQCO52Y5ZUDFKYQBPI/

Apple Daily. (2013, October 12). 母親一言鬧醒徐嘉慎 [Winston Chu was waked up by his mother's word]. *Apple Daily*. Retrieved from https://hk.appledaily. com/local/20031012/NWPM7N7WLQCO52Y5ZUDFKYQBPI/

Castells, M., Lee, G., & Kwok, R. (1990). *The Shek kip Mei syndrome: Economic development and public housing in Hong Kong and Singapore*. Pion.

Census and Statistics Department. (2001). *Hong Kong 2001 population census— Summary results*. Census and Statistics Department.

Census and Statistics Department. (2017). *Hong Kong 2016 population by-census— Summary results*. Census and Statistics Department.

Chan, K. W. (1999). 房屋政策:香港房屋問題的根源 [housing policy: The origin of Hong Kong's housing problems]. In K. J. Lee, S. Chiu, L. C. Leung, & K. W. Chan (Eds.), 新社會政策 *[New Social Policy]* (pp. 173–194). Chinese University Press.

Chen, Y. C., & Pun, N. (2007). Neoliberalization and privatization in Hong Kong after the 1997 financial crisis. *The China Review, 7*(2), 65–92.

Cheng, K. Y. (2019, January 20). 【中環繞道】填海貴推高樓價 徐嘉慎:新界建屋才是唯一正當選擇. [[Central Bypass] Reclamation will push up property prices. 'Building a house in the New Territories is the only legitimate choice,' said Winston Chu]. *Apple Daily*. Retrieved from https://hk.appledaily.com/local/20190120/6CKZQYT5KXFV5XKWCL73F4QXLU/

Cheung, S. N. (1979). Rent control and housing reconstruction: The Postwar experience of Prewar premises in Hong Kong. *Journal of Law & Economics, 22*(1), 27–53.

Chiu, S. W. (2019a, July 26). Making Sense of Recent Events in Hong Kong: A Perspective from Popular Opinions. Presentation made at Hong Kong Studies Initiative, the University of British Columbia.

Chiu, S. W. (2019b, July). Public comments on the current situation and prospects of Hong Kong on the 22nd anniversary of the reunification.

Chiu, S. W. (2019c, December 2). 「檢討深層次矛盾」不提政治無助解困 [Not mentioning politics, "reflect on deep-rooted contradictions" is not cure to the situation]. *Mingpao*. Retrieved from https://news.mingpao.com/ins/文摘/article/20191202/s00022/1575208908831/

Chiu, S. W. (2020, January 3). 研反高鐵傘運 斥一直逃避「政治才是深層次矛盾」趙永佳:政府勿阻市民參與制度 [Studying on the Anti-Speed Rail Movement and the Umbrella Movement, "politics is the deep-rooted contradiction," Stephen Chiu asked the government not to block public participation in the system]. *Mingpao*. Retrieved from https://news.mingpao.com/pns/%E6%B8%AF%E8%81%9E/article/20200103/s00002/1577990343315

Chiu, S. W., & Hung, H. F. (1997). The paradox of stability revisited: Colonial development and state building in rural Hong Kong. *China Information, 12*(1–2), 66–95.

Chiu, S. W., Hung, H. F., & Lai, O. K. (1999). Environmental Movements in Hong Kong. In A. Y. So & F. Y. Lee (Eds.), *Asia's environmental movement: Comparative perspectives* (pp. 55–89). Routledge.

Chiu, S. W., Shum, K. C. & Yip, T. S. (2018, July 9). 回歸逾20年 香港人不滿些什麼? [What are the dissatisfactions of Hong Kong people after over 20 years handover?]. *Mingpao*. Retrieved from https://news.mingpao.com/ins/%E6%96%87%E6%91%98/article/20180709/s00022/1531053494051

Civic Exchange. (2010). Harvest 10th Anniversary Publication and Annual Report 2010. Retrieved from https://civic-exchange.org/dev/wp-content/uploads/2015/10/AR2010_en.pdf

Civic Exchange. (n.d.). *MR WINSTON KA-SUN CHU*. Retrieved from https://civic-exchange.org/person/mr-winston-ka-sun-chu/

Consumer Council. (1996). *Competition policy: The key to Hong Kong's future economic success*. Consumer Council.

Demographia. (2019). The 15th Annual Demographia International Housing Affordability Survey: 2019.

Development Bureau. (2019). Government's Response to Report of Task Force on Land Supply [DEVB(PL-CR) 13/2006]. HKSAR Government: Legislative Council Brief.

Doling, J., & Ronald, R. (2010). Home ownership and asset-based welfare. *Journal of Housing and the Built Environment, 25*(2), 165–173.

Faure, D. (Ed.). (2003). *Hong Kong: A reader in social history*. Oxford University Press (China).

Finlayson, A. (2009). Financialisation, financial literacy and asset-based welfare. *The British Journal of Politics and International Relations, 11*(3), 400–421.

Glaser, R., Haberzettl, P., & Walsh, R. P. D. (1991). Land reclamation in Singapore, Hong Kong and Macau. *GeoJournal, 24*(4), 365–373.

Grydehøj, A. (2015). Making ground, losing space: Land reclamation and urban public space in island cities. *Urban Island Studies, 1*, 96–117.

Hacker, J. S. (2004). Privatizing risk without privatizing the welfare state: The hidden politics of social policy retrenchment in the United States. *American Political Science Review, 98*(2), 243–260.

Harvey, D. (1974). Class-monopoly rent, finance capital and the urban revolution. *Regional Studies, 8*(3–4), 239–255.

Harvey, D. (1982). *The limits to capital*. Blackwell.

HKSAR Government. (2015, November 18). *LCQ1: Small House Policy* [Press release]. Retrieved from https://www.info.gov.hk/gia/general/201511/18/P201511180491.htm

HKSAR Government. (2019, October 16). The Chief Executive's 2019 Policy Address. Retrieved from https://www.policyaddress.gov.hk/2019/eng/index.html

HKSAR Government. (2020, February 27). The 2020–21 Budget. Retrieved from https://www.budget.gov.hk/2020/eng/lr.html

Ho, L. S. (2014, April 1). HK's high land price policy: Myth or reality?. *China Daily*. Retrieved from http://www.chinadaily.com.cn/hkedition/2014-04/01/content_17393905.htm

Ho, L. S., & Wong, G. W. (2006). Privatization of public housing: Did it cause the 1998 recession in Hong Kong? *Contemporary Economic Policy, 24*(2), 262–273.

Hong Kong Connection. (2018, June 30). 《鏗鏘集》公布回歸二十一週年民調結果 年輕人最不滿教育、房屋政策, 對言論自由收窄感憂慮 [Hong Kong Connection announces the results of the 21st anniversary of the reunification: Young people are most dissatisfied with education and housing policies, and worry about the narrowing of freedom of speech]. Retrieved February, from https://www.facebook.com/rthk.HKConnection/posts/1713451935370548

Hong Kong Housing Authority. (1994). *Long term housing strategy: A policy statement; a report on the mid-term review; final report on the mid-term review*. Hong Kong Housing Authority.

Hong Kong Housing Authority. (1996). *Memorandum for the housing authority and the home ownership committee: Sale of flats to sitting tenants scheme*. Hong Kong Housing Authority.

Housing Commission. (1938). *Report of the housing commission 1935*. The Local Printing Press.

Huang, J., Shen, G. Q., & Zheng, H. W. (2015). Is insufficient land supply the root cause of housing shortage? Empirical evidence from Hong Kong. *Habitat International, 49*, 538–546.

Hudson, B. J. (1970). Land reclamation in Hong Kong (Thesis). University of Hong Kong, Pokfulam, Hong Kong SAR. Retrieved from doi:https://doi.org/10.5353/th_b3122884.

Hui, E. C., & Ho, V. S. (2003). Does the planning system affect housing prices? Theory and with evidence from Hong Kong. *Habitat International, 27*(3), 339–359.

Hwang, U., Fang, D., & Zhu, Y. X. (2019, September 4). 沉重的底色与扭曲的方向——香港修例风波背后的一些社会深层根源[Heavy undertones and distorted directions: Some deep social roots behind Hong Kong's Fugitive Offenders amendment bill controversy]. *Xinhua News Agency*. Retrieved from http://www.xinhuanet.com/gangao/2019-09/04/c_1124961699.htm

Ip, I. C. (2011). Welfare good or colonial citizenship? In A. S. Ku & N. Pun (Eds.), *Remaking citizenship in Hong Kong: Community, nation and the global city* (pp. 34–48). Routledge.

Ip, R. & Sat, L. (2018, August 2). The Basic Law means land resumption in New Territories to build more housing isn't so simple. *South China Morning Post*.

Retrieved from https://www.scmp.com/comment/insight-opinion/hong-kong/article/2157744/basic-law-means-land-resumption-new-territories

Jones, M. (2003). Tuberculosis, housing and the colonial state: Hong Kong, 1900-1950. *Modern Asian Studies, 37*(3), 653–682.

Kilpatrick, R. (2018, June 2). Feudalism, not overpopulation or land shortage, is to blame for Hong Kong's housing problems. *Hong Kong Free Press.* Retrieved from https://hongkongfp.com/2018/06/02/feudalism-not-overpopulation-land-shortage-blame-hong-kongs-housing-problems/

Kim, A. M. (2012). The evolution of the institutional approach in planning. In R. Crane & R. Weber (Eds.), *The Oxford handbook of urban planning* (pp. 69–86). Oxford University Press.

Kwan, S. (2019, December 20). Major Hong Kong Developer Donates Land to Mitigate Housing Crisis. *Bloomberg.* Retrieved from https://www.bloomberg.com/news/articles/2019-12-30/top-hong-kong-developer-donates-land-to-mitigate-housing-crisis

La Grange, A. (1997). *Privatization of public housing in Hong Kong: a policy evaluation* (Thesis). University of Hong Kong, Pokfulam, Hong Kong SAR. Retrieved from doi:https://doi.org/10.5353/th_b4212845

La Grange, A., & Pretorius, F. (2000). Ontology, policy and the market: Trends to home-ownership in Hong Kong. *Urban Studies, 37*(9), 1561–1582.

Lai, L. W. (1998). *Zoning and property rights: A Hong Kong case study* (Vol. 1). Hong Kong University Press.

Lai, L. W. (1999). Reflections on the Abercrombie report 1948: A strategic plan for colonial Hong Kong. *Town Planning Review, 70*(1), 61.

Lai, L. W. (2004). Spontaneous catallaxis in urban & rural development under planning by contract in a small open economy: The ideas of Hayek and Mises at work in town & country planning in Hong Kong. *The Review of Austrian Economics, 17*(2–3), 155–186.

Lai, L. W. (2005). Neo-institutional economics and planning theory. *Planning Theory, 4*(1), 7–19.

Lai, L. W. (2011). Discriminatory zoning in colonial Hong Kong. *Property Management, 29*(1), 50–86.

Lai, L. W., & Yu, M. K. (2001). The rise and fall of discriminatory zoning in Hong Kong. *Environment and Planning B: Planning and Design, 28*(2), 295–314.

Lai, L. W., & Fong, K. (2000). *Town planning practice: Context, procedures and statistics for Hong Kong.* Hong Kong University Press.

Lai, L. W., & Ho, W. K. (2001). Low-rise residential developments in green belts: A Hong Kong empirical study of planning applications. *Planning Practice and Research, 16*(3–4), 321–335.

Lai, L. W., & Kwong, V. W. (2012). Racial segregation by legislative zoning and company law: An empirical Hong Kong study. *Environment and Planning B: Planning and Design, 39*(3), 416–438.

Lai, L. W., Lam, G. C., Chau, K. W., Hung, C. W., Wong, S. K., & Li, R. Y. (2009). Statutory zoning and the environment. *Property Management, 27*(4), 242–266.

Lai, L. W. (2000). Housing 'indigenous villagers' in a modern society: An examination of the Hong Kong 'small house' policy. *Third World Planning Review, 22*(2), 207–230.

Lai, N., & Wang, K. (1999). Land-supply restrictions, developer strategies and housing policies: The case in Hong Kong. *International Real Estate Review, 2*(1), 143–159.

Lam, B. (2017, June 7). Boxed in: life inside the 'coffin cubicles' of Hong Kong-in pictures. *The Guardian.* Retrieved from https://www.theguardian.com/cities/gallery/2017/jun/07/boxed-life-inside-hong-kong-coffin-cubicles-cage-homes-in-pictures

Lam, K. (2018, July 16). 【政策分析】林鄭倡有條件填海 「傳聞」只為一幢ifc? [[Policy Analysis] Carrie Lam's conditional reclamation "rumored" is only for an IFC?]. *HK01.* Retrieved from https://www.hk01.com/社會新聞/210963/政策分析-林鄭倡有條件填海-傳聞-只為一幢ifc

Lam, K. (2019a, September 12). 【政策分析】引用《收回土地條例》建公屋 民建聯「成功爭取」? [[Policy Analysis] Citing the "Land Resumption Ordinance" to build public housing, the DAB "successfully fought"?]. *HK01.* Retrieved from https://www.hk01.com/社會新聞/374191/政策分析-引用-收回土地條例-建公屋-民建聯-成功爭取

Lam, K. S. (2019b, September 25). New World donates almost a fifth of its farmland reserves towards building public homes to ease Hong Kong's housing woes. *South China Morning Post.* Retrieved from https://www.scmp.com/business/article/3030317/new-world-development-donates-3-million-square-feet-farm-land-ease-hong

Lam, W. F., & Chan, K. N. (2017). Policy advocacy in transitioning regimes: Comparative lessons from the case of harbour protection in Hong Kong. *Journal of Comparative Policy Analysis: Research and Practice, 19*(1), 54–71.

Lau, C., & Ng, K. C. (2019, July 9). Hong Kong government to appeal against court ruling that strips indigenous New Territories villagers of traditional right to build home. *South China Morning Post.* Retrieved from https://www.scmp.com/news/hong-kong/law-and-crime/article/3017931/hong-kong-government-appeal-against-court-ruling

Lau, S. K. (1984). *Society and politics in Hong Kong.* Chinese University Press.

Lee, G. (2019, October 5). Henderson Land to loan 100,000 sq ft of farmland to Hong Kong government for temporary housing. *South China Morning Post.* Retrieved from https://www.scmp.com/business/companies/article/3031650/henderson-land-loan-100000-sq-ft-farmland-hong-kong-government

Lee, J. (2013). Housing policy and asset building: Exploring the role of home ownership in east Asian social policy. *China Journal of Social Work*, 6(2), 104–117.

Lee, J. W., & Tang, W. S. (2017). The hegemony of the real estate industry: Redevelopment of 'government/institution or community'(G/IC) land in Hong Kong. *Urban Studies*, 54(15), 3403–3422.

Legco Panel on Planning, Lands and Works. (1996). *New territories land exchange entitlements (redemption) bill*. Legislative Council, HKSAR.

Legislative Council. (2019, November 26). Panel on Development Meeting on 26 November 2019 Background brief on developing brownfield sites as a land supply option. Retrieved from https://www.legco.gov.hk/yr19-20/english/panels/dev/papers/dev20191126cb1-160-7-e.pdf

Lethbridge, H. J. (1985). *Hard graft in Hong Kong: Scandal, corruption, the ICAC*. Oxford University Press.

Leung, M. Y. (1999). *From shelter to home: 45 years of public housing development in Hong Kong*. Hong Kong Housing Authority.

Li, S. (2013, October 14). Hong Kong peg to US dollar blamed for city's soaring property prices. *South China Morning Post*. Retrieved from https://www.scmp.com/business/economy/article/1331009/hong-kong-peg-us-dollar-blamed-citys-soaring-property-prices

Liber Research Community. (2015). 棕跡:香港棕土政策研究報告 *[brownfield sites in Hong Kong 2015: Tracing causes, distributions and possible policy framework]*. Liber Research Community.

Liber Research Community. (2018a). 合棕連橫:新界棕土發展潛力研究 [A Study on the Development Potential of Brownfield in the New Territories]. Retrieved from https://drive.google.com/file/d/1WpiXvM_k_6MtQAgQ6uSTkQgWgHd4-OJ9/view

Liber Research Community. (2018b). 隔世追棕—— 新界棕土擴張軌跡與現況 [Brownfields in Time: Tracing the course of Brownfields expansion in the New Territories]. Retrieved from https://drive.google.com/file/d/1UdM-BuFxHGikkzlDJHZPglG86MvW6_cC/view

Liber Research Community. (n.d.). Hong Kong Land Research. Retrieved from https://liber-research.com/en/research-categories-en/land-supply/

Lin, T. B., Lee, R. P., & Simonis, U. E. (1979). *Hong Kong: Economic, social, and political studies in development, with a comprehensive bibliography*. Routledge.

Lu, L. (2005, December 17). Civil Society Declares Victory [Press release]. *Civic Exchange*. Retrieved from https://civic-exchange.org/press-release-civil-society-declares-victory/

Lui, T. L., & Chiu, S. W. (2007). Governance crisis in post-1997 Hong Kong: A political economy perspective. *The China Review*, 7(2), 1–34.

Meyer, J. W., & Rowan, B. (1977). Institutionalized organizations: Formal structure as myth and ceremony. *American Journal of Sociology*, 83(2), 340–363.

Meyer, J. W., Frank, D. J., Hironaka, A., Schofer, E., & Tuma, N. B. (1997). The structuring of a world environmental regime, 1870–1990. *International Organization, 51*(4), 623–651.

Ng, J. (2019, September 13). Beijing piles pressure on Hong Kong developers, calling on government to seize land being 'hoarded for profit'. *South China Morning Post*. Retrieved from https://www.scmp.com/news/hong-kong/hong-kong-economy/article/3027064/hong-kong-developers-who-are-hoarding-land-profit

Ng, J. & Wong, O. (2019, September 14). Can the Lands Resumption Ordinance offer a way out of Hong Kong's housing crisis and quell protests? *South China Morning Post*. Retrieved from https://www.scmp.com/news/hong-kong/hong-kong-economy/article/3027209/can-lands-resumption-ordinance-offer-way-out-hong

Ng, K. C. (2019, September 19). Don't take our support for granted, powerful rural body tells Hong Kong leader as it fights suggestion of seizing private land for public housing. *South China Morning Post*. Retrieved from https://www.scmp.com/news/hong-kong/politics/article/3027969/dont-take-our-support-granted-powerful-rural-body-tells

Ng, M. K. (2006). World-city formation under an executive-led government: The politics of harbour reclamation in Hong Kong. *Town Planning Review, 77*(3), 311–337.

Ng, M. K. (2011). Power and rationality: The politics of harbour reclamation in Hong Kong. *Environment and Planning C: Government and Policy, 29*(4), 677–692.

Ng, M. K. (2018a). Transformative urbanism and reproblematising land scarcity in Hong Kong. *Urban Studies, 57*(7), 1452–1468.

Ng, N. (2018b, December 7). More young, single and highly educated Hongkongers on waiting list for public housing, official figures show. *South China Morning Post*. Retrieved from https://www.scmp.com/news/hong-kong/society/article/2176804/more-young-single-and-highly-educated-hongkongers-waiting

Ng, M. K., Lau, Y. T., Chan, H., & He, S. (2021). Dual land regime, income inequalities and multifaceted socio-economic and spatial segregation in Hong Kong. In M. van Ham, T. Tammaru, R. Ubarevičienė, & H. Janssen (Eds.), *Urban socio-economic segregation and income inequality: A global perspective* (pp. 113–133). Springer.

Nissim, R. (2012). *Land administration and practice in Hong Kong* (3rd ed.). Hong Kong University Press.

Pittini, A., Koessl, G., Dijol, J., Lakatos, E., & Ghekiere, L. (2017). *The state of housing in the EU 2017*. Housing Europe, the European Federation of Public, Cooperative and Social Housing.

Poon, A. (2011). *Land and the ruling class in Hong Kong*. Enrich Professional Publishing.

Research Office Information Services Division. (2016, October 24). Statistical Highlights: Land Utilization in Hong Kong. *Legislative Council Secretariat*. Retrieved from https://www.legco.gov.hk/research-publications/english/1617issh04-land-utilization-in-hong-kong-20161024-e.pdf

Riding, T. (2018). 'Making Bombay Island': Land reclamation and geographical conceptions of Bombay, 1661–1728. *Journal of Historical Geography, 59*, 27–39.

SCMP Reporter. (2005, December 30). No easy solution to deep-rooted problems. *South China Morning Post*. Retrieved from https://www.scmp.com/article/530930/no-easy-solution-deep-rooted-problems

Scott, I. (1989). *Political change and the crisis of legitimacy in Hong Kong*. University of Hawaii Press.

Sito, P., & Li, S. (2017, December 23). How Hong Kong land policies help fuel city's ever-rising property prices. *South China Morning Post*. Retrieved from https://www.scmp.com/property/hong-kong-china/article/2125469/hong-kongs-politics-deter-options-alter-land-sales-policy

Smart, A. (2006). *The Shek kip Mei myth: Squatters, fires and colonial rule in Hong Kong, 1950–1963*. Hong Kong University Press.

Smart, A., & Lee, J. (2003). Financialization and the role of real Estate in Hong Kong's regime of accumulation. *Economic Geography, 79*(2), 153–171.

Sorensen, A. (2017). New institutionalism and planning theory. In M. Gunder, A. Madanipour, & V. Watson (Eds.), *The Routledge handbook of planning theory* (pp. 250–263). Routlege.

Stacke, S. (2017, July 26). Life Inside Hong Kong's 'Coffin Cubicles'. *National Geographic Magazine*. Retrieved from https://www.nationalgeographic.com/photography/proof/2017/07/hong-kong-living-trapped-lam-photos/?cmpid=org=ngp::mc=social::src=facebook::cmp=editorial::add=fbp20181014photo-resurfcoffincubicles::rid&sf200017563=1

Sung, Y. W. & Wong, R. Y. (2018, October 30). 「明日大嶼」願景:成本效益的上佳選擇 [Lantau Tomorrow Vision: the Best Cost-effective Choice]. *Hong Kong Economic Journal*. Retrieved from https://www1.hkej.com/dailynews/commentary/article/1978503/

Tang, B. S., & Wong, S. W. (2008). A longitudinal study of open space zoning and development in Hong Kong. *Landscape and Urban Planning, 87*(4), 258–268.

Tang, B. S., Choy, L. H., & Wat, J. K. (2000). Certainty and discretion in planning control: A case study of office development in Hong Kong. *Urban Studies, 37*(13), 2465–2483.

Tang, B. S., Wong, S. W., & Lee, A. K. (2005). Green belt, countryside conservation and local politics: A Hong Kong case study. *Review of Urban & Regional Development Studies, 17*(3), 230–247.

Tang, B. S., Wong, S. W., & Lee, A. K. (2007). Green belt in a compact city: A zone for conservation or transition? *Landscape and Urban Planning, 79*(3–4), 358–373.

Tang, L. T. (2016, September 28). 東涌谷盧文氏樹蛙棲息地起豪宅 九倉護航 逸東居民冀建社區農場 [Mansions will be built at the habitat of Romer's tree frog in Tung Chung Valley. The Wharf supports. Yat Tung residents want to build community farm]. *HK01*. Retrieved from https://www.hk01.com/社會新聞/45390/東涌谷盧文氏樹蛙棲息地起豪宅-九倉護航-逸東居民冀建社區農場

Tang, W. S. (2008). Hong Kong under Chinese sovereignty: Social development and a land (re)development regime. *Eurasian Geography and Economics, 49*(3), 341–361.

Task Force on Land Supply. (2018a). Land for Hong Kong: Our Home, our say!. Task Force on Land Supply. Retrieved from https://www.legco.gov.hk/yr17-18/english/panels/dev/papers/dev20180529-booklet201804-e.pdf

Task Force on Land Supply. (2018b). Insufficient Land Supply leading to Imbalance in Supply-Demand. *How to tackle land shortage?*. Retrieved from https://www.devb.gov.hk/filemanager/en/content_1051/Land_Supply_En_Booklet.pdf

Task Force on Land Supply. (2019). Demand and Supply. Retrieved from https://www.landforhongkong.hk/en/demand_supply/index.php

Taylor, Z. (2013). Rethinking planning culture: A new institutionalist approach. *Town Planning Review, 84*(6), 683–702.

The Economist. (2015, December 12). Green belts: A notch looser. *The Economist*. Retrieved from https://www.economist.com/britain/2015/12/12/a-notch-looser

The Economist. (2017, February 11). Britain's delusions about the green belt cause untold misery. *The Economist*. Retrieved from https://www.economist.com/britain/2017/02/11/britains-delusions-about-the-green-belt-cause-untold-misery

TrailWatch. (n.d.). Retrieved from https://www.trailwatch.hk/

Tse, R. Y. (1998). Housing Price, land supply and revenue from land sales. *Urban Studies, 35*(8), 1377–1392.

Watson, M. (2009). Planning for a future of asset-based welfare? New labour, financialized economic agency and the housing market. *Planning, Practice & Research, 24*(1), 41–56.

Wong, O. (2013, September 20). The uphill battle for our green havens—Hong Kong's country parks. *South China Morning Post*. Retrieved from https://www.scmp.com/news/hong-kong/article/1313224/uphill-battle-our-green-havens-hong-kongs-country-parks

Wong, O. & Lee, A. (2013, March 15). Ex-Tsoi Yuen villagers' HK$500,000 offer for road sees no takers yet. *South China Morning Post. Review, 15*(1),

1–38. Retrieved from https://www.scmp.com/news/hong-kong/article/1190915/ex-tsoi-yuen-villagers-hk500000-offer-road-sees-no-takers-yet

Wong, S. Y., Tsang, W. W., Ip, R. M., Chu, M. T., Tong, F. K., & To, M. S. (2017). *From Large-Scale Reclamation to an Ideal Home* (Land and Housing Policy Advocacy Series 2). Hong Kong: Our Hong Kong Foundation. Retrieved from https://www.ourhkfoundation.org.hk/sites/default/files/media/pdf/LanHse_PolicyAdv_2_en.pdf

Wong, Y. C. (1998). *On privatizing public housing*. City University of Hong Kong Press.

Xinhua News Agency. (2019, September 13). 新华时评:从解决居住难题入手破解香港社会深层次矛盾 [Solve the deep-seated contradictions in Hong Kong society by solving the housing problem]. *Xinhua News Agency*. Retrieved from http://www.xinhuanet.com/gangao/2019-09/13/c_1124992983.htm

Yu, K. H., & Hui, E. C. (2018). Colonial history, indigenous villagers' rights, and rural land use: An empirical study of planning control decisions on small house applications in Hong Kong. *Land Use Policy, 72*, 341–353.

CHAPTER 9

Hong Kong as the Safest Place in the World? From Gangland to Copland to Disneyland

"The implications of this suggest an extended role for planning as a method of social control, and with that role, an intensification of surveillance and constraints over what remains of the public realm."
—Cuthbert & McLinnell, 1997, p. 310

1 INTRODUCTION

Until the summer of 2019, Hong Kong's current crime rates are remarkably low among developed economies as local official statistics and international crime victim surveys testify (Hong Kong Police Force, 2014; van Dijk et al., 2007). Travel guidebooks frequently remind tourists Hong Kong is a safe city. Yet the image of Hong Kong less than a half century ago was far different. One scene from the movie *Enter the Dragon* (1973) more or less reflects reality in the early 1970s: The British government had to employ Bruce Lee's *Kung Fu* "service" to get rid of the criminal boss

Acknowledgement: this chapter is developed with funding support from the South China Programme, Hong Kong Institute of Asia-Pacific Studies: *The historical and social context of the crime boom (1960–1985) in Hong Kong*.

who was the mastermind behind the colony's crime and vice. So how did Hong Kong transform completely over the past 40 years from a crime-ridden metropolis to one of the safest places on earth?

Kung Fu, a Chinese martial art (*Wu Shu*武術), is frequently associated with the fearsome Hong Kong triad society, such as the triad enforcer Jet Li in *Lethal Weapons 4* (1998). Police characters frequently practiced *Kung Fu* too, like inspector Jimmy Wang Yu in *The Man From Hong Kong* (1975), marine police sergeant Jacky Chan in *Project A* (1983), and senior police inspector Donnie Yen in *Kill Zone* (2005). The *Wu Shu* demonstrated in these movies is traditionally considered an art to stop violence or a conflict, as implied by the Chinese character *Wu* (武): "to stop" (止) and the use of "a spear" (戈). Not surprisingly the roles of the police and the triad society were similarly defined by their capacity to *stop a conflict*: the former entails the capacity to use non-negotiable coercive force (Bittner, 1970); whereas the latter the capacity to use reputational violence to settle underground disputes (Chu, 2000). Both the triads and the police are entrenched in *Kung Fu* movie culture—they are the two sides of the same coin of "policing Hong Kong". To chart the trajectory of crime and security in Hong Kong, requires delving into the interplay of informal peace-keeping arrangements of the *society* (triad societies being one kind) and the *state*'s policing strategy within the broader context of social and political changes.

We examine the state's formal social control function under the colonial context. Hong Kong's modern police institution is frequently considered a British legacy. This first *standard-definition image* overemphasizes the role of police in establishing law and order, thereby stabilizing the once lawless settlement and enabling peaceful socio-economic development. By contrast, in *high-definition*, the "police"—a modern institution symbolizing monopolization of the legitimate use of violence by the state—was functionally weak from the start. The public had little confidence in the police's ability to tackle crime (Gaylord & Traver, 1995). Indeed, much "policing" was conducted in unofficial ways in early Hong Kong. The *District Watch Force* was organized by the Chinese merchant class to maintain security in the Chinese quarters. The triad societies—equipped with the "reputation" to bargain backed by the threat of violence—were often summoned to settle societal discord or underworld disputes (Chu, 2000). In this early functioning of parallel systems of peace keeping, conflict resolution, and crime prevention, the *society* apparently assumed a significant role in effecting social control.

A second *standard-definition* image argues that, despite a weak start, the colonial police gained legitimacy gradually by modernizing and learning to respond effectively to growing crime problems. In *high-definition*, recurrent crises actually undermined such police legitimacy. Police power was consolidated amid the postwar political turmoil, but it remained largely unaccountable and fell into the hands of several corruption syndicates within the police organization (Cheung & Lau, 1981). Subsequent corruption charges, revealing police collusion with organized crime groups, shattered the public's confidence that was already eroded by the police's failure to curb surging criminal violence (Lethbridge, 1985). In response, the colonial *state* assumed a more direct and disciplinary role in "policing" the local Chinese society. "Fighting crime" has become the vehicle to exert political control. A key to this was the rapid expansion of the police bureaucracy to absorb working class youths. Some have argued this police reform, along with other reforms in the criminal justice system, aligned with the emerging frame of moral panic over uncontrolled youth largely heightened by the 1966 and 1967 riots (Lethbridge, 1985; Gray, 1991). With the establishment of the Independent Commission Against Corruption (ICAC), the tacit police-underworld co-policing agreement came to an end, leading to more social disorder (Traver, 1991). Overall crime rates reached their historic highs during the 1970s and 1980s because, paradoxically, the state intervened more in this transitional period.

The conventional view of Hong Kong's recent low crime status attributes it to the effectiveness of the now thoroughly professionalized police. This third *standard-definition image* has neglected, however, the emerging influence of the market sphere in the co-production of the safe city image (Wood & Shearing, 2007). In *high-definition*, the onslaught of neoliberalism from the 1990s has reshaped the landscape of social control in Hong Kong by expanding the role of corporations and private security companies in the provision of security. Inside the private realm of shopping malls or supermarkets or Disneyland, deviant acts are imaginably more likely to attract the attention of private security than either *Kung Fu* fighting triads or police! Even in public areas, social order is no longer maintained by naked force but by highly rationalized spatial designs and zoning that preempt the individual's "deviant" actions in a hegemonic way—much like a Disney World (Shearing & Stenning, 1984). We therefore argue that the transformation of Hong Kong into a safe city is a product of the interplay among the state, the society, and the *market*—with the first and the last dominating the scene now.

Several questions guide our enquiry. Which social group was/is defined as most susceptible to committing deviance and subjected to social control in Hong Kong? What were the chief security concerns of the locals and the government at different stages of development? What caused the postwar "crime wave" and how did it affect the local society? What are the social costs of Hong Kong's low crime situation? In what follows, we put aside *Kung Fu* and examine sociological accounts of crime and security within the Hong Kong context. As outlined, we distinguish three distinct phases of social control: *Gangland* (initiative of the society), *Copland* (primacy of the state) and *Disneyland* (dominance of the market). In each phase the juxtaposition of society, state and market determines what constitutes "deviance" and the corresponding social control mechanisms.

2   GANGLAND AND THE SOCIETY (1843—SECOND WORLD WAR)

2.1   *What Caused More Threats in the Early Colony: Gangs Or Chinese?*

The first *standard-definition* image portrayed Hong Kong an almost Hobbesian state of nature where vagabonds—pirates, robbers, and smugglers—frequented the place for gain or to seek refuge soon after it was declared Crown Land. The British colonial state then established law and order by introducing the first modern police force and the law courts targeting criminal activities and triad societies. Here we present a *high-definition* of the crime situation and discuss the "true" security concerns behind various colonial manoeuvres.

In 1841, twelve years after the birth of the modern police force in Metropolitan London in 1829, the first police force was established in Hong Kong with some 93 soldiers from the local British and Indian regiments and 37 Chinese. But law and order did not improve, as the recruits (mostly expelled soldiers) deemed unfit for service, or members of the Chinese secret societies (Gaylord & Traver, 1995, p. 25). Frequented by robbers and pirates, British-owned warehouses like the East Point warehouse of the Jardine and Matheson Company, had to hire and train their own private Sikhs security personnel to guard against the gangsters (Hamilton, 2012).[1]

---

[1] Chinese pirates were in fact not the sole cause of the maritime problem. Piracy in the territorial area was sometimes fuelled by "collusion" between merchants and pirates. Foreign

Given its tight budget, suppressing crime and ensuring a sense of security, especially among the local Chinese, was of less concern for the colonial police (Miners, 1995; Chiu, 1996).[2] The police even rented out their security services to private companies to sustain police operations at the beginning (Hamilton, 2012). Rather than focusing on crime, the primary objective of social control was to subdue the Chinese population, as the new subjects of the Crown became restless and mounted resistance to colonial rule from time to time. The police were tasked to enforce legislation targeting Chinese indiscriminately. Wesley-Smith (1994) categorized such legislation into three main groupings: registration of Chinese people, punishment exclusively for Chinese, and restriction of Chinese movement at night.

In 1844, the Ordinance *Registry of the Inhabitants of the Island of Hong Kong and Its Dependencies* was passed to require all inhabitants to carry a registration card—without which one would run the risk of being fined or worse (especially for Chinese) being deported from the colony (See The University of Hong Kong Libraries, 1989). This Ordinance was suspended in the same year only after Chinese workers staged a strike and threatened to leave Hong Kong. Claiming it was intended to get rid of the robbers and pirates hiding in Hong Kong, the colonial government set up the Census and Registration Office in 1845 to enhance surveillance of the Chinese population (Wesley-Smith, 1994).

An *Ordinance for the suppression of Triads and other secret Societies* was enacted in 1845 primarily targeting the anti-Qing triad societies operating in colonial Hong Kong (Chu, 2000).[3] Although initially targeting Chinese only and the inhumane way of punishing by branding on the cheek and banishing from the territory were limited to the early days, the law was revised as the draconian *Societies Ordinance* which encompasses all kind of legitimate organizations in the colony with the Commissioner of Police

---

companies that smuggled opium and other goods along the South China coast frequently tipped off Chinese pirates on shipments of rival companies. This tradition of intelligence-led piracy against rival merchant shipments had a long maritime history in Europe. Perhaps it is a good reminder that some hundreds of years ago England outcompeted Spain with the help of Sir Francis Drake—himself a pirate and knighted by Elizabeth I of England.

[2] See Chiu (1996) and Miners (1995) for a discussion of the financial stringency of the early colonial government.

[3] Ordinance No.1 of 1845. *Triad and Secret Societies Ordinance.* See The University of Hong Kong Libraries (1989).

becoming the *Registrar of Societies* in Hong Kong (Gaylord & Traver, 1995).[4]

A series of laws were enacted from 1857 onwards to control Chinese mobility—coined as the "light and pass" laws. Chinese inhabitants were no longer free to travel on Hong Kong Island between 8pm (later 9pm) and sunrise.[5] Those wishing to stay on the street after sunset were required to carry a night pass applied from the police. The law was updated in 1870 to mandate Chinese residents to carry a lantern if they travelled within the City of Victoria after dark.[6] All these "light and pass" laws were eventually incorporated as the *Regulation of the Chinese Ordinance* in 1888, which also included administrative restrictions on Chinese social life like religious ceremonies and theatrical performances.[7]

Law and order, however, continued to deteriorate. One of the reasons is that the government, guided by its patriarchal colonial mentality, intervened in a Chinese tradition of social control. Soon after the colony was declared a free port, Chinese began to settle on the northern part of Hong Kong Island and brought with them the traditional watchmen system, a system similar to the one in London before the establishment of the Metropolitan Police in the eighteenth century. Traditionally, the Chinese watchmen would strike a bamboo and gong while patrolling the neighbourhood at regular hours at night, and routinely chanted "Beware of fire" along their way. This organized routine gave the local Chinese community a sense of security and warned potential thieves of the explicit presence of a guardian (Hamilton, 2012).

Nevertheless, the Chinese watchmen system soon was subjected to colonial intervention. *"An Ordinance for the Preservation of Good Order and Cleanliness within the Colony"* was introduced in 1844 which, along with other prohibitions, forbade "the beating of any gong or drum; and the commission of other acts anywhere in the nighttime that would create unnecessary alarm".[8] According to Hamilton (2012, pp. 22–24), "Chinese

[4] Ordinance No.47 of 1911. *Societies Ordinance.* See The University of Hong Kong Libraries (1989).

[5] Ordinance No.9 of 1857. *Peace of the Colony Ordinance.* See the University of Hong Kong Libraries (1989).

[6] Ordinance No. 14 of 1870. *Passes for Chinese Ordinance.* See the University of Hong Kong Libraries (1989).

[7] Ordinance No. 3 of 1888. *Regulation of Chinese Ordinance.* See the University of Hong Kong Libraries (1989).

[8] Ordinance No. 5 of 1844. *Good Order and Cleanliness Ordinance.* See the University of Hong Kong Libraries (1989).

watchmen" was made a special subject to be regulated and the noise they made was considered "a public nuisance". The nickname "Bamboo Ordinance" was introduced with all watchmen prohibited from making any noise under *An Ordinance for the better securing the Peace and Quiet of the Inhabitants of the Town of Victoria and its vicinity during the night-time* of 1844.[9] Without the sound effect the privately-hired watchmen lost their functions and walked silently, whereas many thieves and pirates swiftly took advantage of the situation.

A degree of lawlessness could thus be attributed to the unintended consequence of colonial control of the Chinese. In retrospect, the permissive attitude of the colonial government towards vice businesses that sprung up in the colony was another key reason why Hong Kong was becoming a gangland. Government revenues were generated from taxing and licensing the brothels and opium dens to fund colonial expenses. To regulate prostitutes, an *Ordinance for Checking the spread of Venereal Diseases* was enacted in 1857.[10] Its 1867 version granted the Registrar-General the licensing right and the police the power to root out unregulated sexual commerce (Howell, 2004). The daily governance of these "legal" vice businesses leads us to examine informal "policing" in the South China frontier.

2.2 The Parallel Systems of Social Control: The Good, the Bad and the Ugly in the South China Frontier

Two informal social control agents—triad societies (the bad) and the District Watch Force (the good) shared, with a certain degree of legitimacy, the "use of violence" with the colonial police. Like the Mafia in Sicily (Hobsbawm, 1959/1971, p.41), triad societies,[11] with their unique capacity to perpetrate "violence", grew out of the needs of all classes in the frontier by occupying a precarious niche in a society lacking trustful relations (Gambetta, 1993, p. 2). While triad societies committed a wide range of illegal acts in the south China region including revolutionary

---

[9] Ordinance No.17 of 1844. *Peace and Quiet Ordinance*. See the University of Hong Kong Libraries (1989).

[10] Ordinance No.12 of 1857. *Venereal Diseases ordinance*. See the University of Hong Kong Libraries (1989).

[11] See Chapter 151 Societies Ordinance for definition of Triad Societies.

activities,[12] their presence in Hong Kong could also be viewed in the context of the harsh conditions of survival and discriminatory practices in the colony. Competition for all kinds of job was keen. Coolies and hawkers frequently had to fight for their right to do dock work or to occupy a favourable street corner. Forming their own triad alliances or joining existing ones allowed these male migrant workers not only to outcompete their opponents, but also to avoid cut-throat street competition that undermined their chances of survival (Morgan, 1960).

Alongside maintaining informal social order among the grassroots, triads provided protection services to early "vice economies" like gambling, opium dens,[13] and brothels which were allowed by the colonial state but not protected by the police. For the Chinese compradors or owners of the coolie houses, triad societies provided a ready service to break strikes or to discipline their coolies. Through these coolie houses, secret society rituals and organization spread overseas to places such as San Franciso and Los Angeles, which led to the infamous Tongs Wars in America between the 1850s and 1920s (Chin, 1990). Apart from the coolie businesses, triads even served in an arbitrator's role for semi-legal matters that could not be dealt with formally through the courts (Chu, 2000).

Following a policy that subject Europeans to English law and Chinese to their own law and customs, the District Watch Force (1866–1970), overseen by the District Watch Committee, was established under the Registrar General to "police" the Chinese community (Hamilton, 2012, p. 39). In practice, it was these Cantonese speaking constables who conducted "policing" within the Chinese community rather than their colonial counterparts—who often prioritized serving the European communities rather than their ethnic neighbours. The District Watch Force was hired and trained by the Chinese community with limited funding from the government, after Chinese leaders petitioned for its formation to protect their businesses and properties in the Central and Western districts. On top of crime detection and prevention, the District Watch Force also preserved public peace, conducted censuses for the Registrar,

---

[12] Let's not forget triad's role in rallying grassroots support for the Chinese revolution—Dr. Sun Yat-sen, the founding father of the Republic of China, was himself a triad officer bearer.

[13] According to Table I of (Ref. No. PRO/REF/29 Encl.3): Sales, Revenue and Costs of the HK Government Opium Monopoly, opium revenue as a percentage of total government revenue reached as high as 46.5% in 1918. Opium sales continued to be part of government revenue until its ban after the post-War (British Military Administration, 1945).

assisted the Po Leung Kuk in investigating/tracking trafficked women and minors, and settled disputes. By the 1890s, the District Watch Committee was recognized by the colonial state as the highest advisory body of the Chinese community by the colonial state, surpassing in this respect the Tung Wah Group of Hospitals (Tsang, 2004, p. 70). Although the Chinese community truly had administrative rights over the District Watch Force, the colonial government maintained effective control by appointing the Captain Superintendent of Police as a member of the District Watch Committee in 1894 (Hamilton, 1998).

So what happened to the early Hong Kong police? Perceived as neither good nor bad by the indigenous Chinese, the police, a modern policing institution brought by the British, was best portrayed as playing the ugly face. It was an inefficient law enforcer and an ineffective alien oppressor from the start. Charles May, who was later promoted to the Governorship and narrowly escaped an assassination attempt, came to serve as the Captain Superintendent of Police in 1845. His initial attempt to follow the model of the Metropolitan Police, nowadays known as the Bobbies, was soon abandoned with the deteriorating situation and the difficulties in filling vacancies—remember "police" was then a brand new concept in the East. When Walter Meredith Deane became the top police officer in 1867, he dismissed a majority of the police force, including all of the inspectors (Gaylord & Traver, 1995, pp. 25–26). With little trust in the Chinese themselves, the decision was made to recruit police constables of Sikh origin from province of Sind in colonial India to serve in Hong Kong.[14] As a result, the colonial police were ethnically diverse but racially divided. Chinese could only achieve the rank of Sergeant, and Indians the rank of Inspector, but British and other Europeans the management grades.[15] Initially, police equipment was also racially assigned, with Europeans equipped with a musket and a cutlass, whereas Indian and Chinese were given only a staff, a rattle and later a whistle (Ho & Chu, 2012).[16] Deane also reformed the police following the combat-ready Royal Irish

[14] A similar colonial logic could be seen in British employing the Nepalese Gurkhas to suppress the Indian Rebellion of 1857.

[15] This is documented in an article "The Force's Ethnic Composition" posted by the Hong Kong Police Force (2018b).

[16] Early police uniform was green in colour. "Big head" was a nickname for both the "Sikh Police" and local Chinese who worn a bamboo hat. "ABCD" each stood for regiment from different ethnic groups: "A"—British and European police; "B"—Indian Sikh police; "C"—Chinese police; "D"—Shandong Weihaiwei police. Hence comes the local slang: "A B C D,

Constabulary model, which means all recruits had to go through paramilitary training in preparation for local insurgencies. This paramilitary tradition has deeply shaped the organizational culture of the Hong Kong Police even up to the present.

3   THE BIRTH OF COPLAND (1950s TO 1980s)

3.1   Policing Modernization

In the second *standard-definition* image, the modernization and expansion of the Hong Kong Police was considered a direct response to the post-World War II crime wave. Scholars had long noted the surge of crime and attempted to explain patterns and trends in official statistics and victim surveys with western criminology theories.[17] The two most frequently cited causes of crime, rapid industrialization and urbanization, echoed the official stance that modernization caused crime (Foreign and Commonwealth Office, 1970). These rapid social changes weakened social control and socialization by traditional institutions, like the family, resulting in social disorganization of neighbourhoods and a surge in the crime problem. Another urbanization related explanation was that high density living created social strains which caused individuals to become prone to explode" in violence,[18] as an official report claimed after the 1966 riots.[19] As individualization continued to strengthen, especially among the younger generation, so did the tendency to commit crime out of impulsivity or the socialization influences of "bad cultures" like violent comics or pornography—one explanation that the moral panic over youth typically ascribed to.[20] In this standard view, colonial policing "intensified"

Big Head in Green Uniform, Can't Catch the Thief, Blow their Whistle!" (「ABCD, 大頭綠衣, 追賊唔到, 吹BB」).

[17] For interpreting crime trends, see Cheung et al. (2002) and Leung (1997) for a discussion based on official statistics; see Broadhurst et al. (2008) and Traver (1991) for a discussion based on victim surveys.

[18] For an orthodox explanation for the rising crime rate, see Cheung et al. (2002).

[19] See Commission of Inquiry on Kowloon Disturbances (1967).

[20] Perhaps public responses to Beatles' landing at Kai Tak Airport, Hong Kong in 1964 and the repeated news coverage of "*ah fei*" (teddy boys) from the early 1960s could be seen as the hallmark of rising moral panic over youth deviance. See Lui (1996) for an explanation of the moral panic over youth.

simply because there was more crime and deviance, and eventually the police did their job.

Scholars long questioned the standard explanation for the crime surge in Hong Kong by the modernization thesis aforementioned. Leung (1997) and Traver (1991) argue that, the crime rate remained remarkably low even as industrialization was taking off between the late 1950s and early 1960s, hence the modernization thesis was not able to explain the continual surge of overall crime in official reports from the 1970s to the early 1980s.[21] As discussed in Chap. 1, Hong Kong's state-society structure was transformed as industrialization took place before and after the Second World War, giving rise to heightened consciousness of local Chinese towards nationalism, labour rights and political identity. In response to this, social control in colonial Hong Kong also shifted ideologically from pacifying the Chinese as a whole,[22] to targeting the emerging working class and youth discontent.[23]

Our *high-definition* image presents three missing lacunae towards the post-Second World War crime wave and their complex relation to the shifting "policing boundary': first the curbing of police syndicated corruption led to the gradual dissolution of indirect policing and a surge in crime. The old informal way to solve crimes through arbitrary exercise of "discretion", was now rationalized with tightened administrative control as the police organization further bureaucratized;[24] second the state-society restructuring throughout this period, for instance the increasing intervention of the colonial state in public housing projects, had reshuffled the postwar refugee society while at the same time creating new "policeable" social space (Chiu & Lee, 2013); and third, after the 1966 Star Ferry riots and 1967 Leftist riots, the colonial state abandoned its "laissez faire" approach toward policing and strengthened its political control of the Chinese working class and youth population through various "crime

---

[21] Broadhurst (2000) suggested the high crime status of Hong Kong in the 1980s should take into consideration new opportunities arising from the economic restructuring of China as it opened up its economy.

[22] See Carroll (2007, pp. 53–61) for a discussion of the related historical events.

[23] This was illustrated in the report submitted by Commission of Inquiry on Kowloon Disturbances (1967) and Ng's (1974) study. Both symbolized an ideological shift to a focus on social control of the young Chinese working class.

[24] For example, the internal rule book of Hong Kong Police—Police General Orders Chapter 33 Gambling mandates that "A police officer shall promptly report any information which may come into his possession regarding unlawful gambling."

projects". At the end of this stage the traditional *Gangland* image of Hong Kong had morphed into the birth of *Copland*. The hitherto local society's role of "policing Hong Kong" is now eclipsed by the state.

3.2   The Changing Boundary and Administration of Policing: The End of Indirect Policing and the Rationalization of Police Practices

As noted above, the indirect policing model was a legacy of early colonial rule. In turn, its end signalled a transitional period in which the boundary of policing was redrawn in response to a series of political and social events.

The photo of eight British gentlemen posing behind the decapitated bodies of the Namoa Pirates at the beach outside the Qing occupied Kowloon Walled City (The West Australian, 1891) best illustrates the loosely configured boundary of the colonial policing system in 1891 Hong Kong.[25] Before the turn of the century, pirates and criminals arrested were often directly deported and to be executed right away by the Qing government.[26] Deportation or forced exile of Chinese subjects from colonial Hong Kong did not end with the fall of the Qing Empire but was intensified by political policing as nationalism spread in the region. The years following the Strike-Boycott of 1925–1926 saw the heightened suppression of communism and banning of unionism in Hong Kong. Communists were arrested and deported across the Shenzhen border often to be executed by the Guangdong government who provided the tip-offs (Carroll, 2007, p. 103). After the Chinese Civil War ended in 1949, the colonial government continued to detain and deport secret agents infiltrating Hong Kong, often without trial (Jones & Vagg, 2017).[27] This time the exiles came from both Kuomintang (Nationalist) and Communist

[25] Public execution displays in Hong Kong ended in 1894. Punishment by branding on the cheeks and exiling were abolished by Governor George Bowen in 1880, (public) caning and public display in shackles were also abolished in 1903 and 1909. Governor John Pope Hennessy proposed to Colonial Secretary Earl of Carnarvon in 1877 to abolish caning and to restrict no. of strokes to just the bottom than the back, and to replace the cat o'nine tails with rattan canes. None were accepted. Within the colony, public display of torturous punishment did not end until 1909—just two years before the Chinese Revolution. See Hong Kong Memory Project (2014).

[26] The death penalty was suspended from 1966 and was eventually abolished in 1993. See Vagg (1997) for a discussion of events leading to its abolishment.

[27] See Jones and Vagg (2017) for a discussion of detention without trial in colonial Hong Kong between 1949 and 1971.

backgrounds and were generally deported back to their politically affiliated regimes. Initially, some of these "political" deportees were members of triad societies, like the 14K triad group formed by Kuomintang agents at Canton (Guangzhou) for intelligence and sabotage purposes (Morgan, 1960). On 10th October 1956 the pro-Nationalist factions incited riots in Tsuen Wan and attacked Communist sympathizers, with triad members frequently sighted in the crowd. The riots resulted in massive destruction on the Kowloon side: 59 deaths and at least 440 injuries (Carroll, 2007, p. 146). The mass deportations following the 1956 riots marked a high point of coercive political policing in Hong Kong's history. In 1958 the colonial police responded to its inadequacy in dealing with large scale riots, which were suppressed only with help from the British Army, by forming a new riot control division. This new Police Training Contingent further institutionalized the paramilitary tradition and was the predecessor of today's Police Tactical Unit.

Deportation was used to deal not only with political agents but also the so-called hardcore criminals in Hong Kong until at least 1961, when Kuomintang and Communist Governments became reluctant to accept such deportees (Foreign and Commonwealth Office, 1970). Meanwhile, the colonial authority began to notice a rise in petty crime and suggested several reasons for it:

> "One is the increased price of drugs which is forcing a greater number of addicts to resort to miscellaneous crime in an attempt to obtain money. *Another is the difficulty of deporting convicted or undesirable aliens.* A third is the continued prosperity of Hong Kong which provides the criminal with wealthy victims." (Emphasis ours, Government Press, 1962)

The police considered deportation and detention to be effective tools for fighting crime until the 1970.[28] The British Foreign and Commonwealth Office (FCO) even had to turn down a request from the colonial government to reconsider deportation as a way of dealing with the crime wave—for fear of constructing an image of Hong Kong as a "police state" (Foreign and Commonwealth Office, 1970). The end of "deportation" as

[28] Jones and Vagg (2017) details the debate between London and Colonial Government of Hong Kong concerning the "indefinite detention" of triad members who were rejected from a deportation destination under the Emergency (Deportation and Detention) Regulations 1962.

a solution to crime redrew the "policing boundary" of Hong Kong—police soon needed to find another way to handle recidivists.

Meanwhile, the indirect policing model that the colonial state relied upon had resulted in a racially-divided police force, a factor contributing to syndicated corruption.[29] Political policing had already expanded police power by revitalizing the regime of detention and deportation after the 1956 riots and the revised Emergency (Deportation and Detention) Regulations 1962. The new power to lock up someone indefinitely without trial fell into the hands of the Chinese Staff Sergeants—the head of the rank and file, and became useful weapons to discipline the underworld for their own gain.

By 1962, an extensive corruption network had penetrated the whole police force with the mighty Chinese detective Staff Sergeants like Lui Lok, who excelled at "peacekeeping" in the underworld, becoming the syndicate heads.[30] Externally a symbiotic relationship, as Traver (1991) coined it, was cultivated between the organized criminals and the police. The triads operated vice businesses (gambling and drug dens, brothels) and "policed" their own community, including the prevention of predatory crime, under tacit agreement to pay "tribute" to the police. As an illustration, in 1973 the police complained that the anti-crime campaign was driving up predatory crime inside the Kowloon Walled City; they believed drug addicts had to resort to robbery for survival since low profile organized crime was being curbed (Foreign and Commonwealth Office, 1973, 1974). The underpaid Hong Kong Police sometimes utilized the graft received to pay informant fees.[31] Due to various kinds of "arrangements", it is no surprise the conviction rate in Hong Kong's Magistracies for juveniles was almost 100% in 1957 (Government Press, 1958).

---

[29] In fact, the biggest corruption scandal involved a British Chief Superintendent—Peter Godber. It should be noted that corruption among detectives working on vice was very common in Britain in the 1960s and 1970s, as shown in Sir Robert Mark's massive cleanup of the Scotland Yard when he was Commissioner of the Metropolitan Police. See Cheung and Lau (1981) for a discussion of the police syndicated corruption in Hong Kong.

[30] Lui Lok, who assumed the position of head of all Detective Staff Sergeants in 1962, retired in 1968; Lam Kong, Kowloon head of Detective Staff Sergeants in 1962, retired in 1969. See also *Creating a Legend* (Hong Kong Police Force, 2018).

[31] "Money from gambling and other rackets helped pay for informants in the underworld whose tips helped greatly in curbing crime, leading to the notion that petty graft, at least, was tolerated." cited from *Creating a Legend* (Hong Kong Police Force, 2018).

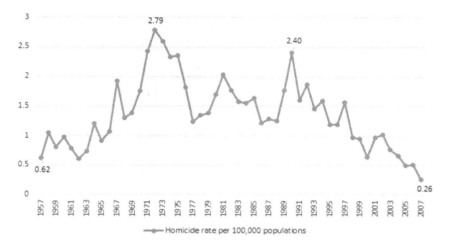

Fig. 9.1 Homicide trend in Hong Kong, 1957–2007. (See: Commissioner of Police (1957–1969); Commissioner of Police (1978–1996); Commissioner of Police (1997–2008))

Nonetheless, such tacit agreement between the police and the triads to curb violence was dissolving from 1965 onward at both fronts. In fact, the overall homicide rate rose to an historical peak in 1972 at 2.79 (per 100,000 population) (see Fig. 9.1). On one hand, the triad leaders complained that their young gang members increasingly paid little respect to "traditional triad values" like loyalty, and frequently resorted to violence to settle minor disputes (Morgan 1960). On the other hand, the homicide detectives found themselves facing a surge in homicides involving groups of youths:

"There is no question that the use of violence especially [sic] by groups of persons in the course of committing other crimes especially Robbery and merely as a method of settling any form of dispute has now reached epidemic proportions." (Police Internal Memo: Homicide—S.S.P./ C.I.D./K. to D.C.I. Date 3rd February 1971). (Information Services Department, 1971–1975)

The police came under enormous pressure for their inability to curb the rising gang violence between 1965 and 1971. One police official claimed in an internal memo that the low conviction rate for murder—out of some 381 persons charged with murder in this period only 15 were convicted—was due to a change in the law and the courts' leniency (Information Services Department, 1971–1975). The police apparently tried to blame the situation on the judiciary, which was making significant advances in protecting defendants' legal rights at the time. The divergence between a modernizing legal system and a colonial policing system lagging behind was obvious.[32] The machinery that was once geared towards the easy conviction of Chinese seems no longer at work by 1971 with the emerging ideology of human rights. Whether this divergence caused the surge of extreme gang violence remains debatable but at least the homicide detectives believed this was the case. It was apparent that a crisis in policing was developing, not just in terms of the obvious corruption problem but due to the police's declining capacity to maintain basic social order. Against the backdrop of working class youth's political mobilizations in 1966 and during the 1967 riots, the policing crisis triggered the subsequent reform of the colonial police, administratively and financially.

The administrative reform clearly violated former financial secretary Cowperthwaite's stringent financial control. There was a large expansion of the police force in the 1970s that incorporated working class youths and that paid junior police officers better than the average working class wage—as seen in the repeated emphasis on "good pay in cash" in police recruitment commercials in the 1970s.[33] A budget was also allocated to establish the Junior Police Call Scheme (JPC) in 1974—the largest organized youth group in Hong Kong history—to recruit young people for community surveillance of triad infiltration and criminal activity. Within the police, Commissioner Charles Sutcliffe broke up the monopoly of the Chinese Staff Sergeants by promoting hundreds of young Non-Commissioned

---

[32] "To amplify my first point the amendments to the law which have made it almost impossible to obtain convictions for Murder and in particular GANG MURDERS have been the abolition of constructive malice ..." (Information Services Department, 1971–1975); "These amendments were brought about in the U.K. by the current permissive and muddled thinking in the legal profession and it may well be that they can afford such luxuries, however, we with a Murder rate which in 1970 was over 4 times the U.K. rate and includes a much larger percentage of Gang Murders cannot afford them" (Information Services Department, 1971–1975).

[33] The number of applicants for the position of police constable increased 2.5 times in 1973–74 (12,460 compared to 4,898 in 1972–73) followed by the implementation of a pay increase from $482 to $660 per month plus fringe benefits. See Lee (1981, pp. 191–192).

Officers to a new rank of Station Sergeants (Hong Kong Police Force, 2018a), while the powerful Staff Sergeants were promoted to the lowest management rank of Inspector, thereby stripping them of their power.[34] Similar promotions have also bridged the racial gap in the administrative structure and promoted "localization" of the colonial police. Police power now flowed from the administrative core rather than from the dispersed power base of the Staff Sergeants within the community. During the reign of the Staff Sergeants, only three cases of rape were reported in a population estimated to be 2,677,000 in 1957. The figure fell to just one case of rape in 1961 for a population of more than three million (Government Press, 1958; Government Press, 1962). Following the power structure reform, there was less of an incentive for the police to paint a "peaceful scene" so that a rise in crime rate was to be expected. With increased public concern and victims becoming more willing to come forward under the influence of the local feminist movement, some 101 cases of rape were reported to the police by 1974 (Lethbridge, 1980).

Financially, the move to regulate *Tsz Fa* (字花) and other illegal gambling was based on the recommendations of the Working Party on Policy on Gambling to divert gambling proceeds away from organized crime syndicates to the government in order to finance the expansion of welfare programs as part of the hegemonic restructuring of the state-society relationship (City District Commissioner Kowloon, 1970–1973).[35] Under the directive of the Secretary of Home Affairs, the Working Party (1971–1973) conducted a secret investigation into the *Tsz Fa* system and scale of illegal gambling—known in the 1960s to be under the tight control of the Staff Sergeants. Police quickly responded by producing their own version of an illegal gambling report but the Working Party had already established the fact that illegal gambling was rampant and that *Tsz Fa* had spread to every Hong Kong district with proceeds routed to powerful syndicates controlling them (City District Commissioner Kowloon, 1970–1973). The colonial state began to take over the regulation of a popular working class leisure activity, gambling, from hands of the police corruption syndicates

---

[34] Personal interview with a retired senior police officer.

[35] *Tsz fa* is Chinese game in which players try to guess a number out of 36, with each number represented by a symbolic icon like a poem or a Chinese historical figure. Newspapers would regularly publish "tips" associated with the symbolic icon. Most *tsz fa* dens were operated by triads and "protected" by the corruption syndicate. Stephen Chiu's late father was a loyal fan of the *Tsz fa* activity and as a young boy he was often tasked to purchase the lottery ticket. Never won any of the grand prizes, however.

in order to tax the revenues. Gambling offences surged rapidly within a year following the colonial government's establishment of the Mark Six in 1975 to replace *Tsz Fa* (Traver, 1991).[36] From this angle, crime increased because the state started to regulate a social practice through administrative measures. In addition, the indirect policing model could no longer be informally financed by the *Tsz Fa* system and the like, and a new policing model solely dependent on government funding began to emerge, hence also tightening the administrative control of the police and increasing accountability.

3.3   State-Society Restructuring: Enhancing Stability But Not Necessarily Security

The regulation of Tsz Fa was one of the many state-society restructuring projects during the 1960s–1970s. Some scholars suggested public housing projects were a form of social control intended to pre-empt the political influence of the Communists in squatter areas (see Smart, 2006) and to divert labour to industrializing districts (Castells et al., 1990; Chap. 8). The view that the colonial housing projects had a stabilizing effect is paradoxical because it was popularly believed these new resettlement and public housing estates were "crime hotspots".

Interestingly, both police and police critics like Elsie Elliot shared the view that public housing had become crime-ridden by the end of the 1960s.[37] Since public housing projects entailed the state's direct intervention into the local Chinese society and their everyday life (see Chap. 8), the associated problem of crime could be seen as an unintended consequence of the restructuring of state-society relations. For many tenants, living in clusters of high-rise public housing was a new experience that required adjustment in their spatial reasoning. New spaces created, such as a park, a public staircase or a corridor, became "unclaimed" territory that was socially and politically ambiguous and contestable by tenants as well as

---

[36] Mark Six is a lottery game operated by the Hong Kong Jockey Club. Winners have to correctly guess six numbers out of 1–49. Apart from Mark Six, the Hong Kong Jockey Club monopolizes all gambling activities related to horse racing (Gambling Ordinance (Chapter 148) of 1977) and soccer betting (Gambling (Amendment) Bill of 2003) in Hong Kong—both online and offline (Chan et al., 2016). Club membership is still restricted to economic and social elites of Hong Kong like the old days (see Chap. 2).

[37] See Elliot (1971) for the view that police corruption caused the crime problem in public housings.

trespassers, often with primitive means—violence (Newman, 1972). For example, neighbours might fight over the use of public area whereas predatory criminals viewed the staircases favourably as a zone free not only from residents' intervention but also from the police. Initially, no one would have expected the state to have any role in ensuring security in such liminal area—public spaces that are perceived as private property.

At first (1969–1970) the police were "puzzled" by what they perceived as burgeoning robberies and burglaries in the resettlement areas, and tried to learn from Police Departments in Hawaii and San Francisco (rather than the United Kingdom!) their crime prevention methods (Royal Hong Kong Police Force, 1968–1975). Special files were also opened by the colonial police to collect crime data concerning resettlement estates from 1968–1975 (Royal Hong Kong Police Force, 1968–1975) and crime data in housing estates from 1971–1977 (Royal Hong Kong Police Force, 1971–1977). The proportion of arrests made against public estate tenants inside and outside their public estates were then tabulated monthly between 1973 and 1975 to illustrate specifically the pattern of crime committed by working class members.[38] By reorganizing people into a fixed abode that required name registration, the public housing projects had become de facto method of social surveillance over the working class.

Despite its ability to know who's who, the government was unable to achieve "full" administrative control of the public housing areas until the 1970s. As an example, tenants of resettlement and public housing estates were required to pay monthly rent to estate officials at their front door, but resistance to paying rent was not infrequent. To collect the rent "smoothly", some estate officers would employ the service of a Chinese boxing class—sometimes under the influence of triad societies like *Sun Yee On* (新義安) (Royal Hong Kong Police Force, 1971–1977)—to accompany them. In some cases, the Chinese boxing class even provided "security service" to the new resettlement estates when the estate management failed to do so (Royal Hong Kong Police Force, 1971–1977), functioning much like the "District Watch Force" mentioned earlier. The state's failure to provide adequate facilities like markets near the public housing resulted in triads' racketeering activities targeting hawkers and other illegal commercial enterprises in ways much like the early days (Royal Hong Kong

---

[38] For example, in December 1975 majority of crime committed by tenants of public housing estates were outside their estates (196 arrests for crime committed outside vs. 115 arrests for crime committed inside). See Royal Hong Kong Police Force (1968–1975).

Police Force, 1969–1971). In this regard, the colonial housing projects might have enhanced "political stability" but not "security" in the modern sense.[39] New "policeable" social space was created but without being adequately "policed".

The situation was no better in the urban centre where robberies and burglaries were mushrooming in privately-owned buildings. Muggings in the lifts and staircases of private high rise apartment buildings were also common experiences for people living in Hong Kong during the 1970s, including the authors. Unlike today, those encounters frequently resulted in serious injuries and sometimes deaths. Scholars attributed this increase in predatory crime to the improvement in the economy which brought about a more affluent lifestyle but also greater economic inequality (Traver, 1991; Cheung et al., 2002). Cowperthwaite's "laissez faire" approach to social welfare of the Chinese failed to insulate their personal well-being from being harmed by market forces. The resulting harsh living conditions in Hong Kong might have played an important role in causing the level of criminal violence to rise (homicide rates in Hong Kong peaked around the time of Cowperthwaite's retirement in 1972).[40] At the height of the homicide wave (see Fig. 9.1), the colonial state came up with plans to mobilize the whole community against crime—by establishing the Fight Violent Crime Committee (FVCC) in March 1973 with sub-branches in each district and assisting tenants of private and public housing in forming their own Mutual Aid Committees (MAC) to look after their buildings (City and New Territories Administration, 1972–1973; City and New Territories Administration, 1973a).

Both FVCC and MAC plans were pushed by the then Governor Murray MacLehose, who assumed office in 1971, the same year as Financial Secretary Philip Haddon-Cave (known for his policy of "positive noninterventionism"). Modelled after the Keep Hong Kong Clean campaigns, the FVCC campaign, set out in 1972 to involve the community to fight crime, and was also overseen by the colonial Information Services Department (which specialized in psychological warfare) in Hong Kong. Through well-orchestrated propaganda, the campaign penetrated into all aspects of life of the local Chinese society.

---

[39] See Wood and Sharing (2006) for a discussion of the multidimensional meaning of security, in contrast with the traditional sense of "law and order".

[40] For example, Messner and Rosenfeld (1997) found homicide rates higher in countries where economic institution dominated all aspects of life.

On the cultural side, "law and order" television programs were tailor-made in Chinese to influence the "lowest common social denominator" but in English to target the wealthier middle class; schools were now considered better agents of social control in reducing juvenile crime than the home (family); social studies, economics and public affairs courses were introduced in schools to cultivate social awareness to discuss the colonial machinery; Confucian teaching was introduced in the Chinese subject to cultivate morality and respect for authority; vacant sites would be developed into active recreational areas; and suggestions were even made to regulate public playground activities to highlight civic responsibility and healthy leisure pursuits (City and New Territories Administration, 1972–1973).

The colonial government perceived the ambiguous and unclaimed new spaces in and around the mushrooming "multi-storey buildings" the core of the crime problem, and conducted a massive survey to justify their view (City and New Territories Administration, 1973b). The survey studied 600 building blocks and found half (281) of those valid cases without proper supervisory management like hiring a caretaker (City and New Territories Administration, 1973b). To facilitate the setting up of the Mutual Aid Committees (MACs), they were deliberately exempted from the Societies Ordinance with approval required only from the colonial consultative machinery, the City District Offices (City and New Territories Administration, 1973a). By 1974 some 1500 MACs had been established by local residents to work closely with the Fight Violent Crime Committee to discourage crime by installing alarm systems and engaging watchmen to patrol premises (Government Press, 1974).[41]

Tensions still existed during this initiation of the society into co-production of security under the colonial state's direct intervention. In one of the Steering Committee meetings for MACs, the massively sponsored campaign was considered to be incompatible with Cowperthwaite's financial logic and very likely would be banned if he were still in office (City and New Territories Administration, 1973a). MACs were officially introduced to public housing estates, industrial buildings, temporary housing and squatter areas (Home Affairs Department, 2020)—but unknown to the public was the initial hesitation of the colonial government to establish MACs in Mark I and II Public Housing for fear of the

---

[41] Rebuilding grassroot society. HE the Governor, Address in the Legislative Council, (Government Press, 1974).

MACs becoming transformed into pressure groups (City and New Territories Administration, 1973a). The police were also concerned over the idea of arming the *Kaifongs* in public housing to fight crime for fear of turning them into vigilante groups (Royal Hong Kong Police Force, 1971–1977).[42]

Reform was also carried out to incorporate Chinese people "fully" into the system of policing. Although no change was made immediately after the Chinese Language Committee completed its third report in June, 1971, on exploring the use of both English and Chinese in court proceedings and laws (Hong Kong Government, 1971), Cantonese as an official language in the court system had become part of the fight crime campaign as a way to strengthen Chinese trust in the legal system (City and New Territories Administration, 1972–1973) and was eventually implemented in 1974. The multi-dimensional fight crime campaign set out to boost public confidence in the government in terms of law and order, but it was well recognized that the result could be contradictory. It was predicted that crime reports would increase so that the way crime statistics were presented needed to be "revised" in a way to shift public attention away from the inevitable rising level of crime (i.e., indicating that police were failing in their mission) to focus on police effectiveness (i.e., detection and conviction) as performance indicators (Hong Kong Government, 1971). Overall crime in fact continued to increase in the 1970s, because the colonial state actively intervened in the local Chinese society (Chiu & Lee, 2013).

3.4   Copland Constituted: The Moral Panic Over Youth and the End of Laissez Faire Policing

The riots triggered by So Sau Chung's hunger strike against Star Ferry's fare increase in 1966 signalled another shift in the colony's social control mechanism. This time the colonial state drew an analogy between the mass mobilizations in 1966, the 1967 riots and the rising level of crime—the youth problem (Adorjan & Chui, 2013).[43] Some ten years earlier, juvenile crime was not yet considered officially as a "problem". In 1957

---

[42] Kaifong is comprised of people coming from the same neighbourhood.

[43] For example, Adorjan and Chui (2013, p. 165) found that the government attempted to depoliticize the 1967 Leftist Riots by pinpointing the high proportion of youth participating in these crimes of violence.

out of the 125,677 persons charged in the Magistracies in Hong Kong, only 13.1% (16,427) were juvenile defendants although their conviction rate were unbelievably high at 99.3% compared to that for adults (also high at 94.7%) (Government Press, 1958, p.227).

Internally, police had long recognized the *"ah fei"* problem by forming a Juvenile Liaison Section in each police district as early as in 1963, and by collecting juvenile crime statistics for the period 1965–1969 with purpose of feeding information to various police operatives, especially the Security Branch (Colonial Secretariat Administration Branch, 1965–1969). This sudden enthusiasm for collecting "statistics" for social surveillance is noteworthy, given that the colonial police were "encouraged" to follow British practice in using "standard tables" for crime reports just a couple of years previously (Colonial Secretariat Administration Branch, 1954–1965), while the then Financial Secretary of Hong Kong, Sir John Cowperthwaite (1961–1971), famously declared, "They should abolish the office of national statistics" to encourage *Lassize Faire* (Singleton, 2006). These *"ah fei"* related policies arguably accumulated to become a systemic response to youth and juvenile crime in the late 1960s and early 1970s following the two riots (Adorjan & Chui, 2014).

The recruitment of large numbers of young Chinese police officers during the police reform implied the expanding bureaucracy could now handle more crime reports and initiate proactive interrogation of people on the street. How active interrogation led to an increase in arrests was explained in a 1975 FVCC meeting: during the post-World War Two period people would carry an ID card with them, though it was not legally compulsory until 1980, for fear of deportation. As risk of deportation faded, offenders tended not to have their I.D. card when they committed crimes. This made it necessary for the police to arrest a suspect even for very minor offences (or simply a pedestrian) to ascertain her/his identity (City and New Territories Administration, 1973–1975).

On the other hand, the widespread moral panic over youth—partly sustained by the Fight Violent Crime Campaign itself—had made youth delinquency more visible than ever. At this juncture, the new diversion scheme like the Police Superintendent's Discretion Scheme (PSDS) formalized the long existing practice of "street-level discretion" into bureaucratic procedures, resulting in the unintended consequence of boosting arrests of young people (Gray, 1991). The moral panic over working class youth extended into the 1980s and 1990s as disciplinary welfare emerged in the late 1970s to manage the juvenile crime problem by professionalizing their care and early intervention (Gray, 1997).[44] Crime continued to increase during the 1970s and 1980s because the colonial state intervened into the life of working-class youth and, whether intended or not, widened the justice net.

No doubt public policing in Hong Kong has professionalized over the years, but this should not be viewed as simply a direct response to rising crime. Rather, "policing crime" has become a political project of the state to resolve the internal crisis of the police organization, to enhance political stability amid the rapid process of state-society restructuring, and to reconfigure the governability of colonial subjects through consolidation of disciplinary power. When overall crime began to drop from the mid-1980s onward, the Hong Kong police received credit and enjoyed the high level of legitimacy they had long sought. Intriguingly, the policing of Hong Kong has undergone a major transformation during the same period—from the state's disciplinary indoctrination to ideological preemption of deviance through manipulation of urban space and rules.

4   COMETH THE MARKET AND THE DISNEYLAND (1980s TO THE PRESENT)

4.1   "Security Unlimited"

"Sir, you cannot sit down on this planter." (Lee's personal experience at the public space at Times Square, 2006)

Being reminded by a security guard to stand up under the silver screen of Times Square was a common experience for locals before the area was "discovered" to be a public space in 2008 so that such a restriction should never have been imposed.[45] The developer of Times Square initially told an enquiring academic that "no sitting is allowed" was intended to "keep an appropriate image of the open space" (Too, 2007, p. 92). What constitutes "an appropriate image" is of course defined in such a case by the nature of the shopping mall as a consumers' citadel. Yet similar non-state

---

[44] "Disciplinary welfare" refers to social programs that aim to indoctrinate juveniles with normative ideals of industrial capitalism and of the family. See Gray (1997).

[45] See C.Y. Yau (2008) for a report of how the discovery of the public space at Time Square unfolded.

policing of public areas by private security,[46] considering the uncountable number of massive private property sites developed under the "freest" economy (see Chap. 8 for land hegemony), has in fact come to dominate the urban life of Hong Kong.

The movie "Security Unlimited" (摩登保鑣) perhaps marked a milestone in Hong Kong's private policing development. Written and directed by, and starring Michael Hui and his brothers, it achieved the highest box office record in Hong Kong's history in 1981. The story depicted Hui, a senior security personnel as inept but pretending to be quick-witted. The Huis were assigned to guard some government money but then got entrapped to steal a national treasure of China. The popularity of the movie was a significant indicator of how private policing had already penetrated social life by the 1980s. Given the negative depiction of Michael's character in the movie one could infer that entrusting policing power to the private sector was still not well received by the general public at that time. Certainly, private security was nothing new in colonial history; we have already discussed the District Watch Force and how British merchants once hired warehouse security. The influence of private security in the past, however, was never all-encompassing, if not "unlimited", as we experience it nowadays.

In our third *standard-definition*, the current low crime status is typically referred to as a colonial legacy and a manifestation of the core values of Hong Kong: law and order upheld by the government in power with community support in crime prevention. Little research has been done, however, to explore the logics and impact of private policing and its co-production of security with public police in maintaining the capitalist social order in Hong Kong. For those who did, like Gaylord and Galliher (1991) who found Hong Kong's MTR as the most successful social control model in terms of its low crime rate (except for the sheer amount of underreported indecent assaults targeting mainly females), credit was given firstly to the effectiveness of the MTR District Police and then the (actually more important) built-in security design of the stations and trains. Little was mentioned about "private policing" conducted by MTR staff and the draconian rules that regulate what one could do in these premises (for example drinking water is prohibited). If one violates such

---

[46] See Kempa et al. (2004) for a discussion of the privatization of policing amid development of mass private property.

rules, it is not the police who intervene but MTR staff—acting as security personnel at this point—who issue tickets fining rule violators.

4.2   Deviance Redefined: Breaker of Law Or Capitalist Order?

Hong Kong's MTR system has been extremely efficient not only in transporting passengers but also in detecting risks that may hinder its smooth operation. This risk aversive model of social control has been projected to premises directly above or linked to the rail system. Quite a number of these linked premises are mega shopping malls that manage public space in ways much like the Times Square (Ho, 2009, pp. 22–23). A good example would be the skybridges that connect multiple shopping malls (retail shops), private estates and MTR stations in the Tseung Kwan O District. The network design allows residents direct connections to the MTR station and consumption sites, which evidently adds a premium to flat prices with the enhanced pedestrian experience (Cervero & Murakami, 2009). These connected premises, as well as other large private estates, employ a similar logic of private policing: social exclusion of undesirables and complete surveillance by CCTV and security guards.

Critics have long argued that privatized public space in Hong Kong, in addition to its undemocratic nature, is inherently anti-social for the only activity encouraged in these sites is consumption (Cuthbert, 1995). Any activity that may obstruct the pursuit of "efficiency" and "profit" would be marginalized if not banned. Corporate owned shopping malls in Hong Kong's urban center seem to have replaced the town hall that represents the state, and churches/temples that represent the traditional society, to become the sites of moral order (Shearing & Stenning, 1984). Hence in our third *high-definition* image, we follow Shearing and Stenning's use of "Disneyland" to delineate the prevailing market constitution of social control in Hong Kong—one that transcends each privately policed zone where the powerful corporations reside and penetrates into every segment of our society or even the state itself.

But how exactly does this "Disneyland" vision of social control influence overall crime rates? Perhaps Cuthbert and McKinnell's (1997) study of space in Hong Kong best illustrates this. They reviewed the development of public accessible space in Central such as the circulating pedestrian bridges linking the Citibank Plaza, Hong Kong Park, Pacific Place/Queensway complex, bus terminus and MTR stations, and found the owners (public space crossings) were granted the security and control over behaviour of the general public apart from an increase in permitted plot ratio to overbuild. Private security personnel would actively question and intervene into any behaviour irrelevant to what the site symbolizes—capital. The two authors assert rightly that such an arrangement follows the "laissez faire" or minimalist planning logic which allows development capital, the state and the planning apparatus to collaborate in "squeezing the last ounce of profit from social space" under circumstances of non-democratic politics and pragmatic pursue of profit (Cuthbert & McKinnell, 1997, p. 310).

In fact, there is little chance for the security guard to encounter something exciting. Direction markings, signs, and guards in costume (uniforms), like what one would see inside Disneyland (or MTR), convey the hidden messages the public space is merely a place for efficient access between checkpoints. Citizens enter the private policing zone of shopping malls alike in consensual terms, without "overt" coercion, of exhibiting certain kinds of behaviour much like one would behave in Disneyland (Shearing & Stenning, 1984). Barriers and physical settings are designed so that citizens are guided naturally to take the shortest path as well as the shortest stay in these privately owned public spaces, while making them spend most of their time in the consumer space enclosed. Security is extremely "efficient" when it is provided by the market realm. This hegemonic preemption of individual thoughts to exhibit disorderly behaviour, not to mention crime, in public or private areas reaches the highest level of *Wu Shu* (武術)—to stop a conflict before one could even think of it.

So, does the logic governing private policing influence state policing in Hong Kong or vice versa? The answer is both. In 2016, up to 305,404 citizens, or 4163 per 100,000 population, have acquired a security personnel permit (Fig. 9.2). This was more than five times the number 20 years ago and 10 times that of the 29,021 regular police strength in the same year (excluding auxiliary police and civilian staff). (Hong Kong Police Force, 2016b; Security Bureau, 2018) One should note that the growth in the number of persons with security permits merely reflects the formalization of a traditional occupation, the caretakers, following the enactment of the 1995 *Security and Guarding Services Ordinance* (Cap.460), which required all persons working in the security professions to acquire a license. All applications are made to, vetted and approved by the Commissioner of Police, thereby effectively putting the whole security business under regulation by the Hong Kong Police (on behalf of the state). On the other hand, management reform modelled after that of

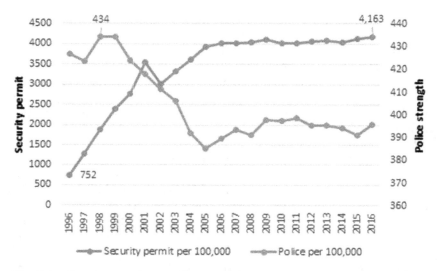

Fig. 9.2 Security permit vs. police strength per 100,000 (1996–2016) (Hong Kong Police Force, 2016b; Security Bureau, 2018, Table 1)

private corporations has also taken place within the Police—for example the service culture movement and the decentralization of command control by assigning tailor-made performance targets to police districts, which together formed a significant part of the larger public sector reform movement under former Governor Chris Pattern (Scott, 2010). The influence is two-way, but both reflect the logics of neo-liberalism.

4.3   Is Hybrid Model Democratizing the Policing of Hong Kong?

Wood and Shearing (2007) present an optimistic view of the privatization of policing, arguing that it allows the democratization of policing by encouraging a co-production of security by both the state and multiple non-state actors—hence, civilizing security. Through market means, people finally have a democratic say over how security shall be achieved. Critics, however, point out the negative side of such commodification of policing (Loader, 1999). First, corporate financial logic, like outsourcing, impacts on the security guards. Being working class themselves, the guards are paid much less, have a lower social status and enjoy far less legitimacy than the public police, although the two often share a largely equivalent role of patrolling an assigned area.

Second, security guards are responsible to the company hiring them, whereas public police are the "people's servant" and theoretically impartial in enforcing Hong Kong's laws. The more private policing is used in a neighbourhood or shopping area, the more likely police would devote their resources to disadvantaged or marginalized neighbourhoods lacking the resources to purchase security through the market. An unintended consequence of uneven or overly public policing in poorer areas of Hong Kong may be to increase the "criminalization" of the grassroots and generate greater antagonism between the society and the state. Hence in Hong Kong, the districts with the highest crime rates are often also the poorer ones with a lower perception of police legitimacy, both being possible outcomes of higher intensity of public policing in such areas.

A recent conflict arising from the "co-policing" of hawking activities demonstrates how private security, public police, and even an alleged triad society group together failed in the co-production of security for the local community, much less to talk about democratizing policing. (Lo, 2016). The conflict took place in Leung King Estate at Tuen Mun between February 2nd and 10th 2016 during the Chinese Lunar New Year holidays in Hong Kong. As background, the Tenants Purchase Scheme (1988) in Hong Kong allowed public housing tenants in Leung King Estate to purchase their own flats. While some of the tenants privatized their flats, others didn't. This created a semi-private zone at the publicly accessible open area under Leung King Estate that was co-managed by Owners' Corporation and the Tuen Mun West District Tenancy Management Office of the Hong Kong Housing Authority, and they hired the Kong Shun Union Property Management for the management purpose. Meanwhile, the Housing Authority had privatized its public assets of retail spaces and car park spaces in 2005 under the Link Real Estate Investment Trust (Link REIT). This created a totally privatized shopping mall complex with a wet market right next to the Leung King Estate. The Link REIT further leased the market to the Uni-China (Market) Management, which further subcontracted the management to an unknown party. Interestingly, neither the public police nor the residents' management company had jurisdiction in managing hawker activities that took place in the now privatized former public space.

Cooked food hawkers have operated in the Leung King Estate open area for some twenty years and are backed by the local community for providing a variety of food choices although complaints over hygiene and safety issues could also be heard from time to time. Between February 2nd and 10th 2016 a group of persons wearing windbreakers bearing the Chinese word "management personnel" obstructed the hawkers from operating near the Leung King Estate Market owned by Link REIT. Soon the event escalated into violent conflicts between the "management personnel" and the hawkers, but also the local residents who were barred from passing through the open area and civil society groups in support of grassroots street vendor activities. It was soon discovered these "management personnel" or private security was neither directly hired by the Housing Authority, the Leung King Estate Owners' Corporation, the Link REIT, nor the subcontracted management of the market. Allegedly, the "management personnel" were supported by triad society groups (Lo, 2016). Complicating this situation is that the open area in which the conflict took place is owned by the Leung King Estate and *not* by Link REIT, but was "voluntarily" managed by a sub-subcontractor of the Leung King Estate Market of Link REIT. In a High Court ruling responding to an application for an interlocutory injunction by Uni-China Market Management against illegal hawkers in the *whole* Leung King Estate, the judge specifically argued the prohibition order applied only to the tiny space just outside the shopping mall but not the entire estate (Lee, 2016).

It was alleged the conflict intensified after the Leung King Estate Market expanded its cooked food stalls just months earlier—with rent set as high as HKD38,000 per month (Yeung et al., 2016). This expansion of the private realm to turn food vendors operated by local grassroots society into profit-making activities for global Link REIT share-holders perhaps best demonstrates the undemocratic aspect of private security—it serves the interests of capital only. The public police faced a paradoxical situation when they were summoned to the scene—the blocked area is a public accessible area put under private management. On one hand the hawkers were not licensed, on the other the "management personnel" did not produce any private security licenses (as required by law) and allegedly were triad members as well. Perhaps this hybridized form of policing will only occur in Hong Kong, where the traditional triad society meets modern police force in the freest economy in the world. The ensuing conflict demonstrates the co-policing is far from an ideal democratic form—given that it is the global shareholders of Link REIT, not the local public housing residents, who have a say over how the privatized public market area should be policed.

5 Concluding Remarks

"You better stop here and do not advance, please tell your commander, we don't welcome you in the shopping mall (authors' translation)." (original: 你哋(警察)最好停喺度唔好再向前, 話番畀你哋指揮官聽, 我哋唔歡迎你入嚟商場!) (Security of IFC refusing riot police entry on July 29, 2019) (Topick, 2019)

The saga of co-policing contemporary Hong Kong by a modernized state police and an efficient market security force experienced a sudden twist in 2019. A group of riot police, in pursuing protestors opposing the Fugitive Offenders and Mutual Legal Assistance in Criminal Matters Legislation (Amendment) Bill 2019 (or, anti-extradition protests), were refused entry by security of the International Finance Centre (IFC) in Central Hong Kong on July 29, 2019. Two months later five security guards were arrested by the Hong Kong Police for blocking riot police from entering a shopping centre at Ma On Shan in the New Territories in pursuit of anti-extradition protestors (Lo, 2019). These were not isolated incidents in which security personnel, often subjected to the demand of the local consumers or residents, tried to prevent frontline riot police from entering the private premises—both shopping malls and residential area (AM730, 2019). As the political crisis unfolded—one that see also the alliance between the local capitalist and the state administrator shattered,[47] so did the cleavage between the security sector that normally polices the private property and the police that usually guards the public, as protestors seek temporary sanctuary at and take strategic advantage of the limbo zone of privatized public space which connected various part of the city—a tactics named as "Be Water". On the other hand, the citizen-police relationship has reached an all-time low.

During the Umbrella Movement protest in 2014, individual police was seen sharing water with thirsty protestor—and vice versa in some other early occasions despite the heightened tension and antagonistic attitudes

---

[47] Abraham Shek, the representative of the real estate and construction industry interest in the Legislative Council, stated he never supported the Fugitive Offenders and Mutual Legal Assistance in Criminal Matters Legislation (Amendment) Bill 2019. See Edigest (2019).

between the two (Mingpao, 2014). In just six years' time, police-community relationship has deteriorated to a point beyond recognition. As some 900 protests, processions and public assemblies were organized in the global city between June and November in 2019 (Lee, 2019),[48] protestors and police showered each other with bricks, petrol bombs, tear gas, water cannon, pepper sprays and pepper balls, and rubber bullets. The movement initially demanded the withdrawal of the extradition bill, but soon centred on policing and later the MTR subway system after the Yuen Long white shirt mob attack incident, andtriggered even more urban unrest (Hale, 2019).

The Anti-Extradition Bill Movement protest is not the first time in Hong Kong's history the legitimating accounts, compliance and consent concerning policing Hong Kong has significantly shifted. Vagg (1996) identified three such periods in the past—roughly matching our *high-definition* image of Gangland, Cops-land and Disneyland. The three periods were marked by a change in the nature of the state, hence yielding different answers towards the questions: "whose law?" and "whose order?".

The first period Vagg (1996) suggested was strictly colonial. The problem of police legitimacy largely arose from the colonial and paternalistic intention to rule the colony through the retention of Chinese law and customs—hence creating a policing vacuum among the local Chinese community. It was a time when the colonial state, with limited administrative muscle, could not quite claim the monopolization of legitimate force. Rather, various groups in the local society made competing claims to exercising such force. The racially divided structure of the police force led, ironically, to bigger issues of policing in the years to come.

Our depiction of Copland echoes the second period proposed by Vagg (1996)—the rise of the "administrative state" governed by consultation. The rising leaders of various pressure groups were co-opted into consultative positions as one way to pacify street politics, thus reducing the threat to police legitimacy. The more local Chinese entrusted their property and life to the colonial police and less to informal ways as we saw in the earlier discussion of *Gangland*, the greater the colonial state's legitimacy and its capacity to monopolize the legitimate use of physical force as Weber

---

[48] See: Lee (2019) which is a written reply by the Secretary for Security in the Legislative Council.

(1919/1965) so defined.[49] While the *standard-definition* typically explains the crime wave in Hong Kong with reference to the modernization thesis derived from the experience of western societies, our *high-definition* demonstrated various causes specifically arising from Hong Kong's colonial context. The crime wave was, nonetheless, a genuine one, but it was amplified by various institutional changes arising from state-society restructuring.[50] Police reform, the establishment of the ICAC and the regulation of illegal gambling like *Tsz Fa*, on the other hand, led to a transition period where the overall crime rates rose further. The colonial state's public housing projects and flourishing multi-story private buildings created ambiguous new spaces lacking clear-cut modes of political and social intervention hence the opportunity for unchecked predatory crimes. With a change in financial logic, the public was mobilized under schemes like FVCC and MACs, to actively police these new spaces by themselves, thus being disciplined into "citizens" by the colonial state.[51] Crime increased because people now felt obliged to report it.[52]

Yet, this is not the end of the story of the evolution of social control in Hong Kong. Hitherto discussions typically neglected an emerging dimension in policing, namely, the market! In 2015, 1827 MACs, 10,069 Owners' Corporations throughout Hong Kong (Home Affairs Department, 2020), along with shopping malls, public parks, and mass transit railways, contributed to the maintenance of social order by private

---

[49] By 1999, Hong Kong's police-citizen ratio was among the world's highest. Shiu, Susan. 1999. "Police ratio among the world's highest." SCMP 27 June. In 2012 alone, Hong Kong police conducted 1.6 million stop-and-search checks on pedestrians among a 6.9 million population, a figure four times higher than New York's and London's. But little attention was given to these figures—not just because locals felt satisfied given the low crime status—but of the panopticon that was set upon them with the policing of the crime wave in Hong Kong some thirty years ago. See Boehler (2013).

[50] Overall crime rates continued to rise until mid-1980s. FVCC, MACs and the ICAC apparently succeeded in rallying Chinese in reporting crime to the police which they formerly wouldn't, as demonstrated in successive waves of crime victim surveys conducted. See Broadhurst et al. (2008) and Traver (1991).

[51] Local Chinese even became more willing to assist the police in exercising "citizen's arrest" therefore embodying "citizenship" (City and New Territories Administration, 1973–1975).

[52] The rationalizing society relations also had a share in boosting overall crime: shop theft surged as corporate owned convenience stores and supermarkets gradually replaced traditional community stores, as their staffs and security were required to report all offences that took place in the premises to the police regardless of offenders' age. See Leung (1997) for related discussion.

policing. Provision of security became externalized/outsourced, professionalized, corporatized yet privately owned and put up for sale in the market. "Policing" is now highly rationalized and permeates our everyday experience as we wander into the "well-policed" spatial-design environment.

In the same period up until 1996, the decolonization process increased the number of elected members of the legislature while a resemblance of democratization appeared, resulting in realignments of political power. Police complaints were for the first time overseen by both government officials and elected legislators. The democratization movement also impacted on police organization and culture (Vagg, 1996). There were more "crime control" demands from the now elected District Boards—with one subcommittee functionally known as the District Fight Crime Committees. It was exactly in the same period when "community policing" resurrected along with the diffusion of service culture in the police organization. "Community policing" in fact suggests policing can be anything and that community should participate—especially through market mean such as the outsourcing of "security" to the much cost-effective private sector; hence our *high-definition* image of Disneyland order appeared to be more than fitting image.

While it remains academically debatable if the privatization of policing could really achieve some sort of democratic ideal or even become a defender of civil liberties, the policing of large scale political events in recent years (see Fig. 9.3), has received much more public attention due to its explicit and direct impact on the quest for democracy.[53] As the police are increasingly freed from policing the private realm of capital in the Disneyland era, its law enforcement focus would likely converge on those politicized and marginalized groups. Such increased police attention to public order policing was recognized by the Police Commissioner in 2016.[54] As a consequence, an increase of 500 and 900 new posts was proposed for the budget year 2016 and 2017 respectively to boost emergency

[53] It seems puzzling that the number for 2019 was lower than that of previous years and especially 2016, but we need to know that the Police counted only officially approved public meetings that included such events as festivals. Many such social activities were cancelled last year, whereas quite a lot of the public assemblies for staging protests were in fact spontaneous without official approval.

[54] "In addition to combating crime, public order policing has become an increasingly heavy commitment for the Police Force in recent years, and 2016 was no exception" (Hong Kong Police Force, 2016a).

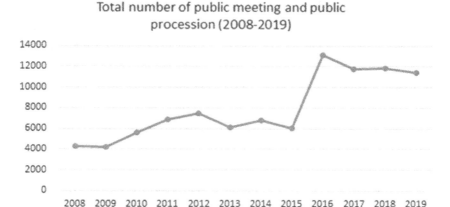

Fig. 9.3 Total number of public meetings and public processions (2008–2019). (Source: Hong Kong Police Force (2020))

and tactical units to handle large-scale events (Fraser, 2015; Qiu, 2016). In the latest government budget announcement, the Hong Kong Police will recruit additional 2543 or additional 7% personnel, with a 24.7% rise in operating expenses—the biggest increase since 1997 (Lum et al., 2020).

Following Vagg (1996), here we suggest our generation is witnessing the advancement of a fourth period of policing, again marked by a significant change in the nature of the state. Central to the debate onthe nature of policing and public order in contemporary Hong Kong, perhaps again are the questions "whose law?" and "whose order?".

References

Adorjan, M., & Chui, W. H. (2013). Colonial responses to youth crime in Hong Kong: Penal elitism, legitimacy and citizenship. *Theoretical Criminology, 17*(2), 159–177.

Adorjan, M., & Chui, W. H. (2014). *Responding to youth crime in Hong Kong: Penal elitism, legitimacy and citizenship.* Routledge.

AM730. (2019, November 14). 保安員與防暴警理論 嘆警民關係「唔係咁樣」 ["Police-public relations should not be managed this way," said a security guard contending with riot police]. *AM730.* https://www.am730.com.hk/news/%E6%96%B0%E8%81%9E/%E3%80%90%E6%9C%89%9%E7%89%87%E3%80%91%E4%BF%9D%E5%AE%89%E5%9

3%A1%E8%88%87%E9%98%B2%E6%9A%B4%E8%AD%A6%E7%9
0%86%E8%AB%96%E3%80%80%E5%98%86%E8%AD
%A6%E6%B0%91%E9%97%9C%E4%BF%82%E3%80%8C
%E5%94%94%E4%BF%82%E5%92%81%E6%A8%A3%E
3%80%8D-196467

Bittner, E. (1970). *Functions of the police in modern society.* National Institute of Mental Health, Center for Studies of Crime and Delinquency.

Boehler, P. (2013, November 24). Hong Kong Police stop-and-search tactics questioned after 1.6m spot checks last year. *South China Morning Post.* https://www.scmp.com/news/hong-kong/article/1364087/police-tactics-queried-after-16m-spot-checks-last-year

British Military Administration. (1945). *Opium proclamation no. 13.* British Military Administration.

Broadhurst, R. (2000). *Crime trends in Hong Kong.* Centre for Criminology, University of Hong Kong.

Broadhurst, R., Chan, C. Y., & Lee, K. W. (2008). Crime trends. In W. H. Chui & T. W. Lo (Eds.), *Understanding criminal justice in Hong Kong* (pp. 45–68). Willan Publishing.

Carroll, J. M. (2007). *A concise history of Hong Kong.* Rowman & Littlefield.

Castells, M., Goh, L., & Kwok, R. Y.-W. (1990). *The Shek Kip Mei syndrome: Economic development and public housing in Hong Kong and Singapore.* Pion.

Cervero, R., & Murakami, J. (2009). Rail and property development in Hong Kong: Experiences and extensions. *Urban Studies, 46*(10), 2019–2043.

Chan, C. C., Leung, E. C., & Li, W. W. (2016). *Problem gambling in Hong Kong and Macao: Etiology, prevalence and treatment.* SPRINGER.

Cheung, T. S., & Lau, C. C. (1981). A profile of syndicate corruption in the police force. In R. P. Lee (Ed.), *Corruptions and its control in Hong Kong* (pp. 199–221). The Chinese University Press.

Cheung, W. T., Cheung, Y. W., & Chu, Y. K. (2002). Crime and deviance. In J. Xie (Ed.), *Our place, our time: A new introduction to Hong Kong society* (pp. 411–448). Oxford University Press.

Chin, K. L. (1990). *Chinese subculture and criminality: Non-traditional crime groups in America.* Greenwood.

Chiu, S. W. (1996). Unravelling the Hong Kong exceptionalism: The politics of industrial takeoff. *Political Power and Social Theory, 10,* 229–256.

Chiu, S. W., & Lee, K. W. (2013). The Crime Wave in Hong Kong, 1960s–1970s: Unintended Consequence of Colonial Governance Reform? *Social Transformations in Chinese Societies, 9*(1), 79–116.

Chu, Y. K. (2000). *The triads as business.* Routledge.

City and New Territories Administration. (1972–1973). *Community involvement against crime – Agenda and minutes of meetings of the working party (HKRS684-5-79).* Government Press.

City and New Territories Administration. (1973–1975). *Fight violent crime committee – Agenda and minutes (HKRS684-5-72)*. Government Press.
City and New Territories Administration. (1973a). *Community involvement – Fight Violent Crime / Clean Hong Kong Campaigns: Steering Committee On Matual Aid Committee & Building Management (HKRS684-5-82)*. Government Press.
City and New Territories Administration. (1973b). *Community involvement – Fight Violent Crime / Clean Hong Kong Campaigns: Pilot Survey Of Building Management & Security (HKRS684-5-81)*. Government Press.
City District Commissioner Kowloon. (1970–1973). *Working party on policy on gambling (HKRS488-3-12)*. Government Press.
Colonial Secretariat Administration Branch. (1954–1965). *Crime Statistics – Standard Tables For .... (HKRS 41-1-8200)*. Government Press.
Colonial Secretariat Administration Branch. (1965–1969). *Juvenile Crime Statistics (HKRS 41-2-570)*. Government Press.
Commission of Inquiry on Kowloon Disturbances. (1967). *Kowloon disturbances 1966: Report of commission of inquiry*. Government Press.
Commissioner of Police. (1957–1969). *Annual reports of the commissioner of police*. Government Printer.
Commissioner of Police. (1978–1996). *Royal Hong Kong police review*. Government Printer.
Commissioner of Police. (1997–2008). *Police review*. Hong Kong Government Printer.
Cuthbert, A. R. (1995). The right to the city. Surveillance, private interest and the public domain in Hong Kong. *Cities, 12*(5), 293–310.
Cuthbert, A. R., & McKinnell, K. G. (1997). Ambiguous space, ambiguous rights – Corporate power and social control in Hong Kong. *Cities, 14*(5), 295–311.
Edigest. (2019, October 30). 石禮謙專訪 – 論逃犯條例風波: 從不支持逃犯條例修定 狠批政府「無用人之道, 無容人之心!」 [An interview with Abraham SHEK on the extradition bill controversy: Never supported the bill and critically the government for not knowing to choose the right person for the right job and lacking tolerance]. *Edigest*. https://www.edigest.hk/article/121356/%e7%b6%93%e4%b8%80%e6%8b%86%e5%b1%80/%e7%9f%b3%e7%a6%ae%e8%ac%99-%e5%bb%ba%e5%88%b6%e6%b4%be-%e6%94%bf%e5%ba%9c-%e9%80%83%e7%8a%af%e6%a2%9d%e4%be%8b/
The West Australian. (1891, July 16). "Execution of Chinese Pirates." *The West Australian*. https://trove.nla.gov.au/newspaper/article/3022220
Foreign and Commonwealth Office. (1970). *Problem of increase in crime rate in Hong Kong – Report of Crime in Hong Kong*. Government Press.
Foreign and Commonwealth Office. (1973, 1974). *Microfilm / digital images of registered files of far eastern department*. Hong Kong: Government Press

Fraser, N. (2015, February 14). Hong Kong police force set for manpower boost after shortcomings exposed by Occupy. *South China Morning Post*. https://www.scmp.com/news/hong-kong/article/1712450/hong-kong-police-force-set-manpower-boost-after-shortcomings-exposed

Gambetta, D. (1993). *The Sicilian Mafia the business of private protection*. Harvard University Press.

Gray, P. (1991). Juvenile crime and disciplinary welfare. In H. Traver & J. Vagg (Eds.), *Crime and justice in Hong Kong* (pp. 25–41). Oxford University Press.

Gaylord, M., & Galliher, J. (1991). Riding the underground dragon. Crime control and public order on Hong Kong's Mass Transit Railway. *British Journal of Criminology, 31*(1), 15–26.

Gaylord, M. S., & Traver †, H. (1995). Colonial policing and the demise of British Rule in Hong Kong. *International Journal of the Sociology of Law, 23*(1), 23–43.

Government Press. (1958). *Hong Kong annual report 1957*. Government Press.

Government Press. (1962). *Hong Kong: Report for the year 1961*. Government Press.

Government Press. (1974). *Hong Kong Hansard*. Government Press.

Gray, P. (1997). The emergence of the disciplinary Welfare Sanction in Hong Kong. *The Howard Journal of Criminal Justice, 36*(2), 187–208.

Hale, E. (2019, October 13). Hong Kong protesters use new flashmob strategy to avoid arrest. *The Guardian*. https://www.theguardian.com/world/2019/oct/13/hong-kong-protesters-flashmobs-blossom-everywhere

Hamilton, S. (1998). The district watch force. *Journal of the Hong Kong Branch of the Royal Asiatic Society, 38*, 199–228.

Hamilton, S. (2012). *Watching over Hong Kong: Private policing 1841–1941*. Hong Kong University Press.

Ho, L. K., & Chu, Y. K. (2012). *Policing Hong Kong 1842–1969 insiders' stories*. City University of Hong Kong Press.

Ho, S. (2009). Shopping Mall as Privately Owned Public Space. *Thesis Report, Hong Kong: School of Architecture: The Chinese University of Hong Kong*.

Hobsbawm, E. (1959). *Primitive Rebels: Studies in Archiaic forms of Social Movement in the 19th and 20th centuries*. Manchester University Press.

Home Affairs Department. (2020). *Mutual Aid Committees*. Home Affairs Department. Retrieved from http://www.had.gov.hk/en/public_services/district_administration/mutual.htm

Hong Kong Government. (1971). *The Third Report of the Chinese language Committee*. Government Press.

Hong Kong Memory Project. (2014). *Central police station tour foreword*. Hong Kong Memory Project. http://www.hkmemory.org/central-police/text/station-tour-eng.php

Hong Kong Police Force. (2014). *Police review* (2000–2014, various editions). Hong Kong Police Force. https://www.police.gov.hk/ppp_en/01_about_us/police_review.html

Hong Kong Police Force. (2016a). 2016 Hong Kong police review. Hong Kong Police Force. https://www.police.gov.hk/info/review/2016/text/en/index.html

Hong Kong Police Force. (2016b). *Statistics.* Hong Kong Police Force. https://www.police.gov.hk/ppp_en/09_statistics/

Hong Kong Police Force. (2018a). *Chapter 3 creating a legend – 1967–1994.* Hong Kong Police Force. https://www.police.gov.hk/ppp_en/01_about_us/ph_03.html

Hong Kong Police Force. (2018b). *The force's ethnic composition.* Hong Kong Police Force. Features. http://www.police.gov.hk/offbeat/777/eng/f03.htm

Hong Kong Police Force. (2020). *Public order event statistics.* Public Order Event Statistics. Hong Kong Police Force. https://www.police.gov.hk/ppp_en/09_statistics/poes.html

Howell, P. (2004). Race, space and the regulation of prostitution in Colonial Hong Kong. *Urban History, 31*(2), 229–248.

Information Services Department. (1971–1975). *Death Inquest – Encl. 1971–1975 (HKRS 70-6-386-2).* Information Services Department.

Jones, C., & Vagg, J. (2017). *Criminal justice in Hong Kong.* Routledge-Cavendish.

Kempa, M., Stenning, P., & Wood, J. (2004). Policing communal spaces: A reconfiguration of the 'Mass Private Property' hypothesis. *British Journal of Criminology, 44*(4), 562–581.

Lee, J. (2019). *Numbers of tear gas rounds used in police operations (in chronological order) (Including tear gas grenades and tear gas rounds).* https://gia.info.gov.hk/general/201911/27/P2019112700593_331105_1_15748492 08959.pdf

Lee, P. N. (1981). The causes and effects of Police corruption. In R. P. Leung, P. N. Lee, & T. S. Cheung (Eds.), *Corruption and its control in Hong Kong: Situations up to the late seventies* (pp. 167–198). Chinese University Press.

Lethbridge, H. J. (1985). *Hard graft in Hong Kong: Scandal, corruption, the ICAC.* Oxford University Press.

Lethbridge, J. (1980). Rape, reform, and feminism in Hong Kong. *Hong Kong Law Journal, 10,* 260–291.

Leung, B. K. (1997). Deviance, crime, and social control. In *Perspectives on Hong Kong society* (pp. 94–114). Oxford University Press.

Lo, C. (2016, February 19). Police nab suspected Hong Kong triad member in connection with hawker-related brawl in Tuen Mun. *South China Morning Post.* https://www.scmp.com/news/hong-kong/law-crime/article/1914076/police-nab-suspected-hong-kong-triad-member-connection

Lo, C. (2019, October 9). Hong Kong security guards arrested on suspicion of blocking police from shopping centre to investigate vandalism at Ma On Shan MTR station. *South China Morning Post.* https://www.scmp.com/news/hong-kong/law-and-crime/article/3032205/hong-kong-security-guards-arrested-suspicion-blocking

Lui, C. W. (1996). 現代性、社會控制與香港青少年問題 1945–1979 [Modernity, Social Control and Youth Problem in Hong Kong, 1945–1979]. *Hong Kong Journal of Social Sciences, 8*, 59–83.

Loader, I. (1999). Consumer culture and the commodification of policing and security. *Sociology, 33*(2), 373–392.

Lum, A., Leung, C., & Lo, C. (2020, February 26). Hong Kong police to ramp up manpower by more than 7 per cent with 2,500 new posts in 'biggest boost since 1997. *South China Morning Post.* https://www.scmp.com/news/hong-kong/law-and-crime/article/3052542/hong-kong-police-ramp-manpower-more-7-cent-2500-new

Messner, S. F., & Rosenfeld, R. (1997). Political restraint of the market and levels of criminal homicide: A cross-national application of institutional-anomie theory. *Social Forces, 75*(4), 1393.

Miners, N. (1995). *The Government and politics of Hong Kong* (5th ed.). Oxford University Press.

Mingpao. (2014, October 18). 警與佔領者分水飲 獲網民讚「警隊男神」 [Sharing a bottle of water with a protestor, officer praised as "idol in the Police Force" by netizens]. *Mingpao.* Retrieved from https://news.mingpao.com/ins/%E6%B8%AF%E8%81%9E/article/20141018/s00001/1413622921542

Morgan, W. P. (1960). *Triad societies in Hong Kong.* Government Press.

Newman, O. (1972). *Defensible space: Crime prevention through urban design.* Macmillan.

Ng, A. M. (1974). *Social causes of violent crimes among young offenders in Hong Kong.* Social Research Centre, The Chinese University of Hong Kong.

Qiu, C. (2016, December 21). HK Police to recruit around 900 new frontline officers. *China Daily Asia.* https://www.chinadailyasia.com/hknews/2016-12/21/content_15545601.html

Royal Hong Kong Police Force. (1968–1975). *Crime in resettlement estates (HKRS415-1-2).* Government Press.

Royal Hong Kong Police Force. (1969–1971). *Hawker control (HKRS434-1-25-1).* Government Press.

Royal Hong Kong Police Force. (1971–1977). *Crime in housing estates (HKRS732-1-1).* Government Press.

RTHK. (2019, August 4). Police group calls protesters 'cockroaches'. *RTHK.* https://news.rthk.hk/rthk/en/component/k2/1472494-20190804.htm

Scott, I. (2010). *The public sector in Hong Kong.* Hong Kong University Press.

Security Bureau. (2018). *Table 1: Age Distribution of Valid Permit Holders 1995–2021, in Age Distribution of Valid Security Personnel Permit Holders (Year 1995–2021).* Security Bureau, HKSAR Government. Last access: January 10, 2022 at https://www.sb.gov.hk/eng/links/sgsia/pdf/ageprofile(eng).pdf

Shearing, C., & Stenning, S. (1984). From the Panopticon to Disney World: The development of discipline. In A. N. Doob, E. L. Greenspan, & J. L. J. Edwards (Eds.), *Perspectives in criminal law: Essays in honour of John Ll.J. Edwards* (pp. 335–349). Canadian Law Book.

Singleton, A. (2006, February 8). Obituary: Sir John Cowperthwaite. *The Guardian*. http://www.theguardian.com/news/2006/feb/08/guardiano-bituaries.mainsection

Smart, A. (2006). *The Shek Kip Mei Myth: Squatters, fires and colonial rule in Hong Kong, 1950–1963*. Hong Kong University Press.

The University of Hong Kong Libraries. (1989). *Historical Laws of Hong Kong online*. https://oelawhk.lib.hku.hk

Too, W. T. (2007). *A study of private/public space in Hong Kong*. Unpublished PhD thesis, The University of Hong Kong, Hong Kong. http://hub.hku.hk/handle/10722/159159

Topick. (2019, July 29). 防暴警中環清場欲進IFC 商場要求警停步:我哋唔歡迎你入嚟 [Riot police demand entrance to the IFC; "you are not welcome here" said a representative of the mall]. *Topick*. Retrieved from https://topick.hket.com/article/2413177/%E3%80%90%E5%8F%8D%E4%BF%AE%E4%BE%8B%E3%80%91%E9%98%B2%E6%9A%B4%E8%AD%A6%E4%B8%AD%E7%92%B0%E6%B8%85%E5%A0%B4%E6%AC%B2%E9%80%B2IFC%E3%80%80%E5%95%86%E5%A0%B4%E8%A6%81%E6%B1%82%E8%AD%A6%E5%81%9C%E6%AD%A5%EF%BC%9A%E6%88%91%E5%93%8B%E5%94%94%E6%AD%A1%E8%BF%8E%E4%BD%A0%E5%85%A5%E5%9A%9F

Traver, H. (1991). Crime trends. In H. Traver & J. Vagg (Eds.), *Crime and justice in Hong Kong* (pp. 10–24). Oxford University Press.

Tsang, S. S. (2004). *A modern history on Hong Kong*. Hong Kong University Press.

Vagg, J. (1996). The legitimations of policing in Hong Kong: A non-democratic perspective. In O. Marenin (Ed.), *Policing change, changing police: International perspectives* (pp. 107–134). Garland.

Vagg, J. (1997). Robbery, death, and irony: How an armed robbery wave in Hong Kong led to the abolition of the death penalty. *The Howard Journal of Criminal Justice, 36*(4), 393–405.

van Dijk, J., van Kesteren, J., & Smit, P. (2007). *Criminal victimisation in international perspective: Key findings from the 2004–2005 Icvs and Eu Ics*. Boom Juridische Uitgevers.

Weber, M. (1919/1965). *Politics as a vocation*. (H. H. Gerth & C. Wright, Trans.). Fortress Press.

Wesley-Smith, P. (1994). Anti-Chinese legislation in Hong Kong. In M. K. Chan (Ed.), *Precarious balance: Hong Kong between China and Britain, 1842–1992* (pp. 91–106). Routledge.

Wood, J., & Shearing, C. D. (2007). *Imagining security*. Willan.

Yau, C. Y. (2008, April 13). Don't even think about sitting on that planter. Big brother is watching you. *South China Morning Post*.

Yeung, T. K. 楊梓勤, Tse, W. Y. 謝蘊然, & Ho, J. Y 何哲瑩. (2016, February 11). 【良景之亂】街坊稱管理員 – 月已出現 揭領費曾「招安」小販 [(Chaos in Leung King Estate) Residents witnessed 'caretakers' since January; The Link REIT's attempt to incorporate hawkers revealed]. *Inmediahk*. https://www.inmediahk.net/node/1040547

CHAPTER 10

Hong Kong as a City of Protest: Social Movement as Motor for Social Change

Be like water making its way through cracks. Do not be assertive, but adjust to the object, and you shall find a way around or through it. If nothing within you stays rigid, outward things will disclose themselves. Empty your mind, be formless. Shapeless, like water. If you put water into a cup, it becomes the cup. You put water into a bottle and it becomes the bottle. You put it in a teapot, it becomes the teapot. Now, water can flow or it can crash. Be water, my friend.
—Bruce Lee *(A famous quote from Bruce Lee in an interview. The video can be found on YouTube, see https://youtu.be/cJMwBwFj5nQ)*

1 INTRODUCTION

Social movement is often seen as motor for social change. Any analysis leaving behind Hong Kong's social movements, especially the ones occurred after 1997, is incomplete. This is the last thematic chapter of this book, and is devoted to recount the story of Hong Kong's social movements.

This chapter is co-authored with Lai Tsz Chung, who is the second author of this chapter (order of authorship: Kaxton Siu, Lai Tsz Chung, Stephen Chiu).

© The Author(s), under exclusive license to Springer Nature   329
Singapore Pte Ltd. 2022
S. W. K. Chiu, K. Y. K. Siu, *Hong Kong Society*, Hong Kong Studies
Reader Series, https://doi.org/10.1007/978-981-16-5707-8_10

The past decade of Hong Kong witnessed the most flourishing era for the city's social movement history. Massive and successive social movements came wave after wave which turns Hong Kong into the object of interests to many local, national and international observers. One common puzzle to these observers is: *What is going on in Hong Kong? Why were there so many Hong Kong people, especially the younger generation, took to the streets to voice their discontents?* For academics, the question is in what way are these social movements link to social political change happening in both local and global context. In this chapter, we try to provide some answers to this puzzle from the perspective of social movement theories and state-market-civil society relations. In doing so, we would like the counter the four *standard-definition* images in public discourses.

The first *standard-definition* image concerns Hong Kong's civil society: Hong Kong is usually dubbed as a city of protest and thus it is easy to consider Hong Kong has a strong civil society. However, as will be seen in this chapter, through our historical survey, Hong Kong's civil society is not as strong and cohesive as expected. In different historical periods, the city's civil society was constrained by various local, regional (national) and international factors, and was fragmented along various ideological lines. To hint, the 2000s witnessed an emergence of a new divide within the civil society along the traditional democrats and localists. That said, this chapter shall take a longer historical view of Hong Kong's civil society in different historical moments and revisit how it had indeed played crucial roles in fostering social movements local and abroad.

The second *standard-definition* image examines the recent phenomenon of politicization and radicalization of Hong Kong youth. This *standard-definition* image suggests that the introduction of the Liberal Studies as a core subject for senior secondary education led to politicization and radicalization among teenagers. Besides, the loss of hope in upward mobility was another main cause of radical actions in the recent years. In *high-definition*, this is insufficient to explain why youngsters have come to the state of *cognitive dissonance* even though Liberal Studies had provided a new cognitive framework for Hong Kong youngsters to make sense of the world. Essentially, the gap between how one perceives the world and the action one decides to take is not addressed. On the other hand, the loss of hope in upward mobility is only a materialistic explanation that does not consider the youngsters' cultural understanding. It reduces the whole phenomenon to an instrumental problem.

The third *standard-definition* image suggests the rise of Hong Kong's social movement as a response to external changes such as a tightened grip over Hong Kong's affairs by the Beijing government. The corollary of this is that local social movements can be explained by the discontents of Hong Kong people held to the loss of autonomy towards local governance. In *high-definition*, the changing openness or closing up of the political opportunity structure throughout Hong Kong history has been totally neglected. On one hand, the rise of localism reflects a dissatisfaction with the traditional way of mobilizing social movements and how pro-democrats use institutional politics to resolve social problems. On the other hand, political responses from various governments including Beijing, Hong Kong, the US and the UK towards the situation in Hong Kong have collectively shaped the trajectory, outcomes and patterns of the city's social movements. The evolving trajectory of the political opportunity structure in Hong Kong actually entails a rather dynamic, rather than a linear, process of change.

The fourth *standard-definition* image holds the view that recent social movements in Hong Kong were an extension of power struggles among the major powers, primarily the United States and China. In high-definition, the international factor should be treated as a structural context, while the agency of Hong Kong people should be emphasized within the context of a vibrant global civil society. "Glocal" social movements (e.g. the 2005 anti-WTO protests in Hong Kong) and various overseas movements (e.g. Sunflower Student Movement in Taiwan) have inspired local activists, changing their perceptions of the world and imaginations of the "repertoires of contention". Connected through network society, activists engaged in an active learning process and adopted skills and organization method developed by the global civil society, resulting in a multiway diffusion process where local social movements in various places inspire each other.

2 Explaining Collective Action: Insights from Social Movement Theories

The 1960s is the watershed of Hong Kong history. This was also the time when a new wave of social movements like the American Civil Rights Movement, anti-war movements, anti-nuclear movements, the hippie movement, feminist movements and others suddenly emerged around the globe. These movements, together with all others that happened after WWII, attracted unprecedented interests among social movement studies scholars. Much earlier, the field had been dominated by the Collective Behaviour School. Gustave LeBon (1896) published his classic *The Crowd: A Study of the Popular Mind*, which emphasized the irrationality of the crowd. While Neil Smelser (1962) suggested structural strain and tension built up in society would lead to collective behaviour, others analysed what makes people join the crowd, who would join the crowd (Allport, 1924; Miller & Dollard, 1941), the emergence of situational norms in the crowd (Turner & Killian, 1957).

However, after witnessing the social movements in the 1960s, analysts started to consider the role of rationality in collective actions. John D. McCarthy and Mayer Zald put forward the resource mobilization theory (McCarthy & Zald, 1977), which, as opposed to the collective behaviour theories, argued the mere existence of grievance itself cannot lead to social movements without effective means of mobilization. By assuming individuals being rational to weigh the cost and benefit of taking different forms of action, they tried to explain how organizations, the resources available and the ability of these organizations in aggregating resources that could determine the development of a social movement.

On the other hand, while the resource mobilization theory focuses on how civil society organizations or social movement organizations utilize resources available to channel grievances into direct actions, other scholars believed social movements can be shaped by the opportunities and constraints in the formal institutional structure. Charles Tilly, Doug McAdam, and Sidney Tarrow put emphasis on the effects of institutionalized politics on social movements (see Tilly, 1978; McAdam, 1982; Tarrow, 1983), aka the political process theory or the political opportunity theory. They examined changes in institutional settings and informal power relations, and the changes given rise to different formats and outcomes of social movements.

Even so, resources and political opportunities cannot immediately lead to the emergence of a social movement, without people identifying the problem they are facing and realizing the opportunities to change the status quo. Observers often count on the framing process to refer to the "conscious strategic efforts by groups of people to fashion shared understandings of the world and of themselves that legitimate and motivate collective action" (McAdam et al., 1996, p. 6). This perspective brings the elements of ideas and sentiments back to the study of social movements.

Mainly in the late 1970s and 1980s, theorists emphasized cultural elements such as identity, meaning and new ideas on their effects on movement mobilization.[1]

Back to the context of Hong Kong, studies analysing the social movements in Hong Kong were plenty. In particular, Stephen Chiu and Li Hang utilized the perspective of political opportunity structure to analyse the development of Hong Kong social movements (Chiu & Li, 2014). Chiu and Li (2014) adopted the political opportunity curve derived from Eisinger (1973) and Meyer (2004) to explain how the likelihood of social movements can vary with the openness of political opportunity. According to Li (2013), in Fig. 10.1 below, there are four possible paths of the varying political opportunity structure. Paths A and D represent the trajectories of "expanding opportunity", while paths B and C represent those of "constricting opportunity" (p. 51). Path A indicates the increasing openness of the political opportunity structure tending to invite activists to take direct actions, but "further expanding opportunity" means more channels for institutionalized participation are available, resulting in declining likelihood for extra-institutional strategies (Li, 2013, p. 52). Similarly, the initial shrinkage in political opportunity tends to provoke resistance, as following path B, but "further constricting opportunity"

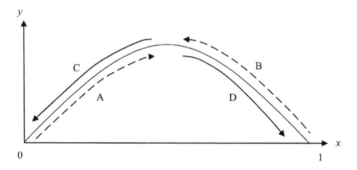

x: Openness of political opportunity structure (1: fully open; 0: fully closed)

y: Likelihood for social movement to employ extra-institutional strategy

Fig. 10.1 Political opportunity curve. (Source: Li, 2013, Fig. 2.1)

[1] For example, see Gamson (1992); Inglehart (1977); McAdam (1982); Melucci (1980, 1985); Tarrow (1983, 1989); Tilly (1978); Touraine (1981).

tends to restrict social movements, as following path C (Li, 2013, p. 52). The political opportunity curve is useful to understand the development of social movements in Hong Kong as it effectively captures the dynamic development in Hong Kong—for example, Li (2013) argued that Hong Kong followed paths A and D since 1982, but switched to path B after 1997.

3   Shifting Landscapes of Hong Kong Social Movements: A Historical Survey

This section outlines the historical trajectory of social movements in Hong Kong before 1997, partially in response to the first *standard-definition* image. While some observers argued that Hong Kong people were politically indifferent and that Hong Kong had curiously high political stability when compared to countries with similar socio-economic and political status (Kuan, 1979; Lau, 1982; Leung, 1996), waves after waves of collective actions were also observed, leading many to have a completely different perception that Hong Kong has a long tradition of a strong and vibrant civil society. In fact, the earliest social movements in Hong Kong can be traced back to the 1840s. Due to the limits of scope and length, this section cannot cover much on the pre-1997 period, but the historical trajectory is crucial to our understanding of the changing roles of social movements in Hong Kong and the factors contributing to such a trajectory.

3.1   Before the 1960s

In the early British colonial days, free population flows existed between Hong Kong and the mainland, contributing to the rapid development of the economy, but simultaneously posing challenges for the British to maintain order in the colony. Hong Kong at that time was not only rich in local social movements, it was also the centre for regional, national and international movements.

The 1844 general strike, against the Registration Ordinance, was considered the first-ever strike in Hong Kong history (Zhou, 2013; Kwantailo, 2013; Tsai, 2004).[2] According to Zhou (2013), there were 10 large-scale

[2] In 1844, just 2 years after the British officially claimed Hong Kong Island, Governor John Davis passed the Registration Ordinance (No. 16 of 1844), requiring all residents on Hong Kong Island to register and pay for an annual fee ($1 for Chinese and $5 for

strikes from 1844 until the end of the nineteenth century, including the coolie strike in 1872 and the rickshaw driver strike in 1883. Later on, labour-related movements continued to be the core of social movements in Hong Kong, and their regional, national and international significance cannot be overlooked. The Seamen's strike of 1922 stemmed from the seamen's demand for higher wages, but soon escalated into a general strike involving tens of thousands of workers from other sectors and disrupted shipping, public transport and other businesses in Hong Kong. Apart from fighting for better treatment to local seamen, the strike inspired labour movements in other parts of China such as Shanghai and Wuhan (Mo, 2011). It also had its impacts on, and was itself part of, regional politics (see Tsai, 2004; Zhang, 2010; Deng, 1957; Yu & Liu, 1995)—for example, the Guangdong Kuomintang government supported the strike by providing aids for workers who had returned to Guangdong.

The Seamen's strike of 1922 paved the way for the Canton–Hong Kong strike started in 1925, which started off as an anti-imperialist movement in response to the May 30 Movement shooting incidents in Shanghai.[3] Starting from June 1925 until October 1926, hundreds of thousands of workers in Hong Kong left their posts; teachers and students participated in class boycotts; Chinese people boycotted British goods; many headed to Canton (Guangzhou). In Hong Kong, the Strike Committee made demands for improved rights for Chinese citizens and workers. With help from the Guangdong Kuomintang government in providing financial aids to workers and imposing a blockade on Hong Kong, the strike lasted for 16 months and was considered the most influential strike in modern Chinese history.[4] The ups and downs of the strike were influenced by, and also had impacts on, local, regional (between Guangdong and British Hong Kong), national (between Kuomintang and the Chinese Communist Party; between the right and left wings within Kuomintang; between Kuomintang and the warlords in the North), and

Europeans)—a poll tax in disguise. The Registration Ordinance encountered vigorous opposition from both Europeans and especially the Chinese, leading to a 12-day general strike and successfully forcing the colonial government to cancel the annual fee.

[3] In the May 30 Movement shooting incidents, Chinese protestors, who are fighting for labour rights against the Japanese-owned cotton mills in the area, were shot by British police officers in the Shanghai International Settlement.

[4] However, the social status of Chinese citizens in Hong Kong was not improved much immediately after the strike (see also Tsai, 2004; Zhang, 2010; Deng, 1957; Yu & Liu, 1995).

international (between Kuomintang, the CCP, the Soviet Union and the UK) politics (see Tsai, 2004).

Beyond labour-related movements, Hong Kong also played significant roles in revolutions in pre-War period. Sun Yat-sen studied in Hong Kong and established the Revive China Society (or Hsing Chung Hui [*Xingzhonghui*]) with the headquarter in Hong Kong and the colony was used as the base for the Chinese Revolution. Even the Communist Party of Vietnam was founded by Ho Chi Minh in Hong Kong in 1930.[5] Other than the aforementioned movements, there had been movements in different forms from time to time, such as the Anti-American Boycott (1905–1906), Anti-Japanese Boycotts (1908; 1919), Tram Boycott (1912–1913), etc. But among all of them, the Anti-Mui Tsai Movement in the 1920s and the 1930s stood out to be the most special one by ending the last slavery system in Hong Kong (see Leung, 2017).

After the Second World War, the Hong Kong government concentrated in recovering from the war and maintaining social stability, while labour movements continued to be the most prominent theme of social movements as making a living was still the major concern for Hong Kong citizens. In the 1940s, labour movements were vibrant as the workers were aware of the power of unionism due to previous experience. Labour movements in this period fostered class consciousness and unionism of the working class, but the struggle between the CCP and the Kuomintang could also be observed locally as labour unions were increasingly divided by ideological differences. Such local conflicts reached the climax at the Double Tenth riots (or the 1956 riots) which led to the decline in rightist support in local society. Later on, the post-war socio-economic background, influences from the political environment in China, increasing ideological divergence of labour unions, all laid the foundation for the 1967 riots (see Chap. 4).

3.2   1960s

In the 1960s, two major social conflicts stood out: the 1966 riots and the 1967 riots. The direct cause of the 1966 riots was the fare increase (from

---

[5] As the French Indochina government sentenced him to death for organizing subversive activities, he was later detained in the Victoria Prison of Hong Kong and escaped from death after his solicitor, Frank Loseby, successfully appealed to the Privy Council in London against the British Hong Kong government's decision to deport him to a French ship (Hong Kong Memory, n.d.).

HKD$0.2 to HKD$0.25 for first-class) of Star Ferry cross-harbour foot passenger ferry (the only public transport across the Victoria Harbour at that time). The peaceful demonstration escalated after a hunger-striking protestor was arrested and sentenced to jail. The 1966 riots lasted for 2 nights and resulted in one death, more than ten injuries and more than 1000 arrests. A month later, Governor David Trench's government set up the Kowloon Disturbances Commission of Inquiry to investigate into the cause of the riots. The inquiry report identified that there was a gap between the government and the people, and recommended administrative reforms to improve channels of communication with the people (see Scott, 2017). However, there were limited immediate reforms. Before any substantial reform could be implemented, the 1967 riots had broken out.

The 1967 riots have been portrayed as the watershed of Hong Kong history (see Cheung, 2009; Bickers & Yep, 2009). It started off as a series of labour disputes, especially at the Hong Kong Artificial Flower Works. Nonetheless, under the direct influence of the Cultural Revolution in China, and also the waves of global decolonization movements, labour movements had connected with leftist and Chinese nationalist movements against British colonial rule. The 7-month riots recorded 51 deaths, more than 800 injuries and nearly 2000 arrests. After the 1966 and 1967 riots, the colonial government became determined to carry out substantial social reforms, including the establishment of District Offices (now the Home Affairs Department) and the City District Officer Scheme to improve communication with local communities, to fix its relationship with the people. Moreover, the riots forced the government to reconsider its governing strategies and push forward significant improvements in its youth and labour policies, and housing, education and public health provisions. Simultaneously, support for leftist organizations among the general public started to decline sharply after the 1967 riots for the violence and chaos they provoked.

Overall, in the 1960s, Hong Kong was highly influenced by the regional political atmosphere. Among all, the Cultural Revolution started in the PRC had profound effects on promoting the anti-colonialism and anti-capitalism awareness in Hong Kong, leading to the riots in the decade. In fact, the Civil right movement and Vietnam War protests in the US could also have impacts on Hong Kong people's sentiments against imperialism and colonists. Moreover, while civil society organizations such as labour unions were further politicized, the colonial government was forced to rethink its social policies in an attempt to fix the problematic state-society relations, which in turn also laid the groundwork for the rapid development of civil society later on.

3.3   1970s

In the 1970s, under the shadow of the 1967 riots, both the government and the general public emphasized more on social stability and economic growth. Cheung and Louie (1991) found that social conflicts between 1975 and 1986 were mostly related to labour and housing issues; Lui and Chiu (1997) also suggested that collective actions in the 1970s were mainly driven by community-based and work-related interests, and that most collective actions in the 1970s were in the form of protests, determined by factors such as limited mass mobilization resources people possessed and the "consultative democracy" institutional setting. The long tradition for "administrative absorption of politics" (King, 1975) also played a part in co-opting local elites into consultative bodies, and thus partially bridging with local society.

Student activism became the main field for collective actions addressing political and ideological issues (Lui & Chiu, 1997). College students in this era, as postwar baby boomers, were born and raised in Hong Kong. They had a stronger sense of belonging to Hong Kong and comparatively cared more about local affairs, while most of their parents' generation were refugees from Mainland China who once treated Hong Kong only as a temporary station. Under such a transition, they had divided identities and opinions on the PRC and the colonial government. The ideological gap was widened after the "Anti-corruption, Arrest Godber" movement. In universities, student activists were divided into the pro-China nationalist camp (*Guocuipai* 國粹派) and the social activist camp (*Shehuipai* 社會派) in the 1970s; the former fraction influenced by the Cultural Revolution and the PRC's rise in the international order (the PRC replaced the Republic of China as the formal representative of "China" in the United Nations in 1971; improved relationship with the US and Western countries in early 1970s), emphasized recognition of the Chinese identity and sympathy to socialist thoughts; the latter fraction, while upholding anti-capitalism and anti-colonialism values, rejected Chinese socialism and focused much more on the wellbeing and immediate needs of local citizens.

In the early 1970s, the pro-China nationalist camp was active in nationalist movements such as the Baodiao movement (保釣運動, literally

Defend the Diaoyu Islands movement), but after the death of Mao Zedong and the downfall of the Gang of Four, they soon lost their ideological basis, and their leading roles in student movements were replaced by the social activist camp. In the late 1970s, student movements mainly focused on community issues—for example, in the "Golden Jubilee Secondary School Incident", college students supported the protests of students of the Golden Jubilee Secondary School against the alleged corruption of the school management; this incident also marked the emergence of the Hong Kong Professional Teachers' Union (HKPTU). As a more general picture, we can take Lui and Chiu's (1997) observation that "identity politics gradually faded into the background and was replaced by a series of collective actions centring on the allocation of resources" (p. 106).

Therefore, in the 1970s, apart from local contexts, social movements in the decade generally followed the varying political atmosphere outside Hong Kong. The rise of the pro-China nationalist camp among student activists was closely tied to the Cultural Revolution, but when the Cultural Revolution ended with the downfall of the Gang of Four, the social activist camp soon assumed leadership roles in student organizations. Student activism, as the major subject of social movements at the time, then turned to community affairs and issues related to allocation of resources. Student activists in the 1970s were among the major contributors to the bloom of civil society organizations such as community-based groups and pressure groups in the 1980s.

3.4 1980s–1997

The 1980s was characterized by the emergence of pressure group politics. In fact, some pressure groups, for instance, the HKPTU and the Society for Community Organization, were formed in the early 1970s and started to gain importance at the end of the 1970s. In the post-1967 era, the government attempted for a closer integration with society, but this had also led to its increasing role as a problem solver and target for social demands of people (Cheung & Louie, 1991). The effect had unfolded gradually. The study by Cheung and Louie (1991) between 1975 and 1986 found that the annual average count of social conflicts was 56 in 1975–1980, but the number grew to 90 in 1981–1986; in addition, there was a significant increase in conflicts related to transport, education, environmental and political issues, showing a tendency of Hong Kong people becoming more socially aware and right-conscious. Collective actions became more and more organized. Participants went from loose groups of individuals to more permanent community groups and single-issue standing groups (Cheung & Louie, 1991).

At the beginning of the 1980s, the government carried reforms to widen the electoral base for Urban Council elections and launched the first District Board election. These reforms had, on the one hand, undoubtedly played important roles in further "administrative absorption of politics". For example, Frederick Fung Kin-kee (馮檢基) participated and won in the 1983 Urban Council election as the chairman of the Hong Kong People's Council on Public Housing Policy (PCPHP), but the divided opinion on whether pressure groups and social movements should participate in electoral politics persists until today. On the other hand, the partial opening up of political structure, albeit minimal, also contributed to the increase of participation in public affairs. Frederick Fung and other pressure group leaders who ran for elections argued that taking up seats in the municipal councils could be advantageous for addressing needs in the community or social movements. Councillors could gain access to resources to set up offices and hire full-time assistants, as they argued, and use them as bridgeheads and bases for mobilization for future movements. However, while citizens were more eager to bring their demands into the public arena at that time, under the context of depoliticization in the post-1967 era, they tended to focus on social welfare and their actions were channelled to specific policies and administrative issues, instead of aiming at the nature of colonial rule (Lui & Chiu, 1997). Additionally, some community-based group members found grassroots' level mobilization overshadowed when local elected councillors emerged in communities (Chung, 2015).

Furthermore, the negotiation between the UK and the PRC had substantial impacts on Hong Kong civil society. After rounds of negotiation between the UK and the PRC, the *Sino-British Joint Declaration* was signed in 1984. After signing on the *Joint Declaration*, Beijing started to draft the *Basic Law*, the mini-constitution for post-1997 Hong Kong. This change in the structure of political opportunities also trigger a wave of social movements addressing constitutional matters and other political issues, with both the British as well as the Chinese government becoming the target of their demands from that point onward (Lui & Chiu, 1997). There had been "increased attention for political participation in formal institutional politics on the part of pressure groups, social movement organizations, and grassroots protest groups" (Lui & Chiu, 1997, p. 107);

moreover, Frederick Fung remembered that he was consulted by the Xinhua News Agency Hong Kong Branch[6] (which was the *de facto* agency of the CCP in Hong Kong, a.k.a. CCP Central Working Committee on Hong Kong and Macau) about the institutional settings of post-1997 Hong Kong (Ma, 2012, p. 38). Although the vast majority of the Hong Kong public did not actually play a part in the Sino-British negotiation, the 1997 question seemed open-ended for different political actors to bargain and fill in. This was the time when the struggle for democracy gained paramount importance in activists' agenda.

Soon it was apparent that the democratization process of Hong Kong was determined by the interplay between London and Beijing. When the British government understood Hong Kong had to be handed over to China, they planned to "withdraw from Hong Kong with honour" (Tsang, 2004, p. 229), which meant to protect British political and economic interest as much as possible in Hong Kong. After taking a disadvantaged position in the negotiation, such that the proposal for an exchange of sovereignty for post-1997 administration was rejected by Beijing, the British government started to democratize Hong Kong, but they had to manoeuvre around the bottom-line of Beijing. When the colonial government further open up the political structure, the pro-democratic groups, who also had closer ties with social movements, switched their focus to electoral politics, leading to a "'hollowing out' of political organizations at the grassroots' level" and the gradual separation of grassroots' mobilization and community action from party politics (Lui & Chiu, 1997, pp. 108–109).

In the 1980s, social movements fostered the development of the local civil society, with a bloom of pressure groups and NGOs, leading to the beginning of party politics in the ensuing decade. The opening up of the political structure allowed the opportunities for active players in the civil society to participate in formal political institutions. Political parties and organizations such as the Democratic Party (previously the United Democrats of Hong Kong) and the Hong Kong Alliance in Support of Patriotic Democratic Movements of China assumed leading roles in democratic movement in the 1990s. Besides the development of a strong local civil society, political considerations of the UK and the PRC and the interplay between the two countries were also important factors for why the

---

[6] Xinhua News Agency Hong Kong Branch became the Liaison Office of the Central People's Government in the Hong Kong Special Administrative Region in 2000.

democracy agenda of Hong Kong could be put up to the international level.

All in all, neither were Hong Kong people politically indifferent generally, nor did Hong Kong have a persistently strong and vibrant civil society; the ups and downs of Hong Kong social movements had been closely related to the political opportunity structure determined by the colonial government and the regional and international environment.

As we can recall, the colonial government had been maintaining a closed political system throughout the first half of the colonial rule and until the 1960s (by which we do not mean a constant level of openness). However, other than grievances persistently accumulated from poor living standards (including labour rights) and the absence of channels for addressing demands, regional, national and geo-political factors expanded the political opportunity structure for local movements. The close tie and high human mobility between Hong Kong and Guangdong contributed to numerous strikes, such as the Seamen's strike and the Canton–Hong Kong strike in the 1920s. The 1967 riots were largely agitated by the Cultural Revolution in China and decolonization movements around the globe.

Using the political opportunity curve in Fig. 10.1 and assuming the 1967 riots to be the vertex of the curve at the time, the political opportunity curve is less convincing in explaining the happening of the riots. According to the figure, only path A and path B could lead to the outburst of the riots. Nonetheless, in the 1960s, the political opportunity structure was not expanding (path A), nor was it constricting from an already relatively high openness of the political opportunity structure (path B). Therefore, we are going to suggest adding an outside dimension to the curve at the end of this chapter, in order to better utilize it to a broader period of time.

After the riots, the colonial government paid immense efforts in social reforms and "administrative absorption of politics". The generally depoliticizing atmosphere in the 1970s confined contentious politics to smaller-scale protests for a specific policy, community or administrative issues, mostly related to resource allocation, except for student activism which had been influenced by the political environment in China and social movements around the globe. Furthermore, the colonial government attempted to narrow the gap between itself and the local community through measures such as the City District Officer Scheme, the setting up or opening up of various consultative bodies, and carrying out municipal elections. Under the transforming state-society relations and partial opening up of the political structure in the 1980s, people were able to address their own interests through forming pressure groups and community groups, while some rising local political elites related to those groups were able to gain resources by winning municipal elections. Thus, from the 1970s to the 1980s, Hong Kong saw an expanding political opportunity structure locally.

Nevertheless, the double role of pressure group leaders in social movements and party politics forged a double-edged sword for grassroots mobilization. The 1997 question posed a new political opportunity for political actors in the 1980s; hence, people fancied the chances for altering the existing institutional settings, and democratic movement assumed top priority on the agenda for many civil society organizations. Eventually, as political elites put their emphasis on electoral politics in the 1990s, social movements entered an era of sluggish development. Therefore, as Chiu and Li (2014) argued, Hong Kong went through paths A and D in the political opportunity curve (Fig. 10.1) since the 1980s to 1997. In other words, the upward trajectory of the political opportunity structure led to the increase in institutionalized participation, and hence extra-institutional strategies were less likely to be adopted (Table 10.1).

To sum up, in this section we have briefly outlined the historical trajectory of social movements in Hong Kong; it shows that the civil society of Hong Kong was vibrant but not always strong, while its development followed different phases in the political opportunity structure which was also determined by local, regional, national and international politics.

4 Post-colonial Development of Hong Kong Social Movements

Since 1997, the socio-economic and political environment of Hong Kong has witnessed a drastic transformation. In the run-up to the return of sovereignty, the colonial government seemed to have put Hong Kong on an upward trajectory of democratization. While Hong Kong people saw their "promised democracy" held off by the Chinese central government in the post-1997 era, governance and legitimation crises of the SAR government came wave after wave. After the Handover, the Asian financial crisis in 1998 and a number of public health crises (the H5N1 avian influenza in 1997 and the SARS outbreak in 2003) dampened Hong Kong people's

Table 10.1   Characteristics of Hong Kong social movements before 1997

Periods	Characteristics of Hong Kong social movements	Examples
Before 1949	• Involvement in local, national and regional social movements, and even revolutions	• The 1911 Revolution • The Canton–Hong Kong strike • The Anti-Mui Tsai Movement
1949–1960	• Fostered local working-class consciousness that led to the 1967 riots	• Various strikes in this period
The 1960s–1970s	• Connected to the Cultural Revolution in the PRC – against capitalism in Hong Kong • Connected to global social movements (e.g. the Civil rights movement in the United States)	• The 1966 riots and the 1967 riots • Community-based movements • Student activism: the pro-China nationalist camp versus the social activist camp • The emergence of pressure groups • The start of women's movements
The 1980s–1990s	• Fostered local civil society development (new political parties and NGOs) • Put Hong Kong's democracy agenda put up to the international level • Emergence of organizations and leaders	• Protests and Candlelight Vigils for the 1989 Tiananmen Square Incident • Democracy movement

confidence in the once reputable civil bureaucracy. These factors contributed to a series of social movements between 1997 and the early 2000s. The 500,000-people march on July 1, 2003, signified a new wave of social movements in Hong Kong. Throughout the years, social movements related to labour, LGBT, social inequality, housing, urban development and heritage preservation constituted the more common themes of social movements in Hong Kong, but democratic movements were often seen as the landmarks of Hong Kong social movements in the post-1997 era, as the 1 July March in 2003, the Umbrella Movement in 2014 and the Anti-ELAB Movement in 2019 were able to mobilize hundreds of thousands people, or even millions as some argued, to voice their concerns on the streets. In this part, we use the three examples of large-scale democratic movements to examine the development of social movements in the post-1997 era.

Section 4.1 below outlines the development of social movements after 1997 through discussing the major changes in the forms and strategies of (1) the 1 July March in 2003, (2) the Umbrella Movement and (3) the Anti-ELAB Movement. It also shows the emerging division within the civil society in the post-1997 era, in response to the first *standard-definition* image. Section 4.2 attempts to analyse the factors contributing to the recent changes of social movements in Hong Kong; the second, third and fourth *standard-definition* images are also addressed.

4.1 New Patterns and Forms of Mobilizations

Building Up the Momentum: The 500,000-People March in 2003
The 1 July March in 2003 was the first mega-scale mass protest after the Handover. In fact, after 1997, the Hong Kong Alliance in Support of Patriotic Democratic Movements of China started to organize annual marches on every July 1 (the HKSAR establishment day) to voice political concerns and demand for democracy and freedom. In 2002, the HKSAR government released the *Proposals to Implement Article 23 of the Basic Law*, then written into the proposed *National Security (Legislative Provisions) Bill* in 2003. The Bill invoked the anxiety that Hong Kong people may lose their freedom of speech and political rights, especially when many democratic movements at that time were inspired by or sympathetic to the 1989 Tiananmen Square Incident. At the same time, Hong Kong also experienced an economic recession, while the SARS outbreak further revealed the limitations of the government. On 1 July 2003, around 500,000 marchers[7] showed up and marched from Victoria Park football field to the Government's Central offices. A large variety of demands were made by the participants, including calling for the resignation of Chief Executive Tung Chee-hwa and withdrawal of the National Security Bill.

---

[7] The counting methods and outcomes of attendance numbers depended on different institutions. For the estimation method for the generally accepted figure, see So and Chan (2003).

The Postmodernization of Hong Kong Protests

The protest was described as "an unprecedented awakening of civil society against the state and the largest indigenous movement in Hong Kong history" (Ma, 2005) and the rise of the "post-modern style of mobilization" of social movements (Chan, 2005). It was post-modern in the sense that it was not mobilized by a highly structured, hierarchically organized mass organization, but a network of loosely organized organizations which are relatively small, autonomous and independent from each other (So, 2011). The July 1 protest in 2003 was organized by the Civil Human Rights Front (CHRF), which consisted of 30 social organizations from mixed backgrounds at the time. The member organizations included labour groups, religious groups, student groups, political groups and more.

The diversification of participant groups in the protest can be attributed to the multiple socio-economic and political changes aforementioned. The fear of deteriorating political freedom, the plunging stock market and property market, the surging unemployment rate, the reduced social welfare assistance, the wage cut for civil servants and the "Lexusgate" scandal of Financial Secretary Antony Leung also added onto the grievances towards Chief Executive Tung's government. The protest was a result of the superimposition of economic conflict and political conflict (So, 2011). These conflicts were so widespread that people from disparate backgrounds simultaneously feel their interests threatened or values challenged. With the help of social networks of the many member organizations from different sectors, information technology and mass media, people attended the march with their own banners and slogans without a single, rigid, unifying ideology. There were also other formats of participation, such as wearing costumes, dancing, performing a funeral march and playing music (So, 2011). The July 1 marches have become a carnival-like festive event at which people come together to voice their variegated concerns since then. It is perhaps the earliest large-scale movement that presented the prototype of leaderless movements in Hong Kong.

From 2003 to 2013

After the protest, Financial Secretary Antony Leung and Secretary for Security Regina Ip resigned and the government was forced to withdraw the National Security Bill. The central government took up a more active role in influencing Hong Kong, not only in the political and economic spheres but also in the cultural sphere.

Economically, the implementation of the mainland and Hong Kong Closer Economic Partnership Arrangement (also known as CEPA, signed on 29 June 2003) seemed to be the saviour to Hong Kong's economy from the damage of SARS, but the increasing dependence on the Mainland's economy profoundly reshaped the local economy. For example, the Individual Visit Scheme (IVS) begun on 28 July 2003, brought millions of mainland visitors to the city every year. The influx of mainland visitors over the years gave rise to intensified conflicts between mainland visitors and local people.[8] Politically, in 2004, the National People's Congress shut out universal suffrage for Chief Executive in 2007 and the direct election for all Legislative Council seats in 2008.

Meanwhile, Beijing also stepped up in promoting its cultural influence. Starting from 2004, for example, the national anthem of the PRC, together with the music video "Our Home, Our Country" (心繫家國 *Xinjijiaguo*) to promote national pride, is played on major Hong Kong TV channels every day before the evening news programme.[9] Henceforth, the all-encompassing moves by Beijing have foreshadowed multiple social movements. The Moral and National Education controversy in 2012 led to protests in rejection to Beijing's influence on local education. It gave rise to student activist group Scholarism which demonstrated prominent influence in the Umbrella Movement.

Furthermore, multiple events between 2003 and 2013 had profound implications for later development of social movements. In 2005, the World Trade Organization Sixth Ministerial Conference of the World Trade Organization was held in Hong Kong. A group of Korean peasants gathered outside the venue to protest against the WTO. After days of peaceful demonstration, some radicalized their actions and were forcefully dispelled by the Hong Kong Police with pepper sprays, tear gases, and even bean bag rounds (The Guardian, 2005; Yeung, 2005). Strategies

---

[8] The Scheme was seen as a double-edged sword (Wong et al., 2016): it has created a large number of working opportunities in the service sector (Sung et al., 2015), but also led to the homogeneity of shop types, generating tremendous pressure on public services and daily necessities supply, constituting nuisances to local residents (Legislative Council/Research Office, 2014).

[9] The music video was produced by the National Education Sub-committee under the Committee on the Promotion of Civic Education. As Patrick Ho, the then-Secretary for Home Affairs, described, the promotional video was to reinforce the national identity of Hong Kong people towards China (Ho, 2004).

adopted by the Korean peasants, not only their radical actions, but also milder actions such as the "*kowtow* procession" had been eye-opening for Hong Kong activists (Baptista, 2019; Lee, 2016).

In the following year, a wave of heritage preservation movements—the "New Preservation Movement" (Chen & Szeto, 2015) started from the preservation of the Star Ferry Pier—could be seen as the enlightenment of local culture appreciation and local identity (Chen & Szeto, 2015; Ku, 2012). Then, in 2009–2010 and 2014, the anti-Hong Kong Express Rail Link movement and the anti-Northeastern New Territories development plan movement signalled a rise in awareness for local identity, local community, and growing opposition to Hong Kong-China integration.

Particularly, the anti-Hong Kong Express Rail Link movement from 2009 to 2010 was one of the most momentous sections of the prelude to the Umbrella Movement and the development of Hong Kong civil society. Approaching the end of 2009, the HKSAR announced its plan for the construction of the Hong Kong section of the Guangzhou-Shenzhen-Hong Kong Express Rail Link. The plan stirred controversies on various areas such as concern for public expenditure, location of the terminal and influence on the local community (e.g. pollution and relocation). On 16 January 2010, protestors surrounded the LegCo building, and trapped Eva Cheng (the Secretary for Transport and Housing) and pro-government lawmakers inside. A large part of the strategies adopted, the skills needed to protect themselves from the police, the awareness of local identity, and the core group of activists came from the New Preservation Movement (or even the 2005 WTO protests). In different social movements, the new generations of activists emerged as core participants of social movements—for example, Eddie Chu has been active since the preservation of the Star Ferry Pier in 2006 and the Defence of Choi Yuen Tsuen during the anti-Hong Kong Express Rail Link movement. The same happened to the succeeding social movements like the anti-national education protests in 2012, in which Joshua Wong and other members of Scholarism emerged and remained active in the Umbrella Movement and the Anti-ELAB Movement. In other words, the social movements in Hong Kong seems always able to pass on resources (including social connections and the core activists) and skill set to prepare for the succeeding social movements.

An Increasingly Divided Civil Society: The Umbrella Movement
On the last day of August 2014, the NPC announced its decision on the 2017 Chief Executive Election. The "31 August Decision"[10] insists that candidates for the 2017 election have to be nominated by half of the members of a nominating committee before the popular election and the Chief Executive-elect will have to be appointed by the Central People's Government. It raised concerns that Beijing would use the nomination process to screen out opposition candidates and the appointment power as a veto.

The civil disobedience campaign "Occupy Central with Love and Peace" (OCLP) supported by the traditional pro-democratic camp was just one part of the large-scale social movements in 2014. The trigger was, in fact, pulled by a series of student movements, including the class boycott mobilized by two major student organizations, Scholarism and the Hong Kong Federation of Students (HKFS), and the "reclaim" of the Civic Square outside the Government Headquarters complex on 26 September 2014. It soon developed into the 79-day[11] Occupy Movement in which participants occupied major roads in Admiralty, Causeway Bay and Mongkok. It was estimated that around 1.2 million citizens have taken part in the movement (CCPOS, 2014). The scene of protestors using umbrellas to defend against pepper spray used by the Hong Kong Police became a symbol of the movement among mass media (Molloy, 2014; The New York Times, 2014).

A Thirty-Year Fantasy Crushed

The 2003 protest was already a bolt from the blue for people who thought Hong Kong people were generally politically apathetic before, and there were various new forms of movements developed between 2003 and 2014, still not many researchers or activists were able to foresee the eruption of participation that came afterwards. Even for one of the initiators of

---

[10] The Decision of the Standing Committee of the National People's Congress on Issues Relating to the Selection of the Chief Executive of the Hong Kong Special Administrative Region by Universal Suffrage and on the Method for Forming the Legislative Council of the Hong Kong Special Administrative Region in the Year 2016.

[11] Some said the movement lasted for 81 days counting from 26 September, when student activists occupied the Civic Square, to 15 December, when all occupied sites were finally cleared by the police. Here we use the more widely accepted 79-day duration which counted from 28 September, when tens of thousands of protesters joined at Admiralty to defend against pepper spray and tear gas used by the police.

the OCLP campaign, Chan Kin-man, himself a scholar specializing in social movement and civil society studies, had only expected 3000 to 10,000 to participate in blocking the main roads in the central business district of the city for a few days (Chong, 2019). This may be because, as OLCP initiator Benny Tai admitted later, the Umbrella Movement had replaced OLCP (Apple Daily, 2014b). In fact, when the OLCP initiators announced to start the occupy movement on the stage during the 2014 Civic Square protests organized by Scholarism and the HKFS, the reaction was extremely divided. The OLCP initiators were accused of "hijacking" the movement and were even "booed" by some protestors downstage (i-Cable News, 2014). The values and principles of OLCP were also regarded as encumbrances to the movement. In the later stages of the movement, however, the leadership of Scholarism and the HKFS was heavily challenged as well. The question is then if the leaderships of different leaders and organizations failed to gain a unified recognition, how was such a large scale of movement possible? For what reasons and how were the participants mobilized?

It has to go back to the changes since 2003. Chan Kin-man (2005) described the mobilization of the July 1, 2003 protest as "post-modern". Indeed, the 2003 protest stamped the change in mobilization patterns of collective actions in Hong Kong such as by encouraging the formation of numerous new social groups, while "traditional" pro-democratic protests in Hong Kong faced difficulties in many ways.

First, their "middle-class as agents" tradition implied their tendency to favour social stability and moderate tactics (So, 1999; Lui, 2003). The July 1 protests and the June 4 vigils, despite not directly organized by pan-democratic parties, also showed strong linkages to them who took the protests as a chance to generate support for elections. However, under the political system of Hong Kong, pan-democratic parties have no hope of gaining control of the LegCo, not to say exerting significant influence on the formal policy-making process. This led to an impasse for the democratic movement.

Second, Hong Kong people have had enough of the "ritualistic" protests. Tarrow's (1989) "cycles of protests" can only partially describe the post-2003 situation. The expected "rise and fall" of collective actions turned out to be much less dramatic. In contrast, the wave of protests did not die off after 2003 but held on to a certain level of activity. As Lee and Chan (2011) suggested, the term "ritualistic protests" can better highlight the fact that "the July 1 protests have become a series of regular and repetitive collective actions that drew a substantial number of participants irrespective of contextual changes," (p.12). After years and years of peaceful, ritualistic demonstrations, a new generation of activists became weary of the "boring, stagnant and ritualistic" repertoire (Law, 2018).

When these problems of the traditional pro-democratic protests entwined, the conventional frame for the democratic movement in Hong Kong has lost its ground. Law Wing-sang (2018) argued that it was the "31 August Decision" that manifested the death of the "reunion-in-democracy" discourse that had been used for nearly three decades, while Brian Fong (2014) even described it as the "end of an era" when the NPCSC Vice Chief Secretary Li Fei insisted that the Chief Executive candidates must "love his country and love Hong Kong". The crumbling of the existing frame pushed the movement into a discursive and organizational vacuum, sparking off the Umbrella Movement (Law, 2018).

As a result, the rational choice theory and the resource mobilization approach became inadequate in explaining the Umbrella Movement. The movement relied on indignation towards the "31 August Decision" and the excessive force used by the police. Participants were more motivated by their individual emotions and everyday life connections than adherence to a certain organization (though this was also a relevant factor). It may make researchers reminiscent of the crowd behaviour approach that tends to treat collective behaviours as emotional and chaotic. Nonetheless, a simple binary view of emotion against rational behaviour is ineffective in coping with the recent developments.

It was not that protestors were irrational. Grievance constituted a large part of their motivations but considering the fact that ordinary citizens have had little say in the formal political process, many participants thought fighting on the street was their only "rational" choice. Moreover, in this spontaneous, voluntary movement, individual participants involved in rule-setting and order maintenance in the occupied area, deliberation of strategic moves, online promotion of ideas and many other actions that would be impossible for an irrational crowd of mobs.

A Leaderless Movement: The Rise of the "No Main Stage" Principle

The fact that multiple occupied zones popped up in different areas of the city further demonstrated the leaderless nature of the Umbrella Movement. On 28 September, after riot police's tear gas dispersion and rumours about the use of rubber bullets, citizens spontaneously occupied a few crowded areas at night, including Mongkok, setting up an occupied zone at one of the busiest crossroads in Kowloon, and also Causeway Bay (Apple Daily, 2014a). These occupied zones were not organized by student organizations, political parties, social organizations or the OLCP leaders. Some participants thought they could distract the police by occupying other areas, while some disagreed with the principles and styles of the "leaders" at Admiralty.[12] In general, Occupy Mongkok[13] was spontaneously established and developed its grassroots and "orderly in chaos" image, as opposed to the Admiralty "main stage", but with a similar general goal.

Not only were there alternative occupied zones that refused to recognize the leadership of Scholarism and HKFS, but there was also a divergence of strategies, and factionalism within the Admiralty occupied zone. On one side, some protestors insisted that the movement should strictly follow the non-violence principle.[14] This view suited the pro-democratic protests tradition and was supported by the pan-democratic parties and a majority of the protestors (Cheng & Chan, 2017). They believed that this would help maintain a morally appealing image of the movement. On the other side, some protestors opposed to this moderate tradition of protests. Although not all of them favoured radical direct actions, a group of them named themselves "the valiants" (勇武派), a relatively militant faction who would not shy away from taking more radical actions like confronting the police and breaking into government buildings. During the movement, the two factions heavily criticized each other. The moderate faction accused "the valiants" of stirring up conflicts from within and giving excuses for the police to use larger force against protestors, while "the valiants" called the moderate pan-democrats "leftards" (左膠), criticizing them for being a drag to the movement.

The OLCP proposal, when initiated in 2013, was not a popular idea, but had undoubtedly helped expand the imagination of possible strategies through a year-long discussion on the principles of civil disobedience.

---

[12] In an online article, a participant explained, "I have been to Admiralty and Mongkok. The utopian atmosphere of Admiralty was easily intoxicating … Admiralty has an elitist, blue-blooded feel in it. For more than once, the 'barrier team' and 'defense-line team' felt they were the boss," (Leung, 2014).

[13] See Yuen (2018, 2019) and Liu (2014).

[14] The non-violence principle was usually addressed as "peaceful, rational and non-violent" (「和理非」). The slogan came from "peaceful, rational, non-violent and no swear words" (和平、理性、非暴力、非粗口) suggested by Democratic Party law-maker Emily Lau, who used the slogan to distinguish her party from more radical parties in the pan-democratic camp.

Traditional political parties and leaders still have a certain degree of influence and mobilizing power to democratic movement supporters, but more than a million of protestors came together without a generally recognized leadership. Protestors voluntarily took up duties such as collecting and distributing resources, providing first-aid services, recycling waste, maintaining order, setting up defence lines, making promotion materials, and even giving free tutorial classes to students. Many showed distrusts towards centralized leadership and divergence of stratagems. The "main stage" at Admiralty where different actors give speeches and made announcements became a symbol for leadership. The saying of "no main stage" among protestors has spoken for the leaderless nature of the movement itself. Nevertheless, it does not mean the movement was a complete chaos. Instead, protestors were able to organize themselves within a decentralized network, with a lot of informal leaders and non-hierarchical, horizontal and self-organized groups (Cheng & Chan, 2017).

Other than ideological divergence, online social media and digital media was another essential factor that contributed to such a leaderless movement. As Lee et al. (2015) found out, the use of social media can facilitate a more decentralized formation of collective actions and a weaker leadership of social movement organizations in the digital age. In Hong Kong, studies also found that the active participation of the younger generation was tied to their heavy use of online social media for communication and obtaining information.[15] The use of Facebook had significant effects on both online and offline political participation (Tang & Lee, 2013), while social media's nature of favouring selective exposure and the echo chamber effect would foster the effect of social psychological factors like grievances, efficacy and anger, then channel them into participation (Garrett, 2009; Lee et al., 2017; Lee et al., 2015). Apart from emotion-driven participation, young activists also engaged in a new mode of movement. They were well aware of the importance of playing the "media and information power game" and became "agents of mediatization" themselves (Lee & Ting, 2015). Moreover, a lower threshold for "political amateurs" to gain influence in the cyber public space was enabled by social media. This also contributed to the more dispersed format of organization and mobilization of social movements.

Besides, alternative media—such as Hong Kong In-media, Social Record Channel (SocREC), House News and MyRadio, which provided

---

[15] For example, see Lee et al. (2015); Li et al. (2015); Ma et al. (2014); Wu (2010).

online news reporting, commentaries, podcast programmes and live streams on current affairs and events—actively promoted civic journalism and were popular sources of information for activists. Studies concluded that the social-media-driven consumption of alternative media could facilitate participation in collective actions, lead to the use of unconventional protest tactics, and even radicalization of social movements (Lee, 2018a; Leung & Lee, 2014; Shen et al., 2020). On the other hand, the importance of traditional media should not be overlooked. Tang (2015)'s study showed that TV footages showing the police's use of tear gas against protestors had mobilized a massive group of people to join the Umbrella Movement. More interestingly, many of them expressed distrust against any of the related political organizations. This may mean TV helped mobilize a group of people who were not politically active in the past, when compared to new media which were often found more influential to people holding pre-existing attitudes (Leung & Lee, 2014; Tang, 2015).

From 2014 to 2018: A Prelude to the Anti-ELAB Movement

Undoubtedly, the Umbrella Movement has a far-reaching impact on Hong Kong society, despite not being successful in achieving its main goal—universal suffrage for 2017 Chief Executive Election and 2018 LegCo Election.

First, the movement cradled many new civil society organizations or community organizations, generally known as "post-umbrella groups", while around 30 of them eventually participated in the 2015 District Council elections. Political groups consisted of mainly the "post-90s" and later the "post-millennial" generations—such as Scholarism (some of its leaders formed the political party Demosisto in 2016), Youngspiration and Hong Kong Indigenous—who posed a great challenge to traditional pan-democratic political parties dominated by experienced, middle-aged politicians.

Second, Beijing has become much more determined in tightening its control on Hong Kong society. During and after the movement, the pro-Beijing camp mobilized its supporters to participate in countermovement campaigns.[16] What is more, Beijing and the Hong Kong government denied candidacies of dissidents in elections and disqualified elected

---

[16] Hong Kong government's senior officials, including Chief Executive Leung Chun-ying, even publicly supported and signed on to an anti-Occupy Central petition launched by a countermovement group.

opposition lawmakers. These factors added up to an increasingly polarized society.

Third, the Umbrella Movement saw the rise of localism among activists. During the movement, "the valiant" groups gained popularity among protestors. While their strategy of action connected with localism (which entails anger and hostile sentiments towards the government and the Mainland), multiple protests against mainland parallel traders in 2015 (Chan & Tsang, 2015; BBC, 2015) and the 2016 Mong Kok civil unrest (also known as the "Fishball Revolution" to its supporters, and the Mongkok Riot to the pro-government camp) (Jenkins & Iyengar, 2016; Chu & Blundy, 2016) signified their popularity among young activists. However, after the violent clash with the police and the large-scale arrests afterwards, the following three years were a period of stillness in terms of mass protests.

The Anti-ELAB Movement

In April 2019, the HKSAR government proposed an amendment to the Fugitive Offenders Ordinance and Mutual Legal Assistance in Criminal Matters Ordinance, the purpose of which, as the government claimed, was to facilitate the extradition of murder suspect Chan Tong-kai[17] to Taiwan. However, the Bill proposed to allow extraditions not only to Taiwan, but also Mainland China and Macau when being requested. This gave rise to overwhelming worries and fear that dissidents may be arrested and transferred to Mainland China, meaning that the contentious political space would be further narrowed. Since March 2019, multiple protests, commonly addressed as the Anti-Extradition Law Amendment Bill (Anti-ELAB) Movement, in different forms, scales and locations have taken place.

The Anti-ELAB Movement was at its peak, in terms of scale and intensity, between June and December 2019. Although Chief Executive Carrie Lam finally withdrew the bill (on 4 September 2019) after several large-scale protests and fierce confrontations on the streets, protestors were largely angered by alleged police brutality during the months of protests, and thus continued to act until their demands were met. They put forward the slogan "Five demands, no one less", suggesting they will not back

---

[17] Being investigated in Hong Kong, Chan Tong-kai confessed to killing his girlfriend Poon Hiu-wing in Taiwan. However, Chan could only be prosecuted for money laundering in Hong Kong. After serving a sentence of 29 months in prison, Chan was released on 23 October 2019, but has yet to turn himself in to Taiwan police and receive court trial.

down until all five of their demands are met. The five demands were (1) full withdrawal of the extradition bill, (2) a commission of inquiry into alleged police brutality, (3) retracting the classification of protesters as "rioters", (4) amnesty for arrested protesters, and (5) dual universal suffrage (Wong, 2019b). On the other hand, Beijing and the HKSAR government insist on taking a hardline approach in dealing with the movement (Lee et al., 2019). Consequently, despite facing exhaustive repression (including but not limited to the invocation of the Emergency Regulations Ordinance and the implementation of the "Hong Kong National Security Law"[18]) and being disrupted by the COVID-19 outbreak, different forms of resistance continued into 2020.

"Be Water" as Strategy

In terms of mobilization and organization, the Anti-ELAB Movement inherited the leaderless and decentralized tradition of the Umbrella Movement. Nevertheless, there had been two key changes since the Umbrella Movement.

First, the influence of pan-democratic political parties and traditional social movement organizations had further declined. Moderate pan-democratic parties and organizations, as more radical activists saw them, were only stumbling blocks for democracy movements. They were accused of concerning nothing else than their seats in the LegCo. Apart from increased emphasis on "no main stage", more radical protestors even held hostile attitudes towards these political parties. On 1 July 2019, just before the Storming of the Legislative Council Complex, a few pan-democratic legislators tried to dissuade protestors from breaking into the Complex. The scene pan-democratic lawmaker Leung Yiu-chung being dragged away forcefully from the entrance was the best portrayal of the relations between radical protestors and traditional pan-democratic politicians (Now News, 2019).

Second, the use of information technologies as a platform for mobilization and a channel of information became even more crucial than during the Umbrella Movement.[19] LIHKG, a popular online forum among the younger generations, was where netizens offer suggestions and evaluations

---

[18] Officially the Law of the People's Republic of China on Safeguarding National Security in the Hong Kong Special Administrative Region. The "Hong Kong National Security Law" was passed by the Standing Committee of the National People's Congress on 30 June 2020.

[19] See Wong (2019a); Kow et al. (2020); Ku (2020); Lee et al. (2019).

on protest tactics and strategies. In the forum a to a meme of "air-con strategists" (冷氣軍師) gained popularity to mock those armchair generals who actively comment on strategies instead of fighting on the frontline. On the other hand, the term was a good illustration of the roles of online platforms to the movement. Being literally leaderless, the strategies were deliberated, and mobilization and organization of collective actions were communicated online and anonymously (Lee et al., 2019). Encrypted instant messaging application Telegram was another crucial tool, where people set up groups on Telegram in subtly divided themes such as community-based information sharing, event-based discussions, promotion strategies, direct action strategies, fact checking, etc. (Lee et al., 2019). Facebook, Instagram and Twitter are also essential to information spreading. Online live streaming by alternative media, and even ordinary people, helped record and spread stunning scenes of the movement. These online sharing and live streaming made people feel connected even when they were not on the frontline.

In terms of strategies, the Anti-ELAB Movement showed significant differences from the Umbrella Movement. Perhaps activists also realized the disparity of force between protestors and the police after the Umbrella Movement and various events like the 2016 Mongkok clash, they decided to replace the "stronghold" strategy with a mixed strategy involving the use of guerrilla-style tactics. That being said, the occupation of the Chinese University of Hong Kong and the Hong Kong Polytechnic University, remained two important events in the movement. "Old-fashioned" peaceful demonstrations continued to take place, like a march on 16 June 2019 recorded 200 millions of participants (BBC, 2019; SCMP Reporters, 2019). Yet increasingly activists adopted "blooming flowers everywhere" (遍地開花) tactic that brought protests into different corners of the city, such as Sha Tin, Tseung Kwan O and Yuen Long, or residential districts that had never experienced large scale protests before (Siu et al., 2019). Therefore, what is distinctive here is not the complete abandoning of the old tactics, but the coexistence of various forms of actions.

Taking Bruce Lee's Taoist motto "Be water" as the guiding philosophy means being "formless" and "shapeless" (Anderlini, 2019). When applied to the movement, it is often interpreted by activists as not sticking to a particular location, not limiting themselves to a certain form of actions, not being shameful of retreating when needed, being willing and able to endure and obscure during hard times and being able to strike back when opportunities arise. As we can see, during the movement, protestors took up a large variety of strategies and forms of actions, such as flash mobbing, human chains, Christian hymns singing, art demonstrations, Lennon Walls, public transport obstructions, road blockades, and boycotting and "buycotting". A 79-day occupation did not occur again, but the movement became a series of monumental events accompanied by resistance in everyday life.

Among various forms of actions, boycotting and "boycotting" was a signature of the movement. Drawing on the use of colours by different camps since the Umbrella Movement particularly, stores that showed support[20] to the movement were labelled "yellow shops", while those supporting the government are "blue shops".[21] Supporters of the movement ask people to "punish" the "yellow shops" by visiting them and making them busy, which in fact means "buycotting", while the "blue shops" are boycotted. They call this the "yellow economic circle" (Beech, 2020; Prasso, 2020; Pang, 2020).[22] The "yellow economic circle" provided a mode of participation with lower political costs for those supporters of the movement did not feel safe to join protests and other direct actions. Protestors voluntarily published online maps and mobile phone applications to list out "yellow shops", making "buycotting" and boycotting convenient. On the whole, resistance has been fused into everyday life. It even shaped "taste" in the cultural sphere—people start to boycott certain singers, actors, writers, movie directors and movie companies.[23]

[20] In June 2019, supporters of the movement started to discuss the stances of shops, especially of restaurants. On the 5 August 2019 general strike, some stores and restaurants decided to close on that day to show support for the general strike. Some provided assistance to the movement, such as acting as first-aid stations and rest areas during protests, providing food and water, and donating money. Most of them put posters and slogans promoting the movement.

[21] The use of yellow colour as a symbol for pro-democracy movements in Hong Kong can be dated back to 2005, but it was widely used to represent the Umbrella Movement in which protestors wore yellow ribbons to fight for universal suffrage. In contrast, the pro-government camp launched anti-mobilization campaigns and wore blue ribbons.

[22] Pro-government supporters and media criticized the "yellow economic circle" for politicizing the consumption of people and pseudoeconomic (Takungpao, 2019; Zhou, 2019). There had been groups of radical protestors breaking into "blue shops", who smashed things and graffitied (although no looting has been reported). Moreover, pro-government economist Francis Lui suggested that the "yellow economic circle" did not worth a discussion when writing his 1400-word article claiming that the "yellow shops" have to pay "protection rackets" to the "thugs" (Lui, 2020).

[23] A famous example would be the "#BoycottMulan" action (BBC, 2020b). The action started because ethnic Chinese movie star Liu Yifei (of US citizenship) posted a message on

Solidarity

Another significant distinctive feature of the Anti-ELAB movement was the relations between different factions. During the Umbrella Movement, factionalism posed fatal damage to the morale of the movement. Learning from this lesson, solidarity was highlighted as a principle of the Anti-ELAB movement.

Although surveys showed an overall trend of radicalization and a rise of localist thoughts, they also showed that protestors recognized the importance of the coexistence of, if not cooperation between, the moderates and the radicals (Lee, 2020a). Moderate actions can easily attract a larger number of participants and appeal to the moral conception of the general public and the international community. Radical actions, on the other hand, can put greater pressure on the government and increase its cost of governing. As Francis Lee (2020a) found, solidarity slogans such as "brothers climb a mountain together, each has to make his own effort" (兄弟爬山, 各自努力) and "no snitching, no severing of ties" (不篤灰, 不割席) were frequently mentioned on online communities. These solidarity slogans reminded people not to easily condemn others' actions during the movement. Nevertheless, although solidarity between the moderate and radical flanks were elevated during the movement's peak, arguments between the two flanks resurfaced when the movement cooled down in 2020.

At the same time, the movement also showed, to some extent, solidarity among other identities such as social classes and occupations. According to Lee et al. (2019), 41.7% of protestors identified themselves as from the lower class, while 49.1% from the middle class. A general strike was called on 5 August 2019. The strike was answered by some trade unions and individual workers including bus drivers, flight attendants, while students launched class boycotts and shop owners closed their shops on the day. Around 350,000 people participated in the general strike, as estimated by the Confederation of Trade Unions, although the precise number is impossible to arrive at (Chong, 2019). The link between local and labour identities was not new to Hong Kong (from the Seamen's strike of 1922 to the 2013 Hong Kong dock strike), but the connection between labour movements and democratic movements remained weak in recent years.

social media to support the Hong Kong police back in August 2019. Protestors launched a campaign on social media to boycott the Disney film *Mulan* starred by her. People used the hashtag "#BoycottMulan" to spread the message on Facebook and Twitter. The campaign was answered in many countries like Thailand, Taiwan, the UK and the USA.

During the Anti-ELAB movement, the ties with labour movements were strengthened significantly; many new, but relatively small, labour unions were established since June 2019.[24]

As a remark, solidarity in this movement should be identified but not romanticized. First, it does not mean the divergent views between different factions have narrowed. The difference in opinions (or even in ideologies) are pragmatically tolerated, but not adequately debated and deliberated. Second, right-wing localist thoughts played a central role in the movement. Arguably, despite being recognized at some points, the perspectives of grass roots, ethnic minorities, expats or immigrants, and people of different religions and sexual orientations remained peripheral to the agenda of the movement.

In short, protestors in the Anti-ELAB movement have taken a fluid and flexible approach by mixing a large variety of strategies. This is made possible because solidarity was emphasized throughout the whole movement to gather as many supporters as possible; hence, many different styles of actions (ranging from confronting the police bodily to singing songs in a shopping mall) coexisted and were performed by different groups of supporters. Different ideas and actions were proposed, discussed and organized anonymously on online forums and through instant messaging applications. Thus, the mobilization and organization process became more decentralized. In addition, information and messages were spread instantly through online social media with the help of alternative media, the popularity of live streaming and civic journalism. Even when supporters were away from the frontline of protests, many have chosen to participate in the everyday life perspective. Political views were valued in consumption activities. Subtle decisions—like which restaurants to dine in, which TV channels to watch, or who to make friends with—are now made through the lens of moral and political obligations.

Change in Political Opportunity Structure

The political opportunity structure has significantly changed from the Umbrella Movement to the Anti-ELAB Movement. During the Umbrella Movement, large-scale suppression was absent, while countermovement

---

[24] According to Apple Daily, from June 2019 to early May 2020, there had been 4328 applications for new union registration at the Labour Department, while before June 2019, there were normally less than 10 applications in a month (Apple Daily, 2020; Lam, 2020).

campaigns were launched to wear down the movement (Yuen & Cheng, 2017). This had led to the impression that Beijing and the HKSAR government would not easily adopt large-scale repression. As a result, the perceived costs for protests were relatively low in the post-Umbrella era, but the pro-democracy camp also suffered devastating divergence in paths and ideology. Added to this is the low morale in the civil society after the Umbrella Movement ended, thus preventing large-scale movements from happening in the next few years.

Then, when the Anti-ELAB Movement broke out, most protestors could not imagine the intensity of repression would be as high as what they had eventually encountered. Not only that the government no longer shy away from countering with tear gas and brute force, but no room for conversation and negotiation (present but limited before) were left open by the government after the storming of the LegCo building by the protestors on 1 July 2019. Thus, the government's strategy has changed from no incorporation but no large-scale repression (in the Umbrella Movement's time) to large-scale repression and no dialogue now, further closing up the local political opportunity structure. Additionally, the enactment of the Prohibition on Face Covering Regulation (Cap. 241K) on 5 October 2019 (to ban the wearing of masks at unauthorized assemblies) and the commencement of the Hong Kong national security law on 30 June 2020 have left fewer and fewer spaces for resistance.

In 2014 Chiu and Li (2014) suggested taking the anti-Hong Kong Express Rail Link movement as a new climax of social movement in Hong Kong so far. They argued that starting from the 1980s to 2009, the development of social movement followed the political opportunity curve from paths A to D, and then to path C (Fig. 10.1). On hindsight, the Anti-ELAB Movement in 2019 should certainly be viewed as the vertex of the curve, while the anti- Express Rail Link movement should be viewed perhaps as the announcement for the new phase of protests in Hong Kong.

If the political opportunity curve is followed, treating the Anti-ELAB Movement as the vertex and considering the fact that the local and national political opportunity structure has definitely been contracting, social movements in Hong Kong would then enter a period of a downturn following path C (Fig. 10.1), roughly demonstrating the cycles of protest. Nevertheless, as can be observed, resistance has been submerged into everyday life, while international factors have been more and more influential and recognized.

The first *standard-definition* image perceives Hong Kong civil society as traditionally strong. In *high-definition*, Hong Kong civil society was not coherent nor strong, but its development has been increasingly mature over time. Despite having ups and downs and internal conflicts, Hong Kong civil society is still thriving under difficult circumstances.

During and after the Umbrella Movement and the Anti-ELAB Movement, many new civil society organizations emerged in various aspects of everyday life. The "blooming flowers everywhere" strategy does not only mean multiple protests in different locations simultaneously, but it can also mean submerging resistance in different realms of everyday life. In other words, many previously non-political (as perceived by the general public) organizations have become arenas in which people holding similar values gather and organize actions to bring changes to that particular aspect of life. For example, labour movements in Hong Kong were generally depoliticized and limited to blue-collar workers, but the general strike during the Anti-ELAB Movement has led to the start of the new labour union movement.

Besides, the awareness of participation in public affairs has successfully spread to the neighbourhood level. New neighbourhood-based organizations were set up, aiming to gain control of the previously overlooked arena of neighbourhood affairs;[25] some participated and triumphed in elections for the management committee of owners' corporations (for example, see the case of Richland Gardens in Kowloon Bay[26]). Apart from labour unions and neighbourhood-based organizations, religious organizations such as churches, and numerous anti-Extradition Bill concern groups in campuses were set up by university students, secondary school students and alumni were also active during the movement.

Not only has Hong Kong civil society acquired advanced skill-set through learning from past and foreign experiences, its development has also shown signs of the "submerged networks". While large-scale

---

[25] During the Anti-ELAB Movement, many homeowners realized that their owners' corporations (if present) were often monopolized by members from pro-Beijing affiliated organizations or political parties, and the operation of the owners' corporations was highly intransparent and undemocratic. The Anti-ELAB Movement magnified the long-existing management issues such as the choice of management companies (for example, some homeowners were strongly discontent of the management company for letting the police enter the housing estate without a warrant).

[26] See Apple Daily (2019); Inmedia (2020).

collective actions may not be feasible under the current circumstances, resistance has penetrated everyday life. Pro-democratic supporters look to continue accumulating social capital and building up a civic tradition through participating in different civil society organizations. This could be advantageous to decentralized mobilization in the future.

4.2 Factors Contributing to the Rise of Recent Social Movements

After overviewing the changing forms of post-1997 social movements, this section attempts to answer the question of why Hong Kong has experienced such an evolution in only 23 years from the Handover. It also recalls the *standard-definition* images we brought up for discussion at the beginning of the chapter. The second *standard-definition* image accounts for the radicalization of the youth, while the third *standard-definition* image suggests increasing intervention from Beijing is the major factor for the radicalization of social movements. The fourth *standard-definition* image focuses on realist politics behind social movements. In this section, we argue that these *standard-definition* images are inadequate in understanding the situation of Hong Kong. A comprehensive explanation needs to take into account not only local and regional factors, but also global factors and the dynamic change in the openness of the political opportunity structure.

Local and Regional Factors

One significant feature of the recent development of social movements in Hong Kong is, as some observers believe, the radicalization of the youth (for example, Kennedy et al., 2018). In fact, not only in academia, but government officials also tried to make sense of the increasingly radical strategies the younger generations tend to take in the recent years—they believe the loss of hope in upward mobility and the introduction of Liberal Studies as a core subject in the high school curriculum are the answers, such that they and pro-government political elites often draws on reforming the Liberal Studies programme and the need for improved distributive policies or social welfare policies as solutions. This, as we argue, is only an SD image to the situation.

The "Deep-Rooted Contradictions"?[27]

During the anti-Hong Kong Express Rail Link movement, Financial Secretary John Tsang suggested that Hong Kong youngsters actively participate in social movements because they saw no hope in upward mobility. In 2014, Chief Executive CY Leung took up a similar explanation for the Umbrella Movement, while the pro-Beijing camp media and supporters described the protestors as the "useless youths" (廢青 *Feiqing*) to label them as unmotivated and disruptive to the economy. During the anti-ELAB Movement, Chief Executive Carrie Lam said:

> They have no stake in the society which so many people have helped to build, and that's why they resort to all this violence and obstructions causing huge damage to the economy and to the daily life of the people. (HKSAR, 2019b)

On another occasion, she also said:

> I believe they [the Umbrella Movement and the Anti-ELAB Movement] reflect not only one incident but some fundamental and *deep-seated problems* [emphasis added] in Hong Kong. Five years ago, we finished Occupy Central, we moved on without addressing those fundamental problems. But this time, I don't think we could continue to ignore those *fundamental and deep-seated problems* [emphasis added] in Hong Kong society. I hope together with Hong Kong community we could really go deep into those fundamental issues and try to find solutions. (HKSAR, 2019a)

Furthermore, Chinese state-run media Xinhua News Agency published an article on 4 September 2019, again using the "deep-rooted contradictions" to explain the emergence of the Anti-ELAB Movement. The article blamed the skyrocketing house prices and stagnation of real income for letting the younger generation feel desperate about the future; serious social inequality and the lack of upward mobility were also mentioned as main reasons for social unrest (Wang et al., 2019).

This showed a continuity behind the government's understanding of the situation. Material conditions of the people have always been used as

---

[27] The term "deep-rooted contradictions" (深層次矛盾) being used in the official discourse can be dated back to 2005 when Wen Jiabao, Premier of the PRC, commented that Hong Kong has "deep-rooted contradictions" in society that the HKSAR government needed to tackle (BBC Chinese, 2005).

an explanation for frequent civil unrest in Hong Kong. However, the "deep-rooted contradictions" they perceived as the main cause of social movements reduced the whole phenomenon to a material problem, which could be misleading if they are looking for a solution.

Indeed, nobody could deny the increasing social structural and material contradictions in the local society. Material concerns—especially severe inequality—have at least added on to the discontent towards the SAR government. The slogan "if we burn, you burn with us," during the Anti-ELAB Movement was definitely an expression for Hong Kong protestors' desperation towards the future. After the economic miracle in the second half of the twentieth century, Hong Kong has developed into one of the wealthiest cities in the world. Similar to many other global cities, however, inequality is acute in Hong Kong. The astronomical prices of apartments are giving rise to the popularity of "coffin homes", subdivided units and other informal housing choices.

On the other hand, many scholars have used Ronald Inglehart's "post-materialism" to suggest that the new generation are generally more concerned about "post-material values" such as freedom of speech, civil rights and environmental protection, rather than material or economic interests, because they were born in wealthier society and their basic needs were more easily met (Inglehart, 1977). In Hong Kong, studies have also found that the younger generations (those born in and after the 1980s) showed a greater tendency to incline towards post-materialism (Wong & Wan, 2009; Lee, 2018b). In a poll survey done by the Hong Kong Public Opinion Research Institute (HKPORI) on the Anti-ELAB movement, respondents were asked to pick reasons leading to the youngsters' dissatisfaction. While post-material reasons such as options related to distrust of the government and pursuit of democracy and freedom were more typical (more than 65%), "housing problem" was also chosen by 58% of the respondents (HKPORI, 2019). Chiu (2019a) further stressed that over-emphasis on the so-called "deep-rooted contradictions" would lead to a distraction in finding solutions and that the government should respond to the younger generations' increasing appeal to universal values (Fung, 2020). Tackling social problems may help, but political problems must be solved with political means.

Chiu and Li (2014) summed up the situation as follows: young people dissatisfied with the government apparently were those identifying with cosmopolitan values—commonly associated with their middle-class background—rather than those being deprived of materialistic opportunities.

To begin with, we have already summarized the headline findings of studies that seek to compare mobility chances in the colonial period to the SAR era. No support was found for a picture of diminishing upward mobility, especially for the younger cohorts. But what about their subjective perception, and are the downtrodden ones in Hong Kong most eager to take part in the protests?

A HKIAPS report (2016) provided solid evidence against the materialist argument. No statistically significant relationship could be found between respondents' occupational mobility and satisfaction towards the government, support for a democratic regime, or support for specific political parties. In terms of political behaviour, no statistically significant relationship could be found between social mobility and voting behaviour or support for radical protest methods. Contrary to common-sense views, those staying at the highest service class and those achieving upward occupational mobility were significantly more likely to participate in the 2014 Umbrella Movement (HKIAPS, 2016; Hsiao & Wan, 2016).

Other than occupational mobility, however, the report (HKIAPS 2016, pp. 124–125) does found some revealing relationship between perceptions of mobility and support for the Occupy Movement. In fact, multivariate analyses suggest that those who were at the higher strata or reached the top were more likely to support the movement. Moreover, those who believed that they had upward mobility were also more supportive. Nevertheless, the HKIAPS team also pointed out respondents who felt that young people in general had sufficient opportunities for upward mobility were less supportive of the Occupy Movement. In other words, as Chiu (2019b) argued, it is not young people's own mobility experiences but their perception of youth upward mobility *in general* that motivates support for protests. Instead of instrumental motivations, it is their aspiration for social justice and equality for all young people in Hong Kong that fuels the discontents over the current regime.

Liberal Studies and the "Battle of the Generations"?

But how do the differences in values and cultural understandings contribute to the radicalization of social movements? The pro-Beijing camp suggested the subject of Liberal Studies should take the blame.

Since 2009, senior secondary education in Hong Kong has switched to a new system, in which the first HKDSE (Hong Kong Diploma of Secondary Education) public examination held in 2012 replaced the two public examinations that secondary students had to go through under the old system. The Liberal Studies subject was introduced to new examination as one of the four core subjects (together with Chinese Language, English Language and Mathematics). The subject expected students to critically assess issues in a large variety of themes including current affairs. Due to the recent social movements, some, including former Chief Executive Tung Chee Hwa, argued that the introduction of Liberal Studies was a cause for increasingly negative views among teenagers towards the government; some thought it was the teachers and the quality of teaching materials that misled the teenagers; some believed the subject has exposed teenagers to political issues prematurely (Ran, 2019). In other quarters of the establishment, Liberal Studies was also said to be under American influence.[28] On the other hand, Stephen Chiu, who participated in the design of the Liberal Studies curriculum, has examined the subject's influence on the students. In the report, Chiu et al. (2018) concluded that there was no evidence to say the subject significantly boosted the anti-establishment consciousness and political engagement of secondary school students; "critical thinking" advocated by the subject only encouraged students to discuss public issues with multiple perspectives instead of radicalizing the students.[29]

By blaming Liberal Studies, the underlying argument is to emphasize the different values upheld by the younger generations as a reason for the recent social unrests. Whether the recent social movements in Hong Kong can be seen as the younger generations against the older generations is largely debatable, as it may involve an unrealistic assumption that there is a uniform set of values and political orientation within an age group. Generally speaking, it is reasonable, however, to assume there are differences in worldviews among different generations. This kind of "battle of the generations" argument stresses how the younger generations are different from the older generations because of their life experiences in a

[28] At one point, it was alleged in pro-establishment media that the Fulbright Scholars in Hong Kong exerted influence on development of Liberal Studies, but in fact they were merely involved in the development of the Chinese University of Hong Kong's General Education (that share the same Chinese translation of Liberal Studies) programme because of its affinity to the Liberal Education tradition in the States. There was no evidence of course of any American influence on Liberal Studies.

[29] The paper was actually based on a research commissioned by the Central Policy Unit, the former government think tank. See Chiu (2016).

different era. During the anti-Express Rail Link Movement, Lui Tai Lok's *Four Generations of Hong Kong People* (2007) was frequently quoted to understand the active roles of the so-called "post-80s" (who were born in and after the 1980s) in social movements (Mok, 2010). Lui's fourth generation of Hong Kong people is similar to another widely used term of "post-80s".[30]

Irrespective of the validity of the argument that Liberal Studies was behind the rise of the generation of protest in Hong Kong, in the post-National Security Law era, the government appears to be adamant that it was responsible. In 2020, it was announced that the subject would be scraped and it was announced in the next year that it would be replaced by a new "Citizenship and Social Development" subject but with substantially reduced lesson hours and a vastly different syllabus with an emphasis on national education and "positive" values. Still, even if the younger generations generally hold a completely different set of values (such as democracy and freedom) and understanding the world from their seniors, this does not automatically result in direct actions. The political opportunity structure and the well-developed global civil society can provide a more comprehensive understanding. These two factors will be discussed later in this chapter.

The Rise of Local Identity

As mentioned in previous sections, one of the reasons why there have been increasingly radicalized protests is the tightening direct control and influence from Beijing on local policies and democratic arrangements, and that Hong Kong people feel their concerns are ignored whatever actions they take. First, after 1997 the NPC made five interpretations of the Basic Law (the mini-constitution of Hong Kong) to override judgements of Hong Kong courts. The actions were seen as political interventions in Hong Kong's legal system. Second, despite having promised in the Basic Law that universal suffrage for both Chief Executive and Legislative Council

---

[30] However, whether the recent social movements in Hong Kong can be seen as the younger generations against the older generations is largely debatable. In an interview by the South China Morning Post, both Xiaogang Wu and Brian Fong agreed that the "post-80s" should not be simplified as a uniform group of social activists (Chan, 2014b). Stephen Chiu also found that there were variations between the "post-80s", the "post-90s" and the "post-Millennials" in their confidence in authorities (Chiu, 2019c; Chiu & Ye, 2017). Moreover, onsite surveys during the Anti-ELAB Movement found that 10.1% of participants were 50 years old or above, and nearly 19% were 40 years old or above (Lee et al., 2019).

elections would be achieved, Beijing showed no sign of keeping its promise—this was exactly the direct cause of the 2014 Umbrella Movement.

Furthermore, the rise of localism and local identity has been another factor that contributes to the recent development of social movements. In the first decade of the new millennium, a wave of heritage preservation movements—the "New Preservation Movement" (Chen & Szeto, 2015)—was ignited against the government's redevelopment plans on historical sites such as the Star Ferry Pier, the Queen's Pier and Lee Tung Street. These preservation movements often drew on narratives of local identity and collective memory (Ku, 2012). To Chen and Szeto (2015), this kind of localism arose from the "New Preservation Movement" was "open localism" which attempted to rebuild local communities and was based on progressive values, in contrast to the anti-China and exclusionary localism (maybe even xenophobic) that has been more popular in recent years; but various brands of Hong Kong localism exist and that the above dichotomy is not always accurate in defining them (Lam, 2018).

As discussed in Chap. 4, the increasing social and economic integration, and then the uneasy encounters with Mainland China (including increased interactions, the influx of immigrants and tourists, cultural conflicts, etc.), have catalysed the emergence of a generally anti-China localism in recent years (Lam, 2018; Ma, 2016). In the last update of the poll on identity issues in June 2019, respondents identifying themselves purely "Chinese" have dropped to 10.8% from 34.4% at the peak in 2008 (the year when the Beijing Olympic Games and the Sichuan earthquake occurred); those identifying themselves as purely "Hongkonger" has reached a new peak at 52.9% (Public Opinion Programme, 2019). Then, there was no surprise when Hong Kong people treated Mainland China as the "others", and when they felt their rights threatened, strong reactions could be expected (see also Ma, 2017; Chan, 2014a).

Therefore, the third *standard-definition* image which used the intervention from Beijing to explain the radicalization of protests can undoubtedly provide part of the explanation. In addition, in this section and when overviewing the Umbrella Movement and the Anti-ELAB Movement, we have briefly discussed the rise of localism which is the result of the increasing social and economic integration, dissatisfaction to the traditional way of mobilizing social movement and the way democrats use institutional politics to resolve social problems. Global and institutional factors should also be added into account.

The Relevance of Global Context

As a global city, Hong Kong society cannot prevent itself from being shaped by the international situation. Geographically, Hong Kong shares its land border in its north with the Mainland, but the colonial history of the city has given it a distinctive geopolitical meaning between the East and the West. Consequently, the PRC, Western countries, and Hong Kong itself have divided agendas in the city. Recent social conflicts could partly be seen as a clash of these agendas.

Since early days of British rule, Hong Kong has been a window for foreign trade to China. During the Korean War in the 1950 (when the international trade embargo on China), and the time when China was more or less shut out of the door of international trade afterwards, Hong Kong had further secured its importance to China. More recently, the rapid development of Shanghai and Shenzhen had seemingly undermined Hong Kong's prestigious position in China's economy.

On the other hand, China's leadership is not satisfied with the nominal and practical "return" of Hong Kong, but want a "return of the will of the people" (人心回歸 *Renxinhuigui*). Wang Gungwu (1996) used "restorative nationalism" to describe Chinese nationalism, meaning under a historical narrative emphasizing China's history of being bullied by the Western countries that the mission of the CCP is to lead the country back to its glorious days (Ho, 2015). As such, Hong Kong, as a consequence of the Treaty of Nanking, was seen as a lost territory waiting for restoration. In traditional Confucianist culture, a strong empire emphasizes on its cultural superiority and recognition by the peripherals. Jiang Shigong (a legal theorist previously worked at the Hong Kong Liaison Office) suggested the "One Country, Two Systems" could be understood as the restoration of this mindset, and that Beijing should focus on winning Hong Kong people's hearts (Jiang, 2008). Beijing, then, is inclined to both to circumscribe Hong Kong's autonomy and exert its cultural influence on Hong Kong to its colonial legacies.

Needless to say, Hong Kong also has salient economic and political functions to the West, making the geopolitical environment another factor directing protests in Hong Kong. During the Cold War, British Hong Kong was China's only window to the Western world. In 1949, British Prime Minister Clement Attlee and Foreign Secretary Ernest Bevin compared Hong Kong with Berlin and called it the "Berlin of the East" for it is the frontline to observe, communicate with, and contain Communist China. Even after the end of the Cold War, Hong Kong's importance in geopolitics remains. While influence from the British fades after the Handover, the US, as a superpower economically and politically, continues to hold massive interests in Hong Kong.

Politically, since Donald Trump was elected President of the United States, the tension between the US and China has heightened. The Trump administration started the so-called "Trade War" against China in 2018. During the Anti-ELAB movement, Donald Trump and President Xi Jinping both mentioned the situation of Hong Kong in negotiations as a strategic move. Eventually, after the "Hong Kong National Security Law" was passed, Trump signed the Hong Kong Autonomy Act to end the city's preferential trade status; the US also imposed sanctions on major Hong Kong officials for playing a major role in suppressing freedom and democratic process, while Beijing condemned the US for interfering Hong Kong's internal affairs (Berger, 2020; Churchill, 2020; BBC, 2020a; Myers, 2020).

Hong Kong people have always been aware of the city's position in the world. In the early days of Hong Kong, most local elites were the comprador-merchants, who acted as "middlemen" between the colonists and the Chinese to mediate and facilitate trades (Hao, 1970). Sir Robert Ho Tung was the most celebrated example among comprador-merchants in early Hong Kong. "Both confluence and conflict characterized Hong Kong's position at *the edge of the Chinese and British empires* [emphasis added]. This combination offered certain opportunities for Chinese merchants to become an organized, self-conscious business elite," wrote Carroll (2005). In the past, this kind of "global vision" and ability to manoeuvre around China and the West, while utilizing one's privileges in cross-cultural knowledge to maximize one's interests, was arguably rather confined to the local elite class.

In recent years, however, with the help of instantaneous spreading of messages, information and ideas, ordinary citizens have developed their own kind of global visions. What happens in Hong Kong, especially since the Cold War, often comes under the spotlight in the international community. It is also true the other way around that, living in a network society, Hong Kong people are relatively well informed about the global civil society. In a split-second, information can reach the other side of the globe, with the help of the internet and social media. Hence, protests in Hong Kong can easily gain influence internationally and, simultaneously, be inspired by events in other parts of the world. In this "Age of Mass Protests" (Brannen, 2020), "repertoires of contention" (Tilly, 1978) are frequently shared around the world.

For example, the Occupy Wall Street movement in 2011 inspired the Occupy Central (2011–2012), a small-scaled but long-lasting occupation of the plaza beneath the HSBC headquarters, which in turn led to the formation of the Occupy Central with Love and Peace idea. Hong Kong protestors, at the same time, have frequently adopted and localized other "repertoires of contention" from other countries. Apart from occupying public areas, during the Umbrella Movement, protestors created their own version of the Lennon Wall at Central Government Offices, using post-it notes with written messages expressing feelings and support for the movement; during the Anti-ELAB movement, Lennon Walls were set up in every community for promotion purpose. In Taiwan, Japan, New York City, Australia and even on the Berlin Wall in Germany, people replicated the Hong Kong-style Lennon Wall to show support for the Anti-ELAB movement. Another example is the Hong Kong Way, where local protestors gathered on the streets at night to form human chains along MTR lines to call for international attention (Li, 2019). About 1000 hikers even showed up on top of the Lion Rock, turning on torches to make the outline of the iconic mountain visible in many parts of Hong Kong—"to ignite the spirit of Lion Rock in Hongkongers," said one of the Lion Rock gathering organisers (Agnew, 2019). More recently, on 23 August 2020, a human chain was formed in Tokyo, singing songs, showing banners and chanting slogans to commemorate the Hong Kong Way.

We have witnessed waves of mass protests sweeping across the globe like chain reactions, just like the Arab Spring, the Sunflower Student Movement in Taiwan, Catalan protests, the Yellow vests movement in France, and most recently the 2020 Belarusian protests and the Black Lives Matter movement. Mass protests in one place shaped, altered and inspired "repertoires of contention" in another. Protests in Hong Kong were definitely part of the whole global civil society process. In retrospect, while Hong Kong has always been standing between the East and West, the current scenarios cast this in-between position in sharper relief than ever before.

5   Conclusion: Institutional Factors, Political Opportunity Structure, and the Future of Hong Kong Social Movement

When authorities foreclose institutional means of redress, extra-institutional action appears to be the most promising route to influence. Fighting against injustice may not have a good chance of success, for example, but in a situation that is highly repressive or seems hopeless, it may be the best that activists can do. (Alimi & Meyer, 2011, p. 476)

The central government continued to hold firm to maintaining the functional constituency system, which contributed much to the influence of the pro-Beijing camp in the LegCo, and also in Chief Executive elections. Against such institutional settings, the pan-democratic parties have no hope of playing a bigger role in formal political processes against Beijing's will, not to mention becoming a ruling party. In addition to having limited influence in formal policy making processes, 6 newly elected dissident legislators were disqualified in an oath-taking controversy in 2016, while in multiple succeeding elections, some dissidents were rejected for candidacy as the government equated their demands—for greater autonomy for Hong Kong—to not recognizing the Basic Law.

In turn, pro-democracy supporters felt channels to articulate their interests and demands were extremely narrow. As McAdam et al. (1996) summed up, political opportunity structure analyses usually involve dimensions such as the "relative openness or closure of the institutionalized political system," and the "state's capacity and propensity for repression" (p. 10). Social movement theorists often found that the relative openness of the political system, meaning it is more vulnerable to changes at the same time, would be a factor encouraging the emergence of social movements. In the case of Hong Kong, being consistently underrepresented, suppressed and excluded in formal political processes, generating direct actions seemed to be "the best that activists can do", echoing Alimi and Meyer (2011, p. 476)'s words.

As Chiu and Li (2014) explained with the political opportunity curve, Hong Kong experienced a period of "expanding opportunity" before the Handover. It even came to a rather peaceful period when many activists focused on elections and other channels available for institutionalized participation, such as illustrated by path D in Fig. 10.1. However, from the above we have also showed how the political opportunity structure has been closing up and how Hong Kong people increasingly feel excluded from the institutionalized political processes, thus forcing more and more people to participate in extra-institutional politics, as following path B in Fig. 10.1.

But as we can observe and expect, Beijing's control over Hong Kong society is tighter than ever. Hong Kong now has been going down to path C ("further constricting opportunity") in Fig. 10.1. Meanwhile, analysis of the process of social movements in Hong Kong, one should look beyond the local political opportunity curve and realist politics like those originated from the Cold War era, and explore the role of global civil society in shaping, and being shaped by, these large scale mobilizations in this 'City of Protests'. This chapter alone certainly could not do justice to the tremendous transformation of social movements in the last few years. While we await for a richer and more in-depth account, we could only offer some preliminary observations.

REFERENCES

Agnew, M. (2019, August 24). Lion Rock 'Hong Kong Way' shines light on united spirit as trail runners and nature lovers spread 'hope, peace and love'. *South China Morning Post.* https://www.scmp.com/sport/outdoor/trail-running/article/3024196/lion-rock-hong-kong-way-shines-light-united-spirit

Alimi, E. Y., & Meyer, D. S. (2011). Seasons of change: Arab Spring and political opportunities. *Swiss Political Science Review, 17*(4), 475–479. https://doi.org/10.1111/j.1662-6370.2011.02041.x

Allport, F. (1924). *Social psychology.* Houghton Mifflin, The Riverside Press.

Anderlini, J. (2019, December 22). Year in a word: Be water. *Financial Times.* https://www.ft.com/content/c34b9582-1da2-11ea-97df-cc63de1d73f4

Apple Daily. (2014a, September 29). 萬人佔領 銅鑼灣 旺角 [Ten thousands of people occupied Causeway Bay and Mong Kok]. *Apple Daily.* https://hk.appledaily.com/local/20140929/KQUAS2J6GRTE53SVOB2W6BINUQ/

Apple Daily. (2014b, December 2). 戴耀廷:雨傘運動出現已替代了佔中 ["The Umbrella Movement has emerged as a replacement for Occupy Central," said Benny Tai]. *Apple Daily.* https://hk.appledaily.com/local/20141202/BL3A7KD3VISI665CERI6SPGFA4/

Apple Daily. (2019, September 14). 8.24麗晶遭克警硬闖後誓立法團 街坊團結冀光復家園 [8.24 Richland Gardens vow to set up owners' corporation after police break-in Neighbours unite to restore their homes]. *Apple Daily.* https://

hk.appledaily.com/local/20190914/H54NMDNKHBBBUNANA6
VHTF272Q/

Apple Daily. (2020, May 7). 過去1年4,328宗新工會申請僅5%獲批 團體發起聯署
轟勞處違服務承諾 [Only 5% of the 4,328 new trade union applications in the
past year have been approved, and organisations have launched a joint campaign against the Labour Department for breaching its performance pledge].
Apple Daily. https://hk.appledaily.com/local/20200507/M6CAYAUEZ7
5X6GVJYHN2OCHVWQ/

Baptista, E. (2019, November 29). Hong Kong demonstrators look to Korea for
inspiration. *Nikkei Asia*. https://asia.nikkei.com/Spotlight/Hong-Kong-
protests/Hong-Kong-demonstrators-look-to-Korea-for-inspiration2

BBC. (2015, March 2). Hong Kong arrests after protest against mainland tourists.
BBC. https://www.bbc.com/news/world-asia-china-31689188

BBC. (2019, June 17). Hong Kong protest: 'Nearly two million' join demonstration. *BBC*. https://www.bbc.com/news/world-asia-china-48656471

BBC. (2020a, May 30). Trump targets China over Hong Kong security law.
BBC. https://www.bbc.com/news/world-us-canada-52856876

BBC. (2020b, September 4). Mulan: Why Disney's latest reboot is facing boycott
calls. *BBC*. https://www.bbc.com/news/newsbeat-54024810

BBC Chinese. (2005, December 28). 溫家寶:香港仍有深層次矛盾未解決 [Wen
Jiabao: Hong Kong still has deep-rooted contradictions to be solved]. *BBC
Chinese*. http://news.bbc.co.uk/chinese/trad/hi/newsid_4560000/new-
sid_4563400/4563430.stm

Beech, H. (2020, January 19). Yellow or blue? In Hong Kong, businesses choose
political sides. *The New York Times*. https://www.nytimes.com/2020/01/19/
world/asia/hong-kong-protests-yellow-blue.html

Berger, M. (2020, August 9). The U.S. sanctions against Hong Kong officials,
explained. *The Washington Post*. https://www.washingtonpost.com/
world/2020/08/08/faq-us-sanctions-hong-kong-officials/

Bickers, R., & Yep, R. (2009). *May days in Hong Kong: Riot and emergency in
1967* (Vol. 1). Hong Kong University Press.

Brannen, S. (2020). *The age of mass protests: Understanding an escalating global
trend*. Center for Strategic and International Studies. https://www.csis.org/
analysis/age-mass-protests-understanding-escalating-global-trend

Carroll, J. M. (2005). *Edge of empires: Chinese elites and British colonials in Hong
Kong*. Harvard University Press.

Centre for Communication and Public Opinion Survey [CCPOS]. (2014,
December 18). Public opinion & political development in Hong Kong: Survey
results [Press Release]. http://www.com.cuhk.edu.hk/ccpos/images/news/
TaskForce_PressRelease_141218_English.pdf

Chan, C. K. (2014a). China as "other": Resistance to and ambivalence toward
national identity in Hong Kong. *China Perspectives, 2014*(1), 25–34.

Chan, K. M. (2005). Civil society and the democracy movement in Hong Kong: Mass mobilization with limited organizational capacity. *Korea Observer, 36*(1), 167.

Chan, S. (2014b, July 14). Rebels with a cause: How the 'post-80s' generation is rejecting old ways of protest in Hong Kong. *South China Morning Post.* https://www.scmp.com/news/hong-kong/article/1553471/post-1980s-generation-radicalises-hong-kongs-protest-movement

Chan, S., & Tsang, E. (2015, March 1). Hong Kong protest sees violence, pepper spray and arrests, but triads stay away. *South China Morning Post.* https://www.scmp.com/news/hong-kong/article/1726912/scuffles-break-out-over-mainland-traders-yeun-long

Chen, Y. C., & Szeto, M. M. (2015). The forgotten road of progressive localism: New Preservation Movement in Hong Kong. *Inter-Asia Cultural Studies, 16*(3), 436–453.

Cheng, E. W., & Chan, W. Y. (2017). Explaining spontaneous occupation: Antecedents, contingencies and spaces in the Umbrella Movement. *Social Movement Studies, 16*(2), 222–239.

Cheung, A. B., & Louie, K. S. (1991). *Social conflicts in Hong Kong: 1975–1986 trends and implications.* Hong Kong Institute of Asia-Pacific Studies, CUHK.

Cheung, G. K. (2009). *Hong Kong's watershed: The 1967 riots* (Vol. 1). Hong Kong University Press.

Chiu, S. W. (2016). *A Study on Civic Values and Engagement of 'Post-90s' in Hong Kong.* Hong Kong: Public Policy Research Centre, Hong Kong Institute of Asia-Pacific Studies, The Chinese University of Hong Kong.

Chiu, S. W. (2019a, December 12). 「檢討深層次矛盾」不提政治無助解困 [Not mentioning politics, "reflect on deep-rooted contradictions" is not cure to the situation]. *Mingpao.* https://news.mingpao.com/ins/%E6%96%87%E6%91%98/article/20191202/s00022/1575208908831

Chiu, S. W. (2019b, July 10). 青年問題真的那麼難懂嗎 [Are youth issues really that difficult to understand?]. *Mingpao.* https://news.mingpao.com/ins/文摘/article/20190710/s00022/1562754678964/青年問題真的那麼難懂嗎(文-趙永佳)

Chiu, S. W. (2019c, September 13). 「千禧後」世代非隨便支持勇武 [The "post-Millennials" are not casually supporting the valiant]. *Mingpao.* https://news.mingpao.com/ins/%E6%96%87%E6%91%98/article/20190913/s00022/1568293367573

Chiu, S. W., & Li, H. (2014). *Contentious politics in two villages: Anti-high-speed-rail campaigns in Hong Kong and Taiwan.* Hong Kong Institute of Asia-Pacific Studies, The Chinese University of Hong Kong.

Chiu, S. W., & Ye, J. H. (2017, November 13). 傘運世代效應 年長者也政治覺醒 [The generational effects of the Umbrella Movement: The older age groups are also politically awaken]. *Mingpao.* https://news.mingpao.com/pns/%e8%a 7%80%e9%bb%9e/article/20171113/s00012/1510509400911

Chiu, S. W., Yuen, J. K., & Leung, Y. K. (2018). How liberal studies influences HK secondary school students? *Hong Kong and Macau Journal, 2018*(1), 63–73.

Chong, H. T. (2019, April 10). 「串謀犯公眾妨擾」罪成 官:三子2013年逐漸形 成犯罪 宣布佔中時已想到放催淚彈 ["Conspiracy to commit public nuisance" found guilty—"The Trio started to commit crimes in 2013, and when they announced that they were occupying Central, they thought of facing tear gas," said the judge]. *Citizen News.* https://www.hkcnews.com/article/19733/佔 中三子-陳仲衡-佔中審訊-19733/【九子案判詞】「串謀犯公眾妨擾」 罪成-官:三子2013年逐漸形成犯罪-宣布佔中時已想到放催淚彈

Chu, L., & Blundy, R. (2016 February 9). In pictures: Mong Kok hawker protest turns violent on first night of Lunar New Year. *South China Morning Post.* https://www.scmp.com/news/hong-kong/law-crime/article/1910852/ pictures-mong-kok-hawker-protest-turns-violent-first-night

Chung, Y. W. (2015, September 19). 羅就訪談:代議政制攆走居民運動 [An inter-view with Law Chau: The representative political system kicked out the resident movements]. *The Initium.* https://theinitium.com/article/20150920-opinion-residence-movement-council-law/

Churchill, O. (2020, July 15). US President Donald Trump signs Hong Kong Autonomy Act, and ends the city's preferential trade status. *South China Morning Post.* https://www.scmp.com/news/world/united-states-canada/ article/3093200/donald-trump-signs-hong-kong-autonomy-act-and-ends

Deng, Z. (1957). 中國職工運動簡史 *[A brief history of the Chinese labour move-ment].* People's Publishing House.

Eisinger, P. K. (1973). The conditions of protest behavior in American cities. *The American Political Science Review, 67*(1), 11–28.

Fong, B. (2014, August 28). 一個時代的終結 [The end of an era]. *Inmedia.* https://www.inmediahk.net/node/1025635

Fung, L. L. (2020, January 3). 研反高鐵傘運 斥一直逃避「政治才是深層次矛 盾」 趙永佳:政府勿阻市民參與制度 [Studying on the Anti-Speed Rail Movement and the Umbrella Movement, "politics is the deep-rooted contra-diction," Stephen Chiu asked the government not to block public participation in the system]. *Mingpao.* https://news.mingpao.com/pns/%e6%b8 %af%e8%81%9e/article/20200103/s00002/1577990343315

Gamson, W. A. (1992). *Talking politics.* Cambridge University Press.

Garrett, R. K. (2009). Echo chambers online?: Politically motivated selective exposure among Internet news users. *Journal of Computer-Mediated Communication, 14*(2), 265–285.

Hao, Y. P. (1970). A new class in China's treaty ports: The rise of the comprador-merchants. *The Business History Review, 44*(4), 446–460.

HKSAR. (2019a, July 9). *Transcript of remarks by CE at media session before ExCo meeting (with video)*. Press Releases, The Government of the HKSAR. https://www.info.gov.hk/gia/general/201907/09/P2019070900608.htm

HKSAR. (2019b, August 9). *Transcript of remarks by CE at media session (with video)*. Press Releases, The Government of the HKSAR. https://www.info.gov.hk/gia/general/201908/09/P2019080900869.htm

Ho, J. (2015, September 23). 何以人心不「回歸」? [Why there is no "reunion of the will of the people"?]. *Master-Insight*. https://www.master-insight.com/何以人心不「回歸」?/

Ho, P. C. (2004, October 13). 立法會二題:《心繫家國》宣傳短片 [LegCo question no. 2: "Our Home, Our Country" promotion video]. Press Releases, The Government of the HKSAR. https://www.info.gov.hk/gia/general/200410/13/1013175.htm

Hong Kong Institute of Asia-Pacific Studies [HKIAPS] (2016). Impact of Social Mobility on the Political Attitudes and Behaviours of Young People: A Comparative Study of Hong Kong, Taiwan, and Macao [2015.A4.011.15C]. Retrieved from https://www.pico.gov.hk/doc/en/research_report(PDF)/2015_A4_011_15C_Final_Report_Dr_Zheng.pdf

Hong Kong Memory. (n.d.). Who were the famous persons in Victoria Prison? *Hong Kong Memory*. http://www.hkmemory.org/central-police/text/prison-q5-eng.php

Hong Kong Public Opinion Research Institute. (2019). *Opinion survey on the "extradition bill"—Survey results*. Research Reports, Hong Kong Public Opinion Research Institute. https://static1.squarespace.com/static/5cfd1ba6a7117c000170d7aa/t/5d5a081034ee48000 18f491f/1566181400708/pcf_anti_extradition_ppt_english_v2_pori.pdf

Hsiao, M. H., & Wan, P. S. (2016). 2014 學生運動與民意: 台灣與香港的比較 [2014 Student Movement and Public Opinion: Comparing Taiwan and Hong Kong]. In M. H. Hsiao, S. W. Chiu, & P. S. Wan (Eds.), *Youth and Social Change in Taiwan and Hong Kong* (pp. 119–162). Hong Kong: Hong Kong Institute of Asia-Pacific Studies, The Chinese University of Hong Kong.

i-Cable News. (2014, September 28). 【現場反應】【有支持啟動佔中 亦有感被騎劫】 [*"Reaction at the scene": "Some support the activation of the occupation, but also feel hijacked"*]. https://www.facebook.com/186040714921338/videos/303575183167890/

Inglehart, R. (1977). *The silent revolution: Changing values and political styles among Western publics*. Princeton University Press.

Inmedia. (2020, August 17). 麗晶居民踢走民建聯業委 居港新加坡參選人:我始終會離開, 但這是我的責任 [Richland Gardens residents kick out DAB member from the owners' committee Singaporean candidate: I'll leave after all, but this is my responsibility]. *Inmedia*. https://www.inmediahk.net/node/1076511

Jenkins, N., & Iyengar, R. (2016, February 9). Hong Kong sees violent start to Chinese new year as protesters clash with police. *Time*. https://time. com/4213191/hong-kong-riot-protest/

Jiang, S. (2008). 中國香港—文化與政治的視野 *[China's Hong Kong: A political and cultural perspective]*. Oxford University Press (China).

Kennedy, K. J., Li, L. J., & Ng, H. Y. (2018). *Youth radicalism in Hong Kong: Exploring changes in adolescents' civic consciousness and attitudes to the nation [2015.A5.019.16B]*. Public Policy Research.

King, A. Y. (1975). Administrative absorption of politics in Hong Kong: Emphasis on the grass roots level. *Asian Survey, 15*(5), 422–439.

Kow, Y. M., Nardi, B., & Cheng, W. K. (2020, April). Be water: Technologies in the leaderless Anti-ELAB Movement in Hong Kong. In *Proceedings of the 2020 CHI Conference on Human Factors in Computing Systems* (pp. 1–12).

Ku, A. (2020). New forms of youth activism–Hong Kong's Anti-Extradition Bill Movement in the local-national-global nexus. *Space and Polity, 24*(1), 111–117.

Ku, A. S. (2012). Remaking places and fashioning an opposition discourse: Struggle over the Star Ferry pier and the Queen's pier in Hong Kong. *Environment and Planning D: Society and Space, 30*(1), 5–22.

Kuan, H. C. (1979). Political stability and change in Hong Kong. In T. B. Lin, R. P. Lee, & U. Simonis (Eds.), *Hong Kong: Economic, social and political studies in development*. M.E. Sharpe.

Kwantailo [阿群帶路]. (2013, March 2). 香港故事:《香港第一次罷工》 [Hong Kong story: The first strike in Hong Kong]. *Kwantailo*. https://kwantailo. wordpress.com/2013/03/02/香港故事:《香港第一次罷工》/

Lam, J. (2020, June 14). Hong Kong protests: Why trade unions have mushroomed as demonstrators push for workers' rights. *South China Morning Post*. https://www.scmp.com/news/hong-kong/politics/article/3088938/hong-kong-protests-why-trade-unions-have-mushroomed

Lam, W. M. (2018). Hong Kong's fragmented soul: Exploring brands of localism. In W. M. Lam & L. Cooper (Eds.), *Citizenship, identity and social movements in the New Hong Kong: Localism after the Umbrella Movement* (pp. 72–93). Routledge.

Law, W. S. (2018). 身份政治往何處去 [Where to go with identity politics]. In E. W. Cheng & S. W. Yuen (Eds.), 社運年代:香港抗爭政治的軌跡 *[An epoch of social movements: The trajectory of contentious politics in Hong Kong]* (pp. 19–36). The Chinese University of Hong Kong Press.

LeBon, G. (1896). *The crowd: A study of the popular mind*. Cherokee Publishing Company.

Lee, A. Y., & Ting, K. W. (2015). Media and information praxis of young activists in the Umbrella Movement. *Chinese Journal of Communication, 8*(4), 376–392.

Lee, D. (2016, February 14). 'The Siege of Wan Chai': How a WTO protest descended into a riot. *South China Morning Post*. https://www.scmp.com/

news/hong-kong/law-crime/article/1912829/siege-wan-chai-how-wto-protest-descended-riot

Lee, F. L. (2018a). Internet alternative media, movement experience, and radicalism: The case of post-Umbrella Movement Hong Kong. *Social Movement Studies, 17*(2), 219–233.

Lee, F. L. (2018b). The role of perceived social reality in the adoption of postmaterial values: The case of Hong Kong. *The Social Science Journal, 55*(2), 139–148.

Lee, F. L. (2020a). Solidarity in the anti-extradition bill movement in Hong Kong. *Critical Asian Studies, 52*(1), 18–32.

Lee, F. L., & Chan, J. M. (2011). Media, social mobilization, and the pro-democracy protest movement in post-handover Hong Kong: The power of a critical event.

Lee, F. L., Chen, H. T., & Chan, M. (2017). Social media use and university students' participation in a large-scale protest campaign: The case of Hong Kong's Umbrella Movement. *Telematics and Informatics, 34*(2), 457–469.

Lee, F. L., Yuen, S., Tang, G., & Cheng, E. W. (2019). Hong Kong's summer of uprising. *The China Review, 19*(4), 1–32.

Lee, P. S., So, C. Y., & Leung, L. (2015). Social media and Umbrella Movement: Insurgent public sphere in formation. *Chinese Journal of Communication, 8*(4), 356–375.

Legislative Council/Research Office. (2014). Individual visit scheme (RB06/13-14). *Legislative Council.* https://www.legco.gov.hk/research-publications/english/1314rb06-individual-visit-scheme-20140507-e.pdf

Leung, B. K. (1996). *Perspectives on Hong Kong society.* Oxford University Press.

Leung, D. K., & Lee, F. L. (2014). Cultivating an active online counterpublic: Examining usage and political impact of Internet alternative media. *The International Journal of Press/Politics, 19*(3), 340–359.

Leung, P. L. (2017, March 7). 十九世紀香港妹仔解放運動 [Anti-Mui Zhai Movement in the nineteenth century]. *WKNews.* https://wknews.org/node/1385

Leung, P. S. (2014, November 13). 相比金鐘, 其實我更愛旺角的真實 [I love the authenticity of Mongkok more than Admiralty]. *Inmedia.* https://www.inmediahk.net/node/1029022

Li, H. (2013). *Contentious politics in two villages: Comparative analysis of anti-high-speed-rail campaigns in Hong Kong and Taiwan.* Doctoral dissertation, The Chinese University of Hong Kong.

Li, S. L. (2019, August 27). The 'Hong Kong Way': How over 200,000 strangers joined hands and became fellow travellers on the road to freedom. *South China Morning Post.* https://www.scmp.com/comment/letters/article/3024369/hong-kong-way-how-over-200000-strangers-joined-hands-and-became

Li, X. X., Tam, H. W., Yeung, K. L., Yip, T. W., & So, C. Y. K. (2015, January 21). The role of social news media in the Occupy Movement. *Media Digest*. http:// app3.rthk.hk/mediadigest/content.php?aid=1990. [In Chinese].

Liu, M. H. (2014, November 26). 隨筆:佔領旺角的回憶與反思 [Essay: Memories and reflections on occupy Mongkok]. *BBC*. https://www.bbc.com/zhongwen/trad/china/2014/11/141126_hk_mongkok_life

Lui, F. T. (2020, January 10). 雷射針—這樣的經濟圈易被擊潰 [Such an economic circle is vulnerable]. *Headline Daily*. https://hd.stheadline.com/news/ columns/849/20200110/826149/專欄-雷射針-這樣的經濟圈易被擊潰

Lui, T. L. (2003). Rearguard politics: Hong Kong's middle class. *The Developing Economies, 41*(2), 161–183.

Lui, T. L. (2007). 四代香港人 *[Four generations of Hong Kong people]*. Step Forward Multi Media Company Limited.

Lui, T. L., & Chiu, S. W. (1997). The structuring of social movements in contemporary Hong Kong. *China Information, 12*(1–2), 97–113.

Ma, N. (2005). Civil society in self-defense: The struggle against national security legislation in Hong Kong. *Journal of Contemporary China, 14*(44), 465–482.

Ma, N. (2012). 香港80年代民主運動口述歷史 *[An oral history of democratic movement of Hong Kong in the 1980s]*. City University of Hong Kong Press.

Ma, N. (2016). The making of a corporatist state in Hong Kong: The road to sectoral intervention. *Journal of Contemporary Asia, 46*(2), 247–266.

Ma, N. (2017). Changing identity politics: The democracy movement in Hong Kong. In W. M. Lam & L. Cooper (Eds.), *Citizenship, identity and social movements in the New Hong Kong* (pp. 34–50). Routledge.

Ma, W. K., Lau, H. C., & Hui, Y. H. (2014, September 12). 2014 news and social media use survey. *Media Digest, RTHK*. http://app3.rthk.hk/mediadigest/ content.php?aid=1960. [In Chinese].

McAdam, D. (1982). *Political process and the development of black insurgency, 1930–1970*. University of Chicago Press.

McAdam, D., McCarthy, J. D., & Zald, M. N. (1996). Introduction: Opportunities, mobilizing structures, and framing processes – Toward a synthetic, comparative perspective on social movements. In D. McAdam, J. D. McCarthy, & M. N. Zald (Eds.), *Comparative perspectives on social movements: Political opportunities, mobilizing structures, and cultural framings* (pp. 1–20). Cambridge University Press.

McCarthy, J. D., & Zald, M. N. (1977). Resource mobilization and social movements: A partial theory. *American Journal of Sociology, 82*(6), 1212–1241.

Melucci, A. (1980). The new social movements: A theoretical approach. *Information (International Social Science Council), 19*(2), 199–226.

Melucci, A. (1985). The symbolic challenge of contemporary movements. *Social Research, 52*, 789–816.

Meyer, D. S. (2004). Protest and political opportunities. *Annual Review of Sociology, 30*, 125–145.

Miller, N., & Dollard, J. (1941). *Social learning and imitation.* Yale University Press.

Mo, S. (2011). 中山革命在香港 *(1895–1925) [Sun Yat-sen revolution in Hong Kong (1895–1925)]*. Joint Publishing (Hong Kong).

Mok, D. (2010, January 17). Scholar of generation gaps looks past the post-80s. *South China Morning Post.* https://www.scmp.com/article/703936/scholar-generation-gaps-looks-past-post-80s

Molloy, A. (2014, September 30). Hong Kong protests in pictures: The 'Umbrella Revolution'. *The Independent.* https://www.independent.co.uk/news/world/asia/hong-kong-protests-pictures-umbrella-revolution-9761617.html

Myers, S. L. (2020, August 12). China vows to retaliate after Trump signs Hong Kong sanctions bill. *The New York Times.* https://www.nytimes.com/2020/07/15/world/asia/china-trump-hong-kong.html

Now News. (2019, July 1). 【衝擊立會大樓】泛民多名議員圖勸阻無效 [Storming the LegCo building: Pan-democratic lawmakers failed to dissuade the protestors]. *Now News.* https://news.now.com/home/local/player?newsId=353786

Pang, J. (2020, May 1). Business booms for 'yellow' firms backing Hong Kong protest movement. *Reuters.* https://www.reuters.com/article/us-hongkong-protests-mayday/business-booms-for-yellow-firms-backing-hong-kong-protest-movement-idUSKBN22D577

Prasso, S. (2020, May 20). Hong Kong's businesses show their pro-democracy colors. *Bloomberg Businessweek.* https://www.bloomberg.com/news/features/2020-05-20/hong-kong-protesters-helped-local-businesses-survive-coronavirus

Public Opinion Programme, The University of Hong Kong. (2019). National issues. People's ethnic identity. Retrieved September 20, 2020, from https://www.hkupop.hku.hk/english/popexpress/ethnic/eidentity/poll/datatables.html

Ran, R. (2019, October 31). 香港通識課:被中國官媒批評的必修科「教壞」年輕人? [Hong Kong Liberal Studies: A compulsory subject criticised by Chinese official media for having bad influence on young people?]. *BBC Chinese.* https://www.bbc.com/zhongwen/trad/chinese-news-50216924

SCMP Reporters. (2019, June 16). As it happened: A historic day in Hong Kong concludes peacefully as organisers claim almost 2 million people came out in protest against the fugitive bill. *South China Morning Post.* https://www.scmp.com/news/hong-kong/politics/article/3014695/sea-black-hong-kong-will-march-against-suspended

Scott, I. (2017). Bridging the gap: Hong Kong senior civil servants and the 1966 riots. *The Journal of Imperial and Commonwealth History, 45*(1), 131–148.

Shen, F., Xia, C., & Skoric, M. (2020). Examining the roles of social media and alternative media in social movement participation: A study of Hong Kong's Umbrella Movement. *Telematics and Informatics, 47*, 101303.

Siu, P., Low, Z., & Lam, J. (2019, July 14). Pitched battles on Hong Kong streets and inside shopping malls as police move to clear extradition bill protesters after stand-off. *South China Morning Post.* https://www.scmp.com/news/hong-kong/politics/article/3018531/thousands-gather-hong-kong-park-latest-rally-against

Smelser, N. J. (1962). *Theory of collective behavior.* Free Press.

So, A. Y. (1999). *Hong Kong's embattled democracy: A societal analysis.*

So, A. Y. (2011). The development of post-modernist social movements in the Hong Kong Special Administrative Region. In J. Broadbent & V. Brockman (Eds.), *East Asian social movements* (pp. 365–378). Springer.

So, C. Y., & Chan, J. S. (2003, July 15). 如何統計「七一大遊行」人數 [How to count the number of participants in the "July 1 rally"]. *Media Digest, RTHK.* https://app3.rthk.hk/mediadigest/content.php?aid=185

Sung, Y. W., Ng, A. C., Wu, Y., & Yiu, A. W. (2015). *The economic benefits of mainland tourists for Hong Kong: The individual visit scheme (IVS) and multiple entry individual visit endorsements (M-Permit).* Shanghai-Hong Kong Development Institute, Occasional Paper, (34).

Takungpao. (2019, December 31). 「黃色經濟圈」激化撕裂 [The 'yellow economic circle' intensifies the tear]. *Takungpao.* http://www.takungpao.com.hk/news/232109/2019/1231/398168.html

Tang, G. (2015). Mobilization by images: TV screen and mediated instant grievances in the Umbrella Movement. *Chinese Journal of Communication, 8*(4), 338–355.

Tang, G., & Lee, F. L. (2013). Facebook use and political participation: The impact of exposure to shared political information, connections with public political actors, and network structural heterogeneity. *Social Science Computer Review, 31*(6), 763–773.

Tarrow, S. G. (1983). *Struggling to reform: Social movements and policy change during cycles of protest* (Vol. 15). Center for International Studies, Cornell University.

Tarrow, S. G. (1989). *Struggle, politics, and reform: Collective action, social movements and cycles of protest* (Vol. 21). Center for International Studies, Cornell University.

The Guardian. (2005, December 13). WTO protesters clash with riot police. *The Guardian.* https://www.theguardian.com/world/2005/dec/13/wto.development

The New York Times. (2014, October 5). Images of Hong Kong's Umbrella revolution. *The New York Times.* https://www.nytimes.com/interactive/2014/10/01/world/asia/hong-kong-protest-photos.html

Tilly, C. (1978). *From mobilization to revolution.* McGraw-Hill.

Touraine, A. (1981). *The voice and the eye: An analysis of social movements.* Cambridge University Press.

Tsai, Y. (2004). *The Hong Kong people's history of Hong Kong 1841–1945* 香港人之香港史 *1841–1945.* Oxford University Press (China).

Tsang, S. Y. (2004). *A modern history of Hong Kong.* Hong Kong University Press.

Turner, R. H., & Killian, L. M. (1957). *Collective behavior.* Prentice-Hall.

Wang, G. (1996). *The revival of Chinese nationalism* (Lecture Series Vol. 6). International Institute for Asian Studies, International Institute for Asian Studies.

Wang, X., Fang, D., & Zhu, Y. (2019). 沉重的底色与扭曲的方向—香港修例风波背后的一些社会深层根源 [Heavy undertones and distorted directions: Some deep-rooted social roots behind Hong Kong's Fugitive Offenders amendment bill controversy]. *Xinhua News.* http://www.xinhuanet.com/gangao/2019-09/04/c_1124961699.htm

Wong, J. (2019a, December). *Protests decentralised: How technology enabled civil disobedience by Hong Kong anti-extradition bill protesters* [Paper presentation]. 8th Asian Privacy Scholars Network Conference Paper 2020, Singapore. https://doi.org/10.31228/osf.io/efvwn

Wong, K. T., Zheng, V., & Wan, P. S. (2016). The impact of cross-border integration with Mainland China on Hong Kong's local politics: The individual visit scheme as a double-edged sword for political trust in Hong Kong. *The China Quarterly, 228,* 1081–1104.

Wong, K. Y., & Wan, P. S. (2009). New evidence of the postmaterialist shift: The experience of Hong Kong. *Social Indicators Research, 92*(3), 497–515.

Wong, T. (2019b, August 20). Hong Kong protests: What are the 'five demands'? What do protesters want? *Young Post.* https://www.scmp.com/yp/discover/news/hong-kong/article/3065950/hong-kong-protests-what-are-five-demands-what-do

Wu, X. (2010). *Hong Kong's post-80s generation: Profiles and predicaments.* The Centre for Applied Social and Economic Research, Hong Kong University of Science and Technology.

Yeung, W. (2005, December 17). Anti-WTO protests intensify. *South China Morning Post.* https://www.scmp.com/article/529722/anti-wto-protests-intensify

Yu, S., & Liu, S. (1995). 二十世紀的香港 *[Hong Kong in the 20th century].* Unicorn Books.

Yuen, S. (2018). Contesting middle-class civility: Place-based collective identity in Hong Kong's Occupy Mongkok. *Social Movement Studies, 17*(4), 393–407.

Yuen, S. (2019). Transgressive politics in occupy Mongkok. In *Take back our future: An eventful sociology of the Hong Kong Umbrella Movement* (pp. 52–73). Cornell University Press.

Yuen, S., & Cheng, E. W. (2017). Neither repression nor concession? A regime's attrition against mass protests. *Political Studies, 65*(3), 611–630.

Zhang, J. (2010). 20世紀初粵港政局之互動 [Interaction between the political situation in Guangdong and Hong Kong in the early 20th century]. In M. Chan & M. Nyaw (Eds.), 嶺南近代史論—廣東與粵港關係 *1900–1938 [A theory of modern Lingnan history – Guangdong and Hong Kong-Guangdong relations 1900–1938]*. The Commercial Press (Hong Kong).

Zhou, C. (2019, December 16). 「黃色經濟圈」是經濟「港獨」 [The "Yellow Economic Circle" is a call for economic "independence of Hong Kong"]. *Takungpao.* http://www.takungpao.com.hk/opinion/233119/2019/1216/391427.html

Zhou, Y. (2013). 香港工運史簡篇 *[The history of Hong Kong labour movement]*. Nice News Publishing.

CHAPTER 11

Postscript

The first draft of this book was completed in early 2019. While we were going through it and making the final touches, a monumental protest movement broke out in the summer initially against the proposed amendment of the Extradition Bill allowing fugitives to be extradited back to the Mainland, among other places. After three months of increasingly violent conflict between police and protesters, Hong Kong Chief Executive Carrie Lam finally announced on 4th September that she would formally withdraw the controversial bill. Opposition to the bill triggered massive protests in June that morphed into a broader protest movement against the government in Hong Kong and authorities in Beijing, calling ultimately for greater democratic freedoms in this semi-autonomous region of China. Contrary to the expectations of more hopeful observers, Lam's "concession" has done little to cool down tensions within Hong Kong society.

Almost nightly, in different streets, neighbourhoods, housing estates and subway stations, violent conflicts between police and protesters continue, and police are escalating their use of force against protestors and even ordinary citizens and journalists. Since the start of the new academic year in September, the social movement has spread into secondary schools and universities, with many students participating in class boycotts, holding hands inside and outside schools and universities to express their sentiments towards alleged police brutality and the government's unresponsiveness over the past three months.

Some parts of this postscript previously appeared in Siu (2019). We are grateful for the permission of *Global Asia* to use materials here.

387

The international community, meanwhile, has begun to express its concern with the increasingly forceful crackdown against protesters. Notably, the US Congress has already passed the "Hong Kong Human Rights and Democracy Act." The bill requires the secretary of state to report annually to Congress on whether Hong Kong is following the Sino-British Joint Declaration, the Hong Kong Basic Law (the city's mini-constitution), and the United Nations Covenant on Civil and Political Rights, in order to adequately protect Hong Kong's autonomy, human rights and democracy. The report must also evaluate whether any Hong Kong government officials should be penalized if their actions violate human rights in Hong Kong.

The rapid deterioration of the situation in the city over the past three months has not only stunned the people of Hong Kong, it has also puzzled the international community (the mainland Chinese government included). Why would a proposed extradition bill set off a massive social movement in Hong Kong? What do the protesters' various demands reveal about Hong Kong's current state-market-civil society relations? More important, what are the implications of the city-wide movement for the world in the context of an increasingly powerful and authoritarian China?

1   THE IDEA OF FREEDOM AS A FUNDAMENTAL SOCIAL VALUE

If we carefully examine the successive waves of mass movements in Hong Kong since 1997—the year of the British handover of Hong Kong to China—it is not hard to discover that almost all of these movements are tightly connected with one of the most fundamental social values in Hong Kong—freedom. That connection has its origins in Hong Kong's postwar history and the development of a Hong Kong identity.

Hong Kong is a society of migrants. Since the end of the Second World War, Hong Kong had been a place that received and settled various types of refugees from war and political disturbances in Mainland China. For these refugees, Hong Kong was a place where they could be shielded from political turmoil and preserve their individual freedoms. To the older generation of Hong Kong people today, these individual freedoms usually mean economic freedom (the ability to choose one's own job and seek to make a decent living), not political freedom. Nevertheless, the aspiration to exercise individual freedom and to be protected from political constraints has been rooted in Hong Kong society since colonial times. As we documented in earlier chapters, the "legacies" that Hong Kong inherited from the colonial times, while are limited in many ways, carry with them a powerful ideological force in framing the protests.

It can be said that Hong Kong society had to wait until the 1960s to experience fundamental change. Demographically, a generation of locally born postwar baby boomers grew up and became the middle class of Hong Kong society. This generation not only inherited the vision of Hong Kong as a "city of freedom" from their predecessors, but compared to their parents, they identified themselves strongly with a distinctive local identity (Hongkonger). To a great extent, as we argued this Hongkonger identity was constructed in relation to the "Mainland Chinese" identity. Understanding these historical details is crucial to making sense of Hong Kong's current situation, especially how the protest movement could bring out onto the streets different generations, mobilizing between one and two million people in successive protests early on. Based on the city's tradition of aspiring to and exercising individual freedom, as well as the construction of a Hongkonger identity, Hong Kong's civil society and social movements started to develop in the 1960s and 1970s. The Sino-British negotiations on the handover of Hong Kong in 1997 began in the early 1980s and resulted in the Sino-British Joint Declaration in 1984, five years before the tragic Tiananmen Square incident in 1989. There was then a period of rapid political reforms in Hong Kong in the final transition period leading up to 1997 that not only turned democracy into one of the key social-development indicators in Hong Kong society, but also consolidated the view among Hong Kong people that the city is a place where individual freedom is guaranteed (in contrast to China as an authoritarian polity).

In its post-handover era, especially after 2003, Hong Kong experienced another drastic social and political transformation. In 2003, the Hong Kong government tabled a controversial national security bill (called for under Article 23 of the Basic Law), thus making Hong Kong citizens feel that their individual rights and freedoms were being severely threatened. Large protests over the bill at the time eventually led the government to back down. In 2012, the Hong Kong government initiated another controversial move for the patriotic curriculum (the so-called civic and national education curriculum) in secondary schools. As a result, it turned secondary schools into a site of political struggles, and incited worries among students, teachers and parents that freedom of speech would be restrained.

At the same time, since 2009, a new subject, Liberal Studies, was introduced into the secondary school curriculum, encouraging Hong Kong
students to use multiple and critical perspectives to understand Hong
Kong and Mainland Chinese social and political affairs. All these social and
political events not only rapidly politicized Hong Kong society down to
the level of schools and families, but also developed another more radical
local identity to resist the increasingly strong and authoritarian
Chinese state.

Then, in 2014 came the so-called Umbrella Movement—a widespread
social protest movement lasting almost 80 days that called for greater
democratic rights. Its far-reaching impacts have been vivid in the sense
that it not only turned social movements into an "everyday affair" in
Hong Kong society, but also enabled youngsters in Hong Kong to learn
using social movements as a means of political struggle by occupying
streets and joining class boycotts. As such, it can be said that the city-wide
protest movement that has gripped Hong Kong over the past months has
its roots in Hong Kong's colonial and post-colonial history and the construction of a local identity. In short, the government's extradition bill
contained all the elements that could touch the political nerves of Hong
Kong people, thus becoming the fuse that set off the current protest
movement.

2   Rapidly Changing Relations Among State, Market and Society

Ever since the outbreak of social movements with much youth participation since the Anti-Express Rail Movement and all the way to the events
in 2019, the establishment has been attributing their causes to a number
of "deep-rooted contradictions" including housing, social mobility and
education afflicting young people. As we discussed in earlier chapters,
while such senses of malaise may not be the direct causes of the widespread
and committed involvement of so many young people to protests, they are
indeed symptoms of genuine problems in the Special Administrative
Region and widely felt among young people. Then, what does the predicaments of Hong Kong today reveal about the city's state-market-civil
society relations?

First, regarding state-society relations, as we discussed in Chapter 1,
several "pillars" of Hong Kong society (freedom of speech, the rule of law

and clean government) that developed in the colonial era have been seriously challenged. Since 21 July 2019, when local gangsters brutally beat protesters and ordinary passengers in the Yuen Long subway station, the Hong Kong police force has been widely blamed for failing to respond and handle those involved in a timely manner. After that, with the police showing more irregularities in enforcement and abandon certain codes of conduct in actions towards protesters and journalists, a legitimacy crisis was looming for the Hong Kong government as well as the Hong Kong police, once dubbed "Asia's finest," as uncorrupted civil servants and law enforcers upholding the principle of the rule of law.

Second, the representative politics that developed in Hong Kong since the 1980s has been shelved over the past few months. Before June 2019, even though the local legislature—known as the Legislative Council, or LegCo—has been dominated by pro-government and pro-Beijing political parties, parties from the two sides still shared LegCo and other institutional channels to engage in political bargaining. At the same time, civil society organizations made use of extra-institutional channels to support political parties in the legislature. But, entering the latter half of June, especially after large-scale protests involving over a million people, Hong Kong's political energy was suddenly released and made many Hong Kong people widely believe that mass movement is the only means to resolve political problems. The situation worsened after the establishment was perceived to make use of its majority in the LegCo and exercise "institutional violence" in passing unpopular laws, greatly reducing the space within existing political institutions to solve political problems. The reluctance of the government to "respond" to protesters' demands besides police crackdown, effectively pushed Hong Kong into becoming a "movement society."

Third, the rapidly changing role of the "market" in Hong Kong society is becoming increasingly important. Traditionally, Hong Kong's status as an international financial centre has been seen as a foundation of its free market economy. It is also widely believed to be one of the characteristics distinguishing Hong Kong from "ordinary" Chinese cities. More importantly, as discussed in Chapter 5, the narrative of Hong Kong as a free market economy has been established on the principle that economic freedom can be exercised in different marketplaces in Hong Kong, and that politics, including the government, should not interfere. Since the current protest movement started, however, this image of a "non-interventionist market" has been increasingly challenged, exposing the vulnerability of

Hong Kong as a free market economy. Once the "free market" has become less hegemonic, protesters have used boycotts (and even sabotages) against companies and shops showing support of the government and police, and talks of building a "yellow" economy (the colour of the movement) has received much attention. Yet again, contradictions generated from the myth of laissez-faire has become another space of struggles in the protest movement.

On the one hand, since the 1980s, the integration of Hong Kong's economy with that of China has proceeded apace. Since 2003, Hong Kong's economy has become even more dependent on China, especially the tourist and retail sectors, which have experienced severe negative effects from the protest movement. On the other hand, precisely because Hong Kong's representative politics and institutional channels have been shelved, civil society organizations (especially professional groups) have demanded the international community to take a greater interest in what is now happening to Hong Kong, which could be seen as inviting "external interventions" from Western countries. As such, Hong Kong's "market" is actually playing a key role in altering the city's future political development.

3   Litmus Test for the Free World

Finally, what are the implications of Hong Kong's current social movement for the rest of the world? Admittedly, we here in Hong Kong are facing a situation where China is increasingly powerful politically and economically, and is directly challenging the set of universal values widely held in the West (such as freedom, democracy and human rights). In the 1980s, many China observers in Hong Kong and in the West thought that with China opening up its economy, the country ultimately would join the league of democratic countries. By now, however, the imagery of "peaceful evolution" has increasingly become a mirage rather than a signpost.

Over the past few years, the Chinese government has tightened its ideological control of the society. At the same time, China has also increasingly used advanced technology to put its citizens under strict surveillance (Dutton & Xu, 2005). All these demonstrate, unfortunately, China is heading towards a more politically authoritarian, if not totalitarian, direction.

Our earlier chapters have argued that Hong Kong's development is always in the intersections of local, regional (national) and global forces.

As a global city, its fates have not been, and will not be, decided just by local conflicts nor even the whims of the national government. To the parts of the world where democracy and freedom are still greatly treasured and exercised, Hong Kong is a litmus test for their faith and determination. Situated at the fringe of two grand ideologies, a retraction of Hong Kong's strong tradition of freedom would have profound implications to the substantive meanings of freedom and democracy in our times. Sadly, it is the people of Hong Kong who will have to pay the highest price.

4 WITHER HONG KONG STUDIES?

To come back to our initial question, why bother to write another book on Hong Kong society? Of course we are doing it both for ourselves and for our readers. For ourselves we are leaving behind a testimony of what we think about the development of the society up to this moment, and for our readers we certainly want to share with you our takes on Hong Kong. It is hopefully a contribution to the academic literature on Hong Kong blossoming in the past few years. When Stephen Chiu was young (the 1980s), Hong Kong was the only thing on our mind. Sociology was Hong Kong studies to a large extent. When it came to Kaxton Siu's youthful days (the 2000s), Hong Kong was no longer the talk of the town. Instead China loomed prominently on the academic agenda among local scholars. For a while it appeared that Hong Kong could be understood as a global city under Chinese sovereignty and the best way is to compare Hong Kong as a city to other major global cities as well as those in the mainland. Reintegration is squeezing Hong Kong studies into a subsection of China studies.

The second decade of the SAR, however, has been pushing upon local academics a new reality and forcing them to reckon with it. Suddenly Hong Kong has become "interesting" again academically. Why did social movements, especially among the young, broke out one after another? Why did the revival of the economy promised by the "China Opportunity" not materialized? Why did the Hong Kong government, long known for its legitimacy and capacity, suddenly become the "walking dead"? Why did Hongkongers, long known for their indifference to politics, suddenly indulged themselves in political activism? All these questions called upon students of Hong Kong to respond to the intellectual challenges of the time. Not just among the ivory towers, but also in the civil society, a burst of energy into research on local developments became evident in the past years.

While research on Hong Kong had much difficulties of landing themselves in the major international journals before the current decade, it has suddenly become trendy to write about Hong Kong. A colleague of us who is an expert on policing, who did not have much luck in publishing internationally even a few years ago, now has journal editors writing to him soliciting submissions. After the Umbrella Movement, hundreds of articles and books have been published about Hong Kong, and it is certain that many more will come out after 2019. Events in 2019 also witnessed the "globalization" of local Hong Kong politics by thrusting it into the new "Cold War" between the two superpowers of China and United States. Hong Kong studies have increasingly attracted an international audience, so much so that there are talks about "worlding Hong Kong studies" around here.

This book does not offer a lot of answers to the many questions hovering above us at the moment. Hong Kong studies could still be a small cottage industry, but it has increasingly gained in size and momentum. While 20 years ago it would have been possible for a text on Hong Kong society to summarize a decent sample of literature, it is no longer possible to do so in some topic areas. We do, however, try our best to capture what we feel to be the gist of the society's development from a macrosociological perspective. This book might still meet with the fate of being outdated the moment it reaches the (now largely virtual) bookstores, but it registered our endeavours in coming to terms with what we observe here, while debunking a couple of what we regarded as "standard definition" images and conjured up a few "high-definition" ones. If we have stimulated some reflections about Hong Kong society and helped some readers into embarking their own understanding of Hong Kong, we would be patting each other's back for a job well done.

REFERENCES

Dutton, M., & Xu, Z. (2005). The Question of Difference: The Theory and Practice of the Chinese Prison. In B. Bakken (Ed.), *Crime, Punishment, and Policing in China*. Rowman & Littlefield Publishers.

Siu, K. (2019). Hong Kong's War Against Authoritarianism: How Did It Start and What Is at Stake for the World? *Global Asia, 14*(3), 58–63.

CPSIA information can be obtained
at www.ICGtesting.com
Printed in the USA
LVHW051735050223
738717LV00009B/1467

9 789811 657061